I. M. Pulkina

A SHORT
RUSSIAN
REFERENCE
GRAMMAR

WITH A CHAPTER
ON PRONUNCIATION

EDITED BY PROF. P. S. KUZNETSOV
DOCTOR OF PHILOLOGY

Eighth edition

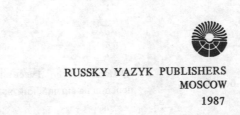

RUSSKY YAZYK PUBLISHERS
MOSCOW
1987

ББК-81.2Р-9
П—88

TRANSLATED FROM THE RUSSIAN

BY

V. Korotky

EDITED

BY

R..Dixon

П $\frac{4306020100-140}{015(01)-87}$ без объявл.

© Издательство „Русский язык", 1975,
перевод на английский язык, 1975

CONTENTS

II. THE NOUN

III. THE ADJECTIVE

IV. THE PRONOUN

V. THE NUMERAL

VI. THE VERB

VII. THE PARTICIPLE AND THE VERBAL ADVERB

VIII. THE ADVERB

IX. THE CONJUNCTION

X. WORD-BUILDING

PREFACE

This book aims at giving a systematic exposition of Russian morphology, pronunciation and spelling for foreigners studying Russian without a teacher and for teachers of Russian.

In this book, syntax is touched upon only briefly and in connection with morphology, when the uses of a morphological form are explained.

Particular attention has been paid to the following points of Russian grammar, which, in the opinion of the author, may prove to be difficult for English-speaking students to grasp: the gender of the noun and the agreement in gender of a word with its head-noun, the meanings and uses of the cases with and without prepositions; the aspects of the verb and their use, the classification of verbs into productive-type and non-productive-type verbs, and word-building.

A short chapter at the beginning of the book deals with the main peculiarities of Russian pronunciation and spelling.

Much attention has been devoted to stress.

Not being a theoretical grammar, the present book contains no definitions of the grammatical categories.

All the grammar material is expounded in tables accompanied by notes giving the most essential explanations.

Each chapter is preceded by General Remarks setting forth the principal peculiarities of the part of speech concerned.

All explanations are based on examples from colloquial Russian, from fiction, newspapers or magazines.

Only the most essential rules of Russian spelling are dealt with.

To facilitate the student's work on the meanings and uses of the cases, the uses are given first without prepositions and then with prepositions; in the tables, the prepositions are arranged in alphabetic order, first those governing one case and then those governing several cases.

The chapters "Main Peculiarities of Russian Pronunciation and Spelling" (pp. 11-33), "Main Types of Stress in Nouns" (pp. 64-73), and "Main Types of Verbs" (pp. 280-288) have been written by Prof. P. S. Kuznetsov. Tables Nos. 79-82 (on the use of the aspects of Russian verbs) and 85, 88, 94, 96-98 have been compiled by V. S. Belevitskaya-Khalizeva.

All suggestions and criticism as to the structure and contents of the book should be forwarded to U.S.S.R., 103012, Москва, Старопанский пер., 1/5. Издательство «Русский язык».

PUBLISHERS' NOTE

The 6th edition of this *Short Russian Reference Grammar* mainly repeats the 1st edition. To meet the numerous requests of students and teachers, all illustrative examples have been supplied with English translations. The translator has kept to the original sentence structure as close as possible to enable the student to see all the peculiarities of Russian construction; for the same reason the examples from poetry have been rendered in English in prose.

ABBREVIATIONS OF NAMES OF AUTHORS QUOTED

Акс. — Акса́ков С. Т.
Арс. — Арсе́ньев В. К.
А. Т. — Толсто́й А. Н.
Бар. — Барати́нский Е. А.
Б. Пол. — Полево́й Б. Н.
Г. — Го́голь Н. В.
Гарш. — Га́ршин В. М.
Герц. — Ге́рцен А. И.
Гонч. — Гончаро́в И. А.
Горб. — Горба́тов Б. Л.
Гр. — Грибое́дов А. С.
Жук. — Жуко́вский В. А.
Заг. — Заго́скин М. Н.
Кр. — Крыло́в И. А.
Кор. — Короле́нко В. Г.
Л. — Ле́рмонтов М. Ю.
Л.-К. — Ле́бедев-Кума́ч В. И.
Л. Т. — Толсто́й Л. Н.

М. — Ма́йков А. Н.
М. Г. — Макси́м Го́рький
Н. Остр. — Остро́вский Н. А.
Нев. — Неве́ров А. С.
Некр. — Некра́сов Н. А.
Ник. — Ники́тин И. С.
О. — Оша́нин Л. И.
П. — Пу́шкин А. С.
Павл. — Павле́нко П. А.
С.-М. — Соколо́в-Микито́в И. С.
Т. — Турге́нев И. С.
Тютч. — Тю́тчев Ф. И.
Фад. — Фаде́ев А. А.
Фурм. — Фу́рманов Д. А.
Ч. — Че́хов А. П.
Эрен. — Эренбу́рг И. Г.
Яз. — Язы́ков Н. М.

I. MAIN PECULIARITIES OF RUSSIAN PRONUNCIATION AND SPELLING

The Russian language comprises various dialects. Since Moscow as far back as the 14th century became the centre and, later, the official capital of the Russian State, the Russian literary language was formed on the basis of the Moscow dialect (though it adopted certain peculiarities of other dialects). Basically the standard pronunciation of Modern Russian conforms to the pronunciation of the Moscow dialect. In the present chapter we shall, therefore, deal mainly with the standard Moscow pronunciation.

Under Peter I the capital was transferred from Moscow to Petersburg (now Leningrad). It was only in 1918 that Moscow once more became the state capital. Petersburg, being a new city, failed to create a dialect of its own differing from the Moscow dialect. Besides, a large section of its population were Moscow-born. There were, however, some deviations from the Moscow standard pronunciation; these shall be discussed as we go along.

SPEECH SOUNDS AND LETTERS

The Russian alphabet comprises 33 letters. They are: *а, б, в, г, д, е, ё, ж, з, и, й, к, л, м, н, о, п, р, с, т, у, ф, х, ц, ч, ш, щ, ъ* (hard mark),* *ы, ь* (soft mark),** *э, ю, я.*

There are more sounds than letters in Russian. To understand how various sounds are represented by letters, we must first dwell on the individual sounds in the Russian language and their classification.

RUSSIAN VOWELS AND CONSONANTS

As in any other language, sounds in Russian fall into *vowels* and *consonants*. The difference between these lies in that while in the pronunciation of vowels the outgoing air passes freely through the

---

* The hard mark (*твёрдый знак*) is so called because — before the Reformed Spelling came into force — it was used to show that the final consonant of the word must not be softened (palatalized).

** The soft mark (*мягкий знак*) is generally used to show that the preceding consonant is softened.

11

mouth cavity, which acts only as a resonator, in the pronunciation of consonants the outgoing air meets with various obstructions formed in the mouth cavity. All Russian vowels are voiced, whereas the consonants may be either voiced or voiceless. All Russian vowels are generally syllabic, whereas the consonants are not. Speech consists of syllables. A syllable is a sound or a number of sounds pronounced at one breath. The syllabic sound is pronounced more vigorously than all the other sounds of the syllable and is, therefore, more audible. There can be only one syllabic sound in a syllable (which in some cases consists only of one sound). All the other sounds in a syllable are non-syllabic. There can be several non-syllabic sounds in a syllable. Thus, in the word *хóдит* '(he) walks' there are two syllables (*хó-дит*) and, consequently, two syllabic sounds (*о, и*). The first syllable contains one non-syllabic sound (*х*), and the second syllable two (*д, т*).

RUSSIAN VOWEL SOUNDS

The character of a vowel sound depends primarily on the position of the tongue (see Table 1). Vowels are classified according to (1) what part of the tongue articulates them and (2) the height of the tongue in the mouth. According to the articulating part of the tongue, the vowels are classified into *back*, *central* and *front* vowels. In pronouncing the back vowels, the back part of the tongue is raised towards the back of the palate; in pronouncing the central vowels, the central part of the tongue is raised towards the central part of the palate, and in pronouncing the front vowels, the central part of the tongue is raised towards the front of the palate. According to the height of the tongue in their pronunciation, the vowels are divided into *open*, *half-open* and *close*. In pronouncing the open vowels,

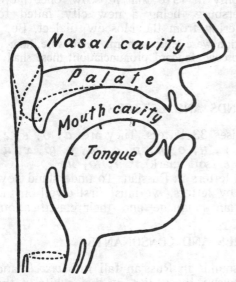

the tongue lies low and is spread flat in the mouth, in pronouncing the half-open vowels, it is raised but not very high, while in pronouncing the close vowels, the tongue is raised very high in the mouth cavity. Depending on what part of the tongue is raised and to what height, the size and form of the mouth cavity (which acts as a resonator) are changed. These changes account for the different vowel quality given in the mouth cavity to the voice produced in the larynx.

In Table 1, the sound *ы* is placed in brackets; since it is not so independent as the sound *u; ы* is pronounced only after hard consonants,* while *u* occurs at the beginning of a word or after a soft consonant (later on this question is dealt with in greater detail).

In pronouncing the vowels *o* and *y*, not only the position of the tongue is important, but the work of the lips as well. In articulating *o*, the lips are rounded, and in pronouncing *y*, they are not only rounded but also slightly protruded. These lip-movements also change the size and shape of the mouth cavity, and, therefore, the vowel quality of the voice.

Table 1

Russian Vowels

Front	Central	Back	Articulating part of tongue / Height of tongue in mouth
u	*(ы)*	*y*	close
э		*o*	half-open
	a		open

RUSSIAN CONSONANTS

Consonants are classified according to (1) the place of the obstruction to the outgoing breath, (2) the manner of forming the obstruction and (3) the work of the vocal cords.

According to the place of obstruction to the outgoing breath, Russian consonants are divided into *bilabial, labio-dental, dental, palato-dental, medio-palatal* and *back-palatal*. In pronouncing the bilabial consonants *(п, б, м)*, the obstruction is formed by the upper and lower lips pressing together. In pronouncing the labio-dental consonants *(в, ф)*, the outgoing breath passes between the lower lip and the upper teeth. In pronouncing the dental consonants *(m, д, c, з, etc.)*, the tip of the tongue is pressed against, or brought close to,

---

* This term is applied to the non-palatalized consonants, i. e., those consonants whose pronunciation is not accompanied by any additional raising of the central part of the tongue towards the front of the palate. The palatalized consonants, whose pronunciation is accompanied by an additional raising of the tongue, are called *soft*.

the upper teeth. In pronouncing the palato-dental consonants *(ж, ш, щ, ч)*, the tip and the centre of the tongue are pressed against, or brought close to, the upper teeth and the front of the palate respectively. The dental and palato-dental consonants are also called *fore-lingual*. In pronouncing the medio-palatal consonant *(й)*, the obstruction is formed between the centre of the tongue and the centre of the palate. The medio-palatal consonant is also called *medio-lingual*. In pronouncing the back-palatal consonants *(к, г, х)*, the obstruction is formed between the back of the tongue and the back of the palate. The back-palatal consonants are also called *back-lingual* (see Table 2).

Table 2

Classification of Consonants according to Place of Obstruction

Bi-labial	Labio-dental	Den-tal	Palato-dental	Medio-palatal	Back-palatal		
п		*m*			*к*	Voiceless	Plosive
б		*д*			*г*	Voiced	
	ф	*с*	*ш, щ*		*х*	Voiceless	Fricative
	в	*з*	*ж, жж*	*й*		Voiced	
		ц	*ч*				Affricative
м		*н*				Nasal	Sonants
		л, р				Liquid	

Hard and Soft Consonants

One of the main peculiarities of Russian pronunciation is the presence of so-called *hard* and *soft* consonants (see Table 3). Most Russian consonants go in pairs according to their hardness or softness, the only difference between the hard and the soft consonant of each pair being that the latter has a peculiar soft (or palatalized) sound. It is of the utmost importance to distinguish between a hard consonant and the corresponding soft one, since the meaning of a word will not infrequently depend only on whether a consonant is pronounced hard or soft. Thus, the words *угол* 'corner' and *уголь* 'coal' differ vocally only in that the sound *л* is pronounced hard in the former, and soft in the latter.

Soft consonants differ from their hard counterparts in the position assumed by the tongue in their pronunciation. To pronounce the soft *m, д, с, з, п, б, ф, в, р, л, н, м,* the centre of the tongue is slightly raised towards the front of the palate; this additional tongue movement never occurs in the pronunciation of the hard consonants. For example, the pronunciation of the hard *n* is effected only by the lips (e.g., *цеп* 'flail'). In the pronunciation of the soft *п,* (e.g., *цепь* 'chain'), the lips assume the same position as in the pronunciation of the hard *n,* but, in addition, the centre of the tongue is raised. A number of Russian consonants do not go in pairs according to hardness or softness: some of them are always hard *(ж, ш, ц),* while others are always soft *(ч, щ, й).*

The way softness of consonants is indicated in writing will be dealt with later.

In Table 3, the soft *к, г, x* are placed in brackets, since they are not so independent as other soft consonants. They generally occur only before a front vowel *(э* or *и),* except for a few proper names of foreign origin (e.g., *Кяхта),* where the soft *к* occurs before *а,* and the forms of the present tense second person singular *(ткёшь),* third person singular *(ткёт),* first person plural *(ткём),* and second person plural *(ткёте)* of the verb *ткать* 'to weave' (where *ĕ = o* following a soft consonant). All other soft consonants may occur before the back vowels, before the consonants, or at the end of a word, e.g., *нёс* '(he) carried', *тёс* 'rough-sawn timber', *тяжесть* 'weight', *довольно* 'enough', *огонь* 'fire', *уголь* 'coal', *цепь* 'chain'; the consonant *щ* is pronounced in accordance with the standard Moscow pronunciation as a long (i.e., double) *ш.* Unlike the ordinary *ш* it is always soft. In Leningrad, *щ* is pronounced as a soft *шч.*

The long (double) *ж* is also a soft consonant. There is no special letter in the Russian alphabet to denote this sound: it is rendered in writing by double *ж* (e.g., *жужжать* 'to buzz') or by *зж* (e.g., *езжу* 'I go'). The long soft *ж* may also be rendered in writing by *жд* (*дождú* — plural of *дождь* 'rain', *дождик* 'light rain', etc.). Many Russian speakers, influenced by the spelling, sound both the letters in the combination *жд,* but according to the standard pronunciation *жд* should be pronounced as a long soft *ж.* In Leningrad, a long hard *жж* is pronounced instead of the Moscow soft *жж.*

In Russian, *й* has the function of a consonant: it is never syllabic. In some instances, *й* is pronounced as a consonant in the articulation of which the centre of the tongue is raised towards the front of the palate, thus narrowing considerably the passage for the outgoing breath; in other instances, *й* is pronounced as a non-syllabic vowel. *й* is generally pronounced as a consonant before a stressed vowel, e.g., *яма* 'pit' (pronounced [йáма]), *ёлка* 'fir-tree' (pronounced [йóлка]), *район* 'region'. *й* is pronounced as a non-syllabic vowel after a stressed vowel (e.g., *край* 'edge', *сарáй* 'shed', *кóйка* 'cot'); it may also be pronounced as a non-syllabic vowel before a stressed syllable beginning with a consonant (e. g., *войнá* 'war').

Table 3

Russian Hard and Soft Consonants

Hard Conso-nants	ц	ш	ж	к	г	х	т	д	с	з	п	б	ф	в	л	р	м	н			

			(к)	(г)	(х)	т	д	с	з	п	б	ф	в	л	р	м	н	ч	щ	й	Soft Conso-nants

й preceding a vowel is very rarely rendered in writing by the letter *й* (e.g., *райóн* 'region'). As a rule, in such cases special letters are employed *(я, е, ё, ю)*, which render the combination of *й* with the corresponding vowel sounds, e.g., *яма* 'pit' (*я* is pronounced as [йа]), *éсли* 'if' (*е* is pronounced as [йэ]).

How to Indicate Hard and Soft Consonants in Writing

Since the meaning of a word will often depend on whether a hard or soft consonant is sounded, it is necessary to indicate the hardness or softness of consonants in writing. However, there are no separate letters for Russian hard and soft consonants. The softness of consonants is indicated in writing either by placing after them the soft mark *(ь)* or by special letters denoting the vowels which follow them. Thus, *я* is written after a soft consonant instead of *а,* which in the word *ряд* 'row', for example, is pronounced in the same manner as *а* in *рад* 'glad' and only shows that the *р* in the former word is soft.

One of the main difficulties of Russian spelling lies in the fact that most letters used to denote a vowel sound after a soft consonant may also be employed to render the combination of the consonant *й* and the corresponding vowel sound. Thus, *я* in the word *яма* 'pit' is the combination of *й* and *а* [йа].

Note. — *й* occurring before a vowel is rendered by a special letter only in a few words of foreign origin, e.g., *райóн* 'region', *майóр* 'major'.

Vowels following hard consonants are represented by the letters *а, э, ы, о, у*. Vowels following soft consonants are represented by the letters *я, е, и, ё, ю* (see Table 4).

Table 4

Use of the Letters *я, е, ё, ю, ь, ъ*

Letter	Pronun-ciation	When so pro-nounced	Examples	Remarks
я	[йа]	After vowels, after *ъ, ь,* and at the begin-ning of a word:	моя́ 'my', изъ-я́ть 'to with-draw', семья́ 'family', я́ма 'pit'	
я	[a]	After soft consonants:	пять 'five', пя́-тый 'fifth'	
е	[йэ]	After vowels, after *ъ, ь,* and at the begin-ning of a word:	мое́й (gen. of моя́), съезд 'congress', в семье́ 'in one's family', е́сли 'if', ель 'fir-tree'	
е	[э]	After soft consonants:	нет 'no', сесть 'to sit down'	
ё	[йо]	After vowels, after *ъ, ь,* and at the begin-ning of a word:	моё 'my', съём-ка 'shooting', бельё 'linen', ёлка 'fir-tree'	In a few words of foreign origin the com-bination [йо] after a consonant is rendered in writing by *ьо,* e.g., *бульо́н* 'broth', *батальо́н* 'battalion'.
ё	[о]	After soft consonants:	нёс 'he carried', лёд 'ice'	
ю	[йу]	After vowels, after *ъ, ь,* and at the beginning of a word:	мою́ (acc. of моя́), адъю-та́нт 'aide-de-camp', вью́га 'snow-storm', лью 'I pour', юг 'south'	
ю	[у]	After soft consonants:	лю́ди 'people'	

Letter	Pronunciation	When so pronounced	Examples	Remarks
ь	Not pronounced.	When occurring after a consonant or at the end of a word, merely indicates the softness of the preceding consonant:	настóльный 'table', путь 'way'	ь is written only after a consonant.
		When occurring before a vowel, ь shows that the letter rendering the vowel sound is pronounced as a combination of й and the corresponding vowel:	в семьé 'in one's family', в семью 'to one's family', без семьú 'without a family'	
ъ	Not pronounced.	ъ shows that the following letter is pronounced as a combination of й and the corresponding vowel sound:	съезд 'congress', отъéзд 'departure', подъём 'rise'	ъ is written only after a consonant and before a vowel; the pronunciation of the consonant before ъ is identical with its pronunciation before ь.

Note. — 1. э is never written after consonants, except in a number of words of foreign origin, mainly foreign proper names (e.g., Тэн 'Tenn', сэр 'Sir'), since all Russian consonants (except those which are never pronounced soft) are softened when followed by the sound э.

2. The relation between ы and и is different from that between а and я, э and е, etc. The letters а and я represent the same vowel sound, while the letters ы and и (the former occurring after the hard consonants and the latter, as a rule, after the soft ones) render different vowel sounds.

In pronouncing и, the central part of the tongue is raised towards the front of the palate, while in pronouncing ы it is raised towards the centre of the palate.

The student must bear in mind the above peculiarities of Russian spelling when studying the tables. Thus, in the table dealing with the nouns ending in -я (дерéвня 'village', пáртия 'party', etc.) nouns are discussed which, in pronunciation, end in -а preceded by a final soft consonant or и in the stem.

Note that to denote *o* following a soft consonant, the sign *ё* (*e* with the diæresis) is sometimes employed; in most printed texts, however, this sign is dispensed with and is replaced by *e* (in this book *ё* is retained). The sign *ё* always denotes a stressed vowel since in an unstressed position *e* and *o* following a soft consonant do not vocally differ from one another, both being pronounced as a sound intermediate between *e* and *u* (*нёс* 'he carried', but *несла* 'she carried').

Russian Voiceless and Voiced Consonants

It is very important to learn to distinguish Russian voiceless consonants from their voiced counterparts (the former are uttered without vibration of the vocal cords, the latter, with such vibration). Some consonants go in pairs consisting of a voiceless consonant and its voiced counterpart. Others do not go in pairs and are pronounced either only as voiceless consonants or only as voiced ones (see Table 5).

Table 5

Russian Voiceless and Voiced Consonants

Voiceless consonants	ц	ч	щ	х	к	т	с	ш	п	ф

г	д	з	ж	б	в	л	р	м	н	й	Voiced consonants

In the above table, the consonants are classified into *voiced* and *voiceless*, irrespective of their hardness or softness; the softness of a consonant has nothing to do with its being voiced or voiceless (thus, the hard *m* is always voiceless and so is the soft *m*, the hard *д* is, on the contrary, always voiced and so is its soft counterpart, etc.).

As can be seen from the table, the Russian affricative consonants *ц* and *ч* are always voiceless: they have no corresponding voiced consonants (as is the case in some foreign languages). The voiceless *щ* has its voiced counterpart — the long (double) soft *ж* (discussed above). In the Russian alphabet, however, there is no special letter to denote this long soft *ж:* it is rendered in writing either by *жж* or by *зж;* e.g., *жужжа́ть* 'to buzz', *визжа́ть* 'to screech'.

The consonants *л, р, м, н, й* have no voiceless counterparts. The consonants *л, м, н* and *р* are called *sonants*. All sonants have one common feature: in articulating a sonant the organs of speech form an obstruction to the flow of the outgoing air, but there always remains a free passage either in the mouth or in the nasal cavity.

The sonants in the pronunciation of which the outgoing air escapes through the mouth cavity, are called *liquids*. These are *л* and *р*. In the pronunciation of *л* only the tip of the tongue obstructs the passage of the outgoing air, which can flow out on the sides. In the pronunciation of *р,* the tip of the tongue makes a rapid series of taps against the front of the hard palate (above the teethridge), the air passing out between the taps.

19

The sonants in the pronunciation of which the soft palate is lowered, forming a free passage for the outgoing air through the nasal cavity, are called *nasals*. These are *м* and *н*.

Plosive, Fricative and Affricative Consonants

According to the manner of forming the obstruction to the outgoing air, consonants are classified into *plosive*, *fricative* and *affricative*.

In the pronunciation of the plosive consonants (*n, m, к,* etc.), the articulating organs (the lips, the tongue and the teeth, the tongue and the palate) are brought close together. When the obstruction is removed, i.e., when the lips or other obstructing organs are parted, the air issues with plosion. The plosives are pronounced momentarily and cannot be prolonged.

In the pronunciation of the fricative consonants (*в, с, х,* etc.), the articulating organs (the lips and the teeth, the tongue and the teeth, the tongue and the palate) come close together, leaving a narrow passage for the outgoing air. Passing through the narrow passage, the air produces friction against the edges of the articulating organs. The fricatives are pronounced long and can be drawn out.

The affricative consonants (*ц* and *ч*) are essentially a combination of a plosive and a fricative. In the pronunciation of these sounds, the articulating organs forming the obstruction (the tongue and the teeth, the tongue and the palate) are brought close together and then gradually (not suddenly!) drawn apart, leaving a long narrow passage for the outgoing air.

It should be noted that in the standard Russian pronunciation there is only one voiced back-palatal consonant, viz., the plosive *г*. It has no fricative counterpart. However, some Russian speakers who acquired their pronunciation habits in the regions south of Moscow often substitute a fricative (long) *г* for the plosive *г* (for example, they pronounce the *г* in the word *город* 'town' as a long voiced *х*). Such pronunciation, however, does not conform to the standard pronunciation, though, according to the old (pre-Revolutionary) standard pronunciation, the fricative *г* was to be sounded in some words of Old Slavonic origin, such as: *благо* 'blessing', *богáтый* 'rich'. Modern standard pronunciation requires that in these words the plosive *г* be sounded.

MAIN CHANGES OF SOUND VALUES

Nearly all Russian sounds (vowels and consonants) undergo certain changes depending on their position in the word (among the factors effecting such changes are the stress, the neighbouring sounds, or the fact that the sound is at the end of the word).

Unstressed Vowels

Most of the Russian vowels are sounded clearly and distinctly only when they are stressed.

Only the vowel *y* is clearly distinguished from all the other vowels when unstressed.

The vowels *o* and *a,* when unstressed, are indistinguishable in pronunciation. When following a hard consonant in the syllable immediately preceding the stressed one or in any unstressed syllable occurring at the beginning of the word, both *o* and *a* are pronounced as a sound similar to *a,* thus, *водá* 'water', *домá* 'houses', *огурéц* 'cucumber' are pronounced almost as [вадá], [дамá], [агурéц]. In all other unstressed syllables these vowels are replaced by a sound similar to *ы* (more precisely, by a very short, weak, central, half-open vowel, differing from *ы* in that in its pronunciation the central part of the tongue is not raised so high towards the centre of the palate as in the pronunciation of *ы*). Examples: *водянóй* 'water-sprite', *гóрод* 'town', *далекó* 'far', *пóвар* 'cook'.

The vowels *e* and *u,* when unstressed, are also almost indistinguishable from one another and are pronounced as a sound similar to *u,* thus, *делá* 'affairs' is pronounced almost as [дилá]. The unstressed vowels *o* and *a* following a soft consonant are also indistinguishable and are pronounced similarly to *u,* e.g., *нёс* '(he) carried' (the stressed *o* follows a soft consonant), but *неслá* '(she) carried' (pronounced almost as [нислá]); *взял* '(he) took' (the stressed *a* follows a soft consonant), but *взялá* '(she) took' (pronounced almost as [взилá]).

Following a sibilant in the syllable immediately preceding the stressed one, *a* is pronounced as a sound similar either to *u* (when following a soft sibilant) or *ы* (when following a hard sibilant), thus, *часы́* 'watch' is pronounced almost as [чисы́], *шагáть* 'to march' almost as [шигáть]. However, such pronunciation is based on the requirements of the old standard pronunciation. In modern pronunciation, *a* following a sibilant in the syllable immediately preceding the stressed one is often sounded as *a* (*шагú* 'footsteps'). The peculiar changes in vowels occurring after sibilants, somewhat resembling those which they undergo when following soft consonants, are accounted for by the fact that in Old Russian all sibilants were soft.

In unstressed syllables other than those immediately preceding the stressed one (after all soft consonants, soft sibilants included), a very weak sound intermediate between *e* and *u* is pronounced instead of *o, a* or *e*; after hard sibilants the same sound is pronounced as after other hard consonants.

It must be borne in mind that in the unstressed masculine endings of the nominative, singular, of adjectives *(-ый)* a weak central half-open vowel sound is pronounced instead of *ы* (e.g., *крáсный* 'red').

Combinations of Hard and Soft Consonants with Vowels

и occurs only at the beginning of a word or after a vowel or a soft consonant. When following a hard consonant (except the back-palatal *г, к, х*), it always changes into *ы*. Compare, for example, *играть* (an imperfective verb) 'to play' — *сыграть* (a perfective verb) 'to have played', *искать* 'to search for' — *изыскáния* 'research'. This fact accounts for the regular correlation *ы — и* in the endings of nouns whose stems terminate in a hard or soft consonant, e.g., *столы́* 'tables' — *рули́* 'rudders', *вóды* 'waters' — *зéмли* 'lands', etc.

и following *г, к, х* does not change into *ы*, the consonants *г, к, х* becoming palatalized (i.e., changing into the soft *г, к, х*), e.g., *волк* 'wolf' — the plural *вóлки* (with a soft *к*). This fact accounts for the spelling rule that *г, к, х* are hardly ever followed by *ы*. Only a very small number of words of foreign origin do not follow this rule, e.g., *акы́н* 'Kazakh folk poet and singer'.

When two consecutive words are pronounced without a pause between them, the first word ending in a back-palatal consonant and the second beginning with *и*, the back-palatal consonant remains hard and *и* changes into *ы*; thus, *волк и кот* 'a wolf and a cat', *к Ивáну* 'to Ivan' are pronounced as [вóлкыкóт] and [кывáну] respectively.

The sibilants *(ж, ч, ш, щ)* and *ц* are either always hard *(ж, ш, ц)* — except in a very small number of words of foreign origin, such as *парашют* 'parachute', *брошюра* 'brochure', *жюри́* 'jury' — or always soft *(ч, щ)*.

Since the hardness or softness of these sounds is not indicated in writing they are always followed by the letters *а, у, и* (and not *я, ю, ы*), irrespective of whether the preceding sibilant is hard or soft, e.g., *чай* 'tea' (*ч* is soft), *чужóй* 'strange' (*ч* is soft), *жизнь* 'life' (*ж* is hard and, consequently, the following vowel is sounded as *ы*).

Exceptions:

1. In a very small number of words of foreign origin *ю* is written after *ш, ж: брошюра, парашют, жюри́*. In the former two words, *ш* is sounded hard, in the latter, *ж* is pronounced soft.

2. *ц* may be followed in writing either by *и* or *ы*, though in both cases it is sounded as *ы* (since *ц* is always hard). Examples: *ци́ркуль* 'compasses', *концы́* 'ends'.

To denote the sound *э* following sibilants, *е* is always written, whereas to denote the sound *о*, either *о* or *е (ё)* is employed, e.g., *мешóк* 'sack', *кружóк* 'circlet' (pronounced as it is written), but *шел* '(he) walked' or *шёл*, *желтый* 'yellow' or *жёлтый* (pronounced [шол], [жóлтый]).

It should be noted that in the texts provided with the sign *ё* the latter is printed after the sibilants, irrespective of whether they are soft or hard, i.e., *ё* is printed not only in *чётный* 'even' (where the sibilant is soft) but also in *шёл* '(he) walked' (where the sibilant is hard).

o is rarely written after a sibilant in an unstressed syllable. Only very few words of foreign origin make an exception, e.g., *шовинизм* 'chauvinism', *шокировать* 'to shock', *шоколад* 'chocolate', *шоссе* 'main road', *шофёр* 'driver', *Шотландия* 'Scotland'.

All consonants are softened before *э, и* (except those which are never soft, viz., *ж, ш, ц*).

Changes in Voiceless and Voiced Consonants

Voiceless consonants change into the corresponding voiced ones when they precede a voiced consonant (except *й, р, л, м, н, в*), e.g., *сделать* 'to do' (pronounced [зделать]), *отбор* 'selection' (pronounced [одбор]), but: *съехать* 'to slide down', *три* 'three', *слой* 'layer', *смыть* 'to wash away', *снять* 'to take off', *свить* (a perfective verb) 'to weave'. In the latter examples, the voiceless consonants *с, т* are not only written but also pronounced as such.

Voiced consonants change into the corresponding voiceless ones when immediately preceding a voiceless consonant or when occurring at the end of the word, e.g., *вперёд* 'forward' (pronounced [фперёт]).

Changes in the Plosive, Fricative and Affricative Consonants

The character of the obstruction formed in pronouncing a consonant changes extremely rarely, yet in certain instances it undergoes certain modifications. In some words, plosive and affricative consonants change when they occur before a plosive. This change consists in the following: the articulating organs fail to form a complete obstruction, the plosive or affricative consonant turning into a fricative one. Thus, in the words *когти* 'claws' and *мягкий* 'soft', instead of *г* we pronounce a *х*. In the words *что* 'what', *скучно* 'it is dull', *конечно* 'of course', *ш* is pronounced instead of *ч*. According to the way the obstruction is formed, the nasal *н* is plosive, the obstruction being formed by the tip of the tongue pressing against the back of the upper teeth. It should be noted that in bookish or learned words *ч* occurring before *н* is sounded; thus, for instance, *ч* is pronounced in the following words: *конечный* 'finite' (*конечная величина* 'finite quantity'), *бесконечный* 'infinite', *бесконечность* 'infinity'; *ч* is retained in the pronunciation of many words when preceding plosive consonants other than *н*, e.g., *почти* 'almost', *привычка* 'habit', etc.

In the word *бог* 'God' the final *г* is devoiced; however, it changes not into the plosive *к*, but into the fricative *х* (*бог* is pronounced [бох]). Such pronunciation is accounted for by the fact that in this word a fricative *г* was sounded in Old Russian and not a plosive one.

m and *c* occurring in the reflexive forms of verbs fuse into a long (double) affricative *ц*, e.g., *смеяться* 'to laugh' is pronounced [сми-я́цца], *смеётся* 'he laughs' [сми́ёцца]. The final *m* in the root of a word fuses with the *c* in the suffix *-ск-* in a similar manner. In that case, however, the resulting *ц* is short (and not double). The word *де́тский* 'infantile' is pronounced [де́цкий]. In some instances no fusion takes place, as in *отсе́чь* 'to cut off', *отскочи́ть* 'to jump aside' where the combination *mc* is sounded as it is written.

MAIN PRINCIPLES OF RUSSIAN SPELLING

Russian spelling is mainly based on the morphological principle, i.e., it tends to preserve unchanged every meaningful part of the word (the root,* prefix, suffix and the ending), even if in actual pronunciation the sound value of the letters representing this or that part of the word is changed due to a shift of stress or a different combination of sounds. Thus, in the root of the word *дом* 'house' *o* is written in the nominative plural (*дома́*) just as in the singular though the stress in the plural has shifted to the final syllable, changing the pronunciation of the unstressed *o* to *a*.

Few are the cases when Russian spelling departs from the morphological principle to reflect the actual pronunciation of the word. The spelling of the prefixes *из-, воз-, низ-, раз-, без-, чрез-* as they are sounded is an example of such departure: *избега́ть* 'to avoid' but *исходи́ть* 'to proceed', *возбужде́ние* 'excitement' but *восхожде́ние* 'ascent', *низверга́ться* 'to rush down' but *ниспада́ть* 'to fall', *разбега́ться* 'to scamper about' but *расходи́ться* 'to disperse', *безрабо́тный* 'unemployed' but *беспоко́йный* 'restless', *чрезме́рный* 'excessive' but *чересполо́сный* 'strip farming'.

The spelling of a number of words is justified historically; for instance, the second person singular of verbs ends in *-шь* although it is sounded hard: *говори́шь* 'speakest' is pronounced [гъвари́ш]; in Old Russian *ш* was soft.

ALTERNATION OF SOUNDS

When a word is given new forms or new words are made by the addition of derivational suffixes, some sounds (both vowels and consonants) are occasionally interchanged; sometimes vowels in the word root or a suffix may be dropped. The interchanging of sounds is called *alternation* and the vowels that can be dropped are called *unstable* vowels.

In Russian, alternation of consonants occurs much more frequently than alternation of vowels.

---

* The root is the part of a word which contains its lexical meaning.

Table 6

Main Instances of Alternation of Vowels

Alternating Vowels	Examples	Remarks
o — a	ло́мит '(he) breaks' — выла́мывает '(he) breaks out' смо́трит '(he) looks'—просма́тривает ('he) looks through'	This alternation most frequently occurs in verb-roots, the verbs with *a* in the root generally expressing a more prolonged or repeated action.
e — u — o	запере́ть 'to lock up' — запира́ть 'to lock' — запо́р 'bolt' беру́ 'I take' — собира́ть 'to gather'—сбор 'gathering'	This alternation generally occurs in verb-roots and in the roots of nouns formed from verbs. The difference between *e* and *u* exists only in writing since *e* and *u* in unstressed syllables are sounded alike.
o — ы	со́хнуть 'to dry' — засыха́ть 'to dry up' задохну́ться 'to choke'—задо́хся '(he) choked' — задыха́ться 'to choke' вздох 'sigh' — вздыха́ть 'to sigh'	The alternation *o — ы* generally occurs in verb-roots, the verbs with *u, ы* in the root expressing a more prolonged or a repeated action; *o* generally occurs in the roots of verbal nouns.

Table 7

Unstable Vowels

Unstable Vowels	Examples	Remarks
o	сон 'sleep' — сна рот 'mouth' — рта рожь 'rye' — ржи	Vowels are most frequently dropped: (1) In the oblique cases* in the singular and in all cases in the plural in the roots of a number of masculine, occasionally feminine, nouns ending in a consonant.
e	день 'day' — дня лев 'lion' — льва	
o *ё* *e*	стрело́к 'shot' — стрелка́ парено́к 'lad' — паренька́ молоде́ц 'fine fellow' — молодца́	(2) In the oblique cases in the singular and in all cases in the plural of nouns with the suffixes -ок, -ёк, -ец.
o	ло́вок 'adroit'—ловка́—ло́вко	(3) In the feminine and neuter genders of short form adjectives.
e	бо́лен 'sick' — больна́ — больно́	

* i. e., in all the cases, except the nominative.

Unstable Vowels	Examples	Remarks
о	гоню́ 'I drive' — гнать 'to drive'	(4) In the root of the infinitive of a number of verbs which have a vowel in the present tense root.
е	беру́ 'I take' — брать 'to take'	
е (ё)	лев 'lion' — льва уголёк 'small piece of coal' — уголька́ бо́лен 'sick' — больна́	When a vowel is dropped after a soft **л**, the latter retains its soft sound; to indicate this in spelling, **л** is followed by **ь**.
о **е**	па́лка 'stick' (gen. pl. па́-лок) ру́чка 'pen' (gen. pl. ру́-чек)	*o* is inserted after a hard consonant, *e* after a soft consonant, mostly in the genitive plural of feminine nouns with the suffix -**к**- preceded by a consonant.
и **ы**	собира́ть 'to gather' — со-бра́ть 'to gather' начина́ю 'I begin' — начну́ 'I shall begin' посыла́ть 'to send' — по-сла́ть 'to send' ты́кать 'to poke' — ткнуть 'to poke' замыка́ть 'to close' — зам-кну́ть 'to close'	This alternation occurs only in verb-roots, the forms with *u*, *ы* generally expressing a more prolonged or a repeated action.

Table 8

Main Instances of Alternation of Consonants

Alternating Consonants	Examples	Remarks
к—ч **к — ч — ц**	рука́ 'hand' — ру́чка 'small hand', 'pen' пук 'large bunch' — пучо́к 'bunch' му́ка 'torture' — му́чить 'to torture' восто́к 'east' — восто́чный 'eastern' крик 'cry' — крича́ть 'to cry'	*ч, ж* generally occur before suffixes beginning with the vowel *e* or *u*, before the suffixes -*ок(-ек)*, -*к(а)*, -*н*- and also in some verb-roots; *ц* generally occurs before the suffix -*к(ий)* of adjectives formed from nouns; *з* alternating with *г, ж* occurs in a few isolated instances.

26

Alternating Consonants	Examples	Remarks
г — ж	крéпкий 'strong' — крéпче 'stronger' лик 'image' — лúчный 'personal' — лицó 'face' рыбáк 'fisherman' — рыбáчить 'to fish' — рыбáцкий 'fishing' ногá 'foot' — нóжка 'small foot' дорóга 'road' — дорóжка 'path' флаг 'flag' — флажóк 'small flag' ногá 'foot' — ножнóй 'foot' ля́гу 'I shall lie down' — лёг 'he lay down' — лежáть 'to lie' — лежý 'I lie' дорогóй 'dear' — дорóже 'dearer' стрóгий 'strict' — стрóже 'more strict'	
г — ж — з	друг 'friend' — дружóк 'pal' — дрýжеский 'friendly' — друзья́ 'friends'	
ц — ч	овцá 'sheep' — овчúна 'sheepskin' — овéчка 'sheep' отéц 'father' — отéческий 'fatherly' лицó 'person' — лúчный 'personal' огурéц 'cucumber' — огýрчик 'small cucumber' пáлец 'finger' — пáльчик 'small finger'	*ч* instead of *ц* generally occurs in derivatives before the vowel *e* or *u* preceding the suffixes *-к(а)*, *-н-*, *-ок*, *-ек*.
х — ш	пахáть 'to plough' — пашý 'I plough' — пáшня 'ploughland' махáть 'to wave' — машý 'I wave' пух 'down' — пушóк 'down' старýха 'old woman' — старýшка 'nice old woman'	*ш* generally occurs in verbs in the present tense, before suffixes or an ending beginning with the vowels *e, u* and also before the suffixes *-ок, (-ек), -к(а), -н-*.

27

Alternating Consonants	Examples	Remarks
	страх 'fear' — стра́шный 'fearful' у́хо 'ear' — у́ши 'ears' сухо́й 'dry' — су́ше 'dryer' глухо́й 'dull' — глу́ше 'duller'	
с — ш *з — ж*	писа́ть 'to write' — пишу́ 'I write' (пи́шешь 'you write') проси́ть 'to ask' — прошу́ 'I ask' (про́сишь 'you ask') носи́ть 'to bear' — ношу́ 'I bear' (но́сишь 'you bear') — но́ша 'burden' высо́кий 'high' — вы́ше 'higher' лиза́ть 'to lick' — лижу́ 'I lick' вози́ть 'to carry' — вожу́ 'I carry' ни́зкий 'low' — ни́же 'lower'	*ш, ж* generally occur: (1) At the end of verb-roots in the present tense (*с, з* occur in the same verbs in the infinitive); in verbs ending in -*ать* (e.g., *писа́ть* 'to write', *лиза́ть* 'to lick') the sibilant is retained in all the present tense forms, in verbs ending in -*ить* (e.g., *проси́ть* 'to ask', *вози́ть* 'to carry') the sibilant occurs only in the first person singular. (2) In verbal nouns with the ending -*а* following the root. (3) In the comparative degree of adjectives.
т — ч	отве́тить 'to reply' — отве́чу 'I shall reply' (отве́тишь 'you will reply') — отвеча́ть 'to reply' колоти́ть 'to beat' — колочу́ 'I beat' (коло́тишь 'you beat') — покола́чивать 'to beat' молоти́ть 'to thresh' — молочу́ 'I thresh' (моло́тишь 'you thresh') — обмола́чивать 'to thresh' хоте́ть 'to want' — хочу́ 'I want' (хо́чешь 'you want') круто́й 'steep' — кру́че 'steeper'	*ч* occurs in the first person singular (occasionally in other persons) of the present or simple future tense of verbs, in imperfective verbs formed from perfective ones, and also in the comparative degree of adjectives.

Alternating Consonants	Examples	Remarks
т—ч—щ	свети́ть 'to shine' — свечу́ 'I shine' (све́тишь 'you shine') — свеча́ 'candle' — свече́ние 'luminescence' —освеща́ть 'to light' — просвеща́ть 'to enlighten' —освеще́ние 'lighting' — просвеще́ние 'enlightenment' трепета́ть 'to tremble' — трепещу́ 'I tremble' (трепе́щешь 'you tremble') похи́тить 'to kidnap' — похи́щу 'I shall kidnap' (похи́тишь 'you will kidnap') — похища́ть 'to kidnap'—похище́ние 'kidnapping'	*щ* mainly occurs in verbal nouns ending in *-ение* and also in imperfective verbs formed from perfective ones. **Note.** — In nouns ending in *-ение* there also occurs *ч* (*све-че́ние* 'luminescence'). *щ* alternating with *т* occurs in words and word-forms of Old Slavonic origin.
д — ж	ви́деть 'to see' — ви́жу 'I see' (ви́дишь 'you see') сиде́ть 'to sit' — сижу́ 'I sit' (сиди́шь 'you sit') — поси́живать 'to sit' молодо́й 'young' — моло́же 'younger' молодо́й 'young' — омолоди́ть 'to rejuvenate' — омоложу́ 'I shall rejuvenate' (омолоди́шь 'you will rejuvenate') — омоложа́ть 'to rejuvenate' — омоложе́ние 'rejuvenation'	*ж* mainly occurs in the first person singular of the present tense of verbs, in imperfective verbs formed from perfective ones and in the comparative degree...
д — ж — дж	ходи́ть 'to walk' — хожу́ 'I walk' (хо́дишь 'you walk') — поха́живать 'to walk' — хожде́ние 'walking'	*жд* mainly occurs in the verbal nouns ending in *-ение*, in imperfective verbs formed from perfective ones and also in past participles passive.

29

Alternating Consonants	Examples	Remarks
	охлади́ть 'to cool' — охлажда́ть 'to cool' — охлажде́ние 'cooling' проводи́ть 'to see off' — провожа́ть 'to see off' — сопровожда́ть 'to accompany' — сопровожде́ние 'accompaniment' роди́ть 'to bear' — рожу́ 'I shall bear' (роди́шь 'you will bear') — рожа́ть 'to bear' — рожда́ть 'to bear' — рождён 'born' — рожде́ние 'birth'	**Note.**—*ж* occasionally occurs in nouns ending in *-ение* (e.g., *омоложе́ние* 'rejuvenation'). *жд* alternating with *д* occurs in words and word-forms of Old Slavonic origin.
ск — щ	доска́ 'board' — доще́чка 'plank' иска́ть 'to look for' — ищу́ 'I look for' тре́скаться 'to crack' — тре́щина 'crack' — треск 'crackling' — треща́ть 'to crackle'	*щ* generally occurs before suffixes beginning with the vowels *e, u* and also in present tense of verbs when the final *-ть* is preceded by *а*.
ст — щ	пусти́ть 'to let' — пущу́ 'I shall let' (пу́стишь 'you will let') блесте́ть 'to shine' — блещу́ 'I shine' (блести́шь 'you shine') густо́й 'thick'—гу́ще 'thicker' просто́й 'simple' — про́ще 'simpler' то́лстый 'thick' — то́лще 'thicker'	*щ* instead of *ст* generally occurs in a number of verbs in the first person singular and also in the comparative degree of adjectives.

Alternating Consonants	Examples	Remarks
п — пл	топи́ть 'to drown' — топлю́ 'I drown' (то́пишь 'you drown') — затопля́ть 'to flood' —затопле́ние 'flooding' топи́ть 'to heat' — топлю́ 'I heat' (то́пишь 'you heat') — ота́пливать 'to heat' — отопле́ние 'heating' терпе́ть 'to endure' — терпе́ние 'patience'—терплю́ 'I endure' (те́рпишь 'you endure')	In all the instances *л* is soft. Combinations with *л* generally occur in the first person singular of the present tense of verbs ending in *-ить* (e.g., *я люблю́* 'I love'), in imperfective verbs formed from perfective ones, in verbal nouns and also in the comparative degree of adjectives. **Note.** — In verbal nouns ending in *-ение* the bilabial consonant may not be followed by *л* (*терпе́ние* 'patience').
б — бл	люби́ть 'to love' — люблю́ 'I love' (лю́бишь 'you love') оскорби́ть 'to insult' — оскорблю́ 'I shall insult' (оскорби́шь 'you will insult')—оскорбле́ние 'insult'	
в — вл	лови́ть 'to catch' — ловлю́ 'I catch' (ло́вишь 'you catch') — ло́вля 'catching' дешёвый 'cheap' — деше́вле 'cheaper'	
ф — фл	графи́ть 'to rule' — графлю́ 'I rule' (графи́шь 'you rule')	
м — мл	ломи́ть 'to break' — ломлю́ 'I break' (ло́мишь 'you break') — преломля́ть 'to refract' — преломле́ние 'refraction'	

Alternating Consonants	Examples	Remarks
	томи́ть 'to torment' — томлю́ 'I torment' (томи́шь 'you torment') — томле́ние 'languor'	
л — л (soft)	стлать 'to spread' — стелю́ 'I spread' стол 'table' — насто́льный 'table' комсомо́л 'Young Communist League' — комсомо́льский 'Young Communist League' генера́л 'general' — генера́льша* 'wife of a general'	A soft л generally occurs in the present tense of some verbs containing a hard л in the infinitive, and also before the suffixes -н-, -ск-, -ш(а).
р — р (soft)	бу́рный 'stormy' — бу́ря 'storm' секрета́рский 'secretarial' — секрета́рша* 'woman secretary' — секрета́рь 'secretary'	A hard р generally occurs before the suffixes -н-, -ш(а).
н — н (soft)	гнать 'to drive' — гоню́ 'I drive' ко́нский 'horse's', 'horses'' — конь 'steed', 'horse'	A soft н occurs in the present tense of some verbs containing a hard н in the infinitive, a hard н occurs before the suffix -ск-.

Occasionally vowels and consonants alternate simultaneously, e.g., хо́дит 'he walks' — поха́живает 'he walks'; но́сит 'he carries' — зана́шивает 'he wears (clothes) to holes'; лежу́ 'I lie' — ля́гу 'I shall lie down' — лёг 'he lay down' — положи́ть 'to put'.

SOME REMARKS ON STRESS IN RUSSIAN

In Russian, the stress may fall on any syllable in the word.

In some instances, the meaning of the word, or of its grammatical form, will depend on what syllable in it is stressed, e.g., за́мок

* Occurs in colloquial speech.

'castle' — *замо́к* 'lock', *руки́* (gen. sing. of *рука́* 'hand') — *ру́ки* (nom. pl.), *му́ка* 'torture' — *мука́* 'flour', *страны́* (gen. sing. of *страна́* 'country') — *стра́ны* (nom. pl.), *кру́гом* (instr. sing. of *круг* 'circle') — *круго́м* (an adverb) 'round', *отреза́ть* (an imperfective verb) 'to cut off' — *отре́зать* (a perfective verb) 'to have cut off', *сбега́ть* (an imperfective verb) — *сбе́гать* (a perfective verb).

In the last example, both the grammatical and lexical meanings of the word depend on the position of the stress *сбега́ть* 'to run down' — *сбе́гать* 'to go running to some place and then return'.

As a rule, the stress is indicated in dictionaries. When a word is given new forms (i. e., when it is declined or conjugated), the stress is either retained on the same syllable or shifted to some other syllable. In this brief chapter it is impossible to set out in detail the laws determining the shifting of the stress. Therefore, we shall point out only the most important of these laws.

The stress *is retained* on the same syllable in all forms:

1. In feminine and neuter nouns, and also in masculine nouns ending in the nominative plural in **-ы, -и,** if in the nominative singular the stress falls neither on the final nor on the initial syllable, as in the nouns *побе́да* 'victory', *зага́дка* 'riddle', *строе́ние* 'building', *руководи́тель* 'leader'. In masculine nouns ending in the nominative plural in **-а (-я)** and stressed in the nominative singular neither on the final nor on the initial syllable, the stress falls on the same syllable in all the forms in the singular and on the ending in all the forms in the plural, e. g., *профе́ссор* 'professor' — gen. sing. *профе́ссора*, etc., nom. pl. *профессора́*, gen. pl. *профессоро́в*, etc.; *учи́тель* 'teacher' — gen. sing. *учи́теля*, etc., nom. pl. *учителя́*, gen. pl. *учителе́й*, etc.*

It should not be assumed that the position of stress remains unchanged only in the above type of nouns. Indeed, the stress is retained on the same syllable in other types of nouns, e. g., *студе́нт* 'student', *тетра́дь* 'exercise-book'.

2. In verbs not stressed on the final syllable in the infinitive, for example, in the verbs *па́дать* 'to fall', *слу́шать* 'to listen', *ду́мать* 'to think'.

It should be noted that in some verbs stressed in the infinitive on the final syllable the stress also remains unchanged, e. g., *чита́ть* 'to read' — *чита́ю* 'I read', *нести́* 'to carry' — *несу́* 'I carry'.

3. In the declension of adjectives the stress is retained on the same syllable, except in the degrees of comparison and in the feminine short form, e. g., *кра́сный* 'red' — *кра́сного* but *красне́е*; *кра́сен* but *красна́*.

---

* This instance is dealt with in greater detail in Table 24.

II. THE NOUN

GENERAL REMARKS

The main grammatical categories of the Russian noun are *gender*, *number* and *case*.

Gender is one of the most characteristic features of the noun. All Russian nouns fall into three genders: *masculine*, *feminine* and *neuter*.

The gender of nouns denoting persons or certain animals is determined by the sex of the persons or animals they denote; the grammatical gender of other nouns is determined by their endings.

The gender of nouns is expressed in their agreement, i. e., in the adjectives, most of the pronouns, the ordinal numerals and past tense verbs changing their endings according to the gender of the noun they refer to. Examples: *большо́й дом* 'a large house' (masc.), *больша́я ко́мната* 'a large room' (fem.), *большо́е окно́* 'a large window' (neut.); *наш пе́рвый уро́к* 'our first lesson' (masc.), *на́ша пе́рвая рабо́та* 'our first job' (fem.), *на́ше пе́рвое зада́ние* 'our first task' (neut.); *пруд за́мёрз* 'the pond has frozen' (masc.), *река́ замёрзла* 'the river has frozen' (fem.), *о́зеро замёрзло* 'the lake has frozen' (neut.). (This question is dealt with in greater detail in the relevant tables.)

Nouns may be *singular* (*заво́д* 'plant', *кни́га* 'book', *окно́* 'window') or *plural* (*заво́ды* 'plants', *кни́ги* 'books', *о́кна* 'windows') (see Table 13).

A number of nouns are used only in the singular; others, only in the plural (see Table 14).

Nouns also change according to *case*. There are six cases in Russian: nominative (which answers the questions *кто?* 'who?', *что?* 'what?'), genitive (which answers the questions *кого́?* 'of whom?', *чего́?* 'of what?'), dative (which answers the questions *кому́?* 'to whom?', *чему́?* 'to what?'), accusative (which answers the questions *кого́?* 'whom?', *что?* 'what?'), instrumental (which answers the questions *кем?* 'by whom?', *чем?* 'with what?'), and prepositional (which answers the questions *о ком?* 'about whom?', *о чём?* 'about what?').

The principal meanings of the cases (which in many instances correspond to the meaning of the cases in some foreign languages) are as follows:

The *nominative case* denotes the subject of the action (*това́рищ чита́ет* 'the friend is reading').

The *genitive case* denotes possession (*кни́га това́рища* 'the friend's book').

The *dative case* denotes the person for whom the action is performed (*пишу товáрищу* 'I write to my friend').

The *accusative case* denotes the object to which the action passes (*получил письмó* 'I received a letter', *видел товáрища* 'I saw my friend').

The *instrumental case* denotes the instrument of action (*пишу мéлом* 'I write with chalk').

The *prepositional case* is only used with a preposition (for its meaning, see Table 33).

There are a few Russian nouns which are indeclinable; these are words of foreign origin, mainly of the neuter gender, e.g., *пальтó* 'overcoat', *кинó* 'cinema', *метрó* 'underground', *рáдио* 'radio', *бюрó* 'bureau', *шоссé* 'main road', *жюрú* 'jury', *клишé* 'cliché', etc. (For the gender of such nouns, see Table 11.)

THE GENDER OF THE NOUN

Table 9

Masculine, Feminine and Neuter

Masculine	Feminine	Neuter
Nominative singular ends in:		
a hard consonant	-*a*	-*o*
труд 'labour', колхóз 'collective farm', лес 'forest'	странá 'country', рóдина 'mother country', газéта 'newspaper'	окнó 'window', письмó 'letter', дéло 'affair'
-*й*	-*я*	-*e*, -*ё*
бой 'battle', май 'May', музéй 'museum'	земля 'land', дерéвня 'village', семья 'family', струя 'jet', лúния 'line', револю́ция 'revolution'	мóре 'sea', здáние 'building', ружьё 'gun', пóле 'field', ущéлье 'gorge', копьё 'spear', гóре 'grief', пáстбище 'pasture'
a soft consonant	a soft consonant	-*мя*
день 'day', дождь 'rain', путь 'way'	жизнь 'life', власть 'power', плóщадь 'square'	úмя 'name', врéмя 'time', знáмя 'banner'
a hard or soft sibilant	a hard or soft sibilant (followed by *ь*)	
нож 'knife', карандáш 'pencil', луч 'ray', плащ 'raincoat'	рожь 'rye', тишь 'silence', ночь 'night', пóмощь 'help'	

Note. — 1. Nouns ending in a soft consonant may be either masculine or feminine. Their gender can be determined by their genitive (masc. *дождь* 'rain' — *дождя́;* fem. *пло́щадь* 'square' — *пло́щади*). In some instances the gender can also be determined in the nominative by the suffixes:

(a) all nouns (denoting persons) with the suffix *-тель* (*чита́тель* 'reader', *писа́тель* 'writer', *руководи́тель* 'leader') or *-арь* (*секрета́рь* 'secretary', *библиоте́карь* 'librarian', *па́харь* 'ploughman') are masculine.

(b) all nouns having the suffixes *-ость, -есть* (*ра́дость* 'joy', *но́вость* 'news', *производи́тельность* 'productivity', *све́жесть* 'freshness', *тя́жесть* 'weight') are feminine.

The gender of all other nouns ending in *-ь* should be memorized (see Table 12).

2. We can tell by the spelling whether a noun ending in a hard or soft sibilant is masculine or feminine: feminine nouns always take *-ь* after the final sibilant in the nominative singular (*рожь* 'rye', *тишь* 'silence', *ночь* 'night', *по́мощь* 'help'), while there is no *-ь* after the sibilant at the end of masculine nouns (*нож* 'knife', *каранда́ш* 'pencil', *луч* 'ray', *плащ* 'raincoat').

Some masculine nouns (denoting persons) end in *-а (-я)* (*ю́ноша* 'a youth', *дя́дя* 'uncle') (see Table 10).

3. Masculine nouns with the diminutive suffixes *-ушк-, -ишк-, -онк-, -ёнк-* may end in *-а* (nouns denoting living beings: *де́душка* 'grandfather', *мальчи́шка* 'urchin', *мужичо́нка* 'peasant') or *-о* (nouns denoting inanimate objects: *городи́шко* 'small town', *доми́шко* 'small house'). Nouns with the augmentative suffixes *-ищ-, -ин-* may end either in *-е* or in *-а*; nouns with the suffix *-ищ-*, in *-е* (*парни́ще* 'lad', *дружи́ще* 'old boy', *голоси́ще* 'strong voice'); and nouns with the suffix *-ин-*, in *-а-* (*дети́на* 'husky lad').

4. There are ten Russian nouns ending in *-мя: и́мя* 'name', *вре́мя* 'time', *зна́мя* 'banner', *се́мя* 'seed', *те́мя* 'top of the head', *бре́мя* 'burden', *пле́мя* 'tribe', *пла́мя* 'flame', *вы́мя* 'udder', *стре́мя* 'stirrup'. All these words are neuter.

5. All indeclinable nouns of foreign origin denoting inanimate objects are neuter (*пальто́* 'overcoat', *кино́* 'cinema', *жюри́* 'jury', *пари́* 'bet', *бо́а* 'boa'), with the exception of the word *ко́фе* 'coffee', which is masculine (*люблю́ кре́пкий ко́фе* 'I like strong coffee'); indeclinable nouns of foreign origin denoting living beings (birds, animals) are generally masculine.

Table 10

The Gender of Nouns denoting Persons

I. Masculine and Feminine Nouns with Normal Gender Endings:

	Masculine	Feminine
1. Nouns denoting persons of the male or female sex generally have corresponding gender endings.	брат 'brother' мáльчик 'boy'	сестра́ 'sister' де́вочка 'girl'
2. Feminine counterparts of masculine nouns may differ from the latter not only in their endings but in suffixes as well.	учени́к 'pupil' комсомо́лец 'Young Communist Leaguer' студе́нт 'student' стари́к 'old man' лётчик 'flyer'	учени́ца 'pupil' комсомо́лка 'Young Communist Leaguer' студе́нтка 'student' стару́ха 'old woman' лётчица 'woman flyer'

Note. — 1. In most instances masculine nouns denoting a member of a profession or a position, occupation, calling, etc., may be used for both men and women: *Она́ хоро́ший педаго́г, о́пытный врач.* 'She is a good teacher, an experienced doctor'. *Секрета́рь вы́шла.* 'The secretary has gone out'. *С докла́дом вы́ступила профе́ссор Ивано́ва.* 'The report was made by Professor Ivanova'. *Премирова́ли садово́да Игна́тьеву.* 'The gardener Ignatyeva was awarded a prize'.

2. Some feminine nouns, such as *до́кторша, дире́кторша*, are used to denote (1) a woman member of a profession or holder of a rank or appointment: 'doctor', 'director'; (2) the wife of a man of the profession, rank or appointment concerned: 'the wife of a doctor', 'the wife of a director'. Such words are never used in the literary language.

3. The masculine nouns *челове́к* 'person', *друг* 'friend', *това́рищ* 'comrade' have no feminine counterparts: *Она́ прекра́сный челове́к.* 'She is a fine person'. *Пришла́ това́рищ Ивано́ва.* 'Comrade Ivanova has come'.

II. Masculine Nouns with the Ending -а, -я:

1. Here belong a number of masculine nouns ending in *-а, -я*: *мужчи́на* 'man', *ю́ноша* 'a youth', *дя́дя* 'uncle', *судья́* 'judge', *ста́роста* 'monitor', and the old words *воево́да* 'commander of an army in mediæval Russia', *вельмо́жа* 'grandee'.

2. Many names of men also end in *-а, -я (Лука́, Кузьма́, Илья́)* as do also diminutives of men's names (*Алёша, Во́ва, Се́ва, Ва́ня,* etc.).

3. Masculine nouns with diminutive suffixes also have the ending *а:* *де́душка* 'grandfather', *старичи́шка* 'small old man', *старика́шка* 'wretched old man', *мужичо́нка* 'peasant'.

III. Masculine Nouns with the Ending -е:

The following nouns have the ending *-е:*

(a) nouns with augmentative suffixes: *дружи́ще* 'old boy' (*мой дружи́ще* 'my old boy'), *мастери́ще* 'expert workman'.

Послу́шай-ка, дружи́ще, ты, ска́зывают, петь вели́кий мастери́ще! (Кр.) 'Look here, old boy, they say you are a great singer!'

(b) the word *подмасте́рье* 'apprentice'.

IV. The noun *дитя́* 'child' is neuter.

V. Nouns with the Ending -а belonging to the so-called Common Gender:

There are a number of nouns ending in *-а* whose gender depends on whether they refer to persons of the male or female sex. If a person of the female sex is meant these nouns are feminine, and adjectives, pronouns and verbs (in the past tense) agree with them accordingly. If a person of the male sex is meant adjectives, pronouns and verbs (in the past tense) may take either masculine or feminine endings.

сирота́ 'orphan', кале́ка 'cripple', зева́ка 'idler', неря́ха 'sloven', запева́ла 'leader (of a choir)', вы́скочка 'upstart', пла́кса 'cry-baby', у́мница 'clever person', тупи́ца 'dullard', неве́жа 'boor', неве́жда 'ignoramus', etc.

Эта де́вочка — *кру́глая сирота́.* 'This girl is a complete orphan'.

Этот ма́льчик — *кру́глый сирота́* (and: *кру́глая сирота́*). 'This boy is a complete orphan'.

Како́й ты неря́ха! 'What a sloven you are!' (but one may also say to a boy: *Кака́я ты неря́ха!*)

Table 11

The Gender of Nouns denoting Animals, Birds, Fishes, Insects

	Masculine	Feminine
1. The male and the female of certain species of animals and birds (mainly domestic) are denoted by nouns formed from different roots and having the corresponding gender endings.	бара́н 'ram' бык 'bull' бо́ров 'boar' пету́х 'cock' се́лезень 'drake'	овца́ 'ewe' коро́ва 'cow' свинья́ 'sow' ку́рица 'hen' у́тка 'duck'
2. Nouns denoting the male and the female have different endings; the feminine nouns also have special suffixes.	волк 'he-wolf' лев 'lion' медве́дь 'he-bear' тигр 'tiger' слон 'bull-elephant' индю́к 'turkey-cock'	волчи́ца 'she-wolf' льви́ца 'lioness' медве́дица 'she-bear' тигри́ца 'tigress' слони́ха 'cow-elephant' индю́шка 'turkey-hen'
	Male and Female	Male and Female
3. In most cases the same word is used for both males and females of animals, birds and fishes, the gender of the word being determined by its form: (a) nouns ending in a hard consonant or sibilant (e.g. *ёж* 'hedgehog') are masculine and nouns ending in -*а* (-*я*) or a sibilant (with a final -*ь* in spelling, e.g. *мышь* 'mouse') are feminine; (b) the gender of nouns ending in a soft consonant should be memorized.	ёж* 'hedgehog' крот 'mole' кро́лик* 'rabbit' кит 'whale' носоро́г 'rhinoceros' уж 'grass-snake' дя́тел 'woodpecker' ко́ршун 'kite' со́кол 'falcon' я́стреб 'hawk' ёрш 'ruff' сом 'sheatfish' грач 'rook' жук 'beetle' клоп 'bed-bug' конь 'horse', 'steed' лось 'elk' оле́нь 'deer'	бе́лка 'squirrel' змея́ 'snake' кры́са 'rat' лягу́шка 'frog' лиса́ (лиси́ца) 'fox' обезья́на 'monkey' соба́ка 'dog' я́щерица 'lizard' га́лка 'jackdaw' куку́шка 'cuckoo' ца́пля 'heron' аку́ла 'shark' щу́ка 'pike' блоха́ 'flea' му́ха 'fly' ло́шадь 'horse' мышь 'mouse' рысь 'lynx'

* In fables, the feminine nouns *ежи́ха* 'she-hedgehog' and *крол763и́ха* 'doe-rabbit' are occasionally used.

	Masculine	Feminine
	Male and Female	Male and Female
These nouns differ in their form only in the oblique cases (masc. *олéнь — олéня — олé-ню,* etc.; fem. *рысь — рýси — рýси,* etc.)	сóболь 'sable' тюлéнь 'seal' глухáрь 'wood-grouse' гóлубь 'pigeon' гусь 'goose' журáвль 'crane' лéбедь 'swan' снегúрь 'bullfinch' карáсь 'crucian' óкунь 'perch' пескáрь 'gudgeon' шмель 'bumble-bee'	стéрлядь 'sterlet'
4. Nouns with the suffixes *-онок, -ёнок* denoting the young offspring of animals are masculine.	волчóнок 'wolf-cub' котёнок 'kitten' ягнёнок 'lamb'	
5. Indeclinable nouns of foreign origin denoting living beings are generally masculine, irrespective of the sex of the animal or bird (a number of these nouns end in *-и, -у,* which is unusual for Russian words).	кенгурý 'kangaroo' какадý 'cockatoo' колúбри 'humming-bird' шимпанзé 'chimpan-zee'	

Note. — In the sentences *Шимпанзé кормúла детёныша.* 'The chimpanzee was feeding her little one.' *Кенгурý кормúла детёныша.* 'The kangaroo was feeding her little one' the form of the verb shows that the nouns *шимпанзé, кенгурý* denote female animals.

Table 12

The Gender of Nouns denoting Inanimate Objects and ending in -ь

The most common nouns denoting inanimate objects and ending in -ь (besides those ending in a sibilant) are as follows:

Masculine		Feminine	
автомобиль 'motor-car'	перстень 'seal-ring'	артель 'association of workmen for collective work'	осень 'autumn'
ансамбль 'ensemble'	пластырь 'sticking-plaster'		ось 'axle'
бинокль 'binoculars'	плетень 'wattle-fence'	бандероль 'printed matter'	оттепель 'thaw'
бредень 'drag-net'	полдень 'noon'	боль 'pain'	очередь 'queue'
букварь 'ABC book'	портфель 'brief-case'	высь 'height'	память 'memory'
бюллетень 'bulletin'	поршень 'piston'	гавань 'haven'	печаль 'grief'
вексель 'note of hand'	профиль 'profile'	гармонь 'accordion'	печать 'stamp'
вихрь 'whirlwind'	пузырь 'bubble'	гарь 'anything burnt'	печень 'liver'
волдырь 'blister'	пустырь 'waste land'	гибель 'destruction'	площадь 'square'
вопль 'howl'	путь 'way'	грань 'brink'	полынь 'wormwood'
гвоздь 'nail'	ремень 'belt'	грудь 'breast'	поросль 'verdure'
госпиталь 'hospital'	рояль 'grand piano'	грязь 'mud'	постель 'bedding'
гребень 'comb'	рубль 'rouble'	даль 'distance'	прибыль 'profit'
груздь 'milk agaric'	руль 'steering-wheel'	дань 'tribute'	пристань 'landing stage'
двигатель 'engine'	словарь 'dictionary'	дверь 'door'	прорубь 'ice-hole'
дёготь 'tar'	спектакль 'performance'	дробь 'shot'	пыль 'dust'
день 'day'	ставень 'shutter'	дрожь 'trembling'	роль 'role'
дирижабль 'air ship'	стебель 'stem'	ель 'fir-tree'	ртуть 'mercury'
дождь 'rain'	стержень 'pivot'	желчь 'bile'	сажень 'sagene'
жёлудь 'acorn'	стиль 'style'	жердь 'perch'	связь 'connection'

инвентарь 'stock'
календарь 'calendar'
камень 'stone'
картофель 'potatoes'
кашель 'cough'
кисель 'thin jelly'
ковыль 'feather grass'
контроль 'control'
корабль 'ship'
корень 'root'
костыль 'crutch'
куль 'sack'
лагерь 'camp'
лапоть 'bast sandal'
ларь 'bin'
локоть 'elbow'
ломоть 'chunk'
монастырь 'cloister'
ноготь 'finger nail'
нуль 'nought'
огонь 'fire'
панцирь 'test'
пароль 'password'
пень 'stump'

сухарь 'rusk'
табель 'table'
уголь 'coal'
уровень 'level'
фитиль 'wick'
флигель 'wing (of a house)'
фонарь 'lantern'
хмель 'hop'
хрусталь 'crystal'
циркуль 'pair of compasses'
штемпель 'stamp'
штепсель 'plug'
штиль 'calm'
щавель 'sorrel'
щебень 'road metal'
якорь 'anchor'
янтарь 'amber'
ясень 'ash'
ячмень 'barley'

жизнь 'life'
йзгородь 'fence'
канитель 'gold or silver thread'
колыбель 'cradle'
копоть 'soot'
корь 'measles'
кровать 'bed'
ладонь 'palm (of the hand)'
лазурь 'azure'
лень 'laziness'
любовь 'love'
мазь 'ointment'
медаль 'medal'
медь 'copper'
мель 'sandbank'
метель 'snow-storm'
мечеть 'mosque'
мозоль 'corn'
мораль 'morality'
мысль 'thought'
нефть 'mineral oil'
нить 'thread'
озимь 'winter crop'
опухоль 'tumour'

сеть 'net'
сирень 'lilac'
скатерть 'table-cloth'
смерть 'death'
соль 'salt'
сталь 'steel'
степь 'steppe'
тень 'shadow'
тетрадь 'copy-book'
ткань 'fabric'
цель 'purpose'
честь 'honour'
шерсть 'wool'
шинель 'great-coat'
ширь 'wide expanse'
щель 'chink'

Nouns denoting the months of the year ending in a soft consonant: январь 'January', февраль 'February', апрель 'April', июнь 'June', июль 'July', сентябрь 'September', октябрь 'October', ноябрь 'November', декабрь 'December'.

Note. — 1. Nouns denoting inanimate objects and ending in *-знь, -сть, -сь, -вь, -бь, -пь* are feminine: *жизнь* 'life', *честь* 'honour', *высь* 'height', *любо́вь* 'love', *про́рубь* 'ice-hole', *степь* 'steppe'.

2. Nouns with the suffixes *-ость, -есть* are feminine: *ста́рость* 'old age', *мо́лодость* 'youth', *све́жесть* 'freshness'. See Table 9. Note 1 (b).

THE PLURAL OF NOUNS

Table 13

1. Changes occurring in the Endings in the Formation of the Plural

1. Masculine and Feminine Nouns with the Plural ending in *-ы* or *-и*.

Masculine and Feminine		Remarks
Singular	Plural	In the Plural:
Nominative		
	-ы	**-ы**
заво́д 'plant'	заво́ды	Ending of:
колхо́з 'collective farm'	колхо́зы	(a) masculine nouns with a final hard consonant in the nominative singular (except nouns whose stem ends in a sibilant or *г, к, х* and the nouns *сосе́д* 'neighbour' — *сосе́ди*, *чёрт* 'devil' — *че́рти*).
маши́на 'machine'	маши́ны	
газе́та 'newspaper'	газе́ты	
страна́ 'country'	стра́ны	(b) feminine nouns whose nominative singular ends in *-а*.
	-и	**-и**
a) геро́й 'hero'	геро́и	Ending of:
бой 'battle'	бои́	(a) masculine nouns with a final *й* in the nominative singular;
музе́й 'museum'	музе́и	
трамва́й 'tram'	трамва́и	
b) дере́вня 'village'	дере́вни	(b) feminine nouns whose nominative singular ends in *-я;*
статья́ 'article'	статьи́	
ли́ния 'line'	ли́нии	
струя́ 'jet'	стру́и	
c) вождь 'leader'	вожди́	(c) masculine and feminine nouns with a final soft consonant in the nominative singular;
пло́щадь 'square'	пло́щади	
d) това́рищ 'comrade', 'friend'	това́рищи	(d) masculine and feminine nouns whose stem ends in a sibilant;
ро́ща 'grove'	ро́щи	
нож 'knife'	ножи́	
межа́ 'border'	ме́жи	
врач 'doctor', 'physician'	врачи́	
ночь 'night'	но́чи	
каранда́ш 'pencil'	карандаши́	
мышь 'mouse'	мы́ши	

Masculine and Feminine		Remarks
Singular	Plural	In the Plural:

Nominative

e) фа́брика 'factory' звук 'sound' нога́ 'leg', 'foot' враг 'enemy' стару́ха 'old woman' пасту́х 'shepherd'	фа́брики зву́ки но́ги враги́ стару́хи пастухи́	(e) masculine and feminine nouns whose stem ends in *г, к, х.*

Note. — Though *ы* is pronounced after a hard sibilant, it is rendered in spelling as *и* (*ножи́* 'knives').

2. Neuter Nouns with the Plural ending in *-a* or *-я*.

Neuter		Remarks
Singular	Plural	In the Plural:
	-a	*-a*
де́ло 'affair' пра́во 'right' госуда́рство 'state' письмо́ 'letter' хозя́йство 'economy' сре́дство 'means'	дела́ права́ госуда́рства пи́сьма хозя́йства сре́дства	Ending of: neuter nouns whose nominative singular ends in *-o.*
	-я	*-я*
по́ле 'field' мо́ре 'sea' собра́ние 'meeting' зда́ние 'building' ружьё 'gun'	поля́ моря́ собра́ния зда́ния ру́жья	Ending of: neuter nouns whose nominative singular ends in *-e, -ё.* Special ways of forming the plural: *у́хо* 'ear' — *у́ши, плечо́* 'shoulder' — *пле́чи, коле́но* 'knee' — *коле́ни, ве́ко* 'eyelid'—*ве́ки, я́блоко* 'apple'—*я́блоки.*

Masculine Nouns with the Plural ending in -*а* or -*я*.

Monosyllabic Words	Dissyllabic Words	Trisyllabic Words
бок 'side' — бока́ век 'century' — века́ глаз 'eye' — глаза́ дом 'house' — дома́ край 'edge' — края́ лес 'forest' — леса́ луг 'meadow' — луга́ снег 'snow' — снега́ рог 'horn' — рога́ сорт 'sort' — сорта́	бе́рег 'shore' — берега́ ве́чер 'evening' — вечера́ го́лос 'voice' — голоса́ го́род 'city' — города́ до́ктор 'doctor' — доктора́ ма́стер 'foreman' — мастера́ но́мер 'number' — номера́ о́стров 'island' — острова́ по́греб 'cellar' — погреба́ по́яс 'belt' — пояса́ па́рус 'sail' — паруса́ по́езд 'train' — поезда́ по́вар 'cook' — повара́	профе́ссор 'professor' — профессора́ учи́тель 'teacher' — учителя́

Note. — A number of masculine nouns take a stressed -*а* or -*я* as their ending for the nominative plural. The following should be noted:

1. In modern literary Russian the forms *профе́ссоры* 'professors', *дире́кторы* 'directors', *реда́кторы* 'editors' occur alongside *профессора́*, *директора́*, *редактора́*; however, the words *ре́ктор* 'rector', *ле́ктор* 'lecturer', *инспе́ктор* 'inspector' always form their plural in -*ы*: *ре́кторы*, *ле́кторы*, *инспе́кторы*.

2. In colloquial Russian the form *договора́* (nom. pl. of *догово́р* 'agreement') is used, but in the literary language the form *догово́ры* is preferred.

3. The nominative plural of the word *год* 'year' is *года́* or *го́ды* (прошлй года́ 'years went by', прошлй до́лгие го́ды 'long years went by').

II. Changes occurring in the Stems and the Endings in the Formation of the Plural

1. Masculine	Remarks
граждани́н 'citizen' — гра́ждане крестья́нин 'peasant' — крестья́не волжа́нин 'native of the Volga region' — волжа́не англича́нин 'Englishman' — англича́не армяни́н 'Armenian' — армя́не	Masculine nouns ending in -*анин* (-*янин*) take -*ане* (-*яне*) in the plural, the suffix -*ин*- being dropped and the ending -*е* added. The following are examples of the plural of nouns ending in -*ин*: *господи́н* 'gentleman' — *господа́*, *хозя́ин* 'master' — *хозя́ева*, *тата́рин* 'Tartar' — *тата́ры*, *болга́рин* 'Bulgarian' — *болга́ры*.

1. Masculine	Remarks
ребёнок 'child' — ребя́та телёнок 'calf' — теля́та волчо́нок 'wolf-cub' — волча́та котёнок 'kitten' — котя́та утёнок 'duckling' — утя́та	Masculine nouns ending in *-онок,* *-ёнок* and denoting young living be- ings take *-ата, -ята* as their ending for the nominative plural. The word *де́ти* 'children' is gener- ally used as the plural of *ребёнок* 'child'.

2. Masculine and Neuter

брат 'brother' — бра́- тья муж 'husband' — му- жья́ лист 'leaf' — ли́стья стул 'chair' — сту́лья прут 'twig' — пру́тья ко́лос 'ear (of a plant)' — коло́сья	друг 'friend' — друзья́ (alternation *г — з*) сук 'bough' — су́чья клок 'rag' — кло́чья (alternation *к — ч*) сын 'son' — сыновья́	перо́ 'feather'—пе́рья крыло́ 'wing' — кры́- лья де́рево 'tree' — дере́- вья звено́ 'link' — зве́нья

Note. — A number of masculine and neuter nouns take the ending *-ья* in the plural.

In the literary language the archaic form of the word *друг* 'friend' — *дру́ги* survives.

Но не хочу́, о *дру́ги*, умира́ть; я жить хочу́, чтоб мы́слить и страда́ть. (П.) 'I do not wish to die, o friends; I want to live so that I can think and suffer'.

The plural forms *сыны́* 'sons' and *мужи́* 'men' occur only in elevated style and in poetry: Как я люблю́, Кавка́з мой велича́вый, твои́х *сыно́в* войнствен- ные нра́вы... (П.) 'How I like, my stately Caucasus, thy sons' warlike dispo- sition'. In modern Russian, the form *сыны́* 'sons' often occurs in the sense of *сыны́ Ро́дины* 'their mother-country's sons'.

3. Neuter	Remarks
вре́мя 'time' — времена́, стре́мя 'stirrup' — стремена́, зна́мя 'banner' — знамёна, се́мя 'seed' — семена́, и́мя 'name' — имена́, пле́мя 'tribe' — племена́	Some neuter nouns have different stems in the singular and the plural. These include: (a) neuter nouns ending in *-мя;*

3. Neuter	Remarks
не́бо 'sky' — небеса́, чу́до 'miracle' — чудеса́	(b) two neuter nouns ending in -*o*: *не́бо* 'sky' and *чу́до* 'miracle'.

Note. — 1. The words *вы́мя* 'udder', *пла́мя* 'flame', *бре́мя* 'burden', *те́мя* 'top of the head' are never used in the plural.

The plural of the word *вре́мя* 'time' has a special meaning (which corresponds to the meaning of the English 'times'):

В тяжёлые *времена́* ца́рского самодержа́вия... 'In the hard times of tsarist autocracy...'; В те далёкие *времена́*... 'In those remote times...'.

2. The word *небеса́* 'skies' occurs mostly in poetry:

Сине́я бле́щут *небеса́*. (П.)
'The skies sparkle as they show blue.'

Ясне́ли хо́лмы и леса́,
И просыпа́лись *небеса́*. (П.)
'The hills and woods became more visible,
And the skies were awakening.'

Звёзды га́снут в *небеса́х*. (Заг.)
'The stars are going out in the skies.'

III. A number of masculine nouns have two plural forms with different meanings.

Singular	Plural	
лист 'leaf' (of a book, of a tree, etc.), 'sheet'	*листы́* 'sheets', 'leaves' (of a book, etc.) Мы пригото́вили больши́е *листы́* бума́ги для диагра́мм. 'We prepared large sheets of paper for the diagrams.' До́лго сих *листо́в* заве́тных не каса́лся я перо́м... (П.) 'It is long since I set my pen to these cherished leaves.'	*ли́стья* 'leaves' (of a tree, etc.), 'foliage' На дере́вьях жёлтые *ли́стья*. 'There are yellow leaves on the trees.' In poetry, however, the form *листы́* also occurs with the meaning of 'leaves' (of a tree, etc.): Уж ро́ща отряха́ет после́дние *листы́* с наги́х свои́х ветве́й... (П.) 'The grove is already shaking the last few leaves from naked boughs...'

Singular	Plural	
ко́рень 'root' (of a living plant)	*ко́рни* 'roots' (of a living plant) *Ко́рни* де́рева глубоко́ ушли́ в зе́млю. 'The roots of the tree went deep into the earth.'	*коре́нья* '(culinary) roots' Мы чи́стили *коре́нья* для су́па. 'We were cleaning roots for the soup.'
про́пуск 'non-attendance'; 'pass', 'permit'	*про́пуски* 'non-attendance' У э́того ученика́ есть *про́пуски* заня́тий по боле́зни. 'This pupil missed some lessons owing to illness.'	*пропуска́* 'passes', 'permits' Часово́й проверя́л *пропуска́*. The sentry checked the passes.
счёт 'account'	*счёты* 'abacus' Я купи́л конто́рские *счёты.* 'I bought an office abacus.'	*счета́* 'accounts' Коми́ссия проверя́ла *счета́.* 'The commission were checking the accounts.'
по́вод 'pretext'; '(bridle) rein'	*по́воды* 'pretexts' *По́воды* для ссо́ры. 'Pretexts for a quarrel.'	*пово́дья* '(bridle) reins' Он опусти́л *пово́дья,* и ло́шадь останови́лась. 'He dropped the reins and the horse stopped.'

Note the following:

1. The plural of *цвето́к* 'flower' is *цветы́* (На лугу́ запестре́ли *цветы́.* 'Varicoloured flowers showed gaily in the meadow.'); the plural of *цвет* 'colour' is *цвета́* (Люблю́ я́ркие *цвета́.* 'I like bright colours.').

2. The word *лю́ди* 'people' is used as the plural of *челове́к* 'person'. The plural form of *челове́к* is used mainly in the genitive with the pronouns *ско́лько* 'how many', *сто́лько* 'so many' (*ско́лько челове́к?* 'how many people?') and with numerals (*пять челове́к* 'five people').

3. The plural of *счёт* 'account' is *счета́* (Коми́ссия проверя́ла *счета́.* 'The commission were checking the accounts.'); the word *счёты* 'abacus' has no singular (Я купи́л конто́рские *счёты.* 'I bought an office abacus.').

Table 14

Nouns used Only in the Singular or Plural

A. The following words are used only in the singular:

---

1. Nouns denoting various materials and substances:	желе́зо 'iron', серебро́ 'silver', зо́лото 'gold', медь 'copper', чугу́н 'cast iron', молоко́ 'milk', вода́ 'water', снег 'snow', соль 'salt', мука́ 'flour', вино́ 'wine', etc.

Note. — A number of this type of nouns are used in the plural in the following cases:

(a) when denoting different varieties of a material or substance:
дороги́е, дешёвые ви́на 'expensive, cheap wines', *минера́льные во́ды* 'mineral waters', *лече́бные во́ды* 'medicinal waters', *минера́льные со́ли* 'mineral salts';

(b) in poetry:

Мосты́ нави́сли над *вода́ми*. (П.) 'Bridges overhung the waters.'

Гони́мы ве́шними луча́ми, С окре́стных гор уже́ *снега́* Сбежа́ли му́тными ручья́ми На потоплённые луга́. (П.)	'From nearby hills the snows, Driven by the spring sun's rays, Had already flowed down Into the flooded meadows.'

---

2. Nouns denoting vegetables, cereals, berries, technical crops:	карто́фель 'potatoes', морко́вь 'carrots', лук 'onions', рожь 'rye', овёс 'oats', лён 'flax', мали́на 'raspberries', клубни́ка 'strawberries', земляни́ка 'wild strawberries'
3. Collective nouns:	молодёжь 'young people, youth', крестья́нство 'peasantry', студе́нчество 'the students', листва́ 'foliage'
4. A number of abstract nouns:	эне́ргия 'energy', бо́дрость 'cheerfulness', ра́дость 'joy', мо́лодость 'youth', белизна́ 'whiteness', темнота́ 'darkness', социали́зм 'socialism', материали́зм 'materialism'

Note. — Certain nouns of group 4 are occasionally used in the plural; but in that case the lexical meaning of the plural is somewhat different from that of the singular: Ка́ждый вто́рник устра́ивались литерату́рные *чте́ния*. 'Each Tuesday literary recitals were arranged.' Ма́ленькие *ра́дости* жи́зни. 'Life's little joys.' «Пе́рвые *ра́дости*» — рома́н К. Фе́дина. '*Early Joys* is a novel by K. Fedin.'

5. Nouns denoting the cardinal points and the months of the year:	се́вер 'north', юг 'south', за́пад 'west', восто́к 'east', янва́рь 'January', февра́ль 'February'

B. The following words are used only in the plural:

1. Nouns denoting objects consisting of two similar parts:	но́жницы 'scissors', очки́ 'spectacles', брю́ки 'trousers', са́ни 'sledge', щипцы́ 'tongs', весы́ 'scales', воро́та 'gates'
2. A number of nouns in common use:	бу́дни 'week days', де́ньги 'money', дрова́ 'firewood', дро́жжи 'yeast', духи́ 'perfume', жму́рки 'blind man's buff', имени́ны 'name day', кани́кулы 'holidays', обо́и 'wall paper', пери́ла 'handrail', по́хороны 'funeral', се́ни 'entrance hall', сли́вки 'cream', су́мерки 'dusk', счёты 'abacus', су́тки 'twenty-four hours', часы́ 'clock', 'watch', черни́ла 'ink'

Note. — 1. All the words that agree with the above nouns are also used in the plural: Начали́сь *ле́тние кани́кулы*. 'The summer holidays started'. Я люблю́ *вече́рние су́мерки*. 'I like dusk.' Мы принесли́ *сухи́х дров*. 'We brought some dry firewood.' Он купи́л *кра́сных черни́л*. 'He bought some red ink.'

2. The word *часы́* in the sense of 'a clock', 'a watch' (стенны́е *часы́* 'wall-clock', карма́нные *часы́* 'watch', etc.) is used only in the plural; in the sense of 'hours' *часы́* is used in both singular (*час* 'hour') and plural (*часы́* 'hours'): Прошёл до́лгий *час* ожида́ния. 'A long hour of expectation had gone by.' Прошли́ до́лгие *часы́* ожида́ния. 'Long hours of expectation had gone by.' Приду́ че́рез *час*. 'I'll come in an hour.' Приду́ че́рез пять *часо́в*. 'I'll come in five hours.'

3. The word *очки́* in the sense of 'spectacles' is used only in the plural (Я потеря́л свои́ но́вые *очки́*. 'I lost my new spectacles.'); in the sense of 'points' (in games, etc.) the word *очки́* is used in both singular (*очко́* 'point') and plural (*очки́* 'points'): Мой това́рищ получи́л на одно́ *очко́* бо́льше, чем я. 'My friend scored one point more than I did.'

THREE TYPES OF DECLENSION OF THE NOUN

I. According to their case inflexions in the singular, Russian nouns fall into three types of declension:

1. *The first declension* includes (a) *masculine* nouns without any ending in the nominative, whose stem ends in a hard or soft consonant (*го́род* 'city', *день* 'day', *май* 'May'); (b) *neuter* nouns ending in *-о(-ё),-е* (*письмо́* 'letter', *ружьё* 'gun', *по́ле* 'field', *зда́ние* 'building').

Note. — Masculine nouns with diminutive or augmentative suffixes plus the ending *-о* or *-е* (*городи́шко* 'small town', *доми́шко* 'small wretched house', *доми́ще* 'enormous house') also belong to the first declension.

2. *The second declension* includes *feminine* nouns ending in *-а (-я)* (*страна́* 'country', *земля́* 'land', *а́рмия* 'army').

Note. — Masculine nouns ending in *-а (-я)*: *ю́ноша* 'a youth', *ста́роста* 'monitor', *судья́* 'judge', *дя́дя* 'uncle', *Кузьма́* (a masculine name), *Ва́ня* (a diminutive masculine name) and nouns of common gender ending in *-а (-я)*: *сирота́* 'orphan', *у́мница* 'clever person', *рази́ня* 'gawk' also belong to the second declension.

3. *The third declension* includes *feminine* nouns without any ending in the nominative, whose stem ends in a soft consonant or a hard or soft sibilant (with a final *-ь* in spelling): *тень* 'shadow', *степь* 'steppe', *ночь* 'night', *рожь* 'rye', *мышь* 'mouse'.
The nouns *мать* 'mother' and *дочь* 'daughter' have some peculiarities in their declension (see Table 22).

II. Some nouns do not belong to any of the above types of declension and are declined in a special way; they are: the masculine noun *путь* 'way', the neuter nouns ending in *-мя: и́мя* 'name', *вре́мя* 'time', etc., and the neuter noun *дитя́* 'child'.

III. There are some nouns which are indeclinable and do not change according to number: *пальто́* 'overcoat', *кино́* 'cinema', *метро́* 'underground', *шоссе́* 'highway', *жюри́* 'jury', *кенгуру́* 'kangaroo', *ко́фе* 'coffee', etc. These nouns, borrowed from foreign languages, are neuter, except *ко́фе* 'coffee', which is masculine.

FIRST DECLENSION

Declension of Masculine and Neuter Nouns (with the Stem ending in a Hard or Soft Consonant)

Table 15

Singular

Cases	Masculine						Neuter		Endings
Nom.	ученик 'pupil'	завод 'plant'	вождь 'leader'	огонь 'fire'	герой 'hero'	бой 'battle'	дело 'affair'	поле 'field'	
Gen.	ученика	завода	вождя	огня	героя	боя	дела	поля	-а, -я
Dat.	ученику	заводу	вождю	огню	герою	бою	делу	полю	-у, -ю
Acc.	ученика	завод	вождя	огонь	героя	бой	дело	поле	as Nom. or Gen.
Instr.	учеником	заводом	вождём	огнём	героем	боем	делом	полем	-ом, -ём, -ем
Prep.	(об) ученике	(о) заводе	(о) вожде	(об) огне	(о) герое	(о) бое	(о) деле	(о) поле	-е

Cases	Masculine		Neuter	
Nom.	пролетарий 'proletarian'	санаторий 'sanatorium'	собрание 'meeting'	
Gen.	пролетария	санатория	собрания	
Dat.	пролетарию	санаторию	собранию	
Acc.	пролетария	санаторий	собрание	
Instr.	пролетарием	санаторием	собранием	
Prep.	(о) пролетарии	(о) санатории	(о) собрании	

Note. — 1. Nouns whose stem ends in a hard consonant take -а in the genitive, -у in the dative, -ом in the instrumental; but when the stem ends in a soft consonant these endings are spelt: -я in the genitive, -ю in the dative, -ём (if the ending is stressed) or -ем (if it is unstressed) in the instrumental.

2. The accusative of the following nouns is identical with the nominative: (a) of all neuter nouns, and (b) of all masculine nouns denoting inanimate objects: завод 'plant', бой 'battle'.

3. The accusative of masculine nouns denoting living beings is identical with the genitive (вождя gen. sing. of вождь 'leader', героя gen. sing. of герой 'hero'), except when they have a collective meaning, in which case their accusative is identical with the nominative (вижу народ 'I see some people', веду отряд 'I lead a detachment').

4. Masculine nouns ending in -ий and neuter nouns ending in -ие take -ии in the prepositional (пролетарий 'proletarian' — о пролетарии, собрание 'meeting' — о собрании).

Note on Spelling. — After sibilants (ж, ч, ш, щ) and ц the instrumental of masculine and neuter nouns with the ending stressed ends in -ом: ножом (instr. of нож 'knife'), плечом (instr. of плечо 'shoulder'), шалашом (instr. of шалаш 'hut'), плащом (instr. of плащ 'raincoat'), борцом (instr. of борец 'fighter'), кольцом (instr. of кольцо 'ring'); it ends in -ем when the ending is unstressed: сторожем (instr. of сторож 'watchman'), товарищем (instr. of товарищ 'comrade', 'friend'), сердцем (instr. of сердце 'heart').

Table 16

Peculiarities in Some Case-Forms of Masculine
Nouns belonging to the First Declension

I. Genitive Case ending in *-у (-ю)*

In the genitive singular, a number of masculine nouns end either in *-а (-я)* or in *-у (-ю)*. The ending *-у (-ю)* occurs in the following instances:

1. When the noun denotes a certain quantity or part of some substance or material: Note that *хлеб* 'bread' and *овёс* 'oats' never take the ending *-у* in the genitive.	кусóк сáхару 'a lump of sugar'; стакáн чáю 'a glass of tea'; килогрáмм мёду 'a kilogramme of honey'; килогрáмм пескý 'a kilogramme of granulated sugar'; купúть сáхару, рúсу, шёлку 'to buy some sugar, rice, silk stuff'; вы́пить чáю 'to drink some tea'; попрóбовать мёду 'to taste honey'; набрáть хвóросту 'to gather some brushwood' Я поднёс емý *чáшку чáю.* (П.) 'I treated him to a cup of tea.' Ворóне гдé-то бог послáл *кусóчек сы́ру.* (Кр.) 'Once upon a time a Crow was sent a small piece of cheese by Heaven.'
2. When the noun indicates: (a) place (after the prepositions *из* 'from', 'out of', *до* 'to'):	он вы́шел *из дóму* 'he came out of the house', *из лесу* 'out of the forest'; он шёл *дó дому* цéлый час 'it took him a whole hour to get to his house' (the stress is generally shifted to the preposition, the noun becoming enclitic). Волк *из лесу* в дерéвню забежáл... (Кр.) 'Out of the wood a Wolf into a village scampered...' Однáжды в студёную зúмнюю пóру Я *из лесу* вы́шел... Был сúльный морóз... (Некр.) 'One frosty day out of the wood I came... 'Twas mighty cold...'

(b) time (after the prepositions *до* 'till', *с* 'from', *óколо* 'about'):	*Дó дóму* ещё бы́ло вёрст вóсемь. (Т.) 'It was still about eight versts to my house.' Я ждал тебя́ *с чáсу* дня. 'I've been waiting for you since one o'clock in the afternoon.' Он ждал тебя́ *до чáсу* дня. 'He waited for you till one o'clock in the afternoon.' Мы броди́ли *пó лесу óколо чáсу*. 'We roamed the woods for about an hour.'
(c) cause (after the preposition *с (со)* 'from', 'for'):	Он побелéл *с испýгу, со стрáху*. 'He turned white with fright, with fear.' . . . . Онá заболéла *с перепýгу*. (Ч.) 'She fell ill with fright.'
3. In some special constructions with certain prepositions:	Я упусти́л э́то *из виду*. 'I did not take that into consideration.' Я не ви́дел егó *óт роду*. 'I've never seen him in my life.' Мы ждём егó *с чáсу на час*. 'We expect him to come any moment.' *С бóку нá бок*. 'From side to side.' *Бéз году недéля*. 'Only a few days.' *Бéз толку*. 'To no purpose.' . . . . *Час óт часу* огóнь слабéе становился. (Кр.) 'From hour to hour the fire became weaker.' Вéтер мéжду тем *час óт часу* становился сильнéе. (П.) 'Meanwhile the wind grew stronger and stronger from hour to hour.' А бéдный пруд *год óт году* всё глох. (Кр.) 'But the poor pond from year to year grew shallower.' А сéрдце во мне бьётся, как *óт роду* не би́лось. (Т.) 'And my heart is beating as it never did in all my life.' *Óт роду* не встречáл я счастли́вца столь блистáтельного. (П.) 'Never in my life have I met such a lucky man and so brilliant.'

53

4. When the noun is used in a negative construction:	Он не пришёл ко мне *ни рáзу.* 'He did not come to see me even once.' О нём *ни слýху, ни дýху.* 'Nothing has been heard of him.' . . . . .До сáмого концá декабря́ *не вы́пало снéгу.* (Т.) 'Till the very end of December no snow fell.' *Не покáзывай* дáже *вйду.* (Т.) 'Give no sign whatsoever.' — Помúлуй, мне и óт роду *нет гóду,* — ягнёнок говорúт. (Кр.) ' "Good gracious! I'm not even a year old," says the Lamb.' Из кóжи лéзут вон, а вóзу всё *нет хóду.* (Кр.) 'They strain, they nearly burst their skins, and yet the cart stands still.' Так пóтчевал сосéд Демья́н сосéда Фóку И не давáл емý *ни óтдыху, ни срóку.* (Кр.) 'Thus Demian feasted his neighbour Foka And gave him no time to rest or even breathe.'

Note. — The ending *-y (-ю)* in the genitive generally occurs in colloquial speech and also in fables, proverbs and sayings (*Не спрося́сь брóду, не сýйся в вóду;* cf. 'Look before you leap').

II. Prepositional Case ending in *-y (-ю)*

In the prepositional case following the prepositions *в* 'in', *на* 'on' (mostly indicating place), a number of masculine nouns take the stressed ending *-y (-ю).* They are mostly monosyllabic words: *лес* 'forest', *сад* 'garden', etc. In this table, the most frequently used nouns of this type are given (in alphabetic order).

в		*на*	
бор 'pine forest'	в борý	бéрег 'shore'	на берегý
бой 'battle'	в боıó	бок 'side'	на бокý
бред 'delirium'	в бредý	борт 'side'	на бортý
быт 'private life'	в бытý	вал 'shaft'	на валý
глаз 'eye'	в глазý	век 'century'	на векý

в		на	
год 'year'	в году́	воз 'cart'	на возу́
долг 'debt'	в долгу́		
дым 'smoke'	в дыму́		
жар 'fever'	в жару́		
край 'land'	в краю́	край 'edge'	на краю́
круг 'circle'	в кругу́	круг 'circle'	на кругу́
лоб 'forehead'	во лбу́	лоб 'forehead'	на лбу́
лес 'forest'	в лесу́	луг 'meadow'	на лугу́
лёд 'ice'	во льду́	лёд 'ice'	на льду́
мёд 'honey'	в меду́	мёд 'honey'	на меду́
мех 'fur'	в меху́	мех 'fur'	на меху́
мозг 'brain'	в мозгу́	мост 'bridge'	на мосту́
мох 'moss'	во мху́	мох 'moss'	на мху́
		мыс 'promontory'	на мысу́
нос 'nose'	в носу́	нос 'nose'	на носу́
плен 'captivity'	в плену́	плот 'raft'	на плоту́
полк 'regiment'	в полку́	пол 'floor'	на полу́
порт 'port'	в порту́	пост 'post'	на посту́
пруд 'pond'	в пруду́	пруд 'pond'	на пруду́
пух 'down'	в пуху́		
ров 'ditch'	во рву́		
род 'family'	в роду́	род 'family'	на роду́
рот 'mouth'	во рту́		
ряд 'row'	в ряду́		
сад 'garden'	в саду́		
снег 'snow'	в снегу́	снег 'snow'	на снегу́
сок 'juice'	в соку́	сук 'bough'	на суку́
строй 'formation'	в строю́		
тыл 'rear'	в тылу́		
у́гол 'corner'	в углу́	у́гол 'corner'	на углу́
ход 'circulation'	в ходу́	ход 'motion'	на ходу́
цвет 'blossom'	в цвету́		
шкаф 'cupboard'	в шкафу́	шкаф 'cupboard'	на шкафу́
Крым 'the Crimea'	в Крыму́	Дон 'the Don'	на Дону́

Хорошо́ *в бору́* дыша́ть сухи́м смоли́стым во́здухом. 'It is good to breathe dry resinous air in a pine wood.'

В порту́ стои́т большо́й кора́бль. 'There is a large ship in the port.'

Маши́на останови́лась *на по́лном ходу́*. 'The motor-car stopped dead.'

На лугу́ пестре́ли цветы́. 'Varicoloured flowers showed gaily in the meadow.'

· · · · · · · · · · ·

Дере́вья *в по́лном цвету́*. 'The trees are in full blossom.'

Больно́й три дня был *в бреду́*. 'The patient had been delirious for three days.'

. . . .

В лесу́ раздава́лся топо́р дровосе́ка. (Некр.) 'The sound of a wood-cutter's axe was heard in the wood.'

Кро́ет уж лист золото́й
Вла́жную зе́млю *в лесу́*. (М.)
'Golden leaves are already covering the moisty ground in the woods.'

В саду́ во тьме́ лени́во сы́плется тёплый дождь. (Л.Т.)
'In the garden, a warm rain is falling lazily in the darkness.'

Что и́щет он в стране́ далёкой?
Что ки́нул он *в краю́* родно́м? (Л.)
'What does he seek in a far country?
What has he left in his native land?'

...А сыр *во рту́* держа́ла. (Кр.)
'...But she held the cheese in her beak.'

Ры́льце у тебя́ *в пуху́*. 'Thy snout is covered with fluff.'

На берегу́ пусты́нных волн
Стоя́л он, дум вели́ких полн,
И вдаль гляде́л... (П.)
'On the shore, by the desolate billows,
He stood, full of great thoughts,
And gazed into the distance...'

На краю́ горизо́нта тя́нется сере́бряная цепь снеговы́х верши́н. (Л.) 'On the edge of the horizon there stretches a silvery chain of snow-capped mountains.'

Вчера́ я прие́хал в Пятиго́рск, на́нял кварти́ру *на краю́* го́рода. (Л.) 'Yesterday I arrived at Pyatigorsk, and engaged lodgings on the edge of the town.'

На по́лном бегу́ на́ бок сала́зки — и Са́ша в снегу́. (Некр.)
'At full-speed the sled turns on its side and — Sasha's in the snow.'

Bear in mind that when denoting the year or hour the prepositional case also requires the ending *-у (-ю)*: *В како́м году́?* 'In what year?' — *В 1947 году́.* 'In the year 1947.' *В про́шлом году́.* 'Last year.' *В кото́ром часу́?* 'At what hour?' — *В пе́рвом часу́.* 'Past twelve.' Also: *на своём веку́* 'in one's day': Мно́го ви́дел я люде́й *на своём веку́*. 'I saw many people in my day.'

Note. — 1. When preceded by other prepositions all these nouns take the usual prepositional case-ending *-е: о ле́се* 'about a forest', *о Кры́ме* 'about the Crimea', *о го́де* 'about the year', *о ча́се* 'about the hour', etc.

2. The archaic form *в ле́се* 'in the forest' sometimes occurs in folk songs: *В тёмном ле́се за реко́й стои́т до́мик небольшо́й.* 'In the dark forest beyond the river there is a small cottage.'

3. When the preposition *в* does not indicate place, the prepositional case ending is *-е*, e.g.: Он знáет толк *в лéсе.* 'He is quite an expert with timber.'

4. When used as names of books these nouns take the prepositional case ending *-е:* В «*Лéсе*» Острóвского... 'In "The Forest" by Ostrovsky...', В «Вишнёвом *сáде*» Чéхова... 'In "The Cherry Orchard" by Chekhov...'.

5. In Lermontov's poem «*Соснá*» "The Pine" the noun *край* 'land' is used in the prepositional case with the ending *-е: В том крáе,* где сóлнца восхóд... 'In the land whence the sun rises...'.

SECOND DECLENSION

Table 17

Feminine Nouns ending in -*а* (-*я*)

1. Nouns with the Stem ending in a Hard Consonant

			Endings		Nouns with the Stem ending in *г, к, х*		Endings
Nom.	странá 'country'	жéнщина 'woman'	-*а*	рукá 'arm' 'hand'	мýха 'fly'	дорóга 'road'	-*а*
Gen.	страны́	жéнщины	-*ы*	руки́	мýхи	дорóги	-*и*
Dat.	странé	жéнщине	-*е*	рукé	мýхе	дорóге	-*е*
Acc.	странý	жéнщину	-*у*	рýку	мýху	дорóгу	-*у*
Instr.	странóй	жéнщиной	-*ой* (-*ою*)	рукóй	мýхой	дорóгой	-*ой* (-*ою*)
Prep.	(о) странé	(о) жéнщине	-*е*	(о) рукé	(о) мýхе	(о) дорóге	-*е*

2. Nouns with the Stem ending in a Soft Consonant

				Endings		Endings
Nom.	земля́ 'land'	семья́ 'family'	стáя 'flock'	-*я*	áрмия 'army'	-*я*
Gen.	земли́	семьи́	стáи	-*и*	áрмии	-*и*
Dat.	землé	семьé	стáе	-*е*	áрмии	-*и*
Acc.	зéмлю	семью́	стáю	-*ю*	áрмию	-*ю*
Instr.	землёй (-ёю)	семьёй	стáей	-*ёй* (-*ёю*) -*ей* (-*ею*)	áрмией	-*ей*
Prep.	(о) землé	(о) семьé	(о) стáе	-*е*	(об) áрмии	-*и*

57

Note. — 1. Nouns with the stem ending in a hard consonant take the ending *-a* in the nominative, *-ы* in the genitive (but *-и* if the stem ends in *г, к* or *х: нога́* 'leg' — *ноги́, рука́* 'arm' — *руки́, му́ха* 'fly' — *му́хи*), *-е* in the dative, *-у* in the accusative, and *-ой (-ою)* in the instrumental.

2. Nouns whose stem ends in the hard sibilant *ж* or *ш (межа́* 'boundary', *кры́ша* 'roof') take *-и* in the genitive singular (*межи́, кры́ши*), which is pronounced as *-ы*.

3. Nouns whose stem ends in a soft consonant take *-я* in the nominative, *-и* in the genitive, *-е* in the dative, *-ю* in the accusative, and *-ей (-ею), -ёй (-ёю)* in the instrumental; nouns ending in *-ия (а́рмия* 'army', *ли́ния* 'line') take *-и* in the dative and the prepositional (*а́рмии, ли́нии*).

4. Masculine nouns and nouns of common gender ending in *-а (-я)* are also declined according to the second declension.

Note on Spelling. — After sibilants *(ж, ч, ш, щ,)* and *ц* the instrumental case is formed in *-ой (-ою)* if the ending is stressed: *межо́й* 'by a boundary', *свечо́й* 'with a candle', *овцо́й* 'by a sheep' and in *-ей* if it is unstressed: *кры́шей* 'with a roof', *ро́щей* 'by a grove', *пти́цей* 'by a bird', *ту́чей* 'by a cloud', *лу́жей* 'with a puddle'.

THIRD DECLENSION

Table 18

Feminine Nouns without an Ending and with the Stem ending in a Soft Consonant or a Hard or Soft Sibilant

Cases	Nouns with Stem ending in a Soft Consonant		Nouns with Stem ending in a Hard or Soft Sibilant			Endings
Nom.	жизнь 'life'	пло́щадь 'square'	ночь 'night'	рожь 'rye'	мышь 'mouse'	
Gen.	жи́зни	пло́щади	но́чи	ржи	мы́ши	*-и*
Dat.	жи́зни	пло́щади	но́чи	ржи	мы́ши	*-и*
Acc.	жизнь	пло́щадь	ночь	рожь	мышь	as Nom.
Instr.	жи́знью	пло́щадью	но́чью	ро́жью	мы́шью	*(-ь)ю*
Prep.	(о) жи́зни	(о) пло́щади	(о) но́чи	(о) ржи	(о) мы́ши	*-и*

1. The nominative and the accusative of nouns belonging to the third declension are always identical.

2. The genitive, dative and prepositional end in *-и (жи́зни, но́чи, ржи, мы́ши)*.

3. The instrumental case ends in *(-ь)ю (жи́знью*, etc.).

4. The nouns *мать* 'mother' and *дочь* 'daughter' follow a special pattern of declension (see Table 22).

Table 21

Peculiarities in the Declension of Nouns in the Plural

			Remarks
Nom.	гра́ждане 'citizens'	крестья́не 'peasants'	Masculine nouns ending in *-анин, -янин* (*гражданúн* 'citizen', *крестья́нин* 'peasant') end in *-ане, -яне* in the nominative plural and in *-ан, -ян* in the genitive plural (*гра́ждан, крестья́н*). All the other cases are formed from the stem by adding the normal case-ending (*гра́жданам, крестья́нам,* etc.).
Gen.	гра́ждан	крестья́н	
Dat.	гра́жданам	крестья́нам	
Acc.	гра́ждан	крестья́н	
Instr.	гра́жданами	крестья́нами	
Prep.	(о) гра́жданах	(о) крестья́нах	

			Remarks
Nom.	ребя́та 'children'	волча́та 'wolf-cubs'	Masculine nouns ending in *-ёнок, -онок* (*ребёнок* 'child', *волчóнок* 'wolf-cub') and denoting young living beings end in *-ата, -ята* in the nominative plural and in the stem-consonant in the genitive plural (*ребя́т, волча́т*). All the other cases are formed from the stem by adding the normal case-endings (*ребя́тами, волча́тами*, etc.). But: *бесёнок* 'imp' — *бесеня́та*, *чертёнок* 'imp' — *чертеня́та*.
Gen.	ребя́т	волча́т	
Dat.	ребя́там	волча́там	
Acc.	ребя́т	волча́т	
Instr.	ребя́тами	волча́тами	
Prep.	(о) ребя́тах	(о) волча́тах	

Nominative	Genitive	Remarks
глаза́ 'eyes'	глаз	A number of masculine nouns do not take any ending in the genitive plural, the form of the latter case being identical with that of the nominative singular.
чулки́ 'stockings'	чуло́к	
ва́ленки 'felt boots'	ва́ленок	
солда́ты 'soldiers'	солда́т	
партиза́ны 'guerrillas'	партиза́н	
грузи́ны 'Georgians'	грузи́н	
ту́рки 'Turks'	ту́рок	
башки́ры 'Bashkirs'	башки́р	

		Remarks
Nom.	лю́ди 'people'	The plural of the noun *челове́к* 'person' is used only in the oblique cases in combination with numerals, the form of the genitive plural being identical with that of the nominative singular (*два́дцать челове́к* 'twenty people'). The word *лю́ди* 'people' is used in all the cases in the plural.
Gen.	люде́й	
Dat.	лю́дям	
Acc.	люде́й	
Instr.	людьми́	
Prep.	(о) лю́дях	

Singular

	Neuter		Masculine	Feminine	
Nom.	и́мя	зна́мя	путь	мать	дочь
	'name'	'banner'	'way'	'mother'	'daughter'
Gen.	и́мени	зна́мени	пути́	ма́тери	до́чери
Dat.	и́мени	зна́мени	пути́	ма́тери	до́чери
Acc.	и́мя	зна́мя	путь	мать	дочь
Instr.	и́менем	зна́менем	путём	ма́терью	до́черью
Prep.	(об) и́мени	(о) зна́мени	(о) пути́	(о) ма́тери	(о) до́чери

Plural

	Neuter		Masculine	Feminine	
Nom.	имена́	знамёна	пути́	ма́тери	до́чери
Gen.	имён	знамён	путе́й	матере́й	дочере́й
Dat.	имена́м	знамёнам	путя́м	матеря́м	дочеря́м
Acc.	имена́	знамёна	пути́	матере́й	дочере́й
Instr.	имена́ми	знамёнами	путя́ми	матеря́ми	дочеря́ми (дочерьми́)
Prep.	(об) имена́х	(о) знамёнах	(о) путя́х	(о) матеря́х	(о) дочеря́х

Note. — 1. In the singular all the neuter nouns ending in *-мя* (*вре́мя* 'time', *зна́мя* 'banner', *пла́мя* 'flame', *се́мя* 'seed', *бре́мя* 'burden', *те́мя* 'top of the head', *вы́мя* 'udder', *стре́мя* 'stirrup', *пле́мя* 'tribe') follow the declension pattern of *и́мя* 'name'.

The words *пла́мя, бре́мя, те́мя, вы́мя* are never used in the plural. Unlike *и́мя* and other words in *-мя, зна́мя* has the stress on the suffix *-ён-* in all the cases in the plural. The genitive plural of *се́мя, стре́мя* is *семя́н, стремя́н*.

2. In Modern Russian, the neuter noun *дитя́* 'baby', 'child' is used in the singular only in the nominative and the accusative.

In all the other cases the forms of this word are generally replaced by the corresponding forms of the noun *ребёнок* 'child' (*ребёнку, ребёнком*, etc.). In the plural, both *дитя́* and *ребёнок* are used in all the cases; however, *дитя́* may be considered the more literary of the two, *ребёнок* being used mostly in colloquial speech. In the works of classics the oblique cases of the word *дитя́* occur.

Below we give the declension of the word *дитя́:*

Cases	Singular	Plural
Nom.	дитя́ 'baby', 'child'	де́ти
Gen.	дитя́ти	дете́й
Dat.	дитя́ти	де́тям
Acc.	дитя́	дете́й
Instr.	дитя́тей	детьми́
Prep.	(о) дитя́ти	(о) де́тях

3. The masculine noun *путь* 'way' is declined in the singular and plural as a feminine noun ending in a soft consonant (*кость* 'bone'), except the instrumental case (*путём*).

4. In the declension of the feminine nouns *мать* and *дочь* the stem in all the cases except the nominative singular ends in *-ер-*.

Table 23

Declension of Surnames of Persons and Names of Towns

Masculine Surnames ending in *-ын, -ин* and Masculine and Neuter Names of Towns and Settlements ending in *-ын(о), -ин(о):*

Nom.	Ильи́н 'Ilyin'	Пти́цын 'Ptitsyn'		Unlike masculine nouns, masculine surnames
Gen.	Ильина́	Пти́цына		ending in *-ин, -ын* take
Dat.	Ильину́	Пти́цыну		*-ым* in the instrumental
Acc.	Ильина́	Пти́цына		case.
Instr.	Ильины́м	Пти́цыным	*-ым*	
Prep.	(об) Ильине́	(о) Пти́цынс		

Nom.	Каля́зин 'Kalyazin'	Цари́цын(о)* 'Tsaritsyno'		Masculine and neuter names of towns and
Gen.	Каля́зина	Цари́цына		settlements ending in
Dat.	Каля́зину	Цари́цыну		*-ин(о), -ын(о)* are de-
Acc.	Каля́зин	Цари́цын(о)		clined as masculine nouns
Instr.	Каля́зином	Цари́цыном	*-ом*	ending in a hard conso-
Prep.	(о) Каля́зине	(о) Цари́цыне		nant.

Masculine and Neuter Names of Towns and Settlements ending in *-ов(о), -ев(о):*

Nom.	Сара́тов 'Saratov'	Ку́нцево 'Kuntsevo'		Masculine and neuter names of towns, settle-
Gen.	Сара́това	Ку́нцева		ments and villages end-
Dat.	Сара́тову	Ку́нцеву		ing in *-ов, -ев* are de-
Acc.	Сара́тов	Ку́нцево		clined as masculine nouns
Instr.	Сара́товом	Ку́нцевом	*-ом*	ending in a hard conso-
Prep.	(о) Сара́тове	(о) Ку́нцеве		nant.

---

* Цари́цын 'Tsaritsyn' is now called Волгогра́д 'Volgograd'.

Masculine Surnames ending in *-ов, -ев:*

Nom.	Петро́в 'Petrov'	Серге́ев 'Sergeyev'		Masculine surnames ending in *-ов, -ев* are declined as masculine nouns, but they take *-ым* in the instrumental case.
Gen.	Петро́ва	Серге́ева		
Dat.	Петро́ву	Серге́еву		
Acc.	Петро́ва	Серге́ева		
Instr.	Петро́вым	Серге́евым	*-ым*	
Prep.	(о) Петро́ве	(о) Серге́еве		

Feminine Surnames ending in *-ин-а, -ов-а.*

Nom.	Ильина́ 'Ilyina'	Петро́ва 'Petrova'	Feminine surnames ending in *-ин-а, -ов-а* are declined as feminine adjectives, but in the accusative they take the noun-ending *-y.*
Gen.	Ильино́й	Петро́вой	
Dat.	Ильино́й	Петро́вой	
Acc.	Ильину́	Петро́ву	
Instr.	Ильино́й	Петро́вой	
Prep.	(об) Ильино́й	(о) Петро́вой	

Masculine and Feminine Names and Surnames:

Иваницкий 'Ivanitsky' Бе́льский 'Belsky' Иваницкая 'Ivanitskaya' Бе́льская 'Belskaya'	Surnames with the endings identical with those of adjectives are declined as adjectives.
Ива́н Ива́нович 'Ivan Ivanovich' Мари́я Ива́новна 'Maria Ivanovna'	Names and patronymics are declined separately as nouns with the same endings.
Дурново́ 'Durnovo' Пушны́х 'Pushnykh' Чутки́х 'Chutkikh' Долги́х 'Dolgikh'	Russian surnames with endings uncommon in the Russian language are indeclinable.

Masculine and Feminine Names and Surnames:

Шевче́нко 'Shevchenko' Короле́нко 'Korolenko' Максиме́нко 'Maksimenko' Безборо́дко 'Bezborodko' Хво́йко 'Khvoiko'	Ukrainian surnames ending in *-енко* or *-ко* are generally indeclinable (*у Короле́нко* 'at Korolenko's', *у Хво́йко* 'at Khvoiko's'); if these surnames are declined, they follow the declension pattern of feminine nouns ending in *-а* (*у Максиме́нки* 'at Maksimenko's', *я писа́л Максиме́нке* 'I wrote to Maksimenko', *я ви́дел Максиме́нку* 'I saw Maksimenko', *я говори́л с Максиме́нкой* 'I spoke to Maksimenko').
Мицке́вич 'Mickewicz' Богдано́вич 'Bogdanovich' Боро́дич 'Borodich'	Masculine surnames ending in *-ич* or *-ович* are declined as nouns with the same endings. Feminine surnames with these endings are indeclinable.
Шмидт 'Shmidt' Мо́царт 'Mozart'	Foreign masculine surnames ending in a consonant are declined as nouns with the corresponding endings. Feminine surnames ending in a consonant are indeclinable.
Гариба́льди 'Garibaldi' Салье́ри 'Salieri' Россе́тти 'Rossetti' Золя́ 'Zola' Баку́ 'Baku' Тбили́си 'Tbilisi' Со́чи 'Sochi' Ско́пле 'Skoplje' Чика́го 'Chicago'	Non-Russian surnames ending in a vowel and foreign names of towns ending in *-у, -и, -е, -о* are indeclinable.
Гли́нка 'Glinka'	Non-Russian surnames ending in an unstressed *-а* are declinable.

MAIN TYPES OF STRESS IN NOUNS

1. Fixed stress is stress which falls on the same syllable in a given word in all cases, singular and plural: *победа* 'victory', *победы, победе*, etc.; *студент* 'student', *студента, студенту*, etc.; *движение* movement', *движения, движению*, etc.

Fixed stress is observed in all feminine and neuter nouns and in most masculine nouns whose nominative singular is not stressed on the first or the last syllable, e.g., *победа* 'victory', *палатка* 'tent', *болото* 'swamp', *движение* 'movement', *сапожник* 'shoemaker', *переплётчик* 'bookbinder'. Exceptions to this group are masculine nouns whose nominative plural ends in **-а (-я),** which are stressed on the last syllable in all cases in the plural, e.g., *профессор* 'professor' — *профессора*, gen. pl. *профессоров*, etc.; *учитель* 'teacher' — *учителя*, gen. pl. *учителей*, etc. Fixed stress is also observed in nouns whose nominative singular is stressed differently from those of the above group, e.g., *студент* 'student' (the nominative singular is stressed on the last syllable), *плотник* 'carpenter' (the nominative singular is stressed on the first syllable).

2. The stress is shifted to the beginning of the word in the accusative singular: *рука* 'arm' — acc. sing. *руку, голова* 'head' — acc. sing. *голову*.

3. The stress is shifted to the beginning of the word in the nominative plural: *рука* 'arm' — nom. pl. *руки, голова* 'head' — nom. pl. *головы*.

4. The stress is shifted to the beginning of the word in all the cases in the plural: *письмо* 'letter' — pl. *письма, писем, письмам*, etc.

5. The stress is shifted to the last syllable in all the oblique cases, singular and plural: sing. *конь* 'steed', *коня, коню*, etc., pl. *кони, коней*, etc.

6. The stress is shifted to the last syllable in all the oblique cases in the plural: *волк* 'wolf' — pl. *волки, волков, волкам*, etc.

7. The stress is shifted to the last syllable in the prepositional singular when in combinations with the prepositions **в, на** denoting place or time: *лес* 'wood' — *в лесу* 'in a wood', *мост* 'bridge' — *на мосту* 'on a bridge', *год* 'year' — *в прошлом году* 'last year', *печь* 'stove' — *на печи* 'on a stove', *степь* 'steppe' — *в степи* 'in the steppe'.

Note. — In the masculine gender, the stress is shifted in the prepositional case only if its ending is **-у.**

Table 24

MAIN TYPES OF STRESS-SHIFT IN THE NOUN

A. Feminine nouns ending in a stressed *-a (-я):*

Dissyllabic Nouns	Singular		
1. The stress is shifted to the first syllable in the accusative singular and nominative and accusative plural (in the word *земля* 'land' it is also shifted in all oblique cases plural except the genitive):	Nom. рука́ 'arm', 'hand'	земля́ 'land'	
	Gen. руки́	земли́	
	Dat. руке́	земле́	
	Acc. ──────────→		ру́ку, зе́млю
	Instr. руко́й	землёй	
	Prep. (о) руке́	(о) земле́	
	Plural		
	Nom. ──────────→		ру́ки, зе́мли
	Gen. рук, земе́ль		
	Dat. рука́м		зе́млям
	Acc. ──────────→		ру́ки, зе́мли, зе́млями, (о) зе́млях
	etc.		

	Singular	Plural
2. The stress is shifted to the first syllable in all the cases in the plural:	Nom. страна́ 'country'	стра́ны
	Gen. страны́	стран
	Dat. стране́	стра́нам
	etc.	etc.

	Singular
3. The stress may remain fixed:	Nom. статья́ 'article'
	Gen. статьи́
	etc.
	Plural
	Nom. статьи́
	Gen. стате́й
	etc.

A. Feminine nouns ending in a stressed -*a* (-*я*):

Trisyllabic Nouns	Singular		
1. With the combination -*оро*- or -*оло*- in the root (see Dissyllabic nouns, 1):	Nom. голова́ 'head'	сторона́ 'side'	
	Gen. головы́	стороны́	
	Dat. голове́	стороне́	
	Acc. ⟶		го́лову, сто́рону
	Instr. голово́й	стороно́й	
	Prep. (о) голове́	(о) стороне́	
	Plural		
	Nom. ⟶		го́ловы, сто́роны
	Gen. голо́в	сторо́н	
	Dat. голова́м	сторона́м	
	Acc. ⟶		го́ловы, сто́роны
	etc.		etc.

	Singular	
2. Without -*оро*- or -*оло*- in the root. The stress is shifted one syllable nearer to the beginning of the word in all the cases in the plural:	Nom. широта́ 'latitude'	
	Gen. широты́	
	Dat. широте́	
	Acc. широту́	
	etc.	

	Plural	
	Nom. ⟶	широ́ты
	Gen. ⟶	широ́т
	Dat. ⟶	широ́там
	etc.	etc.

B. Feminine nouns ending in a soft consonant or a sibilant:

1. The stress is shifted to the ending in all the oblique cases in the plural except the accusative:	**Singular** Nom. о́чередь 'queue', пло́щадь 'square', мышь 'mouse' Gen. о́череди, пло́щади, мы́ши etc.	
	Plural Nom. о́череди, пло́щади, мы́ши Gen. ⟶ Dat. ⟶ etc.	 очереде́й, площаде́й, мыше́й очередя́м, площадя́м, мыша́м etc.
2. The stress is shifted to the ending in the prepositional singular and in all the oblique cases in the plural except the accusative:	**Singular** Nom. печь 'stove' Gen. пе́чи Dat. пе́чи Acc. печь Instr. пе́чью Prep. { о пе́чи в печи́	In words of this type the stress falls on the ending in the prepositional case only if the latter is used to indicate place: *в печи́* 'in a stove', but: *о сте́пи* 'about the steppe'.
	Plural Nom. пе́чи Gen. ⟶ Dat. ⟶ etc.	 пече́й печа́м etc.

B. Feminine nouns ending in a soft consonant or a sibilant:

3. The stress may in some instances remain fixed on the same syllable:	Singular Nom. тетра́дь 'copy-book' Gen. тетра́ди Dat. тетра́ди etc. Plural Nom. тетра́ди Gen. тетра́дей etc.

C. Masculine nouns ending in a consonant:

1. The stress is shifted to the ending in all the oblique cases in the singular and in all the cases in the plural. The shifting occurs, among other instances, in all nouns with a stressed unstable *o* or *e* in the last syllable if the latter is stressed in the nominative singular, e.g.: *кусо́к* 'piece', gen. sing. *куска́*, etc.; *бое́ц* 'warrior', gen. sing. *бойца́*, etc. (however, if the last syllable of the word is not stressed in the nominative singular, the stress remains fixed, e.g., *ва́ленок* 'felt boot', gen. sing. *ва́ленка*;	Singular
	Nom. стари́к 'old man'
	  дождь 'rain'
	Gen. ⟶
	Dat. ⟶
	etc.
	
	Plural
	Nom. ⟶
	Gen. ⟶
	Dat. ⟶
	etc.
	
	Singular
	Nom. ого́нь 'fire'
	  оте́ц 'father'
	Gen. ⟶
	Dat. ⟶
	etc.
		
		стари́ка́, дождя́
		старику́, дождю́
		etc.
		
		старики́, дожди́
		старико́в, дожде́й
		старика́м, дождя́м
		etc.
		
		огня́, отца́
		огню́, отцу́
		etc.

C. Masculine nouns ending in a consonant:

	Plural	
комсомо́лец 'Young Communist Lea-guer', gen. sing. *комсомо́льца*):	Nom. ⟶	огни́, отцы́
	Gen. ⟶	огне́й, отцо́в
	Dat. ⟶	огня́м, отца́м
	etc.	etc.

	Singular	
2. The stress is shifted to the ending in the oblique cases in the singular and plural:	Nom. гвоздь 'nail'	
	Gen. ⟶	гвоздя́
	Dat. ⟶	гвоздю́
	etc.	etc.
	Plural	
	Nom. гво́зди	
	Gen. ⟶	гвозде́й
	Dat. ⟶	гвоздя́м
	etc.	etc.

	Singular	
3. The stress is shifted to the ending in all the cases in the plural:	Nom. сад 'garden'	
	Gen. са́да	
	Dat. са́ду	
	etc.	
	Plural	
	Nom. ⟶	сады́
	Gen. ⟶	садо́в
	Dat. ⟶	сада́м
	etc.	etc.

	Singular	
4. The stress is shifted to the ending in all the oblique cases in the plural:	Nom. волк 'wolf'	
	Gen. во́лка	
	Dat. во́лку	
	etc.	
	Plural	
	Nom. во́лки	
	Gen. ⟶	волко́в
	Dat. ⟶	волка́м
	etc.	etc.

C. Masculine nouns ending in a consonant:

	Singular	
5. The stress is shifted to the ending in **all** the cases in the plural:	Nom. го́род 'city', 'town' учи́тель 'teacher' Gen. го́рода, учи́теля Dat. го́роду, учи́телю etc.	
	Plural	
	Nom. ——————→ Gen. ——————→ Dat. ——————→ etc.	города́, учителя́ городо́в, учителе́й города́м, учителя́м etc.
6. The stress may remain fixed:	Singular	
	Nom. студе́нт 'student' Gen. студе́нта Dat. студе́нту etc.	
	Plural	
	Nom. студе́нты Gen. студе́нтов Dat. студе́нтам etc.	

Note. — 1. In masculine nouns ending in a consonant and taking, in the prepositional singular, the ending *-у (-ю)* the latter is always stressed, e.g., *в лесу́* 'in a forest', *в саду́* 'in a garden', *на краю́* 'on the edge'.

2. In masculine nouns ending in a consonant and taking, in the nominative plural, the ending *-a (-я)* the latter is always stressed, e.g., *города́* 'cities', *учителя́* 'teachers'.

D. Neuter nouns ending in *-o, -e (-ĕ):*

Dissyllabic Words	Singular	
1. Words with the stress on the first syllable. The stress is shifted to the ending in all the cases in the plural:	Nom. ме́сто 'place', по́ле 'field', мо́ре 'sea' Gen. ме́ста, по́ля, мо́ря Dat. ме́сту, по́лю, мо́рю etc.	
	Plural	
	Nom. ⟶ Gen. ⟶ Dat. ⟶	места́, поля́, моря́ мест, поле́й, море́й места́м, поля́м, моря́м etc.
	etc.	
2. Words with the stress on the ending. The stress is shifted to the first syllable in all the cases in the plural:	Singular Nom. окно́ 'window', лицо́ 'face', ружьё 'gun' Gen. окна́, лица́, ружья́ Dat. окну́, лицу́, ружью́ etc.	
	Plural	
	Nom. ⟶ Gen. ⟶ Dat. ⟶	о́кна, ли́ца, ру́жья о́кон, лиц, ру́жей о́кнам, ли́цам, ру́жьям etc.
	etc.	
3. The stress may remain fixed:	Singular Nom. жа́ло 'sting' Gen. жа́ла Dat. жа́лу etc.	
	Plural Nom. жа́ла Gen. жал Dat. жа́лам etc.	

D. Neuter nouns ending in *-o, -e (-ё)*

Trisyllabic Words		
	Singular	
1. Words with the stress on the first syllable. The stress is shifted to the second syllable in all the cases in the plural:	Nom. óзеро 'lake' Gen. óзера Dat. óзеру etc.	
	Plural	
	Nom. ⟶	озёра
	Gen. ⟶	озёр
	Dat. ⟶	озёрам
	etc.	etc.
	Singular	
2. Words with the stress on the ending. The stress is shifted to the second syllable in all the cases in the plural:	Nom. ремесло́ 'trade' Gen. ремесла́ Dat. ремеслу́ etc.	
	Plural	
	Nom. ⟶	ремёсла
	Gen. ⟶	ремёсел
	Dat. ⟶	ремёслам
	etc.	etc.
	Singular	
3. The stress may also remain fixed:	Nom. боло́то 'swamp' варе́нье 'jam' Gen. боло́та, варе́нья Dat. боло́ту, варе́нью etc.	
	Plural	
	Nom. боло́та, варе́нья Gen. боло́т, варе́ний Dat. боло́там, варе́ньям etc.	

STRESS IN PREPOSITION + NOUN PHRASES

Sometimes a noun preceded by a preposition throws its stress back on to the preposition and so loses its own stress. This occurs in the following instances:

1. In the accusative singular and plural of feminine nouns ending in *-a (-я)* with the stress on the last syllable if, in the accusative singular, the latter is shifted to the first syllable, e.g., *рука́* 'arm' — *ру́ку* — *за́ руку* 'by the arm' — *за́ руки* 'by the arms'; *голова́* 'head' — *го́лову* — *за́ голову* 'by the head'.

Example: Он схвати́лся *за́ голову.* 'He seized his head.'

2. In the accusative and, occasionally, in the instrumental singular of masculine nouns which have *-оро-* or *-ере-* in the root and end in a consonant if they are stressed on the first syllable, e.g., *го́род* 'city', 'town' — *за́ город* 'to the country', *за́ городом* 'in the country'; *бе́рег* 'shore' — *на́ берег* 'on to the shore'.

Examples: Мы пое́хали *за́ город.* 'We went to the country.'
Я живу́ *за́ городом.* 'I live in the country.'

3. In the dative and accusative singular of a number of monosyllabic masculine nouns ending in a consonant and stressed on the first syllable in the oblique cases in the singular, e.g.:

мост 'bridge', *мо́ста, мо́сту,* etc. — *по́ мосту* 'across the bridge', *на́ мост* 'on to the bridge'.

4. In the dative, accusative, instrumental and prepositional singular of dissyllabic neuter nouns stressed on the first syllable, e.g.:

по́ле 'field', *по́ля,* etc. — *по́ полю* 'across the field', *на́ поле* 'in the field'.
мо́ре 'sea', *мо́ря,* etc. — *по́ морю* 'on the sea', *на́ море* 'on the sea', *за́ морем* 'beyond the sea'.

Note. — In Modern Russian, the stress in the above instances is often placed on the noun and not on the preposition. The stress is always placed on the preposition when the combination of the preposition and noun has an adverbial meaning, e.g., я живу́ *за́ городом* (i.e. 'I live in the country'), but со́лнце сади́лось *за го́родом* (i.e. 'the sun was setting behind the town'); уро́ки за́дали *на́ дом* 'the lessons were to be done at home', but смотре́л *на до́м* '(he) looked at the house'.

73

USES OF CASES WITHOUT PREPOSITIONS

Table 25

Uses of the Genitive Case

The genitive of the noun is used with another noun, an adjective, numeral or a verb.

A. With nouns, adjectives or numerals the genitive is mainly used:

I. With nouns: **1.** To denote possession (the genitive answers the questions *чей?, чья?, чьё?, чьи?* 'whose?'):	— Чей э́то каранда́ш? 'Whose pencil is this?' — Это каранда́ш *бра́та*. 'It is the brother's pencil.' — Чья э́то тетра́дь? 'Whose note-book is this?' — Это тетра́дь *сестры́*. 'It is the sister's note-book.' — Чьё э́то ружьё? 'Whose gun is this?' — Это ружьё *отца́*. 'It is the father's gun.' — Чьи э́то кни́ги? 'Whose books are these?' — Это кни́ги *това́рищей*. 'These are the comrades' books.'
2. To denote the agent of an action:	Речь *учи́теля*. 'The teacher's speech.' Отве́т *ученика́*. 'The pupil's answer.' Пе́ние *де́вушки*. 'The girl's singing.' Выступле́ние *делега́тов*. 'The delegates' speeches.' Бой *часо́в*. 'The striking of a clock.'
3. To denote the object acted upon (the object to which the action passes):	Чте́ние *кни́ги*. 'The reading of a book.' Пе́ние *рома́нса*. 'The singing of a romance.' Слу́шание *ле́кций*. 'The listening to lectures.' Убо́рка *урожа́я*. 'The gathering in of the harvest.'
	Note. — With verbs the accusative is required: *чита́ть кни́гу* 'to read a book', *петь рома́нс* 'to sing a romance', *слу́шать ле́кции* 'to listen to lectures', *убира́ть урожа́й* 'to gather in the harvest'.
4. To denote: (a) a characteristic feature of an object:	Демонстра́ция *дру́жбы* и *еди́нства*. 'A demonstration of friendship and unity.' Пра́здник *пе́сни*. 'A song festival.' Вопро́сы *совреме́нности*. 'Problems of our time.'

(b) a descriptive attribute of an object:

Ма́льчик *высо́кого ро́ста*. 'A tall boy.'
Челове́к *большо́го ума́*. 'A person of great intellect.'
Места́ *порази́тельной красоты́*. 'Places of extreme beauty.'
Бума́га *пе́рвого со́рта*. 'Best-quality paper.'

Note. — A descriptive attribute generally consists not of a noun alone but of a noun qualified by an adjective.

Note. — In most instances, the attribute consisting of a noun qualified by an adjective can be replaced by an adjective (*высо́кий ма́льчик* 'a tall boy', *первосо́ртная бума́га* 'best-quality paper') or by an adjective qualified by an adverb (*о́чень у́мный челове́к* 'a very intelligent person', *порази́тельно краси́вые места́* 'extremely beautiful places').

(c) the possessor of a quality:

Сме́лость *геро́я*. 'The hero's courage.'
Ум *челове́ка*. 'Man's intellect.'
Темнота́ *но́чи*. 'The dark of the night.'
Белизна́ *сне́га*. 'The whiteness of snow.'
Теплота́ *во́здуха*. 'The warmth of the air.'
Просто́р *поле́й*. 'The expanse of the fields.'

II. With the comparative degree of an adjective:

Сестра́ *приле́жнее бра́та*. 'The sister is more diligent than her brother.'
Во́лга *ши́ре Оки́*. 'The Volga is wider than the Oka.'

Note. — There is another way of expressing comparison: Сестра́ *приле́жнее, чем брат*. 'The sister is more diligent than her brother.' Во́лга *ши́ре, чем Ока́*. 'The Volga is wider than the Oka.' In such constructions the conjunction *чем* 'than' is used and the noun denoting the object compared with some other object stands in the nominative.

Утро *ве́чера мудрене́е*. (Proverb) Cf. 'Take counsel with your pillow.'
Охо́та *пу́ще нево́ли*. (Proverb) Cf. 'Where there's a will, there's a way.'

III. With the adjectives *по́лон* 'full (of)', *по́лный* 'full (of)', *досто́ин* 'worthy (of)', *досто́йный* 'worthy (of)':

Дом *по́лон люде́й*. 'The house is full of people.'
Ко́мната *полна́ наро́ду*. 'The room is full of people.'
Се́ти *бы́ли полны́ ры́бы*. 'The nets were full of fish.'

Он принёс корзи́ну, *по́лную я́блок.* 'He brought a basket full of apples.'

Её глаза́ *полны́ слёз, полны́ ра́дости.* 'Her eyes are full of tears, filled with joy.'

Note. — Masculine nouns occurring in such combinations generally take the ending *-y (-ю)* in the singular (*полна́ наро́ду* 'full of people'). With *по́лон* 'full', 'filled' abstract nouns take the genitive ending *-a (-я)* and not *-y (-ю)* (*по́лон восто́рга* 'filled with delight').

. . . .

Оно́ (я́блоко) *со́ку спе́лого полно́...* (П.) 'It (the apple) is full of ripe juice...'

Хлопо́т марты́шке *по́лон рот...* (Кр.) 'The monkey has its hands full of trouble...'

По́лный разду́мья, шёл я одна́жды по большо́й доро́ге. (Т.) 'Plunged in thought, I was once walking along a highroad.'

На берегу́ пусты́нных волн
Стоя́л он, *дум вели́ких полн...* (П.) 'On the shore, by the desolate billows, He stood, full of great thoughts...'

Note. — 1. Although the genitive case is usual in such combinations, the instrumental case occasionally occurs:
Тоско́й и *тре́петом полна́,*
Тама́ра ча́сто у окна́
Сиди́т в разду́мье одино́ком... (Л.)
'Full of melancholy and trepidation,
Tamara would often sit at the window,
Plunged in lonely thoughts...'

2. With verbs derived from *по́лный* 'full' (*наполниться, заполниться* 'to be filled') only the instrumental is used (*Её глаза́ напо́лнились слеза́ми.* 'Her eyes filled with tears.'; but: *Её глаза́ полны́ слёз.* 'Her eyes are full of tears.').

Эта рабо́та *досто́йна награ́ды.* 'This work deserves a reward.'

IV. With words denoting quantity: (1) With cardinal numerals in the nominative or accusative (which is identical with the nominative):	(a) with *два, две* 'two', *о́ба, о́бе* 'both (the)', *три* 'three', *четы́ре* 'four' and compound numerals whose last word is *два, три, четы́ре*	(b) with *пять* 'five', *шесть* 'six', *семь* 'seven', etc. the genitive plural is used:

(e.g., *двáдцать два* 'twenty-two', *стó трúдцать три* 'one hundred and thirty-three') the genitive singular is used:

Numeral	Noun (gen. sing.)
два 'two' óба 'both (the)' три 'three' четы́ре 'four' сто два 'one hundred and two' сóрок три 'forty-three' сто пятьдеся́т четы́ре 'one hundred and fifty-four'	каран-дашá 'pen-cils' альбóма 'al-bums' ученикá 'school-boys'

Numeral	Noun
пять 'five' шесть 'six' семь 'seven' двенáд-цать 'twelve' тринáд-цать 'thirteen' три́дцать пять 'thirty-five' сто пятьдеся́т вóсемь 'one hundred and fifty-eight'	каран-дашéй 'pen-cils' альбó-мов 'al-bums' ру́чек 'pens' тетрá-дей 'exer-cise-books' ученикóв 'school-boys' учени́ц 'school-girls'

Numeral	Noun
две 'two' óбе 'both (the)' три 'three' четы́ре 'four' сто две 'one hundred and two' сóрок три 'forty-three' сто пятьдеся́т четы́ре 'one hundred and fifty-four'	ру́чки 'pens' тетрá-ди 'exer-cise-books' учени́цы 'school-girls'

В э́той гру́ппе бы́ло *два́дцать три* челове́ка. 'There were twenty-three people in this group.'

В кла́ссе *три́дцать пять* ученико́в: *два́дцать де́вочек* и *пятна́дцать ма́льчиков*. 'There are thirty-five pupils in the class: twenty girls and fifteen boys.'

Вчера́ я купи́л *три альбо́ма, четы́рнадцать карандаше́й* и *со́рок две тетра́ди*. 'Yesterday I bought three albums, fourteen pencils and forty-two exercise-books.'

. . . .
Шли *два прия́теля* вече́рнею поро́й.
И де́льный разгово́р вели́ между́ собо́й.
(Кр.)
'Two friends were walking one evening
And were talking busily with each other.'
Прошли́ *две-три мину́ты* — та же тишина́. (Герц.) 'Two or three minutes went by — and the same silence fell again.'

В песча́ных степя́х арави́йской земли́
Три го́рдые *па́льмы* высо́ко росли́...
(Л.)
'In the sandy deserts of Arabia
There grew three tall proud palms...'
Три молоды́х *де́рева* расту́т пе́ред две́рью пеще́ры: ли́па, берёза и клён. (М. Г.) 'Three young trees grow in front of the entrance to the cave: a lime, a birch and a maple.'

(For the agreement of the adjective with the noun, see Table 43.)

Челове́к пять ста́ли мы́ться в го́рном холо́дном ручье́. (М. Г.) 'About five people began to wash in a cold mountain stream.'

Челове́к семь... направля́лось к нам. (М. Г.) 'About seven people ... were approaching us.'

Note. — 1. With the nominative or accusative of a collective numeral (*дво́е* 'two', *тро́е* 'three', *че́тверо* 'four', etc.) the noun takes the genitive plural: *дво́е дете́й* 'two children', *тро́е това́рищей* 'three friends'.

2. If a numeral (from *два* on) is neither in the nominative nor in the accusative (identical with the nominative), the numeral and the noun agree in case: Я встрéтил *трёх товáрищей.* 'I met three friends.' Я придý *к семи часáм.* 'I shall come by seven o'clock.'

3. With the words *тысяча* 'thousand', *миллиóн* 'million', *миллиáрд* 'milliard' ('billion') the noun always takes the genitive plural: В библиотéку привезли *тысячу книг.* 'A thousand books were brought to the library.' Артисты выступили пéред *девятью тысячами зрителей.* 'The actors performed before nine thousand spectators.'

(2) With words denoting indefinite quantity: *мнóго* 'many', 'much', 'a lot', *немнóго* 'some', 'a little', *мáло* 'few', 'little', *немáло* 'not a few', 'many'; 'not a little', 'much', *нéсколько* 'some', 'several', *большинствó* 'the majority (of)', 'most (of)', *меньшинствó* 'the minority (of)', *скóлько* 'how many', 'how much', *стóлько* 'so many', 'so much', etc.:

Мнóго фáбрик и завóдов. 'Many factories and plants.'

Нéсколько библиотéк. 'Several libraries.'

Я прочитáл *нéсколько статéй.* 'I've read several articles.'

Нам пришлóсь приложить *мнóго усилий.* 'It required much effort on our part.'

Мнóго угля, желéза, электроэнéргии. 'Much coal, iron, electric power.'

Note. — When used with the words *мнóго* 'many', 'much', *мáло* 'few', 'little', etc., nouns which have no plural are used in the singular: *мнóго серебрá и желéза* 'much silver and iron', *мнóго счáстья* 'much happiness', *мáло энéргии* 'little energy'.

. . . .

Широкá странá моя роднáя,
Мнóго в ней *лесóв, полéй* и *рек!*

(Л.-К.)

'Spacious is my native country,
Many are its forests, fields and rivers!'

Мнóго звёзд в безмóлвии ночнóм горит.

(Бар.)

'Many stars shine in the silence of the night.'

Мнóжество пчёл, ос и *шмелéй* дрýжно гудит в густых ветвях акáций. (Т.)
'A lot of bees, wasps and bumble-bees are humming all together in the bushy boughs of the acacias.'

Скóлько тут было кудрявых *берёз!...*

(Некр.)

'What a lot of leafy birches there were here!...'

(3) With words denoting a measure:

Кило хлéба. 'A kilo of bread.'
Литр молокá. 'A litre of milk.'
Стакáн воды. 'A glass of water.'
Метр ситца. 'A metre of cotton print.'

B. With verbs the genitive is used:

I. To denote part of a whole quantity (the action involves only part of the whole). Thus *вы́пей воды́* **means 'drink some water', while** *вы́пей во́ду* **means 'drink (the whole of) the water'.**

Наре́жь *хле́ба.* 'Cut some bread.'
Нале́й *молока́.* 'Pour out some milk.'
Принеси́ *дров.* 'Bring some firewood.'
Пое́шь *я́год.* 'Eat some berries.'
Я купи́л *мя́са, со́ли, овоще́й.* 'I bought some meat, salt and vegetables.'

Note. — In such constructions (a) the nouns used are generally the names of some material or substance, (b) the verbs used are generally perfective ones.
Я нае́лся *я́год* и напи́лся *молока́.* 'I've had my fill of berries and of milk.'
Я начита́лся *книг.* 'I've read enough books.'
Я накупи́л *книг.* 'I've bought a lot of books.'

II. To denote the object of a transitive verb preceded by the negative particle (the so-called genitive of negation):

Я не получи́л сего́дня *газе́т, письма́.* 'I have not received any papers, any letter today'
Я не ви́дел э́той *карти́ны.* 'I haven't seen that picture.'
Не люблю́ *ци́рка.* 'I don't like the circus.'

Note. — 1. In colloquial speech transitive verbs preceded by the negative particle are sometimes followed by the accusative: Я не брал *э́ту кни́гу.* 'I didn't take that book.' Смотри́ не потеря́й *тетра́дь.* 'See that you don't lose the exercise-book.' *Зарпла́ту* я ещё не получи́л. 'I haven't received my salary (wages) yet.' The accusative is generally used when the speaker wants to stress the fact that the object in question is a definite one or when he wants to make his statement more categoric.
2. If the verb is used figuratively and its object is not a noun indicating a concrete thing, the accusative is never used: В рабо́те он не знал *уста́лости.* 'He never tired of working.' Его́ предложе́ние не встре́тило *поддержки.* 'His proposal failed to get support.'

. . . .
В ко́мнатах ещё не зажига́ли *огня́.* (Ч.) 'There were no lights in the rooms yet.'
Из пе́сни *сло́ва* не вы́кинешь. (Proverb) 'You can't leave a (single) word out of a song.'

III. In impersonal sentences with the words *нет* 'there is (are) no', *нé было* 'there was (were) no', *не будет* 'there will be no':

Сегóдня *нет собрáния*. 'There is no meeting today.'
Зáвтра *дóктора не будет*. 'The doctor will not be here tomorrow.'
Вчерá *нé было дождя*. 'There was no rain yesterday.'

У меня	нет нé было не будет	бумáги карандашá врéмени	'I	have no had no shall have no	paper pencil time.'

Моегó *брáта (сестры, отцá, мáтери) нет* дóма. 'My brother (sister, father, mother) is not at home.'

Меня Тебя Егó Её Нас Вас Их	нет нé было не будет	дóма.	'I 'You 'He, it 'She, it 'We 'You 'They	am, is, are not was, were not shall, will not be	at home.'

Note. — 1. One may say: Вчерá *мы нé были* дóма. 'We were not at home yesterday', *мы* 'we' being the subject and *нé были* 'were not', the predicate. However, the impersonal construction with the genitive is more literary: Вчерá *нас нé было* дóма. 'We were not at home yesterday.'

2. Some verbs with the particle *не* can be used in the sense of *нет* 'there is (are) no', *нé было* 'there was (were) no', *не будет* 'there will be no', e. g., *не существует* 'does not (do not) exist', *не оказáлось* 'turned out not to be', *не остáлось* 'did not remain', *не встречáлось* 'did not occur', *не произошлó* 'did not happen', etc. Nouns used with these verbs also take the genitive: В этой рабóте ужé *не существует* (or *не встречáется*) никакúх *трудностей*. 'There are no longer any difficulties whatever in this work.' В кáссе теáтра *не остáлось* ни одногó *билéта*. 'There is not a single ticket left at the theatre booking-office.' *Не остáлось* никакúх *сомнéний*. 'There are no longer any doubts left whatever.' В киóске *не оказáлось* нужных нам *книг*. 'They did not have the books we needed at the bookstall.' Пóезд вóвремя остановúлся и *крушéния не произошлó*. 'The train stopped in time, and no accident occurred.'

. . . .

Ветра нет, и нет ни сóлнца, ни свéта,
ни тéни, ни движéния, ни шýма... (Т.)

'There is no wind, and no sun, no light, no shade, no movement, no noise...'

Печа́лен я: со мно́ю *дру́га нет*...   (П.)
'I feel sad: my friend is not with me...'

В теле́ге е́ду по холма́м —
Поро́й для взо́ра *нет грани́ц*,
И всё поля́ по сторона́м,
И над поля́ми ста́и птиц.   (М.)
'I drive in a cart over the hillocks:
At times the view before me is boundless,
And fields upon fields stretch on both sides,
And over them fly flocks of birds.'

Я добра́лся, наконе́ц, до угла́ ле́са, но там *не́ было* никако́й *доро́ги*. (Т.) 'I reached the corner of the forest at last, but there was no road there.'

Луны́ не́ было на не́бе: она́ в ту по́ру по́здно всходи́ла. (Т.) 'There was no moon in the sky: at that time of the year it rose late.'

IV. To denote the object of verbs indicating attainment, loss, deprivation, etc.:

добива́ться, ⎱ 'to
доби́ться ⎰ achieve'
(чего́? 'what?')

Добива́ться (доби́ться) успе́хов, выполне́ния пла́на, разреше́ния вопро́са. 'To achieve success, the fulfilment of a plan, the solution of a problem.'

достига́ть ⎱'to
дости́гнуть ⎰achieve',
дости́чь 'to reach'
(чего́? 'what?')

Достига́ть (дости́чь) це́ли, успе́хов. 'To achieve one's goal, success.'
Серьёзных *успе́хов дости́гла* промы́шленность. 'Industry has achieved considerable success.'
Дости́чь бе́рега, верши́ны. 'To reach the shore, the summit.'
Они́ *дости́гли верши́ны* горы́. 'They reached the top of the mountain.'
Мы уси́ленно рабо́тали вёслами и бы́стро *дости́гли бе́рега.* 'We rowed lustily and soon reached the shore.'

тре́бовать ⎱ 'to de-
потре́бовать ⎰ mand'
(чего́? 'what?')

Тре́бовать (потре́бовать) дисципли́ны, выполне́ния пла́на, объясне́ния, внима́ния, тишины́. 'To demand discipline, the fulfilment of a plan, an explanation, attention, silence.'

Трéбовать бумáги, книг. 'To demand paper, books.'

. . . .

Большо́го напряже́ния и вели́кой стра́сти тре́бует нау́ка от челове́ка. (Па́влов) 'Science requires of man much strain and great passion.'

Note. — When the object of the verb *тре́бовать* 'to demand' denotes part of a certain quantity or number it always takes the genitive (*тре́бовать бумáги, книг* 'to demand paper, books'); in other cases, when the object in question is a definite one, the verb *тре́бовать* requires the accusative (*Я тре́бую свою́ кни́гу.* 'I demand my book.').

проси́ть ⎫
попроси́ть ⎬ 'to ask'
(чего́? 'for what?')

Проси́ть (попроси́ть) воды́, по́мощи, поща́ды, внима́ния, сове́та, извине́ния. 'To ask for water, help, mercy, attention, advice, pardon.'

Больно́й попроси́л воды́. 'The sick man asked for water.'

. . . .

А он, мяте́жный, про́сит бу́ри,
Как бу́дто в бу́рях есть поко́й. (Л.)
'And he, wild rover, asks for tempests,
As if in tempests there was peace.'

Note. — In some instances, the verb *проси́ть* 'to ask' requires the accusative: *Я попроси́л в библиоте́ке интере́сную кни́гу.* 'I asked for an interesting book at the library.' *Больно́й попроси́л сестру́.* 'The patient asked for a nurse.'

иска́ть 'to look for', 'to seek'
(чего́? '(for) what?')

Иска́ть по́мощи, подде́ржки. 'To seek help, support.'

Иска́ть сове́та, слу́чая. 'To seek advice, an opportunity.'

Больно́й иска́л по́мощи. 'The sick man was looking for help.'

Я иска́л слу́чая поговори́ть с дру́гом. 'I was looking for an opportunity to speak to my friend.'

Мы и́щем в иску́сстве глубо́кой жи́зненной *пра́вды, отве́та* на волну́ющие вопро́сы совреме́нности. 'In art we seek profound truthfulness to life, an answer to the burning questions of the day.'

ждать
(ожидáть) } 'to wait'
дожидáться } 'to
дождáться } wait'
(чегó? 'for what?')

Note. — The accusative is required in the following instances: *Я ищý шáпку, кнúгу.* 'I am looking for my cap, my book', and also in the question *Что ты úщешь?* 'What are you looking for?'

Ждать пóмощи, концá, решéния, назначéния, разрешéния вопрóса. 'To wait for help, the end, a decision, an appointment, the solution of a question.'

Ожидáть удáра. 'To expect a blow.'

Онú *ждáли пóезда* двáдцать минýт. 'They waited twenty minutes for the train.'

Мы *дождалúсь решéния вопрóса.* 'We waited until the question was settled.'

Наконéц *дождалúсь теплá.* 'At last warm weather has come.'

Всё в прирóде *ждáло* весéннего *дóждика.* 'Everything in nature longed for a spring shower.'

Note. — 1. The accusative must be used in the following instances: *Я ждал сестрý, брáта.* 'I was waiting for my sister, brother.' However, occasionally the genitive is used, as in Turgenev: *Он всё ждал Лúзы.* 'He was still waiting for Liza.'

2. If the object of the action is a noun denoting a definite specific thing or person the accusative is used after the verbs *трéбовать* 'to demand', 'to require', *искáть* 'to look for', *ждать* 'to wait for', e.g., *Я трéбую* свою *кнúгу.* 'I demand my book'. (but: *Я трéбую возвращéния* кнúги. 'I demand the return of the book.') *Попросú* в библиотéке *нóвую кнúгу.* 'Ask for a new book at the library.' *Я ищý шáпку, рýчку.* 'I am looking for my cap, my pen. (but: *Я ищý слýчая* поговорúть с тобóй. 'I am looking for an opportunity to talk to you.'); *Я жду сестрý, мать.* 'I am waiting for my sister, mother.'

3. Following the above verbs (usually in the imperfective aspect), nouns denoting means of conveyance generally take the genitive: Он *ждал пóезда, трамвáя, самолёта, парохóда,* etc. 'He was waiting for the train, tram, aeroplane, ship.' The word *письмó* also takes the genitive: Онá *ждалá* с нетерпéнием *письмá.* 'She was waiting impatiently for a letter.'

хотéть
захотéть } 'to want'
(чегó? 'what?')

Хотéть чáю, хлéба, печéнья. 'To want tea, bread, biscuits.'

Хотéть мúра, спокóйствия, тишины́. 'To want peace, tranquillity, quiet.'

. . . .
Мать чу́вствовала, что от неё *чего́-то хотя́т, ждут*. (М. Г.) 'The Mother felt they wanted, expected her to do something.'

жела́ть *пожела́ть* } 'to wish' (чего́? 'what?')	*Жела́ть сча́стья, здоро́вья, успе́хов.* 'To wish happiness, good health, success.' *Жела́ю (пожела́ю) вам сча́стья, здоро́вья, успе́хов.* 'I wish (I'll wish) you happiness, good health, success.'

. . . .
Оте́ц *пожела́л* мне *до́брого пути́.* (П.) 'My father wished me a happy journey.'
Мы дру́жбою на́шей могу́чей сильны́,
Мы *сча́стья хоти́м*,
Не жела́ем войны́. (О.)
'We are strong thanks to our great
                                        friendship,
We want happiness,
We don't want war.'

каса́ться *косну́ться* } 'to touch' (кого́? 'whom?', чего́? 'what?')	*Каса́ться стола́, руки́.* 'To touch the table, someone's hand.' *Каса́ться вопро́са.* 'To touch upon a question.' Докла́дчик *косну́лся* трёх *вопро́сов.* 'The speaker touched upon three questions.'

. . . .
Что́-то тёплое *косну́лось Его́рушкиной спины́.* (Ч.) 'Something warm touched Yegorushka's back.'
Мелька́ют ла́сточки, почти́ *каса́ясь земли́* изо́гнутыми кры́льями. (М. Г.) 'Swallows flash about, almost touching the ground with their curved wings.'
Дунове́ние живо́й си́лы *косну́лось се́рдца* ма́тери, будя́ его́. (М. Г.) 'A puff of invigorating strength touched on the Mother's heart, awakening it.'
Я не есте́ственник, и не моё де́ло *каса́ться* подо́бных *вопро́сов.* (Г.) 'I am not a science student, and it is not my business to touch upon such questions.'

держа́ться
придёржи- } 'to keep'
ваться
(чего? 'to what?')

Держа́ться мне́ния, пра́вила. 'To be of an opinion, to keep to a rule.'
Он *де́ржится (придёрживается) стро́гих пра́вил.* 'He is a man of strict habits.'
Больно́й стро́го *придёрживался дие́ты.* 'The patient kept to a rigorous diet.'
Я *держу́сь того́ мне́ния,* что... 'I am of the opinion that...'

слу́шаться } 'to lis-
послу́шаться } ten'
(кого? 'to whom?',
чего? 'to what?')

Слу́шаться (послу́шаться) ма́тери, отца́, това́рищей. 'To listen to one's mother, father, friends.'
Слу́шаться го́лоса со́вести. 'To listen to the voice of one's conscience.'

сто́ить
(in the sense of 'to be worthy', 'to deserve' чего? 'what?')

Это *сто́ит награ́ды.* 'It is worthy of a reward.'
Его́ рабо́та *сто́ит награ́ды.* 'His work is worthy of a reward.'

Note. — The genitive is also used with the adjectives *досто́йный, досто́ин* 'worthy': Он *досто́ин награ́ды.* 'He is worthy of a reward.'

лиша́ться } 'to lose'
лиши́ться }
(кого? 'whom?', чего? 'what?')

Лиши́ться (лиша́ться) зре́ния, слу́ха, поко́я. 'To lose one's sight, hearing, one's peace of mind.'
Лиши́ться сна. 'To suffer from sleeplessness.'
Лиши́ться отца́, ма́тери. 'To lose one's father, mother.'
Больно́й *лиши́лся сна.* 'The sick man suffered from sleeplessness.'
Лиши́ться споко́йствия. 'To become restless.'
Лиши́ться прав. 'To forfeit one's rights.'
Лиши́ться капита́ла, де́нег. 'To lose one's capital, money.'
Лиши́ть себя́ ра́дости. 'To deprive oneself of joy.'

лиша́ть } 'to deprive'
лиши́ть }
(чего? 'of what?')

. . . .
Бе́лый колосса́льный ствол берёзы, *лишённый верху́шки,* поднима́лся из зелёной гу́щи. (Т.) 'The enormous white trunk of a birch, with the crown missing, rose above the green thicket.'

боя́ться 'to be afraid' (кого́? 'of whom?', чего́? 'of what?')

пуга́ться *испуга́ться* } 'to be frightened' (кого́? 'by whom?', чего́? 'by what?')

Боя́ться *темноты́, грозы́, мо́лнии.* 'To be afraid of darkness, a thunderstorm, lightning.'

Он *испуга́лся гро́ма.* 'He was frightened by the thunder-clap.'

Ребёнок *бои́тся соба́ки.* 'The child is afraid of the dog.'

. . . .

Одни́ подде́льные цветы́ *дождя́ боя́тся.* (Кр.) 'Only artificial flowers are afraid of rain.'

Волко́в боя́ться — в лес не ходи́ть. (Proverb) Cf. 'Nothing venture, nothing have.'

Де́ло *ма́стера бои́тся.* (Proverb) Cf. 'He works best who knows his trade.'

избега́ть *избежа́ть* } 'to escape', 'to avoid', 'to shun' (кого́? 'whom?', чего́? 'what')?

Избега́ть (избежа́ть) *опа́сности, после́дствий, неприя́тностей.* 'To escape danger, consequences, trouble.'

Избега́ть *люде́й, встре́чи, разгово́ров, ссо́ры.* 'To avoid people, meeting (someone), talking, a quarrel.'

Путеше́ственники *избежа́ли опа́сности.* 'The travellers escaped danger.'

опаса́ться *остерега́ться* } 'to fear' (кого́? 'whom?', чего́? 'what?')

Опаса́ться (остерега́ться) *после́дствий, осложне́ний.* 'To fear the consequences, complications.'

Врач *опаса́лся осложне́ний* по́сле опера́ции. 'The doctor feared complications following the operation.'

стесня́ться 'to be shy' (кого́? 'of whom?', чего́? 'of what?')

Стесня́ться *люде́й, о́бщества, чужи́х.* 'To be shy of people, society, strangers.'

стыди́ться 'to be ashamed' (кого́? 'of whom?', чего́? 'of what?')

Стыди́ться *своего́ ви́да, своего́ костю́ма.* 'To be ashamed of one's appearance, one's clothes.'

Стыди́ться *незна́ния.* 'To be ashamed of one's ignorance.'

сторони́ться (*чужда́ться*) } 'to avoid', 'to shun' (кого́? 'whom?', чего́? 'what?')

Сторони́ться *о́бщества, чужда́ться люде́й.* 'To shun society, to avoid people.'

Note. — The genitive is used to denote the date: Она́ прие́хала *два́дцать пя́того а́вгуста 1948 го́да.* 'She came on the twenty-fifth of August, 1948.' Заня́тия начну́тся *пятна́дцатого сентября́.* 'Lessons will begin . on the fifteenth of September.' But (a) in cases like Сего́дня *два́дцать пя́тое а́вгуста.* 'Today is the twenty-fifth of August.' *Пе́рвое сентября́* — день нача́ла на́ших заня́тий. 'The first of September is the day when our lessons begin.' the nominative is used; (b) when only the year is given the prepositional is used: Он прие́хал в Москву́ *в ты́сяча девятьсо́т со́рок восьмо́м году́.* 'He came to Moscow in nineteen forty-eight.'

(For the use of the genitive with prepositions, see Table 29.)

Table 26

Uses of the Dative Case

The dative is used with verbs, nouns or adjectives (mostly with verbs).

The Dative is mostly used:

I. With verbs or nouns to denote the indirect object:	*Написа́ть сестре́.* 'To write to one's sister.' *Письмо́ сестре́.* 'A letter to one's sister.' *Помога́ю това́рищу.* 'I help my friend.' *По́мощь това́рищу.* 'Help for one's friend.' *Отвеча́ть учи́телю.* 'To answer the teacher.' *Отве́т учи́телю.* 'An answer to the teacher.' **Note.** — Note the use of the dative in the following combinations: *Па́мятник Пу́шкину* 'A monument to Pushkin', *Па́мятник Го́голю* 'A monument to Gogol'.
II. With the following frequently used verbs & verb phrases: уделя́ть внима́ние } 'to pay удели́ть } attention' внима́ние) (кому́? 'to whom?', чему́? 'to what?')	*Уделя́ть внима́ние де́тям, сестре́, больно́му.* 'To give attention to one's children, sister, a sick man.' Во вре́мя ле́тнего о́тдыха необходи́мо *уделя́ть* мно́го *внима́ния спо́рту.* 'During the summer holidays much attention should be given to sport.' Печа́ть и радиовеща́ние *уделя́ют* большо́е *внима́ние нау́чно-просвети́тельной пропага́нде.* 'The press and radio give much attention to scientific and educational propaganda.'
зав*и́*довать 'to envy' (кому́? 'whom?', чему́? 'what?')	*Зави́довать кому́-нибудь, зави́довать успе́хам.* 'To envy somebody, to envy success.' Все *зави́дуют моему́ здоро́вью.* 'Everybody envies my health.'

The Dative is mostly used:

рáдоваться
порáдоваться } 'to rejoice', 'to be glad', 'to be happy'

(комý? 'at whom?', чемý? 'at what?')

Рáдоваться письмý, успéхам, хорóшей погóде. 'To be glad to get a letter, to rejoice in somebody's success, to be glad of the fine weather.'

Все рáдуются весéннему сóлнцу. 'Everybody rejoices at the spring sun.'

Also with the words: *рад, рáда, рáдо, рáды* 'glad':

Я óчень рад твоемý приéзду. 'I am very glad you came.'

. . . .

И рáды мы прокáзам мáтушки-зимы. (П.) 'And we rejoice in Mother Winter's pranks.'

удивля́ться *удиви́ться* } 'to be surprised'

поража́ться *порази́ться* } 'to be astonished'

(комý? 'at whom?', чемý? 'at what?')

способствовать 'to contribute' (чемý? 'to what?')

Удивля́ться работоспосóбности, спокóйствию, си́ле. 'To be surprised at one's efficiency, composure, strength.'

Пораж́аться мýжеству. 'To be astonished at one's courage.'

Спосóбствовать успéху товáрища. 'To contribute to a friend's success.'

Спосóбствовать развитию дрýжественных отношéний мéжду двумя́ странами. 'To contribute to the development of friendly relations between two countries.'

III. In impersonal sentences, to denote the person required to perform an action or experiencing a certain state:
(1) With the words *нáдо* 'it is necessary', 'one must'; *необходи́мо* 'it is necessary', 'one must'; *нýжно* 'it is necessary', 'one must'; *мóжно* 'one is allowed', 'one may'; *нельзя́* 'it is impossible', 'one cannot', 'one must not',

Моемý брáту необходи́мо вы́ехать сегóдня. 'My brother must leave today.'

Вам нýжно закóнчить рабóту в срок. 'You must finish the work in time.'

Всем сотрýдникам нáдо прийти́ на собрáние к пяти́ часáм. 'All the employees must come to the meeting by five o'clock.'

Мóжно мне кури́ть? 'May I smoke?'

Тебé нельзя́ кури́ть. 'You must not smoke.'

The Dative is mainly used:

etc. followed by the infinitive of a verb:

With an infinitive to denote obligation or inevitability of an action:

Всем сотрудникам собраться в пять часов. 'All the employees are to gather at five o'clock.'

Моему товарищу ехать в два часа. 'My friend is to leave at two .o'clock.'

Куда *тебе ехать* завтра? 'Where are you to go tomorrow?'

. . . .

Быть грозе великой! (П.) 'There will be a terrible storm!'

Быть вам к вечеру! (Фурм.) 'You shall come by night!'

Свадьбе не бывать! (Г.) 'The wedding shall not take place!'

(2) With impersonal verbs ending in the reflexive particle *-ся:*

Мне не спится. 'I cannot sleep.'

Мне сегодня что-то не поётся. 'Today I cannot sing somehow.'

Брату нездоровится. 'The brother does not feel well.'

Мне сегодня не работалось, не читалось, не писалось. 'I could not work, could not read, could not write today.'

Мне здесь нравится. 'I like it here.'

In the same construction but with an infinitive used as part of a complex predicate:

Слушателям не хотелось уходить. 'The listeners did not wish to leave.'

Мне хочется поехать в горы. 'I feel like going to the mountains.'

Товарищу приходится часто *ездить* в командировки. 'My friend has often to go away on business.'

Сестре удалось летом хорошо *отдохнуть.* 'The sister managed to get a good rest in the summer.'

Мне нравится бродить по горам. 'I like to rove the mountains.'

. . . .

Тёмной осённей ночью *пришлось мне ехать* по незнакомой дороге. (Т.) 'One dark autumn night I had to travel along an unfamiliar road.'

The Dative is mainly used:

Взгрустну́лось ка́к-то *мне* в степи́ одно-обра́зной. 'I felt somewhat sad in the monotonous steppe one day.'

О, как глубоко́ и ра́достно *вздохну́лось Са́нину,* как то́лько он очути́лся у себя́ в ко́мнате. (Т.) 'Oh, how happily Sanin breathed as soon as he found himself in his own room.'

Не писа́лось ему́ на э́тот раз. (Ч.) 'He could not write this time.'

Литви́нов взя́лся за кни́гу, но *ему́ не чита́лось.* (Т.) 'Litvinov took a book, but he felt he could not read.'

(3) With adverbs used as part of a compound predicate:

(a) with adverbs ending in **-o** (formed from qualitative adjectives):

Това́рищу	
Сестре́	*ве́село, хорошо́, гру́стно,*
Мне	*ску́чно, сты́дно, хо́лодно,*
Нам	etc.

'The comrade	
'The sister	feel(s) gay, good, sad,
'I	bored, ashamed, cold',
'We	etc.

Note the expressions: *Мне жаль...* 'I am sorry...' *Мне жаль това́рища.* 'I am sorry for my friend.' *Мне жаль сестру́.* 'I am sorry for my sister.' *Мне жаль вре́мени.* 'I grudge the time.' *Мне жаль расста́ться* с това́рищем. 'I am sorry to part with my friend.' *Мне лень...* 'I don't feel like...'. *Мне лень* занима́ться. 'I don't feel like studying.' *Мне пора́...* 'It is time for me...' *Мне пора́ идти́.* 'It is time for me to go.'

(b) with negative adverbs:

Мне не́куда сего́дня *идти́.* 'I have nowhere to go today.'

Мне не́когда гуля́ть. 'I have no time to go for a walk.'

Нам не́куда спря́таться от дождя́. 'There is nowhere for us to shelter from the rain.'

Тебе́ не́зачем э́то *знать.* 'You needn't know that.'

Ему́ не́откуда ждать пи́сем. 'There is nowhere for him to expect letters from.'

91

The Dative is mainly used:

IV. With some adjectives (in both long and short forms): *благода́рный, благода́рен* 'grateful' *ве́рный, ве́рен* 'true', 'faithful' *подо́бный, подо́бен* 'like' *сво́йственный, сво́йствен* 'characteristic (of)'	Я *вам* о́чень *благода́рен.* 'I am very grateful to you.' Оте́ц, *ве́рный* своему́ *обеща́нию*, своди́л сы́на в зоопа́рк. 'As he had promised, the father took his son to the Zoo.' Я не встреча́л люде́й, *подо́бных* э́тому челове́ку. 'I haven't met people like that man.' Он рабо́тал со *сво́йственной ему́* эне́ргией. 'He worked with energy so characteristic of him.'

(For the dative used with prepositions, see Table 30.)

Uses of the Accusative Case

Table 27

The accusative is used with verbs.

The Accusative is mainly used:

I. With a transitive verb to denote the direct object (provided the verb is not in the negative form):	*Чита́ть газе́ту.* 'To read a newspaper.' *Получи́ть письмо́.* 'To get a letter.' *Стро́ить фа́брики, заво́ды...* 'To build factories, plants...' Беззаве́тно *лю́бим свою́ Ро́дину.* 'We love our mother country selflessly.' . . . . Вы *чита́йте, чита́йте ру́сскую литерату́ру* как мо́жно бо́льше, всё чита́йте! (М. Г.) 'You read, read as much Russian literature as possible, read everything!' *Люби́те кни́гу...* (М. Г.) 'Love books...' Он *ро́щи* полюби́л густы́е, *Уедине́нье, тишину́,* И *ночь,* и *звёзды,* и *луну́.* (П.) 'He got to like the thick groves, The solitude, the silence, And the nights, the stars, and the moonlight.' *Люблю́ тебя́,* Петра́ творе́нье, *Люблю́* твой стро́гий, стро́йный *вид.* (П.) 'I love thee, Peter's creation; I love thy austere well-proportioned outlines.'

The Accusative is mainly used:

Below are a number of frequently used verbs which require the accusative:
благодарить ⎱'to
поблагодарить⎰thank'
(кого? 'whom?', что? 'what?')

Благодарю вас, товарищей, сестру, etc. 'I am thankful to you, to my friends, to my sister', etc.

Note. — With the words *благодарен, благодарны* the dative is used: Я *благодарен вам, тебе, товарищам, сестре.*

поздравлять ⎱'to con-
поздравить ⎰gratu-
late'
(кого? 'whom?')

Поздравляю вас, товарищей, сестру, etc. 'I congratulate you, my comrades, my sister', etc.

вспоминать⎱'to recol-
вспомнить ⎰lect'
(кого? 'whom?', что? 'what?')

Я часто *вспоминаю* нашу *дружбу...* 'I often recollect our friendship.'
. . . .
Бойцы *вспоминают* минувшие *дни*
И *битвы,* где вместе рубились они. (П.)
'The warriors recollect the old times,
And the battles where together they fought
side by side.'

II. With verbs:
(a) to denote a period of time or a distance:

Всю зиму стояла тёплая погода. 'The whole winter the weather kept warm.'
Я *работал весь день.* 'I worked the whole day.'
Я *буду месяц* на практике. 'I'll have practice for a month.'
Я *всё лето проживу* в деревне. 'I'll spend the whole summer in the country.'
Я *провёл неделю* на юге. 'I spent a week in the south.'
Шли бой *всю осень и всю зиму.* 'Fighting was on the whole autumn and winter.'
Всю дорогу они *шли* молча. 'They kept silent all the way.'

(b) to denote the price of an object:

Книга стоит рубль. 'The book costs one rouble.'
Почтовый бланк стоит копейку. 'The post form costs one copeck.'

(For the accusative used with prepositions, see Table 31.)

Table 28

Uses of the Instrumental Case

The instrumental is used with verbs and nouns (mainly verbal nouns).

The Instrumental is mainly used:

I. To denote the instrument of action:	Я *пишу мéлом, карандашóм.* 'I write with chalk, with a pencil.' Я *вытирáю (стирáю) тряпкой.* 'I rub off with a duster.' Я *рéжу ножóм, нóжницами.* 'I cut with a knife, scissors.' Я *рублю топорóм.* 'I chop with an axe.' Я *размáхиваю рукáми.* 'I am swinging my arms.' (The instrumental is also used after verbal nouns: *рýбка топорóм* 'chopping with an axe', *размáхивание рукáми* 'swinging one's arms'.) . . . . Старúк *ловúл нéводом* рыбу, Старýха прялá свою прáжу. (П.) 'The old man caught fish with his drag-net, The old woman spun her yarn.' Он ушёл неохóтно, тяжелó *шáркая ногáми.* (М. Г.) 'He left unwillingly, shuffling his feet heavily as he went.' Пахáть — не *рукáми махáть.* (Proverb) 'Ploughing is not (so easy as) swinging one's arms.'
II. To denote the circumstances of action: (1) to denote the place through, along or over which a movement occurs:	*Éхать пóлем, лéсом, мóрем.* 'To go across a field, through a wood, by sea.' *Идтú бéрегом.* 'To go along the bank (shore).' Какóй *дорóгой* мне *идтú?* 'Which road am I to take?' Заяц выскочил из лесу и *побежáл пóлем.* 'The hare rushed out of the wood and ran across the field.' . . . .

94

The Instrumental is mainly used:

	По ни́ве *прохожу́* я у́зкою *межо́й*, Поро́сшей ка́шкою и це́пкой *лебедо́й*. (М.) 'Across a field I thread my way along a narrow borderline, All thickly grown in clovers and stick goose-foots.' Вы бы *ле́сом шли, ле́сом идти́* прохла́дно. (М. Г.) 'Why don't you go through the wood? it is cool walking through the wood.' Я *возвраща́лся* домо́й пусты́ми *переу́лками* станиц. (Л.) 'I was returning home along the deserted streets of Cossack villages.'
(2) to denote time:	*Рабо́тать ноча́ми.* 'To work by night.'
	Note. — Some Russian speakers say *рабо́тать вечера́ми* 'to work in the evening', *рабо́тать утра́ми* 'to work in the morning'. However, the expressions *рабо́тать по вечера́м* 'to work in the evening', *рабо́тать по утра́м* 'to work in the morning' should be preferred. One cannot say *рабо́тать дня́ми* or *рабо́тать по дням*; however, it is possible to say *рабо́тать це́лыми дня́ми* or *рабо́тать по це́лым дням* 'to work all day long', though the meaning of these expressions is somewhat different.
	Ра́нним у́тром он *уходи́л* в по́ле. 'Early in the morning he went to the fields.' *Возвраща́ться по́здней но́чью.* 'To come back late at night.' . . . . *Тёмной осе́нней но́чью пришло́сь* мне *е́хать* по незнако́мой доро́ге. (Т.) 'One dark autumn night I had to travel along an unfamiliar road.'
(3) to denote a difference in time (with a comparative):	*Двумя́ дня́ми* ра́ньше, по́зже. 'Two days earlier, later.' Я прие́хал *двумя́ дня́ми* ра́ньше това́рища. 'I arrived two days earlier than my comrade.'
(4) to denote manner (the instrumental then answers the questions *как?* 'how?', *каки́м о́бразом?* 'in what manner?'):	*Говори́ть шёпотом.* 'To speak in whispers.' *Говори́ть гро́мким го́лосом, ти́хим го́лосом.* 'To speak in a loud voice, in a soft voice.'

The Instrumental is mainly used:

	Широкой полосой тянутся поля. 'Fields stretch in a wide band.'
	. . . .
	Лучше умереть героем, чем *жить рабом!* (Горб.) 'It's better to die like a hero than to live like a slave!'
	Дождь полил ручьями. (Т.) 'The rain fell in torrents.'
	Горит восток *зарёю новой.* (П.) 'A new dawn is glowing in the east.'
	Солнце садилось: широкими багровыми полосами разбегались его последние лучи. (Т.) 'The sun was setting; its last rays were streaming in broad crimson bands.'
	Амфитеатром громоздятся горы. (Л.) 'Mountains tower up amphitheatre-like.'
(5) to denote a means of conveyance:	*Ехать пароходом, поездом.* 'To go by ship, by train.' *Прилететь самолётом.* 'To arrive by plane.'
	Note. — In the literary language the expressions *прилетел на самолёте* 'arrived by plane', *приехал на поезде* 'came by train' are preferred.
III. To denote the agent in passive constructions:	*Дома строятся рабочими.* 'Houses are built by workers.' *Поля обрабатываются колхозниками.* 'Fields are cultivated by collective farmers.'
IV. To denote the agent in impersonal constructions:	(a) *Водой залило* луга. 'The meadows were flooded with water.' *Градом побило* хлеб. 'The corn was beaten by the hail.' *Ветром сорвало* крышу. 'The roof was torn away by the wind.' (b) *Пахнет цветами.* 'It smells of flowers.'

The Instrumental is mainly used:

V. The instrumental is used as part of a compound predicate with the verbs:
быть 'to be'
становиться 'to become'
стать 'to become'
оказаться 'to turn out (to be)'
являться 'to be'

казаться 'to seem'

называться ⎱ 'to be
назваться ⎰ called'

оставаться ⎱ 'to re-
остаться ⎰ main'

считаться 'to be considered'
делаться ⎱ 'to be-
сделаться ⎰ come'

Он *был студентом.* (One may also say: Он был студент.) 'He was a student.'
Он *стал инженером.* 'He became an engineer.'
Он *оказался прекрасным работником.* 'He turned out to be an excellent worker.'
Он *является членом* этой организации. 'He is a member of that organization.'
Этот человек *кажется* очень *опытным и знающим.* 'This man seems to be quite experienced and skilful.'

Бором называется лес, в котором растут хвойные деревья. 'A forest consisting of coniferous trees is called a "bor".'

Она всегда *остаётся спокойной* в минуты опасности. 'She always remains calm in an hour of danger.'

Он *считается прекрасным работником.* 'He is considered to be an excellent worker.'
Он *сделался взрослым человеком.* 'He became a grown-up man.'

. . . .

Пьер *казался растерянным и смущённым.* (Л. Т.) 'Pierre looked confused and embarrassed.'

Она в семье своей родной
Казалась девочкой чужой. (П.)
'In her own family.
She looked a strange girl.'

Через пять минут он перестал *быть гостем,* а *сделался своим человеком* для всех нас. (Л. Т.) 'After five minutes he no longer looked a stranger, but seemed to be quite at home among us.'

The Instrumental is mainly used:

	Слепо́й ма́льчик *оказа́лся прекра́сным музыка́нтом*... (Кор.) 'The blind boy turned out to be a fine musician...'
VI. With the following frequently used verbs:	
руководи́ть 'to lead', 'to supervise'	*На́шим кружко́м руководи́т* преподава́тель. 'Our study group is supervised by a teacher.'
управля́ть 'to govern', 'to drive'	Шофёр *управля́ет маши́ной.* 'A driver drives a car.'
кома́ндовать 'to command'	Това́рищ *кома́ндует ро́той (батальо́ном, полко́м, диви́зией*...). 'The comrade commands a company (a battalion, a regiment, a division...).'
заве́довать 'to be in charge of'	Он *заве́дует моло́чной фе́рмой.* 'He is in charge of a dairy-farm.'
облада́ть 'to have', 'to possess'	Лётчики должны́ *облада́ть больши́м споко́йствием.* 'Flyers must possess great composure.'
владе́ть 'to be able', to use'	Учени́к хорошо́ *владе́ет ру́сским языко́м.* 'The pupil has a good command of Russian.'
овладе́ть 'to master'	Он *овладе́л но́вой профе́ссией.* 'He has mastered a new trade.'
по́льзоваться 'to enjoy', 'to use'	Това́рищ *по́льзуется дове́рием, влия́нием, любо́вью, авторите́том.* 'The comrade enjoys confidence, has influence, is liked, carries authority.'
занима́ться ⎱ 'to take up', 'to deal (with)' заня́ться ⎰	Он *занима́ется спо́ртом.* 'He goes in for sport.' На́до *заня́ться э́тим вопро́сом.* 'This question should be attended to.'
интересова́ться 'to be interested (in)'	Ученики́ *интересу́ются ру́сской литерату́рой.* 'The pupils are interested in Russian literature.'
увлека́ться ⎱ 'to be interested (in)', 'to be carried away' увле́чься ⎰	Они́ *увлека́ются свое́й рабо́той, увлека́ются интере́сными ле́кциями.* 'They are interested in their work, carried away by the interesting lectures.'
горди́ться 'to be proud'	Мы *горди́мся достиже́ниями нау́ки.* 'We are proud of the achievements of science.'

The Instrumental is mainly used:

любоваться 'to admire'

хвалиться 'to boast'

восхищаться 'to admire'

наслаждаться 'to enjoy'

злоупотреблять 'to abuse'

болеть 'to be ill'
заболеть 'to fall ill'

Мы *любуемся природой*. 'We admire nature.'

Мальчик *хвалится своей силой*. 'The boy boasts of his strength.'

Мы *восхищаемся музыкой* Рахманинова. 'We admire Rakhmaninov's music.'

Мы *наслаждаемся весенним солнцем, летним отдыхом*. 'We enjoy spring sunshine, our summer holidays.'

Нельзя *злоупотреблять доверием, хорошим отношением*. 'Confidence, good-will must not be abused.'

Он *заболел гриппом, тифом, тяжёлой болезнью*. 'He was taken ill with the 'flu, typhus, a serious disease.'

Note. — The instrumental is also used with nouns denoting actions and formed from the verbs *руководить* 'to lead', 'to supervise', *управлять* 'to govern' 'to drive', *овладеть* 'to master', etc.: *руководство массами* 'leading the masses' (but: *руководитель масс* 'leader of the masses'), *управление государством* 'government of the state', *овладение техникой* 'mastery of technique', *увлечение математикой* 'enthusiasm for mathematics' (but: *интерес к математике* 'interest in mathematics'), *наслаждение отдыхом* 'enjoyment of holidays', *злоупотребление солнечными ваннами* 'abuse of sunbathing'.

. . . .

Я *наслаждаюсь дуновеньем*
В лицо мне веющей весны. (П.)
'I enjoy the puffs of spring air
Blowing into my face.'

Душой овладевает спокойствие, о прошлом не хочется думать. (Ч.) 'Calmness comes over you and you do not want to think of the past.'

Лев *не нахвалится усердием* друзей. (Кр.)
'The Lion had no words to praise his friends' zeal.'

The Instrumental is mainly used:

VII. With the adjectives: *довóлен* *довóльна* } 'pleased' *довóльны*	Я *довóлен рабóтой*. 'I am pleased with the work.' Онá *довóльна свóими успéхами*. 'She is pleased with her achievements.' Мы *довóльны результáтами рабóты*. 'We are pleased with the results of the work.' . . . . Учúлась Каштáнка óчень охóтно и *былá довóльна свóими успéхами*. (Ч.) 'Kashtanka learned quite willingly and was pleased with her achievements.' Скучнá мне óттепель: вонь, Грязь — веснóй я бóлен... *Сурóвою зимóй я бóлее довóлен*... (П.) 'The thaw displeases me with its stink and mud — I am unwell in spring... The severe winter pleases me better...' **Note.** — The long form of the adjective (*довóльный* 'pleased') is also used with the instrumental: *довóльный свóими успéхами* 'pleased with his achievements.
VIII. With verbs to denote one's occupation, profession, position:	Онá *рабóтает библиотéкарем, машинúсткой*... 'She works as a librarian, as a typist...' Собрáние *выбрало* товáрища Ивáнова *председáтелем*. 'At the meeting Comrade Ivanov was elected chairman.' Меня *назнáчили руководúтелем* грýппы. 'I was appointed head of the group.' **Note.** — *Рабóтает библиотéкарем* 'works as a librarian' can also be expressed by the construction incorporating the words *в кáчестве* 'in the capacity of': Онá *рабóтает в кáчестве библиотéкаря*. 'She works in the capacity of a librarian.'

(For the instrumental used with prepositions, see Table 32.)

Table 29

The Genitive Case

I. Prepositions followed exclusively by the genitive: **без** 'without'	Он пришёл *без шáпки.* 'He came without his cap.' Мой сын написáл рабóту *без ошúбок.* 'My son wrote his exercise without mistakes.' Зимá простоя́ла *без морóзов.* 'The winter passed without frosts.' Путешéственники éхали *без приключéний.* 'The travellers were journeying without any incidents.' Больнóй провёл ночь *без сна.* 'The sick man spent a sleepless night.' . . . . Избýшка там на кýрьих нóжках Стоúт *без óкон, без дверéй...* (П.) 'A hut without windows and without doors Stands there upon hen's feet...' Всю ночь у пýшек пролежáли Мы *без палáток, без огнéй.* (Л.) 'The whole night we lay by the guns Without tents and without fires.' Зáяц хóдит нóчью по поля́м и лесáм *без стрáха* и проклáдывает прямы́е следы́. (Л. Т.) 'At night a hare runs about in the fields and woods without fear, and its tracks form a straight line.' Кто живёт *без печáли и гнéва,* Тот не лю́бит отчи́зны своéй. (Некр.) 'He, who lives not knowing what sorrow or anger is, Has never loved his native land.' *Без трудá* не вы́нешь и ры́бку из прудá. (Proverb) Cf. 'No pains, no gains.' Ды́ма *без огня́* не быея́ет. (Proverb) Cf. 'There is no smoke without fire.'

Expressions in frequent use: *без сомнéния* 'without doubt', *без исключéния* 'without exception', *бéз толку* 'to no purpose'.

близ 'near', 'close to'

Я живý *близ бульвáра*. 'I live near a boulevard.'

Близ рóщи на пригóрке стоѝт стáрый дом. 'On the hill near the grove stands an old house.'

вдоль 'along'

Вдоль стенѝ посáжены дерéвья. 'Along the wall trees are planted.'

Дéти шли *вдоль рекѝ, вдоль опýшки лéса*. 'The children were walking along the river-bank, along the edge of the wood.'

Вдоль дорóги тянýлась молодáя пóросль орéшника. 'Along the road stretched young hazel bushes.'

вмéсто 'instead of'

Вмéсто математики бýдет урóк рýсского языкá. 'Instead of the lesson of mathematics there will be a lesson of Russian.'

Дáйте мне, пожáлуйста, бумáги *вмéсто тетрáдей*. 'Please give me some paper instead of exercise-books.'

. . . .

Так тѝ бы с своегó гнездá слетéла
Да *вмéсто мáтери* к малюткам сéла.

(Кр.)

'You ought to fly down from your nest
And sit by the little ones instead of their
mother.'

вне 'outside'

Вне дóма. 'Outside the house.'

Вне странѝ. 'Outside the country.'

Вне закóна. 'Outside the law.'

Вне врéмени и прострáнства. 'Outside time and space.'

Вѝполнить рабóту *вне плáна*. 'To do work over and above the plan.'

Жизнь больнóго *вне опáсности*. 'The patient's life is out of danger.'

Этот человéк *вне всяких подозрéний*. 'This man is altogether above suspicion.'

внутрѝ 'inside'

Внутрѝ помещéния. 'Inside the house (room).'

Внутрѝ странѝ. 'Inside the country.'

во́зле 'near', 'close to' (synonymous to the prepositions *близ, о́коло*)

Я живу́ *во́зле реки́*. 'I live near a river.'

Во́зле ле́са, на горе́, стоя́л ста́рый деревя́нный дом. 'On the hill near the wood stood an old wooden house.'

. . . .

Случа́лось ли вам сиде́ть в тёплую, тёмную, ти́хую ночь *во́зле ле́са?* (Т.) 'Have you ever happened to sit by a wood on a warm dark, and quiet night?'

вокру́г '(a)round'

Они́ се́ли *вокру́г стола́*. 'They sat down round the table.'

Пионе́ры стоя́ли *вокру́г костра́*. 'The Young Pioneers were standing round the fire.'

Вокру́г расска́зчика собрало́сь мно́го наро́да. 'Many people gathered round the narrator.'

Земля́ враща́ется *вокру́г свое́й о́си*. 'The earth revolves round its axis.'

Постоя́нно возника́л спор *вокру́г одни́х и тех же вопро́сов*. 'An argument always arose about the same questions.'

. . . .

В то вре́мя сто́рож полуно́чный
Оди́н *вокру́г стены́* круто́й,
Сверша́я ти́хо путь уро́чный,
Броди́л с чугу́нною доско́й. (Л.)
'At that time the night guard
Was alone on his usual round
Along the high wall,
With an iron plate in his hands.'

Челове́к два́дцать партиза́н лежа́ло *вокру́г костра́*. (Фад.) 'Some twenty guerrillas were lying round the fire.'

Молодёжь собрала́сь *вокру́г чи́стенького, аккура́тного пло́тника Серафи́ма*. (М. Г.) 'The young people gathered round the neat and tidy carpenter Serafim.'

Вокру́г меня́ всё бы́ло так уны́ло. (Тютч.) 'Everything round me was so gloomy.'

для 'for'

Principal meanings:

(1) the person or object for whose benefit the action is performed:

Ма́льчик купи́л кни́гу *для това́рища*. 'The boy bought a book for his friend.'

У меня́ есть все возмо́жности *для рабо́ты*. 'I have every opportunity for work.'

Чудеса́ мо́жет де́лать наро́д, когда́ он тру́дится *для себя́, для свое́й Ро́дины, для всего́ о́бщества*. 'People can work wonders when they work for themselves, for their mother country, for the whole of society.'

(2) purpose:

Мы останови́лись в пути́ *для о́тдыха*. 'We made a halt on our way for a rest.'

Помеще́ние *для библиоте́ки*. 'A building for a library.'

Посу́да *для молока́*. 'Containers for milk.'

до 'till'; 'up to', 'as far as':

Principal meaning: limit in space or time:

От Ленингра́да *до Москвы́* 649 киломе́тров. 'It is 649 kilometres from Leningrad to Moscow.'

Они́ дошли́ *до ста́нции* за де́сять мину́т. 'They reached the station in ten minutes.'

До отхо́да по́езда оста́лось две мину́ты. 'Two minutes remained till the train's departure.'

Он рабо́тал *до утра́*. 'He worked till the morning.'

Жара́ ле́том доходи́ла *до тридцати́ пяти́ гра́дусов*. 'In the summer the temperature reached thirty-five degrees.'

Во́лосы *до по́яса*. 'Hair reaching one's waist.'

. . . .

С трудо́м добрали́сь мы *до избы́*. (Т.) 'We reached the cottage with difficulty.'

Язы́к *до Ки́ева* доведёт. (Proverb) Cf. 'A clever tongue will take you anywhere.'

От Москвы́ *до са́мых до окра́ин*,
С ю́жных гор *до се́верных море́й*
Челове́к прохо́дит как хозя́ин
Необъя́тной Ро́дины свое́й. (Л.-К.)

'From Moscow to the farthest outlying re-
gions,
From the southern mountains to the northern
seas
Man marches, the master
Of his immense mother country.'

Я рад. Остáнься *до утрá*
Под сéнью нáшего шатрá. (П.)
'I'm glad. Stay till tomorrow
Under the shelter of our tent.'

из (изо) 'from', 'of',
'out of'

Principal meanings:
(1) the starting point
of a movement:

(2) the source of in-
formation, the origin:

(3) the material of
which an object is
made:

(4) the whole from
which some part is
singled out:
(5) the cause of an
action:

Он приéхал *из гóрода, из дерéвни.* 'He
came from town, from the country.'

Мы узнáли об э́том *из газéт.* 'We
learned that from the newspapers.'
Словá *из стихотворéния* Пýшкина.
'Words from a poem by Pushkin.'
Мой товáрищ *из рабóчей семьú, из крес-
тья́н.* 'My friend comes from a worker's
family, a peasant's family.'
Эта посýда *из глúны,* а та *из стеклá.*
'These dishes and plates are made of clay,
and those of glass.'
Костю́м *из сукнá.* 'A suit (made) of
broadcloth.'

Нéкоторые *из рабóчих* вы́полнили задá-
ние досрóчно. 'Some of the workers fulfilled their tasks ahead of time.'
Совершúть пóдвиг *из любвú* к Рóдине. 'To
accomplish a feat out of love for one's
country.'

. . . .

Метéли, снегá и тумáны
Покóрны морóзу всегдá.
Пойдý на моря́-окия́ны*,
Пострóю мосты́ *изо льдá.* (Некр.)
'Snow-storms, snows and fogs
Always obey the frost.
I'll attack the seas and the oceans
And will build bridges of ice.'

* This form is archaic; the modern form is *океáны.*

105

Был оди́н *из тех нена́стных студёных дней*, каки́е ча́сто встреча́ются к концу́ о́сени. (Т.) 'It was one of the cold rainy days which are so frequent at the end of autumn.'

Одна́ *из гла́вных алле́й* была́ уса́жена ли́повыми дере́вьями. (Т.) 'One of the main lanes was lined with lime trees.'

Expressions in common use: *из го́да в год* 'from year to year', *изо дня́ в день* 'day by day'.

из-за 'from (a)round', 'from behind';' owing to', 'because of'
Principal meanings:
(1) the place whence the movement proceeds (in this instance **из-за** combines the meanings of the prepositions **из** and **за**):

Из-за угла́ вы́шел челове́к. 'A man came from round the corner.'

Из-за ле́са восхо́дит со́лнце. 'The sun rises from behind the wood.'

Из-за дере́вьев пробива́ется луч со́лнца. 'A sun beam comes through the trees.'

(2) cause:

Из-за дождя́ отложи́ли экску́рсию. 'The excursion was put off owing to the rain.'

Из-за тума́на не ви́дно пути́. 'The road is invisible owing to the fog.'

Из-за тебя́ я опозда́л. 'I am late because of you.'

. . . .

Он доста́л *из-за по́яса* топо́р, присе́л на́ пол и на́чал коло́ть лучи́ну. (Т.) 'He got an axe from his belt, squatted on the floor and began chopping splinters.'

Из-за ре́чки послы́шалась куку́шка. 'From beyond the river a cuckoo was heard.'

Из-за туч луна́ кати́тся. (П.) 'From the clouds the moon comes rolling.'

Над Москво́й вели́кой, златогла́вою,
Над стено́й кремлёвской белока́менной,
Из-за да́льних лесо́в, из-за си́них гор
Заря́ а́лая подыма́ется. (Л.)
'Over the great, golden-domed Moscow,
Over the Kremlin's white-stone wall,
From beyond the far forests, from be-
        yond the blue mountains
A scarlet dawn is breaking.'

Из-за шу́ма па́дающего ли́вня ничего́ не́ было слы́шно. (Т.) 'Nothing could be heard because of the noise of the pouring rain.'

из-под 'from under'

Principal meanings:
(1) the starting point of a movement (indicating a movement from below; in this instance **из-под** combines the meanings of the prepositions **из** and **под**):

Ма́льчик вы́лез из-под стола́. 'The boy crawled from under the table.'
За́яц вы́скочил из-под куста́. 'A hare rushed from under the bush.'
Из-под большо́го пло́ского ка́мня то́некой стру́йкой лила́сь вода́. 'From under a large flat stone a small stream of water came forth.'
Голубы́е цветы́ показа́лись из-под сне́га. 'From under the snow peeped light-blue flowers.'
Idiomatic expression: *прие́хал из-под Ленингра́да* '(he) came from near Leningrad'; *из-под Москвы́* 'from near Moscow'.
Ба́нка из-под варе́нья. 'A jam jar.'
Кувши́н из-под молока́. 'A milk jug.'
. . . .
Две больши́е чёрные соба́ки подняли́сь из-под крыльца́. (Л. Т.) 'Two big black dogs came from under the porch.'
Из-под куста́ мне ла́ндыш серебри́стый Приве́тливо кива́ет голово́й. (Л.)
'From under the bush a silvery lily-of-the-valley Gives me a welcoming nod.'
Из-под ша́пки широ́кого па́поротника скро́мно улыба́лась спе́лая земляни́ка, а из-под опа́вшей листвы́ го́рдо тяну́лся вверх чума́зый гриб. (Нев.) 'From under the broad cap-like frond of a fern a ripe strawberry smiled shyly, and from under the fallen leaves a smudgy mushroom strove up proudly.'

(2) the purpose of an object:

На ма́ленькой те́сной поля́не валя́лись бо́чки из-под дёгтя. (М. Г.) 'All over the small cramped glade tar barrels were scattered about.'

Note. — Unlike the preposition *под* 'under', used answering the questions *где?* 'where?', *куда?* 'where to?' (*Где сиде́л за́яц?* 'Where did the hare sit?' — *под кусто́м* 'under the bush'. *Куда́ спря-*

та́лся за́яц? 'Where did the hare hide?' — *под куст* 'under the bush'), the preposition *из-под* 'from under' is used answering the question *откуда?* 'from where?' (*Откуда* вы́скочил за́яц? 'Where did the hare rush from?' — *из-под куста́* 'from under the bush').

кро́ме 'except', 'besides'

По состоя́нию здоро́вья я могу́ жить везде́, *кро́ме Ленингра́да*. 'The state of my health enables me to live anywhere except Leningrad.'

На собра́ние пришли́ все, *кро́ме больны́х*. 'The meeting was attended by all except those ill'.

Я никого́, *кро́ме тебя́*, здесь не зна́ю. 'I don't know anyone here except you.'

Кро́ме ла́сточки, здесь посели́лся и скворе́ц. 'Besides the swallow, a starling settled there.'

. . . .

Я ничего́ не ви́жу, *кро́ме бе́лой сте́пи да я́сного не́ба*. (П.) 'I don't see anything except for the white steppe and the clear skies.'

ми́мо 'past', 'by'

По́езд промча́лся *ми́мо ста́нции*. 'The train rushed past the station.'

Он прошёл *ми́мо меня́* и не заме́тил меня́. 'He went by without noticing me.'

Ми́мо э́того фа́кта пройти́ нельзя́. 'This fact must not be overlooked.'

. . . .

Вы прохо́дите *ми́мо де́рева* — оно́ не шелохнётся: оно́ не́жится. (Т.) 'You pass by a tree — it won't stir, it is indulging itself.'

Мне почти́ всегда́ случа́лось проходи́ть *ми́мо уса́дьбы* в са́мый разга́р вече́рней зари́. (Т.) 'I nearly always passed by the country-estate at the height of the evening-glow.'

Вдруг она́ пробежа́ла *ми́мо меня́*, напева́я что́-то друго́е. (Л.) 'Suddenly she tripped past me singing a different song.'

накану́не 'on the eve of'

Meaning: 'on the day preceding the one on which some event takes place'; in a broad-

Накану́не пра́здника. 'On the eve of the holidays.'

Накану́не уче́бного го́да. 'Just before the beginning of the academic year.'

er sense **накануне** means 'shortly before', 'not long before':

около 'by', 'near', 'around'; 'about'
Principal meanings:
(1) by, near, close to somebody or something:

(2) approximation of quantity, distance or time (usually in the sense of 'almost', 'about'):

от (ото) '(away) from'
Principal meanings:
(1) the starting point in time or space; the person (or object) from whom (or which) the action proceeds:

(2) cause:

Мы *накануне великих событий.* 'We are on the eve of great events.'

Самолёт опустился *около леса.* 'The aeroplane landed near a forest.'
Летом я жил *около моря.* 'In the summer I lived at the seaside.'
Тропинка вилась *около дороги.* 'The path wound its way along by the road.'
Мы прошли *около пяти километров.* 'We covered nearly five kilometres.'
Я буду дома *около двух часов.* 'I shall be at home at about two o'clock.'
Я ждал тебя *около месяца.* 'I waited for you for nearly a month.'

От дома до школы четверть километра. 'It is a quarter of a kilometre from the house to the school.'
От дерева ложится длинная тень. 'The tree casts a long shadow.'
Приём у врача *от одиннадцати* до трёх. 'The doctor's consultation hours are from eleven to three.'
Я получил письмо *от брата.* 'I received a letter from my brother.'
Он пришёл *от товарища.* 'He came from a friend.'
Привет *от сестры.* 'Regards from one's sister.'
Ребёнок запрыгал *от радости.* 'The child started jumping with joy.'
Мальчик заплакал *от обиды.* 'The boy began crying with resentment.'
Он не мог говорить *от волнения.* 'He could not speak for nervousness.'
Деревья побелели *от инея.* 'The trees turned white with hoarfrost.'
Трава выгорела *от солнца.* 'The grass faded in the sun.'

(3) the purpose of cure or protection ('for', 'against'):

Лека́рство *от ревмати́зма, от головно́й бо́ли*. 'A medicine for rheumatism, for headache'.

Раски́дистая ель защища́ла *от со́лнца*. 'The branchy fir-tree gave shelter from the sun.'

В кре́пости мы бы́ли защищены́ *от враго́в*. 'In the fortress we were protected against the enemy.'

Note. — The preposition *от* 'of' may be used to introduce the date (generally in official papers): Резолю́ция *от пя́того сентября́*. 'A resolution of September the fifth.' Прика́з дире́ктора *от 1-го а́вгуста*. 'The director's order of August the 1st.' Протоко́л собра́ния *от 3 мая*. 'The minutes of the meeting of May 3.' Письмо́ *от 10 а́вгуста*. 'A letter of August 10.'

. . . .

Дли́нная тень ложи́лась *от гор* на сте́пи. (Л. Т.) 'A long shadow was cast by the mountains on the steppes.'

От дере́вьев, от кусто́в, от высо́ких стого́в се́на — ото всего́ побежа́ли дли́нные те́ни. (Т.) 'The trees, the bushes, the tall haystacks — all cast long shadows.'

Дубо́вый листо́к оторва́лся *от ве́тки роди́мой*
И в степь укати́лся, жесто́кою бу́рей гони́мый...
Засо́х и увя́л он *от хо́лода, зно́я и го́ря*
И вот наконе́ц докати́лся до Чёрного мо́ря... (Л.)
'An oak leaf tore off from its native branch
And rolled into the steppe driven by the cruel storm...
It faded and dried because of the cold, the heat and sorrow
And at last it rolled as far as the Black Sea...'

Его́рушка лежа́л на тюке́ и дрожа́л *от хо́лода*. (Ч.) 'Yegorushka was lying on the bale shivering with cold.'

Волчи́ха вздра́гивала *от мале́йшего шу́ма*. (Ч.) 'The she-wolf started at the slightest noise.'

От рáдости Каштáнка пры́гала. (Ч.) 'Kashtanka was jumping with joy.' Каштáнка взви́згнула *от востóрга*. (Ч.) 'Kashtanka gave a yelp of ecstasy.'

Нóги подкáшивались подо мнóй *от устáлости*. (Т.) 'My legs nearly gave way under me with fatigue.'

Когдá сóлнце поднимáется над лугáми, я невóльно улыбáюсь *от рáдости*. (М. Г.) 'When the sun rises over the meadows I smile involuntarily for joy.'

пóсле 'after'

Пóсле урóка я пойдý к товáрищу. 'After the lesson I'll go to see my friend.'

Пóсле рабóты я поéду отдыхáть. 'After work I'll go and have a rest.'

Всё зазеленéло *пóсле дождя́*. 'Everything became green after the rain.'

посреди́ 'in the middle of'

Посреди́ плóщади стои́т пáмятник. 'There is a monument in the middle of the square.'

. . . .

Посреди́ кóмнаты стоя́л самовáр, шумя́ и испускáя клубáми пар. (М. Г.) 'In the middle of the room stood a samovar, with smoke puffing out noisily.'

Всё жи́во *посреди́ степéй*. (П.) 'All is alive amid the steppes.'

прóтив 'opposite', 'against'

Principal meanings:

(1) relations between objects in space:

Прóтив моегó окнá растёт берёза. 'Opposite my window there is a birch.'

Прóтив теáтра стои́т пáмятник. 'There is a monument opposite the theatre.'

. . . .

Ты, Ми́шенька, сади́сь *прóтив альтá*, Я, при́ма, ся́ду *прóтив втóры*. (Кр.) 'You, Bruin, sit down opposite the viola, And I, first fiddle, will face the second.'

(2) movement in the opposite direction:

Мы плы́ли *прóтив течéния*. 'We sailed against the stream.'

Я шёл *прóтив вéтра*. 'I was walking in the face of the wind.'

(3) opposition to someone or something:	Выступа́ть *про́тив предложе́ния*. 'To oppose a proposal.' Голосова́ть *про́тив резолю́ции*. 'To vote against a resolution.'
ра́ди 'for the sake of'	*Ра́ди сча́стья* свои́х дете́й ма́тери объединя́ются в борьбе́ за мир. 'Mothers unite in the struggle for peace for the sake of their children.'

среди́ (средь) 'in the midst of'
Principal meanings:
(1) relations between objects in space:

Среди́ по́ля сиротли́во стоя́ла берёза (here *среди́* is synonymous with the preposition *посреди́*). 'A lonely birch stood in the middle of the field.'

Доро́га тяну́лась *среди́ бесконе́чных поле́й*. 'The road stretched between endless fields.'

Лю́ди вози́лись *среди́ камне́й* и *утёсов*. 'People were fussing amidst stones and rocks.'

(2) relations of time:

Ребёнок просну́лся *среди́ но́чи* и запла́кал. 'The child awoke in the middle of the night and started crying.'

(3) among other persons, things or events:

Среди́ на́ших ученико́в не́сколько отли́чников. 'Among our pupils there are some who get only the top marks.'

Среди́ делега́тов на конфере́нции мно́го же́нщин. 'Among the delegates to the conference there are many women.'

. . . .

Я уже́ реши́лся ночева́ть *среди́ сте́пи*. (П.) 'I had already made up my mind to spend the night in the steppe.'

Кру́то сверну́л на тропу́, почти́ незаме́тную под хво́ей и *среди́ каки́х-то ма́леньких ёлочек*. (М. Г.) '(He) took a sharp turn to a path which was hardly noticeable under the fir and pine needles and between some small firs.'

Не сты́дно ль, — говори́т, — *средь бе́ла*
дня попа́лся! (Кр.)
"'Aren't you ashamed," he says, "to get
caught in broad daylight!'"
Ве́село бы́ло слы́шать *среди́ мёртвого*
сна приро́ды фы́рканье уста́лой тро́йки и
неро́вное побря́кивание ру́сского колоко́ль-
чика. (Л.) 'It filled you with joy to hear,
amidst the death-like sleep of nature, the
snorting of the tired troika and the unsteady
ringing of a Russian bell...'

у 'by', 'at', 'near'
Principal meanings:
(1) position by, at
or near some object:

a) Стол стои́т *у окна́.* 'By the window
stands a table.'
Мы сиде́ли *у костра́.* 'We were sitting
round a fire.'
Жить ле́том *у мо́ря.* 'To live at the seaside in summer.'
Маши́на останови́лась *у са́мого до́ма.* (syn-
onyms: *во́зле, вблизи́, о́коло*) 'The motor-
car pulled up just in front of the house.'
b) Я был *у до́ктора.* 'I visited a doctor.'
Он был на приёме *у дире́ктора.* 'He
was received by the director.'
Я жил ле́том *у бра́та.* 'I stayed with my
brother in summer.'
Note the expressions: *стоя́ть у вла́сти*
'to be in power', *стоя́ть у руля́* 'to be at
the helm'.

(2) possession, own-
ership, etc.:

a) *У орла́* могу́чие кры́лья. 'The eagle
has powerful wings.'
У лисы́ пуши́стый хвост. 'The fox has a
bushy tail.'
У бра́та краси́вый го́лос. 'The brother
has a beautiful voice.'
У меня́ интере́сная кни́га. 'I have an interesting book.'
b) *У това́рища* мно́го рабо́ты. 'The comrade has a lot of work to do.'
У меня́ боли́т зуб. 'I have a toothache.'
Я взял *у това́рища* кни́гу. 'I borrowed
a book from a friend.'
Я за́нял *у бра́та* немно́го де́нег. 'I borrowed a little money from my brother.'

(3) the origin of
something or the source
from which something
has been acquired or
appropriated:

Жил стари́к со свое́ю стару́хой
У *са́мого си́него мо́ря...* (П.)
'There lived an old man and his old woman
On the very shore of the blue sea...'

Ути́х ау́л: на со́лнце спят
У *са́клей* псы сторожевы́е. (П.)
'The village has become quiet: by the
cottages
The watch-dogs are sleeping in the sun.'

У *ме́льника* вода́ плоти́ну прососа́ла. (Кр.)
'Once the water through a miller's dam
did ooze.'

Кавка́з подо мно́ю. Оди́н в вышине́
Сто́ю над снега́ми *у кра́я стремни́ны.*
(П.)
'The Caucasus is beneath me. I stand alone
At this height, over the snows, by the
edge of the precipice.'

И пусть *у гробово́го вхо́да*
Млада́я бу́дет жизнь игра́ть
И равноду́шная приро́да
Красо́ю ве́чною сия́ть. (П.)
'And let youthful life play
At the tomb's entrance
And let indifferent nature
Shine in its eternal beauty.'

У *стра́ха* глаза́ велики́. (Proverb) Cf.
'Fear takes molehills for mountains.'

II. Prepositions followed by the genitive and also by other cases (for the latter, see Notes):

c (co) 'from', 'from off', 'with'

Used to denote:

(1) relations of space (generally indicating the starting point of motion; the genitive answers the question *отку́да?* 'from where?')

Ма́льчик взял кни́гу *со стола́.* 'The boy took the book from the table.'

Я снял пальто́ *с ве́шалки.* 'I took my coat from the coatstand.'

Парашюти́ст пры́гнул *с самолёта.* 'The parachutist jumped from the aeroplane.'

С о́зера пове́яло прохла́дой. 'Cool air came from the lake.'

Он пришёл *с собрáния, с рабóты, с урóка.* 'He came from the meeting, from work, from the lesson.'

Я получи́л письмó *с рóдины.* 'I received a letter from my mother country.'

(2) relations of time (the genitive answers the question *с какóго врéмени?* 'from what time?'):

Я занимáюсь *с утрá.* 'I study from early morning.'

К экскýрсии нáдо приготóвиться *с вéчера.* 'You must prepare for the excursion from the evening.'

Врач принимáет *с десяти́.* 'The doctor receives patients from ten o'clock.'

Занятия в шкóле начнýтся *с сентября́.* 'School will begin in September.'

С óсени я запишýсь в библиотéку. 'In the autumn I'll enroll at a library.'

Любóвь к кни́ге *с дéтства, с юности.* 'Love for reading from one's childhood, young days.'

(3) cause:

Мáльчик заплáкал *с гóря* (in this instance one can also say: *от гóря*). 'The boy began crying for grief.'

Он сказáл э́то *со злóсти.* 'He said it out of anger.'

Он рассерди́лся *ни с тогó ни с сегó.* 'He got angry for no reason whatsoever.'

(4) permission or consent:

С разрешéния, с позволéния, с соглáсия, с одобрéния. 'With one's permission, by one's leave, with one's consent, with one's approval.'

Учени́к ушёл *с разрешéния* преподавáтеля. 'The pupil left with the teacher's permission.'

(5) the unit employed in calculation:

В прóшлом годý урожáй был 32 цéнтнера *с гектáра.* 'Last year the yield was 32 centners per hectare.'

(6) *с* followed by the genitive may also have various other meanings:

Перевести́ *с рýсского языкá* на роднóй. 'To translate from Russian into one's native language.'

Взять гóрод *с бóю.* 'To take a town by storm.'

Expressions in common use: *с чáсу на час* 'any moment'; *со дня нá день* 'any day';

115

с мину́ты на мину́ту 'any minute' (Жду его *с мину́ты на мину́ту* 'I expect him to come any moment.' Он мо́жет прие́хать *со дня на́ день.* 'He may come any day.'); *с то́чки зре́ния* 'from the point of view of'.

. . . .

С реки́ доно́сится шум и плеск воды́. (М. Г.) 'From the river comes the splashing and the noise of the water.'
С горы́ бежи́т пото́к прово́рный. (Тютч.)
'A swift stream is running from the mountain.'
Уж ме́ркнет со́лнце за гора́ми;
Вдали́ разда́лся шу́мный гул,
С поле́й наро́д идёт в ау́л. (П.)
'The sun was already getting dim beyond the mountains,
A din came from afar;
The people were returning to their village from the fields.'
Октя́брь уж наступи́л — уж ро́ща отряха́ет
После́дние листы́ *с наги́х свои́х ветве́й.* (П.)
'October has already come — the grove is already shedding
The last leaves from naked boughs.'
Уж *с утра́* пого́да зли́тся. (П.)
'The weather has been angry since early morning.'
Вы́пьем *с го́ря*, где же кру́жка?
Се́рдцу бу́дет веселе́й... (П.)
'Let us drink for grief, where is the tankard?
It'll lighten the heart...

Note. — The preposition *с* is also used with the accusative (see Table 31) and the instrumental (see Table 32).

ме́жду (меж) 'between', 'among':

Брожу́ ли я вдоль у́лиц шу́мных,
Вхожу́ ль во многолю́дный храм,
Сижу́ ль *меж ю́ношей безу́мных*,
Я предаю́сь мои́м мечта́м. (П.)
'Whether I roam the noisy streets,
Whether I enter a crowded temple,
Or sit among mad youths,
The same thoughts assail me.'

Меж крутых бережкóв Вóлга-рéчка течёт. (From a Russian folk song) 'The river
Volga flows between its steep banks.'

Note. — The preposition *мéжду (меж)* 'between', 'among' followed by the genitive is mainly used in folk songs, proverbs and sayings and in
some set phrases (*заблудился мéжду двух сóсен*,
cf. 'to lose one's way in broad daylight', *сидéть
мéжду двух стýльев*, cf. 'to sit between two
stools'); occasionally it is used in fiction. In colloquial speech and in fiction the preposition *мéжду
(меж)* is usually followed by the instrumental (see
Table 32).

Table 30

The Dative Case

I. Prepositions fol-
lowed exclusively by
the dative:
к (ко) 'to', 'towards';
'by'
Principal meanings:
(1) indicates direc-
tion, approaching in
time or space; also used
in the sense of 'to
belong' (to an organi-
sation, party, school,
etc.):

Ученик подошёл *к доскé*. 'The pupil went
to the blackboard.'
Автóбус подъéхал *к шкóле*. 'The bus
drove up to the school.'
Лóдка пристáла *к бéрегу*. 'The boat
pulled in to the shore.'
Лётчик ведёт самолёт *к гóроду*. 'The pilot
is navigating the aeroplane towards the city.'
Вчерá я ходил *к дóктору*. 'Yesterday I
went to a doctor.'
Сад спускáется *к рекé*. 'The garden slopes
down to a river.'
Готóвиться *к...* (подготóвка *к...*). 'To prepare for... (preparation for...).'
Мы готóвимся *к экзáменам.* 'We are pre-
paring for the examinations.'
Стремиться *к...* (стремлéние *к...*). 'To
strive for... (striving for...).'
Он стремится *к знáниям.* 'He strives for
knowledge.'
Относиться *к...* (отношéние *к...*). 'To
adopt an attitude to... (attitude to...).
Он серьёзно отнóсится *к своим обязан-
ностям.* 'He takes his duties seriously.'

Обраща́ться *к...* (обраще́ние *к...*). 'To appeal to... (appeal to...).'

Обраща́ться *к организа́ции* за по́мощью. 'To appeal to an organisation for help.'

Присоединя́ться *к...* (присоедине́ние *к...*). 'To join... (joining...).'

Я присоединя́юсь *к ва́шему мне́нию.* 'I subscribe to your opinion.'

Привыка́ть *к...* (привы́чка *к...*). 'To get used to... (getting used to...).'

Я привы́к *к зде́шнему кли́мату.* 'I've got used to the climate here.'

Принадлежа́ть *к...* (принадле́жность *к...*). 'To belong to... (belonging to...).'

Мой това́рищ принадлежи́т *к юнна́тской организа́ции.* 'My friend is a member of the Young Naturalists Group.'

Он принадлежи́т *к лу́чшим ученика́м* шко́лы. 'He is one of the school's best pupils.'

Note. — When possession of some object is indicated the verb *принадлежа́ть* 'to belong' is used without the preposition **к** 'to': Эта кни́га *принадлежи́т бра́ту.* 'This book belongs to my brother.'

(2) denotes time and has various other meanings:

Никола́й придёт *к трём часа́м.* 'Nikolai will come towards three o'clock.'

К ве́черу я зако́нчу рабо́ту. 'I'll have finished my work by the evening.'

К ию́лю мы должны́ верну́ться. 'We are due back by July.'

К ча́ю, к за́втраку. 'For tea, for breakfast.' (*К за́втраку* нам да́ли кака́о. 'We were served cocoa for breakfast.')

Expressions in common use:

a) *к сожале́нию* 'to one's regret', *к сча́стью* 'fortunately', 'luckily', *к несча́стью* 'unfortunately', 'unluckily';

b) *Это вам не к лицу́.* 'It does not become you';

c) *к вопро́су о...* 'concerning...' ('on...') (often used in newspaper headlines and in scientific works)

. . . .

Но́чью мы подъе́хали *к ма́ленькой ста́нции.* (Л.) 'At night we arrived at a small station.'

Кто́-то спуска́лся *к исто́чнику*. (Л.)
'Someone was coming down to the spring.'
Плуто́вка *к де́реву* на цы́почках подхо́-
дит. (Кр.)
'The knave approaches the tree on tiptoe.'
Ягнёнок в жа́ркий день зашёл *к ручью́*
напи́ться. (Кр.)
'One hot day a Lamb went to a brook to
drink.'
Гусе́й крикли́вых карава́н тяну́лся *к ю́гу*...
(П.)
'A caravan of noisy geese headed for the
south...'

благодаря́ 'thanks to', 'owing to'

Благодаря́ по́мощи това́рища я зако́нчил
рабо́ту в срок. 'Thanks to my friend's help
I finished my work on time.'
Благодаря́ хоро́шей пого́де экску́рсия была́
о́чень уда́чной. 'Thanks to the fine weather
the excursion was quite a success.'
Благодаря́ весе́нним дождя́м урожа́й был
прекра́сный. 'Owing to the spring rains the
harvest was excellent.'

согла́сно 'according to', 'in accordance with'

Согла́сно постановле́нию прави́тельства...
'According to the decision of the government...'
Согла́сно статье́ Конститу́ции... 'Under
an article of the Constitution...'
Согла́сно распоряже́нию дире́ктора... 'In
accordance with the director's order...'
Согла́сно реше́нию суда́... 'By decision of
the court...'
Согла́сно директи́вам... 'According to the
instructions...'

Note. — In formal correspondence the preposition
согла́сно is quite often followed by the genitive
(*согла́сно распоряже́ния*... 'in accordance with
the order...'). The literary standard, however, requires that *согла́сно* should be followed by the
dative.

навстре́чу 'to meet'

Чле́ны экспеди́ции шли *навстре́чу всем
опа́сностям*. 'The members of the expedition went on in the face of all dangers.'

. . . .

Уж на равни́не, по холма́м
Грохо́чут пу́шки. Дым багро́вый

Клубами всходит к небесам
Навстречу утренним лучам. (П.)
'And on the plain, and on the hills
The guns are already thundering. The
purple smoke
Rises to the heavens in puffs,
To meet the rays of dawn.'

<table>
<tr><td>

наперекор 'in defiance of', 'against the will of', *вопреки* 'contrary to', 'in spite of'

</td><td>

Он всё делает *наперекор мне*. 'He does everything disregarding what I say.'

Вопреки совету врача, он встал с постели. 'He got out of bed in defiance of the doctor's advice.'

Вопреки всем трудностям, экспедиция выполнила задание. 'In spite of all the difficulties the expedition carried out its task.'

Вопреки закону... 'In defiance of the law...'

. . . .

Вопреки предсказанию моего спутника, погода прояснилась. (Л.) 'Contrary to my companion's prediction, the weather had cleared.'

Рассудку вопреки, наперекор стихиям... (Гр.) 'Contrary to all reason, and in defiance of the elements...'

Герой — это тот, кто творит жизнь *вопреки смерти*, кто побеждает смерть! (М. Г.) 'A hero is one who creates life in defiance of death, who vanquishes death!'

Note. — One cannot say: *Вопреки дождю*, я пошёл гулять. *Вопреки* 'in spite of' is mainly used when something is done against the will of some person or in spite of difficulties.

</td></tr>
</table>

II. Prepositions followed by the dative or by other cases (for the latter, see Notes).

по 'across', 'along', 'at', 'due to', 'in', 'according to', 'on', 'by', 'through(out)'

Principal meanings and uses:

(1) the surface along which a movement proceeds:

Мы шли *по улице, по бульвару, по берегу* реки. 'We were going along the street, along the boulevard, along the river bank.'

Он бродил *по лесу.* 'He roamed the woods.'

Он ехал *по равнине.* 'He was driving across flat country.'

Слёзы текли у неё *по щекам.* 'Tears were streaming down her cheeks.'

Золотые полосы протянулись *по небу.* 'Golden bands stretched across the sky.'

. . . .

Туча *по небу* идёт,
Бочка *по морю* плывёт. (П.)
'A rain cloud is floating in the sky,
A barrel is sailing on the sea.'

По ниве прохожу я узкою межой. (М.)
'Across a field I thread my way along a
                                 narrow footpath.'

Цыгане шумною толпой
По Бессарабии кочуют. (П.)
'A noisy crowd of gypsies roam Bessarabia.'

По дороге зимней, скучной
Тройка борзая бежит. (П.)
'Along a monotonous wintry road
A swift troika is running.'

Дождя отшумевшего капли
Тихонько *по листьям* текли. (А. Т.)
'The drops of the rain that had ceased,
Were running silently down the leaves.'

Note. — In classics, one may find examples of an archaic use of *по* with a pronoun in the prepositional to denote the surface along which a movement proceeds: Лжец ни один у нас *по нём* пройти не смеет. (Кр.) 'No liar here will ever dare go across it (the bridge)...'

(2) the object struck:

Он ударил *по столу.* 'He banged on the table.'

Он ударил его *по руке.* 'He struck him on the arm.'

Он ударил вожжой *по лошади.* 'He whipped the horse with the rein.'

Дождь барабáнит *по крьіше*. 'The rain is pattering on the roof.'

. . . .

Когдá я впустúл егó в избý, он хлóпнул меня *по плечý*. (М. Г.) 'When I let him into the cottage, he slapped me ˉon the shoulder.'

Кот сильнéе вьігнул спúну, зашипéл и удáрил Каштáнку лáпой *по головé*. (Ч.) 'The cat arched its back more, spat at Kashtanka and hit her on the head with its paw.'

Путеводúтель наш... постучáл пáлкой *по стволý* дéрева и мóлча крýто свернýл на тропý. (М. Г.) 'Our guide... knocked on the trunk of the tree with his stick, and without saying a word, turned sharply on to the track.'

Глýхо бьют *по водé* спúцы колёс парохóдов..., гдé-то бьёт мóлот *по железý*, заунь́вно тя́нется пéсня. (М. Г.) 'The blades of the ships' wheels slap on the water dully..., a hammer is heard striking the iron somewhere far away, an endless dreary song drags on.'

Крýпные кáпли дождя́ рéзко застучáли и зашлёпали *по лúстьям*. (Т.) 'Large drops began to beat and slap loudly on the leaves.'

(3) the place to which an action refers:

(a) when the whole of a place is involved:

Прикáз *по шкóле, по инститýту*... 'An order to be announced throughout the school, throughout the institute.'

(b) when several or many places are involved:

По фáбрикам, по завóдам, по всем учреждéниям устрáивались мú́тинги. 'Meetings were ˉ held at factories, plants, at all offices.' (But one can also say: *На фáбриках, на завóдах, во всех учреждéниях* устрáивались мú́тинги.)

(c) when several or many places are involved consecutively:

Я хожý *по магазúнам*, покупáю кнúги. 'I go from shop to shop buying books.'

Коми́ссия ходи́ла *по фа́брикам и заво́-
дам.* 'The commission went round the factories
and plants.' (In this instance one cannot
say: на фа́бриках, etc.)

**(4) the time when a
repeated action takes
place:**

До́ктор принима́ет *по вто́рникам и суб-
бо́там.* 'The doctor receives patients on
Tuesdays and Saturdays.'

Пе́ред экза́менами я мно́го занима́лась
по вечера́м, иногда́ *по ноча́м.* 'Before the
examinations I did a lot of studying in
the evening and sometimes even at night.'
(One cannot say: по дням. One may say: по
це́лым дням, but this phrase means 'all day
.long'.)

**(5) the reason for an
action:**

Я пропусти́л заня́тия *по боле́зни, по ува-
жи́тельной причи́не.* 'I missed the lessons
through illness, for a valid reason.'

Ма́льчик сде́лал э́то *по глу́пости, по не-
осторо́жности, по небре́жности.* 'The boy
did that out of foolishness, through carelessness, through negligence.'

**(6) one's occupation,
speciality:**

Он специали́ст *по матема́тике, по физи-
ке, по исто́рии.* 'He is a specialist in mathematics, in physics, in history.'

Э́то прекра́сная рабо́та *по геогра́фии.*
'This is a brilliant work on geography.'

Он то́карь *по мета́ллу.* 'He is a metal
turner.'

Он чемпио́н *по лы́жам.* 'He is a skiing
champion.'

В э́том зда́нии помеща́ется Общество *по
распростране́нию* полити́ческих и нау́чных
зна́ний. 'This building houses the Society
for the Dissemination of Political and Scientific Knowledge.'

Нам нужны́ тепе́рь специали́сты *по ме-
та́ллу, по тексти́лю, по то́пливу, по хи́-
мии, по се́льскому хозя́йству, по тра́нспор-
ту, по торго́вле, по бухгалте́рии,* etc. 'Now
we need specialists in metal, textiles, fuels,
chemistry, agriculture, transport, trade, book-
keeping,' etc.

(7) used in the sense of 'according to', 'in accordance with', 'after', 'on the ground (of)':	Поезд отхо́дит *по расписа́нию*. 'The train is leaving according to the time-table.' Фильм «Пётр I» сде́лан *по рома́ну* А. Толсто́го. 'The film "Peter I" was made after A. Tolstoy's novel.'

. . . .

Мы избира́ли себе́ труд *по призва́нию*, профе́ссию *по душе́*, подру́гу *по се́рдцу*. (Горб.) 'We chose our work according to our calling, our profession according to our liking, our companion according to our heart.'

По оде́жде встреча́ют, *по уму́* провожа́ют. (Proverb) 'Meeting people, we judge them by their clothes, seeing them off, by their intelligence.'

Expressions in common use: *по прика́зу* 'by the order of', *по сообще́нию*, *по све́дениям* 'according to reports', *по мне́нию* 'in the opinion of', *по преда́нию* 'according to tradition', *по слу́хам* 'from hearsay'.

(8) the object which determines the direction of a movement:	Мы плы́ли *по тече́нию*. 'We were going down stream.' Охо́тник шёл *по следа́м* зве́ря. 'The hunter followed in the animal's tracks.'
(9) relationship:	Ро́дственники *по ма́тери, по отцу́*. 'Relatives on the mother's side, on the father's side.' Я встре́тил това́рища *по шко́ле*. 'I met a school-mate.' Челове́к, бли́зкий мне *по убежде́ниям*. 'A man akin to me by his convictions.'
(10) objects distributed singly:	Да́йте нам, пожа́луйста, *по карандашу́* и *по тетра́ди*. 'Please give each of us a pencil and a note-book.' Ка́ждый из ученико́в получи́л *по кни́ге*. 'Each pupil received a book.'
(11) also used in the following preposition + noun combinations:	*По по́чте* 'by post', *по телегра́фу* 'by telegraph', *по телефо́ну* 'by telephone'.

Note. — The preposition *по* is also used with the accusative (see Table 31) and with the prepositional (see Table 33).

Table 31

The Accusative Case

I. Prepositions followed exclusively by the accusative:	
про 'about', 'concerning' (the meaning of this preposition is close to that of *о*):	Ох ты гой еси, царь Иван Васильевич! *Про тебя* нашу песню сложили мы, *Про твоего любимого опричника*, Да *про смелого купца, про Калашникова.* (Л.) 'Now all hail to thee, Tsar Ivan Vasilyevich, Of thee have we made our song, Of thy favourite oprichnik, And of the bold merchant Kalashnikov.' Я смотрю на его весёлое лицо и вспоминаю бабушкины сказки *про Ивана-царевича, про Иванушку-дурачка.* (М. Г.) 'I look at his gay face and recollect Grandmother's fairy-tales about Crown Prince Ivan, and about Ivanushka the Fool.'

Note. — In the above meaning the preposition *о (об)* followed by the prepositional may be used instead of the preposition *про* followed by the accusative: Расскажу вам *об экскурсии*. Расскажу вам *про экскурсию.* 'I shall tell you about the excursion.'

сквозь 'through' used to denote the object through which someone (or something) passes or forces his (its) way:	*Сквозь сырую мглу* тускло светили огни. 'Through the damp haze lights shone dimly.' *Сквозь крышу* протекала вода. 'Water leaked in through the roof.' . . . . И башни замков на скалах* Смотрели грозно *сквозь туманы.* (Л.) 'The towers of the castles on the rocks Loomed through the mists threateningly.' Я быстро отодвинул занесённую ногу и *сквозь* едва *прозрачный сумрак* ночи увидал далеко под собою огромную равнину. (Т.) 'I quickly pulled back my foot, which I had already raised, and saw, through

---

* This word should normally be pronounced *скалах*. Here the stress is shifted for the sake of rhythm.

the scarcely transparent darkness of the night, a vast valley far beneath me.'

Алый полусвет ложился *сквозь узкие окна* в потемневшую комнату. (Т.) 'A scarlet twilight poured into the darkened room through the narrow windows.'

Месяц смотрит *сквозь сетку* ветвей.

(Ник.)

'The moon peeps through the network of branches.'

Сквозь кусты глядел вечерний луч.

(Л.)

'An evening ray came through the shrubs.'

Он увидел её головку *сквозь золотую сетку* колосьев. (Т.) 'Through the golden network of ears, he saw her head.'

Сквозь стеклянную дверь видна была комната. (Ч.) 'Through the glass door, a room could be seen...'

Expressions in common use: *прошёл сквозь огонь и воду* 'he went through fire and water', 'through thick and thin', *смотреть сквозь пальцы* 'to look through the fingers', 'to close one's eyes to something', *смех сквозь слёзы* 'laughing with one eye and weeping with the other.'

через (чрез) 'across', 'through'

Principal meanings:

(1) used to mean 'crossing some place', 'across some place'

Я перешёл *через улицу.* 'I crossed the street.'

Они построили мост *через реку.* 'They built a bridge across the river.'

Через ручей нужно было переправляться вброд. 'The stream had to be forded.'

Через дорогу был протянут провод. 'A wire was stretched across the road.'

(2) synonymous with the preposition *сквозь* 'through':

Еле заметная тропинка вела *через* почти *непроходимую чащу.* 'A scarcely discernible path led through an almost impenetrable thicket.'

Партизаны бесшумно прошли *через лес.* 'The guerrillas went through the forest noiselessly.'

Кровь просочи́лась *че́рез ма́рлю (сквозь ма́рлю)*. 'Blood had oozed through the gauze.'

(3) used to denote time, in the sense of the English 'in':

Я приду́ *че́рез час*. 'I'll come in an hour.'

Уро́к ко́нчится *че́рез пять мину́т*. 'The lesson will be over in five minutes.'

Че́рез год я уе́ду на пра́ктику. 'In a year, I'll go to my practicals.'

(4) used to denote the means by which something is achieved, in the sense of the English 'through', 'by means of', 'with the help of':

Он пе́редал мне письмо́ *че́рез сестру́*. 'He sent me a letter through his sister.'

Бесе́ду вели́ *че́рез перево́дчика*. 'The conversation was conducted through an interpreter.'

Объявле́ние бы́ло сде́лано *че́рез газе́ту*. 'The announcement was made through a newspaper.'

Че́рез непроходи́мые леса́ и боло́та, че́рез ска́лы и го́ры был проло́жен кана́л. 'Through impenetrable woods and across impassable marshes, through rocks and mountains a canal was built.'

. . . .

Услы́шал он уда́ры топора́ и *че́рез мину́ту* треск повали́вшегося де́рева. (Т.) 'He heard the strokes of an axe and, a minute later, the crash of a falling tree...'

И перево́зчик беззабо́тный
Его́ за гри́венник охо́тно
Чрез во́лны стра́шные везёт. (П.)
'And, willingly the care-free boatman
Carries him over the terrible waves
For ten copecks.'

Expressions in common use: на́до пройти́ *че́рез всё, че́рез все тру́дности* 'you must see it through'.

II. With prepositions followed by the accusative or other cases (for the latter, see Notes).

в 'to', 'into', *на* 'to', 'on to', *за* 'behind', *под (подо)* 'under' (answering the

Я иду́ *в теа́тр*. 'I am going to the theatre.'

Он идёт *на собра́ние*. 'He is going to the meeting.'

question куда́?
'where?'):

Мы е́дем *в дере́вню*. 'We are going to the country.'

Ле́том я пое́ду и́ли *на Кавка́з*, и́ли *в Крым*. 'In summer, I'll go either to the Caucasus or the Crimea.'

Мы се́ли *под де́рево*. 'We sat down under a tree.'

Они́ ста́ли *под наве́с*. 'They stepped under a shed.'

Она́ положи́ла письмо́ *под кни́гу*. 'She put the letter under a book.'

Со́лнце спря́талось *за ту́чи*. 'The sun hid behind the clouds.'

. . . .

Я стал почти́ ка́ждый день проси́ть ба́бушку: «Пойдём *в лес!*» (М. Г.) 'I began to ask Grandmother nearly every day: "Let's go to the woods."'

Голо́дная кума́-лиса́ зале́зла *в сад*.

(Кр.)

'A hungry Reynard once got into a vineyard.'

...Ле́бедь рвётся *в облака́*,
Рак пя́тится наза́д, а Щу́ка тя́нет
в во́ду. (Кр.)

'...The Swan strains towards the clouds,
The Crayfish steps backward, and the
Pike pulls towards the water.'

Мы зары́лись *в се́но* и засну́ли. (П.)
'We buried ourselves in the hay and fell asleep.'

Со́лнце скры́лось *за небольшу́ю оси́новую ро́щу*. (Т.) 'The sun hid behind a small aspen grove.'

Прогля́нет день как бу́дто понево́ле
И скро́ется *за край* окру́жных гор.

(П.)

'The day would arrive as if reluctant
And then it would vanish behind the edge
of the surrounding mountains.'

Журча́ ещё бежи́т *за ме́льницу* ручей,
Но пруд уже́ засты́л. (П.)

'The brook still runs and murmurs behind the mill,
But the pond's already frozen.'

Пти́чка *в да́льние страны́**,
В тёплый край за си́не мо́ре
Улета́ет до весны́. (П.)
'The little bird flies away
To distant lands, to a warm country,
Beyond the dark-blue sea, not to return
before spring.'

Я прилёг *под обгло́данный ку́стик* и
стал гляде́ть круго́м. (Т.) 'I lay down under a small clean-picked bush and began to
look round...'

в 'on', 'at' used to denote:

(1) time (question: *когда́?* 'when?'):

Собра́ние бу́дет *в сре́ду, в семь часо́в*
ве́чера. 'The meeting will take place on
Wednesday at seven o'clock in the evening.'
  В э́ту мину́ту он вошёл в ко́мнату.
'At that moment he entered the room.'
  В день 1-го ма́я бу́дет больша́я демон-
стра́ция. 'On the 1st of May a large de-
monstration will take place.'
  Уны́ло во́ет ве́тер *в дождли́вую холо́д-
ную о́сень.* 'The wind wails dolefully on a
cold rainy autumnal day.'

. . . .

В тот год осе́нняя пого́да
Стоя́ла до́лго на дворе́. (П.)
'That year the autumn weather
Lasted for a long time.'
Одна́жды *в студёную зи́мнюю по́ру*
Я и́з лесу вы́шел... (Некр.)
'One cold winter day
I came out of the wood...'

Note. — To indicate the year or month, the prepositional is used: Снег вы́пал то́лько *в январе́.*
(П.) 'Snow did not fall till January.' *В ты́сяча
девятьсо́т со́рок седьмо́м году́.* 'In the year nineteen hundred and forty-seven.' (see Table 33).

* This word should normally be pronounced *стра́ны.* Here it is made to
rhyme with *весны́.*

(2) a period of time during which the action is accomplished:

Я сде́лал э́ту рабо́ту *в неде́лю, в ме́сяц, в год.* 'I did that work in a week, a month, a year.'

В одну́ мину́ту сбежа́лись все. 'In a minute they all came running.'

на 'for', 'on'

(1) used to indicate a period of time (question: *на како́е вре́мя?* 'for how long?'):

Я уе́ду в дере́вню *на неде́лю.* 'I'll go to the country for a week.'

Он взял рабо́ту *на ле́то.* 'He took some work for the summer.'

(2) used in the sense of *для* 'for':

На э́ту рабо́ту ну́жно 10 дней. 'This work will require 10 days.'

На постро́йку до́ма истра́чено полмиллио́на. 'Half a million roubles was spent on the construction of this house.'

На подгото́вку к экспеди́ции ушло́ два ме́сяца. 'The preparations for the expedition took two months.'

(3) used in comparisons to indicate the extent of difference between the objects compared:

Мой това́рищ *на́ голову* вы́ше меня́. 'My friend is a head taller than I.'

Они́ прие́хали *на неде́лю* ра́ньше. 'They came a week earlier.'

Моя́ ко́мната бо́льше ва́шей *на один квадра́тный метр.* 'My room is one square metre larger than yours.'

(4) used after the words *походи́ть, похо́ж* to denote the person or object whom another person or object resembles:

Ребёнок *похо́ж на отца́.* 'The child resembles his father.'

. . . .

Мы побежа́ли наве́рх одева́ться так, что́бы как мо́жно бо́лее *походи́ть на охо́тников.* (Л. Т.) 'We ran upstairs to dress, so that we might look as much like hunters as possible.'

Note. — The prepositions *в* and *на* are also used with the prepositional case (see Table 33).

за 'for'
Used to indicate:
(1) purpose with verbs (or verbal nouns) implying struggle or denoting an action done in favour of somebody or something:

Боро́ться *за выполне́ние* пла́на, *за дисципли́ну* (борьба́ *за выполне́ние* пла́на, *за дисципли́ну*). 'To strive for the fulfilment of a plan, for discipline (striving for the fulfilment of a plan, for discipline).'

Боро́ться *за свобо́ду и незави́симость* свое́й страны́. 'To fight for the freedom and independence of one's country.'

Голосова́ть *за резолю́цию, за предложе́ние...* 'To vote for a resolution, proposal...'

Note: — To indicate purpose after verbs of motion, the instrumental (and not the accusative) is used: Я ходи́л *за хле́бом.* 'I went for bread.' (See Table 32).

. . . .

Уж посто́им мы голово́ю
За ро́дину свою́! (Л.)
'We'll stand up for our country,
And we won't spare our lives!'

Мы зна́ем, что у нас о́чень мно́го друзе́й, и, голосу́я *за мир,* голосу́ем *за бра́тство* наро́дов, *за сча́стье* всех тру́жеников, где бы они́ ни жи́ли. (Эрен.) 'We know we have very many friends, and in voting for peace, we also vote for fraternity between peoples, for the happiness of all workers people wherever they happen to live.'

(2) reason:

Това́рищ получи́л пре́мию *за хоро́шую рабо́ту.* 'My friend got a bonus for good work.'

(3) used in the sense of 'instead of', '(in exchange) for':

Сде́лай э́то *за меня́.* 'Please do that instead of me.'

Я купи́л кни́гу *за рубль.* 'I bought a book for a rouble.'

(4) a definite period of time:

За э́ту зи́му я мно́го раз быва́л в теа́тре. 'I was at the theatre many times this winter.'

За после́днее вре́мя я прочита́л мно́го книг. 'I've read many books lately.'

(5) *за* is used with certain verbs meaning 'to begin (doing something)':

Приня́ться *за рабо́ту.* 'To get down to work.'

Взя́ться *за де́ло.* 'To set to work.'

Сесть *за кни́гу.* 'To take up a book.'

. . . .

Прими́сь *за про́мысел любо́й:*
Желе́зо куй иль пе́сни пой
И сёла обходи́ с медве́дем. (П.)

'Take up any trade:
Forge the iron, or sing songs
And go from one village
to another with a bear.'

Зубáстой Щýке в мысль пришлó
За кóшачье приня́ться *ремеслó.* (Кр.)
'A sharp-toothed Pike once got it in his
head
To take up a Cat's vocation.'

(6) used in expres-sions of gratitude:

Спаси́бо *за кни́гу, за письмó, за совéт.*
'Gratitude for a book, a letter, advice.'
Благодарю́ вас *за внимáние.* 'Thank you
for your kind attention.'

. . . .
Но так и быть: прости́мся дру́жно,
О ю́ность лёгкая моя́!
Благодарю́ *за наслаждéнья,*
За грусть, за ми́лые мучéнья,
За шум, за бýри, за пиры́,
За все, за все твои́ дары́. (П.)
'But let it be as it may: let's part as friends,
O my light-hearted youth!
I thank you for the enjoyments you gave me,
For the melancholy, the dear sufferings,
For the din, the storms, the feasts,
For all, for all your gifts.'

под '(intended) for',
'(occupied) by'; 'on
the eve of':

**(1) used to denote
the purpose for which
something is intended**

Эту кóмнату отвели́ *под библиотéку,*
а ту — *под читáльный зал.* 'This room has
been set aside for a library, and that one
for a reading-hall.'

Эту зéмлю отвели́ *под огорóды,* а ту —
под пáшню. 'This land has been set aside
for vegetable gardens, and that for plough-
land.'

**(2) used in the sense
of 'on the eve of':**

Под Нóвый год мы устрóили ёлку. 'On
New-Year's eve we decorated the New-Year's
tree.'

Под выходнóй день я всегдá уезжáю зá
город. 'On the eve of my days off I always
go to the country.'

(3) used to denote an attendant action:	Мы шли *под му́зыку.* 'We were marching to music.' Он зако́нчил свою́ речь *под аплодисме́нты.* 'He finished his speech to applause.' *Под весёлые раска́ты* гро́ма зашуме́л ли́вень. 'To the accompaniment of loud claps of thunder, a shower began to pour.' Прия́тно засыпа́ть *под шум дождя́.* 'It is pleasant to fall asleep to the noise of rain.' Я задрема́л *под ти́хое журча́нье ручейка́.* 'I dozed to the soft murmuring of the stream.' Idiomatic construction: *отда́ть под суд* 'to bring to trial'. **Note.** — The prepositions *за* and *под* are also used with the instrumental (see Table 32).
по (1) used to indicate distribution of objects (from two on) in equal groups:	Да́йте всем *по три карандаша́* и *по пять тетра́дей.* 'Give them three pencils and five note-books each.' Ка́ждый получи́л *по два я́блока.* 'They got two apples each.' **Note.** — 1. To denote distribution of objects by one, the dative is used: Ка́ждый получи́л *по я́блоку.* 'They all got an apple each.' (see Table 30). 2. To denote distribution of objects by two and on, the dative can also be used for numerals ending in -ь (i.e., *пять* 'five', *шесть* 'six', *семь* 'seven', etc.): Да́йте всем *по пяти́ (шести́,* etc.) *тетра́дей.* 'Give them five (six, etc.) exercise-books each.' (but one cannot say *по трём, четырём тетра́дям,* etc.).
(2) used to indicate price:	Прошу́ четы́ре биле́та *по два́дцать копе́ек.* 'Please give me four tickets at twenty copecks each' (but: оди́н биле́т *за два́дцать копе́ек* 'one ticket for twenty copecks', where the accusative is used).
(3) used to denote a time limit in the sence of 'up to and including':	Он получи́л о́тпуск *по деся́тое ию́ля.* 'He got a holiday up to the tenth of July (meaning: up to and including the tenth of July).' Отчёт *по пя́тое а́вгуста.* 'An account covering the period up to the fifth of August.'

133

(4) used to denote some limit:	Ма́льчик вошёл в во́ду *по ше́ю.* 'The boy went into the water neck-deep.'

Idiomatic expressions: *рабо́ты по го́рло* '(to háve) work enough and to spare'; *за́нят по го́рло* '(to be) up to the eyes in work'; *влюблён по́ уши* '(to be) over head and ears in love'.

. . . .

Шелкови́стая... трава́ была́ почти́ *по по́яс* на заливно́м ме́сте. (Л. Т.) 'The silky grass... was waist-deep where the land had been flooded.'

Жура́вль свой нос *по ше́ю*
Засу́нул Во́лку в пасть. (Кр.)
'The Crane put its bill as far as his neck
Into the Wolf's mouth.'

Че́рез мгнове́нье мы стоя́ли в воде́ *по го́рло.* (Т.) 'A moment later we stood in the water neck-deep.'

(5) In folklore *по* is used to denote the purpose of an action as an equivalent of *за* followed by the instrumental:	Пошла́ *по́ воду, по грибы́, по я́годы.* 'She went to fetch some water, to gather mushrooms, berries.' (The usual expressions are: *за водо́й, за гриба́ми, за я́годами.*)

Спустя́ ле́то *по мали́ну* не хо́дят. (Proverb) 'After the summer you don't go raspberry-picking.'

с (со) '(the size) of' **(1)** used to denote approximate size:	Я́блоко *с кула́к.* 'An apple the size of a fist.'

Вчера́ вы́пал град *с кури́ное яйцо́.* 'It hailed yesterday and the hailstones were as big as hen's eggs.'

. . . .

Пове́ришь ли? Ну, пра́во, был он
с го́ру. (Кр.)
'Will you believe it? It really was as
big as a mountain.'

Бесспо́рно, огуре́ц и *с дом* величино́й
Дико́винка, коль э́то справедли́во.

(Кр.)

'A cucumber the size of a house is a re-
markable thing
If there really was such a cucumber.'
Ма́льчик *с па́льчик* 'Tom Thumb'.
Он про́был в дере́вне *с ме́сяц*. 'He stayed
in the country for about a month' (it
is also possible to say: *почти́ ме́сяц* or
о́коло ме́сяца).

**(2) used to denote
approximate space or
time:**

Note. — The preposition *c* is used both with the
genitive (see Table 29) and with the instrumental
(see Table 32).

о (об) 'against'
used with a noun
denoting an object
against which some-
thing strikes or with
which something col-
lides:

Ма́льчик уда́рился *об стол*. 'The boy
hurt himself against the table.'
Ло́дка уда́рилась *о ка́мень*. 'The boat
struck against a stone.'
Парохо́д разби́лся *о ска́лы*. 'The steamer
was wrecked on the rocks.'
Как горо́х *об сте́ну* (an idiomatic expression meaning 'like being up against
a stone wall').
Что ему́ ни объясня́й — ничего́ не пони-
ма́ет: как горо́х *об сте́ну*. 'He won't understand anything no matter how hard you
try to explain it to him: it's just like
knocking against a stone wall'.

. . . .
Марты́шка тут с доса́ды и с печа́ли
О ка́мень так хвати́ла их,
Что то́лько бры́зги засверка́ли. (Кр.)
'And at that juncture the Monkey, in its
vexation and grief,
Dashed them (the spectacles) against
a stone, so
That only small splinters sparkled.'
Мо́ре глу́хо рокота́ло, и во́лны би́лись
о бе́рег бе́шено и гне́вно. (М. Г.) 'The
sea was rumbling low, and the waves
beat against the shore wildly and angrily.'
Со скре́жетом уда́рили *о ка́мень* мосто-
во́й ко́ваные копы́та. (Н. Остр.) 'The
iron-clad hoofs struck against the stones of
the paved road with a grinding sound.'

Note. — The preposition *о* is also used with the
prepositional (see Table 33).

135

Table 32

The Instrumental Case

I. Prepositions followed exclusively by the instrumental: *над (надо)* 'over', 'above'

Со́лнце поднима́лось *над го́родом*. 'The sun was rising over the town.'

Над реко́й тума́н сгусти́лся. 'The mist had thickened over the river.'

Ли́стья шуме́ли *над мое́й голово́й*. 'The leaves over my head were rustling.'

. . . .

Облака́ бегу́т *над мо́рем*. (Яз.) 'Clouds are racing over the sea.'

Ве́село сия́ет ме́сяц *над село́м*. (Ник.) 'The moon is shining gaily over the village.'

Па́хнет се́ном *над луга́ми*. (М.) 'Over the meadows there is a smell of hay.'

Я́стреб пролете́л высоко́ *над да́льним ле́сом*. (Л. Т.) 'The hawk flew high above the far woods.'

Летя́т *над мра́чными леса́ми*,
Летя́т *над ди́кими гора́ми*,
Летя́т *над бе́здною морско́й*. (П.)
'They fly over the gloomy forests,
'They fly over the wild mountains,
'They fly over the abyss of the sea.'

У́тки лете́ли *над сжа́тыми поля́ми, над пожелте́вшими леса́ми и над деревня́ми*. (Гарш.) 'The ducks were flying over fields, which had already been reaped, over forests, which had already turned yellow and over villages.'

пе́ред (пе́редо), *пред (пре́до)* 'in front of', 'before' Principal meanings and uses:

(1) used to indicate relations between objects in space:

Пе́ред шко́лой тени́стый ма́ленький сад. 'In front of the school there is a small shady garden.'

Пе́ред о́кнами цветы́. 'There are flowers in front of the windows.'

(2) used to indicate relations between objects in time:	*Пéред заседáнием* я зайдý к тебé. 'Before the meeting I'll call on you.' *Пéред рассвéтом* началáсь грозá. 'Before daybreak a storm broke out.'
(3) various other meanings:	*Пéред нáми* стоя́т больши́е задáчи. 'We face great tasks.' Отвéтственность *пéред нарóдом.* 'Responsibility towards the people.' Обя́занность *пéред óбществом.* 'Duties to society.' Долг *пéред нарóдом.* 'An obligation towards the people.' Не отступáть *пéред трýдностями.* 'Not to retreat in the face of difficulties.' Сохраня́ть спокóйствие *пéред лицóм опáсности.* 'To keep calm in the face of danger.' . . . . Киби́тка остановúлась *пéред деревя́нным дóмиком.* (П.) 'The kibitka stopped in front of a small wooden house.' На хóлмах Грýзии лежи́т ночнáя мгла, Шуми́т Арáгва *предо мнóю.* (П.) 'There is a night haze on the mountains of Georgia, The Aragva is brawling beneath me.' Стáрый Тарáс дýмал о дáвнем: *пéред ним* проходúла егó мóлодость. (Г.) 'Old Taras was thinking about the past: his youth was passing before him.'
II. With prepositions followed by the instrumental and also by other cases (for the latter, see Notes): *c* 'with', 'to' Principal meanings and uses: (1) used in denoting association or joint action:	Пóсле экзáмена я дóлго разговáривал *с преподавáтелем.* 'After the examination I had a long conversation with the teacher.'

137

	Он спо́рил *с това́рищем.* 'He was arguing with his friend.'
	За́втра отправля́юсь *с бра́том* на охо́ту. 'Tomorrow I shall go hunting with my brother.'
(2) used to denote possession or presence of something:	Он отпра́вился на охо́ту *с ружьём.* 'He went hunting with a gun.'
	Он челове́к *с хара́ктером.* 'He is a man of strong character.'
	Тепе́рь в каре́льских леса́х вы́росли благоустро́енные лесны́е посёлки *с прекра́сными дома́ми, клу́бами, шко́лами, больни́цами, столо́выми, магази́нами.* 'Now, well-appointed settlements with fine houses, clubs, schools, hospitals, canteens and shops have sprung up in the Karelian forests.'
(3) used in the sense of 'with', 'against':	Боро́ться *с враго́м.* 'To fight the enemy.'
	Боро́ться *с тру́дностями.* 'To fight difficulties.'
(4) used in expressions denoting manner or attending circumstances:	Он сказа́л э́то *с улы́бкой.* 'He said that with a smile.'
	Я обы́чно чита́ю газе́ту *с больши́м внима́нием.* 'I usually read the newspaper with great attention.'
	Я *с удово́льствием* сде́лаю э́то. 'I'll do that with pleasure.'
	Грачи́ *с кри́ком* кружи́ли над дере́вней. 'The rooks circled over the village, cawing.'
	Соба́ки *с ла́ем* вы́бежали нам навстре́чу. 'The dogs ran towards us, barking.'
(5) used to denote time or simultaneousness:	Пти́цы просыпа́ются *с заре́ю.* 'Birds wake up at dawn.'
	Я встаю́ *с восхо́дом* со́лнца. 'I get up at sunrise.'
(6) used to denote the relation between contents and container:	Буты́лка *с молоко́м,* ба́нка *с варе́ньем.* 'A bottle of milk, a jar of jam.'
(7) used in certain formulas of congratulation:	Поздравля́ю *с Но́вым го́дом!* 'I wish you a Happy New Year!'
	С Но́вым го́дом! 'A Happy New Year!'
	С но́вым сча́стьем! '(I wish you) new happiness!'

Поздравля́ю *с сы́ном, с до́чкой!* 'I congratulate you upon your son's birth, your daughter's birth!'

Поздравля́ю *с оконча́нием* шко́лы! 'I congratulate you on your finishing school!'

Поздравля́ю *с блестя́щими успе́хами!* 'I congratulate you on your brilliant success!'

. . . .

С свое́й волчи́хою голо́дной
Выхо́дит на доро́гу волк. (П.)

'On the road there comes a wolf
With his hungry mate.'

Пришёл не́вод *с одно́ю ры́бкой,*
С не просто́ю ры́бкой, золото́ю. (П.)

'The drag-net brought one fish,
But not an ordinary fish, a gold one.'

Лесо́в таи́нственная сень
С печа́льным шу́мом обнажа́лась. (П.)

'The mysterious canopy of the woods
Bared itself with sad rustling.'

С зарёю у́тки с ля́гушкой сно́ва пусти́лись в путь. (Гарш.) 'At daybreak, the ducks and the frog started on their journey again.'

Note. — The preposition *с* is also used with the genitive (see Table 29) and with the accusative (see Table 31).

за 'behind', 'beyond'
(1) used to denote place (question: *где?* 'where?'):

Ва́ше пальто́ виси́т *за две́рью.* 'Your overcoat is hanging behind the door.'

Сад *за до́мом.* 'The garden is behind the house.'

Со́лнце скры́лось *за ле́сом.* 'The sun had disappeared behind the woods.'

Пе́сня раздаётся *за реко́й.* 'The song is heard beyond the river.'

Я живу́ *за́ городом.* 'I live out of town.'

(2) when following verbs of motion *за* + noun indicates purpose:

Утром я иду́ *за хле́бом*. 'In the morning I go to buy some bread.'
Он побежа́л *за до́ктором*. 'He ran for a doctor.'
Тигр охо́тился *за оле́нем*. 'The tiger hunted the stag.'

. . . .

Покры́та бе́лою чадро́й,
Княжна́ Тама́ра молода́я
К Ара́гве хо́дит *за водо́й*. (Л.)
'Covered with a white yashmak,
The young princess Tamara
Goes to the Aragva to get some water.'

(3) *за* can be used in the sense of 'following someone (or something)', 'after':

Так *за слоно́м* толпы́* зева́к ходи́-ли. (Кр.)
'So there were crowds of idlers following the elephant.'

Note. — Only the context enables the reader (or the listener) to tell in which sense, (2) or (3), the preposition *за* is used. Thus побежа́л *за това́ри-щем* may mean: (1) 'ran for a friend', (2) ran after the friend.'

(4) used in the sense of 'at', 'in the time of'; 'throughout the course of':

Я ча́сто чита́ю газе́ту *за за́втраком*. 'I often read the newspaper at breakfast.'
За рабо́той не замеча́ешь вре́мени. 'You do not heed time when you are working.'
За ча́ем говори́ли о литерату́ре. 'At tea they spoke about literature.'

(5) used in the sense of 'occupied with', 'engaged in':

Моя́ ста́ршая дочь сиди́т *за уро́ками* це́лыми дня́ми. 'My eldest daughter takes whole days over her homework.'
Я провожу́ вечера́ *за чте́нием*. 'I spend my evenings reading.'
Он сиди́т *за кни́гой*. 'He is busy with a book.'
Я его́ всегда́ застаю́ *за рабо́той*. 'I always find him working.'

---

* Normally this word is stressed on the first syllable (*то́лпы*).

(6) used to indicate cause:

Usually in formal speech: *за не-име́нием...* (*lit.* 'owing to the lack of...'), *за отсу́тствием...* 'owing to the absence of...', *за по́здним вре́менем...* 'because of the late hour...', etc.

под 'under', '(occupied) by', 'for'
Principal meanings:
(1) used to denote place (question: где? 'where?'):

Мяч *под столо́м*. 'The ball is under the table.'
За́яц *под кусто́м*. 'The hare is under the bush.'
Самолёты *под облака́ми*. 'The aeroplanes are under the clouds.'
Я живу́ *под Москво́й*. 'I live near Moscow.'

Note. — In the sense of 'in the environs of', 'near' *под* is generally followed by a proper name or by the word го́род: *Под са́мым го́родом* бы́ло село́ Торгу́ево. (Ч.) 'Very near the town there was the village of Torguevo.'

. . . .

Захрусте́ли *под нога́ми* сухи́е сосно́вые ши́шки, наруша́я ва́жную тишину́. (М. Г.) 'The dry pine cones rustled underfoot, breaking the solemn silence.'

И пря́чется в саду́ мали́новая сли́ва
Под се́нью сла́достной зелёного листка́.
(Л.)
'And a crimson plum hides in the orchard
Under the pleasant shelter of a green leaf.'

(2) used in indicating the object (or objects) occupied by some other object (or objects):

По́ле *под пшени́цей, под ро́жью*. 'A field sown to wheat, to rye.'

Note. — In such expressions as *ба́нка из-под варе́нья* 'jam jar', the preposition *из-под* requires the genitive (see Table 29).

(3) used in the following combinations:

Под дождём 'in the rain', *под со́лнцем* 'in the sun', *под я́сным не́бом* 'under a clear sky'.

. . . .

Па́шка шёл с ма́терью *под дождём.* (Ч.) 'Pashka was walking with his mother in the rain.'

Ты знал ли ди́кий край *под зно́йными луча́ми?* (Л.) 'Have you known a wild land under scorching rays?'

Под обстре́лом. 'Under fire'.

Мы до́лго находи́лись *под обстре́лом.* 'We had been under fire for a long time.'

(4) used in the following expressions (meaning 'under the leadership of', 'under the guidance of', 'under the banner of'):

Под руково́дством, под води́тельством, под зна́менем. 'Under the leadership (of), under the guidance (of), under the banner (of).'

ме́жду (меж) 'between', 'among'

Principal meanings and uses:

(1) indicates a relation between objects in space:

Стол стои́т *ме́жду окно́м и две́рью.* 'The table is between the window and the door.'

Река́ течёт *ме́жду гора́ми.* 'The river flows between the mountains.'

Пряма́я ли́ния — кратча́йшее расстоя́ние *ме́жду двумя́ то́чками.* 'A straight line is the shortest distance between two points.'

Ме́жду Ленингра́дом и Москво́й 649 киломе́тров. 'It is 649 kilometres between Leningrad and Moscow.'

(2) indicates a relation between objects in time:

Я пойду́ к дире́ктору *ме́жду уро́ками — ме́жду пе́рвым и вторы́м.* 'I'll go to see the director between the first and second lessons.'

(3) used to indicate distribution between or among certain persons or objects. Also used to denote location between or among things or persons:

Карандаши́ и тетра́ди раздели́ли *ме́жду учениками.* 'The pencils and note-books were distributed among the pupils.'

. . . .

Он *ме́жду на́ми жил...* (П.) 'He lived among us...'

(4) used to indicate relations between or among certain parties or persons:	Догово́р *ме́жду двумя́ стра́нами*. 'A treaty between two countries.' Дру́жба *ме́жду наро́дами* СССР. 'The friendship between the peoples of the U.S.S.R.' Хоро́шие отноше́ния *ме́жду това́рищами*. 'Good relations between friends.'
(5) used to indicate a difference between or among:	*Ме́жду сестро́й и бра́том* больша́я ра́зница в хара́ктерах. 'There is a great difference between the brother's character and the sister's.'

Idiomatic expressions: пусть э́то оста́нется *ме́жду на́ми* 'let it remain between you and me'; я сде́лаю э́то *ме́жду де́лом* 'I shall do it at odd moments'.

. . . .

Снача́ла шли по доро́ге *ме́жду ствола́ми* мо́щных со́сен. (М. Г.) 'At first they walked along the road between the trunks of powerful pine-trees.'

По траве́ *ме́жду чёрными те́нями* протяну́лись я́ркие по́лосы све́та. (Ч.) 'Between the black shadows on the grass there stretched bright stripes of light.'

Лишь кое-где́ *ме́жду куста́ми* выдава́лись кро́хотные поля́нки. (Т.) 'Only in places there were tiny glades between the bushes.'

Чуть ветеро́к там ды́шит *меж листа́-ми*. (Жук.)
'A gentle wind hardly breathes between the leaves.'

Между́ колёсами теле́г,
Полузаве́шенных ковра́ми,
Гори́т ого́нь. (П.)
'A light is burning
Between the wheels of the carts
Half hung with rugs.'

Note. — The preposition *ме́жду (меж)* is also used with the genitive (see Table 29).

143

Table 33

The Prepositional Case

I. Prepositions used exclusively with the prepositional: *при* 'in the time of', 'under', 'near', 'attached to' Principal meanings: Used to indicate: (1) time:	*при царизме* 'under tsarism' *при капитализме* 'under capitalism' *при жизни* 'in one's lifetime' Эти стихи́ бы́ли напеча́таны *при жи́зни* поэ́та. 'These poems were printed in the poet's lifetime.'
(2) place (proximity to something else):	Мой оте́ц жил *при ста́нции.* 'My father lived at the station.' *При до́ме* был огоро́д. 'There was a kitchen garden on the grounds where the house stood.'
(3) possession:	*При заво́де* хоро́ший клуб. 'The factory has a good club of its own.'
(4) indispensable or attendant circumstances:	*При жела́нии; при стара́нии; при уча́стии; при по́мощи.* 'If (you) want it; if (you) try; with... taking part; with the help of, by means of'. . . . . *При свида́нии* по́сле до́лгой разлу́ки, как э́то всегда́ быва́ет, разгово́р до́лго не мог установи́ться. (Л. Т.) 'As it always happens when people meet after a long separation, conversation could not start for a long time.' *При ка́ждом ша́ге* вперёд ме́стность изменя́лась. (Л. Т.) 'With every step forward the country changed.' Чу́ден Днепр *при ти́хой пого́де!..* (Г.) 'Wonderful is the Dnieper in quiet weather!...' Кто *при звезда́х** и *при луне́* Так по́здно е́дет на коне́? (П.)

---

* This word is usually stressed on the first syllable and is pronounced *звёздах*. Here the stress is shifted for the sake of rhythm.

'Who is this man who is galloping on his
steed
So late, in the light of the stars and the
moon?'

При свете солнца далеко и ясно станови́лись видны́ предме́ты, то́чно покры́тые ла́ком. (Л. Т.) 'By sunlight, objects in the distance became clearly visible, as if coated with varnish.'

II. Prepositions used with the prepositional or other cases (for the latter, see Notes):

в 'in', *на* 'at', 'on'

Used to indicate place (question: *где?* 'where?'):

Брат рабо́тает *на заво́де.* 'My brother works at a plant.'

Ле́том я был *в дере́вне.* 'I was in the country during the summer.'

. . . .

В степи́ бы́ло ти́хо, па́смурно. (Ч.) 'It was silent and gloomy in the steppe.'

На не́бе га́снут облака́. (Тютч.)
'Clouds are fading in the sky.'

В ро́ще щёлкал соловей (Т.) 'A nightingale was jugging in the grove.'

Везде́ рабо́та: *на гора́х, в доли́нах, ро́щах и луга́х.* (Жук.)
'Work is under way everywhere: on the hills, in the valleys, the groves and the meadows.'

в 'in'

Used to indicate:

(1) the month or year (question: *когда?* 'when?'):

В а́вгусте я уе́ду на пра́ктику. 'In August I'll go to my practicals'.

Това́рищ прие́хал *в 1974 году́.* 'My friend came in 1974.'

(2) age or period of life:

В де́тстве, в ю́ности, в мо́лодости, в ста́рости. 'In one's childhood, in one's youth, in one's young days, in one's old age.'

(3) emotional state:

В печа́ли, в го́ре, в гне́ве, в восто́рге. 'In sorrow, in grief, in anger, in rapture.'
Я в восто́рге от карти́ны. 'I am delighted with the picture.'
Он был в большо́м го́ре. 'He was very much distressed.'

Note. — The prepositions *в* and *на* are also used with the accusative (see Table 31).

о (об, обо) 'about', 'of', 'on', 'concerning':

Used to indicate the theme or content of a speech, document, book, etc.:

Вчера́ мы слу́шали докла́д о Пу́шкине и Го́голе. 'Yesterday we listened to a report about Pushkin and Gogol.'
Мы говори́ли о литерату́ре. 'We spoke about literature.'
«Ска́зка о рыбаке́ и ры́бке» Пу́шкина. '"A Tale about the Fisherman and the Gold Fish" by Pushkin.'
Во всех газе́тах пи́шут о на́шем стро́ительстве. 'In all the newspapers they write about our construction work.'
спо́рить *о...* 'to argue about...'
ду́мать *о...* 'to think about...'
мечта́ть *о...* 'to dream about...'
Подписа́ние договора *о дру́жбе, о сотру́дничестве* и *о взаи́мной по́мощи.* 'The signing of the treaty of friendship, cooperation and mutual assistance.'

. . . .

Слух обо мне́ пройдёт по всей Руси́ вели́кой. (П.)
'My fame will spread all over vast Russia.'

Note. — The preposition *о* is also used with the accusative (see Table 31).

по 'on'

(1) used in the sense of 'after', '(up)on':

По оконча́нии школы я поступлю́ в университе́т. 'Upon finishing school I'll enter the University.'
Я стал писа́ть расска́з по прие́зде в дере́вню. 'I began writing the story on my arrival at the village.'

По возвращéнии на рóдину он поступи́л в консерватóрию. 'On his return to his native country he entered the Conservatoire.'

Note. — The preposition *по* in the sense of *пóсле* 'after', '(up)on' is used only with verbal nouns and generally in formal speech: *по истечéнии срóка* 'on the expiry of the period', *по рассмотрéнии дéла* 'on considering the matter', etc.

(2) used with pronouns after the verbs:

скучáть 'to miss', *тосковáть* 'to miss badly':

Я *скучáю по вас*. 'I miss you'.
Я *тоскýю по вас*. 'I miss you badly.'

(With pronouns the prepositional is used, while with nouns both the prepositional and the dative are possible: тосковáть *по товáрищу* or *по товáрище* 'to miss a friend badly', скучáть *по дóму* or *по дóме* 'to miss one's home'; in the literary language the dative is preferred.)

Note. — The preposition *по* is also used with the dative (see Table 30) and the accusative (see Table 31).

PREPOSITIONS AND SOME OF THE MOST COMMON PREPOSITIONAL WORDS USED WITH CASES

Table 34 (Summary)

Cases	Prepositions		
	Used only with one case	Used with two cases	Used with three cases
Genitive	без 'without' близ 'near', 'close to' вдоль 'along' вмéсто 'instead of' вне 'outside' внутри́ 'inside' вóзле 'by' вокрýг '(a)round'	мéжду (меж) 'between', 'among' (rarely used with the genitive)	с 'from', 'from off', 'with'

Cases	Prepositions		
	Used only with one case	Used with two cases	Used with three cases
Genitive	для 'for' до 'till', 'up to', 'as far as' из 'from', 'of', 'out of' из-за 'from (a)round', 'from behind', 'because of' из-под 'from under' кроме 'except', 'besides' мимо 'past', 'by' накануне 'on the eve of' около 'by', 'near', 'around', 'about' от '(away) from' после 'after', 'following' посреди 'in the middle of' против 'opposite', 'against' ради 'for the sake of' среди 'in the midst of' у 'by', 'at', 'near'		
Dative	к 'to', 'towards', 'by' благодаря 'thanks to', 'owing to' вопреки 'contrary to' подобно 'like', 'resembling' согласно 'according to', 'in accordance with' наперекор 'in defiance of', 'against the will of' навстречу 'to meet'		по 'along', 'at', 'due to', 'in', 'according to', 'on', 'by'

Cases	Prepositions		
	Used only with one case	Used with two cases	Used with three cases
Accusative	про 'about', 'concerning' сквозь 'through' че́рез 'across', 'through'	в 'on', 'at' на 'for', 'on' за 'for' под '(intended) for', '(occupied) by'; 'on the eve of' о (об) 'about', 'against'	с 'the size of' по 'up to (and including)'
Instrumental	над 'over', 'above' пе́ред 'in front of', 'before'	за 'behind', 'beyond', 'after', 'following' под 'under', '(occupied) by', 'for' ме́жду (меж) 'between', 'among'	с 'with'
Prepositional	при 'In the time of', 'under'; 'near', 'attached to'	в 'in' на 'at', 'on' о (об) 'about', 'of', 'on', 'concerning'	по 'after', 'on'

Note. — A number of other words can be used as prepositions: (a) *во вре́мя* 'during' (*во вре́мя уро́ка* 'during a lesson', *во вре́мя кани́кул* 'during the holidays', *во вре́мя войны́* 'during the war'), *в тече́ние* 'during', *в продолже́ние* 'in the course of' (*в продолже́ние всего́ уче́бного го́да* 'during the whole academic year'), *всле́дствие* 'owing to' (*всле́дствие недоста́точной организо́ванности* 'owing to insufficient organization'), *ввиду́* 'in view of' (*ввиду́ необходи́мости* 'in view of the necessity', *ввиду́ осложне́ний* 'in view of the complications'), *в си́лу* 'because of' (*в си́лу необходи́мости* 'because of the necessity'), *по ме́ре* 'as' (*по ме́ре на́добности* 'as (it) becomes necessary', *по ме́ре разви́тия* 'as (it) develops'), etc. used with the genitive; (b) *несмотря́ на* 'in spite of' (*несмотря́ на тру́дности* 'in spite of the difficulties', *несмотря́ на запреще́ние* 'in spite of the prohibition', *несмотря́ на дождь* 'in spite of the rain', etc.) used with the accusative. Most of the above prepositional words are used in formal speech.

Table 35

Prepositions used with Several Cases (Main Uses)

Preposition	Genitive Case	Dative Case	Accusative Case	Instrumental Case	Prepositional Case
в 'to', 'at', 'in'			1. Indicating place (question: *куда?* 'where to?'): Я иду *в театр*. 'I am going to the theatre.' 2. Indicating time (question: *когда?* 'when?'): Собрание *в семь часов*. 'The meeting is at seven o'clock.' Я уеду *в эту ночь*. 'I am leaving tonight.' 3. Indicating the period of time in which something is completed: Я сделаю это *в один год*. 'I'll do that in one year.'		1. Indicating place (question: *где?* 'where?'): Я был *в театре*. 'I was at the theatre.' 2. Indicating time: month or year (question: *когда?* 'when?'): Я уеду *в августе*. 'I'll leave in August.' Я уеду *в этом году*. 'I'll leave this year.'

на 'to', 'at', 'by'

1. Indicating place (question: *где?* 'where?'): Я рабо́таю *на фа́брике.* 'I work at a factory.'

1. Indicating place (question: *куда́?* 'where to?'): Я иду́ *на фа́брику,* 'I am going to the factory.'

2. Indicating time limit (question: *на како́е вре́мя?* 'for how long?'): Мы взя́ли рабо́ту *на всё ле́то.* 'We took work for the whole summer.'

3. *На* is used in the sense of *для: На э́ту рабо́ту* ну́жно 5 дней. 'This work will take 5 days.'

4. Indicating some difference in a comparison: Моя́ ко́мната *на метр* бо́льше твое́й. 'My room is one metre larger than yours.'

Preposition	Genitive Case	Dative Case	Accusative Case	Instrumental Case	Prepositional Case
за 'for', 'instead of', 'behind'			1. Indicating place (question: *куда?* 'where?'): *Повéсьте пальтó за дверь.* 'Hang your overcoat behind the door.' 2. Indicating a period of time (question: *за какóе врéмя?* 'during what time?'): *За этот год я мнóгое сдéлал.* 'This year I have done a lot.' 3. Indicating the purpose of an action: *Мы бóремся за лýчшую дисциплúну.* 'We strive for better discipline.' 4. Indicating reason (questions: *почемý?* 'why?',	1. Indicating place (question: *где?* 'where?'): *Пальтó за двéрью.* 'The overcoat is behind the door.' 2. Indicating purpose (when following verbs of motion): *Я идý за хлéбом.* 'I am going for some bread.'	

	1. Indicating place (question: *где?* 'where?'): *Мяч под столом.* 'The ball is under the table.'
за что? 'what for?'): *Он получил премию за хорошую работу.* 'He got a bonus for his good work.' 5. Used in the sense of 'instead of', 'in exchange of': *Сегодня я работаю за товарища Иванова.* 'Today I work instead of Comrade Ivanov.' *Я купил книгу за три рубля.* 'I bought a book for three roubles.'	1. Indicating place (question: *куда?* 'where?'): *Он бросил мяч под стол.* 'He threw the ball under the table.' 2. Indicating time (in the sense of 'on the eve of'): *Под выходной день я уезжаю на дачу.* 'On the eve of my day off I go to the country.'

под
'under', 'on the eve of', '(instead) of'

Preposition	Genitive Case	Dative Case	Accusative Case	Instrumental Case	Prepositional Case
			3. Indicating the purpose of an object is intended for: Эту комнату отвели под библиотеку. 'This room was set aside for a library.'		
c (co) 'from', 'with', 'since', 'for' 'about', 'the size of', 'against'	1. Indicating place (question: откуда? 'from where?'): Он взял книгу со стола.' He took the book from the table.'		1. Indicating approximate space of time: Я пробыл в деревне с месяц. 'I stayed in the village for about a month.'	1. Indicating association: Он работал с товарищем. 'He worked with his friend.'	
	2. Indicating a starting point in time (question: с какого времени? 'from what time?'): Он начал эту работу с осени.		2. Indicating approximate size: Град с куриное яйцо. 'Hailstones the size of a hen's egg.'	2. Used in the sense of 'against', 'with': Мы боремся с трудностями. 'We fight the difficulties.'	

по 'at (all the...)', 'along', 'in', 'up to (and including)', 'after', 'on'	1. Indicating that the action occurs simultaneously in several places (question: *где?* 'where?'): *По фа́брикам, по заво́дам, по всем учрежде́ниям* проводи́лись собра́ния. 'Meetings were held at all factories, plants and offices.'	1. Indicating time limit (in the sense of 'up to and including'): *Я пробу́ду в дере́вне по 5 сентября́.* 'I'll stay in the country up to the 5th of September.'	Used in the sense of 'after', '(up) on': *По оконча́нии* шко́лы я пое́ду в дере́вню. 'On finishing school I'll go to the country.'

'He began this work in autumn.'
3. Indicating cause: Он заболе́л *с го́ря.* 'He fell ill with grief.'

Preposition	Genitive Case	Dative Case	Accusative Case	Instrumental Case	Prepositional Case
		2. Indicating movement along, across, through or over: *Я шёл по улице.* 'I was walking along the street.' 3. Indicating time: *По утрам, по вечерам, по ночам.* 'In the mornings, in the evenings, at night.'	2. Indicating some limit: *Мальчик вошёл в воду по пояс.* 'The boy went into the water up to his waist.' 3. Indicating distribution of objects but not singly: *по две* 'two... each,' *по три* 'three... each', etc.: *Дайте нам по два яблока.* 'Give us two apples each.'		
по 'in the field of', 'according to'		4. Indicating occupation: *Он специалист по механике.* 'He is a specialist in mechanics.'			

5. Indicating distribution of objects singly: Дайте нам по яблоку. 'Give us an apple each.' 6. Used in the sense of 'according (to)': Мы рабо́таем по плáну. 'We work according to plan'	Indicating collision of objects: Я уда́рился об стол. 'I knocked against the table.' Парохо́д разби́лся о скáлы. 'The steamer was wrecked on the rocks.'	Indicating the subject spoken about: Мы говори́ли о литерату́ре. 'We spoke about literature.'
о, об 'against' 'on', 'about'		

157

Table 36

Use of the Prepositions *в* and *на* and the Prepositions *из* and *с* Correlative with Them

(Я) рабо́таю '(I) work'	**(Я) пришёл** '(I) came'
в музе́е 'at a museum' *but:* на фа́брике 'at a factory' в конто́ре 'at an office' *but:* на заво́де 'at a plant' в амбулато́рии 'at a dispensary' *but:* на по́чте 'at a post-office' в мастерско́й 'at a workshop' *but:* на телегра́фе 'at a telegraph-office' в магази́не 'at a shop' *but:* на вокза́ле 'at a railway-station'	из музе́я 'from the museum' *but:* с фа́брики 'from the factory' из конто́ры 'from the office' *but:* с заво́да 'from the plant' из амбулато́рии 'from the dispensary' *but:* с по́чты 'from the post-office' из мастерско́й 'from the workshop' *but:* с телегра́фа 'from the telegraph-office' из магази́на 'from the shop' *but:* с вокза́ла 'from the railway-station'
(Я) был '(I) was'	**(Я) пришёл** '(I) came'
на собра́нии 'at a meeting' на заседа́нии 'at a conference' на уро́ке 'at a lesson' на фро́нте 'at the front'	с собра́ния 'from the meeting' с заседа́ния 'from the conference' с уро́ка 'from the lesson' с фро́нта 'from the front'
(Я) жил '(I) lived'	**(Я) прие́хал** '(I) came'
в Крыму́ 'in the Crimea' *but:* на Кавка́зе 'in the Caucasus' в Белору́ссии 'in Byelorussia' *but:* на Украи́не 'in the Ukraine' в Сиби́ри 'in Siberia' *but:* на Ура́ле 'in the Urals', на Да́льнем Восто́ке 'in the Far East'	из Кры́ма 'from the Crimea' *but:* с Кавка́за 'from the Caucasus' из Белору́ссии 'from Byelorussia' *but:* с Украи́ны 'from the Ukraine' из Сиби́ри 'from Siberia' *but:* с Ура́ла 'from the Urals', с Да́льнего Восто́ка 'from the Far East'
(Я) е́ду '(I) shall be away'	**(Я) верну́лся** '(I) came back'
в о́тпуск 'on holiday'	из о́тпуска 'from my holidays'
(Я) иду́ '(I) am going'	**(Я) пришёл** '(I) came back'
в теа́тр 'to the theatre' *but:* на конце́рт 'to a concert'	из теа́тра 'from the theatre' *but:* с конце́рта 'from the concert'

(Я) живу́ ('I) live'	(Я) пришёл ('I) came'
в переу́лке 'in a lane' *but:* на пло́щади Восста́ния 'in Vosstanye Square', на у́лице Го́рького 'in Gorky Street'	из переу́лка 'from the lane' *but:* с пло́щади 'from the square', с у́лицы 'from the street'

Note. — 1. To indicate a means of conveyance, the preposition *на* is generally used: Я *е́ду на по́езде* 'I am going by train', *на трамва́е* 'by tram', *на авто́бусе* 'by bus', *на метро́* 'by the underground', *лечу́ на самолёте* 'I am going by plane', but one may also say: *в по́езде* 'by train', *в трамва́е* 'by tram', *в метро́* 'by the underground', etc.

2. Он *вы́шел из трамва́я* 'He got off the tram', but *сошёл с трамва́я* 'got off the tram'.

3. По́езд идёт *на Москву́* 'The train is bound for Moscow' (here direction is indicated).

Note the use of the correlative prepositions *из — в, с — на* in the set phrases: *изо дня́ в день* 'from day to day', *из ме́сяца в ме́сяц* 'month after month', *из го́да в год* 'year after year', *со дня на́ день* 'any day', *с ча́су на час* 'at any minute', *с мину́ты на мину́ту* 'any moment'.

Table 37

Most Common Uses of Prepositions to Express Relations of Space, Time, Cause and Purpose

I. Place and Direction

1. Prepositions *в, на, из, с; под, из-за, из-под*

где? 'where?'	куда́? 'where to?'	отку́да? 'from where?'
Prepositional	Accusative	Genitive
в 'at' (Я учу́сь *в шко́ле.* 'I go to school.')	*в* 'to' (Я иду́ *в шко́лу.* 'I am going to school.')	*из* 'from' (Я иду́ *из шко́лы.* 'I am coming from school.')
на 'on' (Я сижу́ *на сту́ле.* 'I am sitting on a chair.')	*на* 'on' (Я сел *на стул.* 'I sat down on a chair.')	*с (со)* 'from' (Я встал *со сту́ла.* 'I rose from the chair.')

159

где? 'where?'	куда? 'where to?'	откуда? 'from where?'
Instrumental	Accusative	Genitive
за 'beyond' (*За лесом* поле. 'There is a field beyond the forest.')	**за** 'behind' (Солнце зашло *за тучу*. 'The sun went behind a cloud.')	**из-за** 'from behind' (Солнце показалось *из-за тучи*. 'The sun came from behind the cloud.')
под 'under' (Заяц сидел *под кустом*. 'The hare was sitting under a bush.')	**под** 'under' (Заяц бросился *под куст*. 'The hare dashed under the bush.')	**из-под** 'from under' (Заяц выскочил *из-под куста*. 'The hare dashed from under the bush.')

2. Prepositions *у, от, около, возле, вдоль, среди, против, вокруг, по, к; через; над, перед, между; при*

Genitive	**у** 'at' (Ученик стоит *у доски*. 'The pupil is standing at the blackboard.')	где?
	от 'from' (Ученик отошёл *от доски*. 'The pupil has gone away from the blackboard.')	от чего?
	около 'near' (*Около леса* протекала река. 'Near the forest there was a river.')	где?
	возле 'close to' (*Возле леса* протекала река. 'Close to the forest there was a river.')	где?
	вдоль 'along' (*Вдоль улицы* посажены деревья. 'Trees were planted along the street.')	где?
	среди 'in the middle of' (*Среди леса* стоял домик лесника. 'In the middle of the forest stood the forester's cottage.')	где?
	против 'opposite' (*Против театра* стоит памятник. 'Facing the theatre is a monument.')	где?
	вокруг 'round' (Охотники сидели *вокруг костра*. 'The hunters were sitting round a fire.')	где?

160

Dative	*к* 'to' (Ма́льчик бежи́т *к реке́*. 'The boy is running to the river.')	*куда́?*
	по 'along' (Мы гуля́ли *по у́лицам* большо́го го́рода. 'We were walking in the streets of the large city.')	*где?*
Accusative	*че́рез* 'over', 'across' (Мы е́хали *че́рез мост*. 'We were going over the bridge.')	
Instrumental	*над* 'over' (Карти́на виси́т *над дива́ном*. 'The picture hangs over the sofa.')	*где?*
	пе́ред 'at' (*Пе́ред до́мом* останови́лась маши́на. 'A car pulled up at the house.')	*где?*
	ме́жду 'among' (*Ме́жду со́снами* растёт берёзка. 'A birch-tree grows among the pines.')	*где?*
Prepositional	*при* (*При шко́ле* есть огоро́д и сад. 'The school has a kitchen garden and an orchard of its own.')	*где?*

Ме́лкие пти́цы щебета́ли и и́зредка перелета́ли *с де́рева на де́рево*. 'Small birds were chirping, flying now and again from tree to tree.'

. . . .

В степи́ за реко́й, по доро́гам — везде́ бы́ло пу́сто. (Л. Т.) 'In the steppe beyond the river and along the roads not a soul was to be seen.'

Мы вы́шли *из ро́щи*, спусти́лись *с холма́*... (Т.) 'We came out of the grove and went down the hill...'

Я взгляну́л *в окно́: на безо́блачном не́бе* разгора́лись звёзды. (М. Г.) 'I looked out of the window: the stars were beginning to glow in the cloudless sky.'

Во ржи крича́т перепела́, *в мали́нниках над ручья́ми* сви́щут соловьи́; *че́рез доро́гу* перебежи́т куропа́тка, за́яц метнётся *из-под куста́;* глухо́й те́терев шара́хнется *в сыро́м бору́*. (Т.) 'Quails were whistling in the rye, nightingales were jugging among the raspberry-canes over the streams, (now and then) a partridge would run across the road, a hare would dash from under a bush, a deaf black-cock would shy off in the damp pine woods.'

II. Time

Genitive	**после** 'after' (*После обеда* дети пошли гулять. 'After dinner the children went for a walk.') **до** 'till', 'before' (*До ужина* они сделали уроки. 'Before supper they did their homework.') **накануне** 'on the eve of' (Я встретился с ним *накануне праздника*. 'I met him on the eve of the holiday.') **среди** 'in the middle of' (Ребёнок проснулся *среди ночи*. 'The child awoke in the middle of the night.') **с** 'since' (Я занимался *с утра, с 9-ти часов*. 'I have been studying since morning, since 9 o'clock.') (Занятия начались *с сентября*. 'The lessons have been going on since September.') (Он любил музыку *с детства*. 'He has loved music since his childhood.') (Я изучаю русский язык *с 1979 года*. 'I've been studying Russian since 1979.') **до** 'till' (Я занимался *до вечера, до 10-ти часов*. 'I studied till the evening, till 10 o'clock.') (Занятия продолжались *до июля*. 'The lessons continued till July.') (Он не потерял бодрости *до глубокой старости*. 'He did not lose his cheerfulness till a very old age.') (Я буду жить в Москве *до 1988 года*. 'I'll live in Moscow till 1988.')	*когда?* *с какого времени?* *с каких пор?* *до какого времени?* *до каких пор?*
Dative	**по** 'in' (Я люблю работать *по утрам*. 'I like to work in the morning.') **к** 'towards', 'by' (*К вечеру* он вернулся домой. 'Towards evening he returned home.') (Я приду *к двум часам дня*. 'I'll come by two o'clock in the afternoon.')	*когда?* *к какому времени?*
Accusative	**в** 'in', 'at', 'on' (Я приду *в субботу, в 2 часа*. 'I'll come at 2 o'clock on Saturday.') (Он помог мне *в трудную минуту*. 'He helped me in my hour of need.') (*В эту ночь* был сильный дождь. 'That night it rained hard.')	*когда?*

	на (Приходи́ ко мне *на сле́дующий день* по́сле экза́мена. 'Come to see me next day after the exam.')	
	че́рез 'in' (*Че́рез неде́лю* я е́ду в Ленин-гра́д. 'In a week, I am going to Leningrad.') (*Че́рез 5 мину́т* ко́нчится уро́к. 'In 5 minutes the lesson will be over.')	
	за... до 'before' (Мы прие́хали из дере́вни *за неде́лю до заня́тий*. 'We came from the country a week before classes began.')	
	под 'on the eve of' (Мы встре́тимся *под Но́вый год*. 'We'll meet on New Year's eve.')	
	в 'in' (Я сде́лаю э́ту рабо́ту *в неде́лю*. 'I'll do this work in a week.') (Он собра́лся *в одну́ мину́ту* и уе́хал. 'He got ready in a moment and left.')	*в какой срок?*
	за 'in' (Я прочита́л кни́гу *за один ве́чер*. 'I read the book in one evening.') (Но́вый дом постро́или *за один год*. 'The new house was built in one year.')	*за какой срок?*
	на 'for' (Он уе́хал *на неде́лю*. 'He went away for a week.') (Дай мне, пожа́луйста, кни́гу *на один ве́чер*. 'Will you lend me this book for one evening, please?')	*на какой срок?*
	по 'up to' (Она́ получи́ла о́тпуск *по 20-е а́вгуста*. 'She got a holiday up to the 20th of August.')	*по какой срок?*
Instrumental	*пе́ред* 'before' (*Пе́ред ле́кцией* я зашёл в библиоте́ку за кни́гами. 'Before the lecture I called at the library to get books.')	*когда?*
	ме́жду 'between' (Мы обе́даем *ме́жду двумя́ и тремя́ часа́ми*. 'We have dinner between two and three o'clock.')	
	за 'at' (Я обы́чно чита́ю газе́ту *за за́втраком*. 'I usually read the newspaper at breakfast.')	*когда?*
	с 'at' (Я люблю́ встава́ть ле́том *с восхо́дом со́лнца*. 'In summer I like to get up at sunrise.')	

6*

Preposi-tional	*в* 'in' (Мы на́чали заня́тия *в сентябре́.* 'We began our lessons in September.' Я прие́хал в Москву́ *в 1956 году́.* 'I came to Moscow in 1956.')	*когда́?*
	(*В мо́лодости* он мно́го занима́лся спо́ртом. 'In his youth he went in for sports a great deal.')	*когда́?*
	на (*На про́шлой неде́ле* я был в теа́тре. 'Last week I was at the theatre.')	
	по 'on' (*По оконча́нии* университе́та я уе́ду на пра́ктику. 'On graduation from the University I'll go to my practicals.')	
	при (*При наступле́нии* темноты́... 'When it gets dark...')	

Note. — To indicate a period of time in minutes, hours, weeks, years, etc., the preposition *че́рез* 'in' is used: *че́рез четы́ре го́да* 'in four years', *че́рез пять лет* 'in five years', *че́рез пять мину́т* 'in five minutes', *че́рез два часа́* 'in two hours', etc. In this sense one cannot say *приду́ по́сле двух часо́в*, since it would mean 'I shall come after two o'clock'. But one can say: Я уви́дел его́ *по́сле двух лет* разлу́ки. 'I met him after we had not seen each other for two years.'

III. Purpose

| Accusative | *за* 'for' (*Бо́ремся за* мир. 'We fight for peace.' *Голосу́ем за* резолю́цию. 'We vote for the resolution.' *Выступа́ем за...* 'We stand for...') |
| Instrumen-tal | (Идём *за кни́гами, за пи́сьмами.* 'We are going to get the books, the letters.') |

IV. Cause

| Genitive | *из-за* 'because of', 'owing to' (*Из-за дождя́* не состоя́лась экску́рсия. 'Owing to the rain the excursion did not take place.') (*Из-за тебя́* у меня́ неприя́тности. 'I have trouble because of you.') *от* 'for', 'because of' (*От волне́ния* он не мог говори́ть. 'He could not speak for excitement.') (Урожа́й поги́б *от за́сухи.* 'The crops have perished because of the drought.') |

	из 'out of' (Он спра́шивал э́то *из любопы́тства.* 'He asked that out of curiosity.')
	(*Из скро́мности* он молча́л о свои́х успе́хах. 'He did not say anything about his success out of modesty.')
	с (...*с похва́л* вскружи́лась голова́. (Кр.) 'The praises went to (her) head.')
Dative	*благодаря́* 'thanks to' (Рабо́та шла хорошо́ *благодаря́ уме́лому руково́дству.* 'The work went on well thanks to good leadership.')
	по 'owing to' (Учени́к сде́лал оши́бку *по небре́жности.* 'The pupil made the mistake owing to carelessness.')

Note. — 1. To indicate an external cause, the following prepositions are used: (1) *из-за* 'owing to', 'because of' (*Из-за дождя́* не состоя́лась экску́рсия. 'Owing to the rain the excursion did not take place.' *Из-за шу́ма* я не мог засну́ть. 'I could not fall asleep because of the noise.' *Из-за тебя́* у меня́ неприя́тности. 'I have trouble because of you.') (2) *от* 'because of', 'by' (Всё вы́сохло *от со́лнца.* 'Everything dried up because of the sun.' Всё поги́бло *от пожа́ра.* 'Everything was destroyed by the fire.' Он заболе́л *от потрясе́ния.* 'He fell ill with shock.' Её во́лосы растрепа́лись *от ве́тра.* 'Her hair was ruffled by the wind.' У неё *от жары́* разболе́лась голова́. 'Her head began to ache with the heat.') (3) *с* (*С похва́л* вскружи́лась голова́. 'The praises went to (her) head.')

Some prepositions can be replaced by others: *от похва́л* вскружи́лась голова́ (instead of *с похва́л*); or *от шу́ма* не мог засну́ть (instead of *из-за шу́ма*).

The prepositions *из-за* 'because of' and *благодаря́* 'thanks to' have different shades of meaning, viz., the cause expressed by a noun preceded by the preposition *из-за* produces an undesirable action while the cause expressed by a noun preceded by the preposition *благодаря́* gives a desirable effect: *Из-за за́сухи* поги́б урожа́й. 'The crops have perished because of the drought.' *Благодаря́ дождя́м* бу́дет хоро́ший урожа́й. 'Thanks to the rains good crops are to be expected.' *Благодаря́ твое́й по́мощи* я уже́ зако́нчил рабо́ту. 'Thanks to your help I have already finished the work.'

2. To indicate a cause expressing the state of a person, certain emotions or feelings, the prepositions *от, с, из* are generally used.

The preposition *от* 'for' is usually employed to denote the state of a person: Ма́льчик запры́гал *от ра́дости.* 'The boy began jumping for joy.' *От возмуще́ния и оби́ды* у него́ вы́ступили на глаза́х слёзы. 'Tears of indignation and anger welled up in his eyes.' Ребёнок дрожа́л *от стра́ха.* 'The child was trembling with fear.' Он побледне́л *от испу́га.* 'He turned pale with fright.' Де́вочка пла́кала *от го́ря.* 'The girl was crying for grief.'

The meaning of the preposition *с (со)* is identical with that of the preposition *от* but the former preposition is less frequently used (it usually occurs in colloquial speech).

The cause indicated by the preposition *из* 'out of' is generally a feeling or inclination impelling the agent to act in a certain manner: Она́ э́то сде́лала *из любви́ к де́тям.* 'She did that out of love for the children.'

3. To indicate a cause rising from some internal quality of a person, the preposition *по* 'through' is generally used: Он сде́лал э́то *по рассе́янности (по небре́жности, по глу́пости, по невнима́тельности)* 'He did that through absentmindedness (carelessness, stupidity, carelessness).' Besides, *по* is used in the expressions: пропусти́ть заня́тия *по боле́зни* 'to miss classes through illness', *по уважи́тельной причи́не* 'for good reasons'.

Человéка, котóрый рискýет жúзнью *из тщеслáвия* úли *из лю-
бопúтства* úли *из áлчности*, нельзя́ назвáть хрáбрым. 'A man
who risks his life out of vanity, curiosity or greed cannot be
called brave.'

. . . .

Из-за шýма пáдающего лúвня ничегó нé было слы́шно. (Т.)
'Owing to the noise of the falling rain one could hear nothing.'

Каштáнка взвúзгнула *от востóрга*. (Ч.) 'Kashtanka gave a whine
of delight.'

Когдá сóлнце поднимáется над лугáми, я невóльно улыбáюсь
от рáдости. (М. Г.) 'When the sun rises over the meadows, I cannot help smiling for joy.'

Мать задыхáлась *от волнéния* и чýвствовала — надвигáется
чтó-то нóвое. (М. Г.) 'The Mother was breathless with excitement
and felt that something new was coming.'

Лицó егó стáло грýстным *от переживáемых воспоминáний*. (Арс.)
'His face became sad with the recollection of his past.

Всё мне показáлось молоды́м и чúстым *благодаря присýтствию*
Лúды и Мисю́сь. (Ч.) 'Everything seemed pure and youthful to me
thanks to the presence of Lida and Misyus.'

Вещýньина *с похвáл* вскружúлась головá,
От рáдости в зобý дыхáнье спёрло. (Кр.)
'The praises went to the prophetess's head,
Joy took her breath away.'

Я удавúлась бы *с тоскú*,
Когдá бы на неё хоть чуть былá похóжа. (Кр.)
'I'd have hanged myself for grief
Had I had the slightest resemblance to her.'

Марты́шка тут *с досáды и печáли*
О кáмень тáк хватúла их,
Что тóлько бры́зги засверкáли. (Кр.)

'At that juncture the Monkey, in its vexation and grief,
dashed them (the spectacles) against a stone with such force that
they broke into sparkling splinters.'

Вы́пьем, дóбрая подрýжка
Бéдной ю́ности моéй,
Вы́пьем *с гóря*. Где же крýжка?
Сéрдцу бýдет веселéй. (П.)
'Let's drink,
Of my unlucky youth's genial companion,
Let's drink for grief. Where is the tankard?
Our hearts will become lighter.'

Не зна́я, что нача́ть *со стра́ха*,
Предчу́вствий го́рестных полна́,
Ждала́ несча́стья уж она́. (П.)
'Not knowing in her fear what to do,
Full of sad apprehension,
She expected some misfortune.'

Table 38

List of Common Russian Verbs with the Cases They Require
(The verbs are given in alphabetic order)

благодари́ть 'to thank'	*кого́?* 'whom?'	*что?* 'what?'	(Acc.)
боя́ться 'to fear', 'to be afraid'	*кого́?* 'whom?', 'of whom?'	*чего́?* 'what?', 'of what?'	(Gen.)
владе́ть, овладева́ть 'to possess', 'to take possession'	*кем?* 'whom?' 'of whom?'	*чем?* 'what?', 'of what?'	(Instr.)
восхища́ться 'to admire'	*кем?* 'whom?'	*чем?* 'what?'	(Instr.)
вспо́мнить 'to recollect'	*кого́?* 'whom?'	*что?* 'what?'	(Acc.)
встреча́ть 'to meet'	*кого́?* 'whom?'	*что?* 'what?'	(Acc.)
горди́ться 'to be proud'	*кем?* 'of whom?'	*чем?* 'of what?'	(Instr.)
добива́ться 'to try to get', 'to strive'		*чего́?* 'what?' 'for what?'	(Gen.)
дорожи́ть 'to value'	*кем?* 'whom?'	*чем?* 'what?'	(Instr.)
достига́ть 'to achieve'		*чего́?* 'what?'	(Gen.)
жа́ждать 'to thirst'		*чего́?* 'for what?'	(Gen.)
жела́ть 'to wish'		*чего́?* 'what?'	(Gen.)
же́ртвовать 'to sacrifice'	*кем?* 'whom?'	*чем?* 'what?'	(Instr.)
заболе́ть 'to fall ill'		*чем?* 'with what?'	(Instr.)
заве́довать 'to manage'		*чем?* 'what?'	(Instr.)
зави́довать 'to envy'	*кому́?* 'whom?'	*чему́?* 'what?'	(Dat.)
занима́ться 'to be busy'	*кем?* 'with whom?'	*чем?* 'with what?'	(Instr.)
заража́ть 'to infect'		*чем?* 'with what?'	(Instr.)
злоупотребля́ть 'to abuse'		*чем?* 'what?'	(Instr.)
избега́ть 'to avoid'	*кого́?* 'whom?'	*чего́?* 'what?'	(Gen.)
изумля́ться 'to be amazed'	*кому́?* 'at whom?'	*чему́?* 'at what?'	(Dat.)

интересова́ться 'to be interested'	*кем?* 'in whom?'	*чем?* 'in what?'	(Instr.)
каза́ться 'to seem'	*кем?* 'whom?'	*чем?* 'what?'	(Instr.)
каса́ться 'to touch'	*кого́?* 'whom?'	*чего́?* 'what?'	(Gen.)
кля́сться 'to swear'		*чем?* 'by what?'	(Instr.)
кома́ндовать 'to command'	*кем?* 'whom?'	*чем?* 'what?'	(Instr.)
лиша́ться 'to lose'	*кого́?* 'whom?'	*чего́?* 'what?'	(Gen.)
меша́ть 'to prevent'	*кому́?* 'whom?'	*чему́?* 'what?'	(Dat.)
называ́ться 'to be called'	*кем?* 'whom?'	*чем?* 'what?'	(Instr.)
облада́ть 'to possess'		*чем?* 'what?'	(Instr.)
отста́ивать 'to defend'	*кого́?* 'whom?'	*что?* 'what?'	(Acc.)
подража́ть 'to imitate'	*кому́?* 'whom?'	*чему́?* 'what?'	(Dat.)
по́льзоваться 'to use'		*чем?* 'what?'	(Instr.)
посвяща́ть 'to dedicate'	*кому́?* 'to whom?'	*чему́?* 'to what?'	(Dat.)
пренебрега́ть 'to ignore'	*кем?* 'whom?'	*чем?* 'what?'	(Instr.)
преодолева́ть 'to overcome'		*что?* 'what?'	(Acc.)
препя́тствовать 'to hinder'	*кому́?* 'whom?'	*чему́?* 'what?'	(Dat.)
проти́виться 'to oppose'	*кому́?* 'whom?'	*чему́?* 'what?'	(Dat.)
пуга́ться 'to be frightened'	*кого́?* 'with whom?'	*чего́?* 'with what?'	(Gen.)
ра́доваться 'to rejoice'	*кому́?* 'at whom?'	*чему́?* 'at what?'	(Dat.)
руководи́ть 'to lead'	*кем?* 'whom?'	*чем?* 'what?'	(Instr.)
соде́йствовать 'to assist'	*кому́?* 'whom?'	*чему́?* 'what?'	(Dat.)
сочу́вствовать 'to sympathize'	*кому́?* 'with whom?'	*чему́?* 'with what?'	(Dat.)
спосо́бствовать 'to favour'		*чему́?* 'what?'	(Dat.)
станови́ться 'to become'	*кем?* 'whom?'	*чем?* 'what?'	(Instr.)
стесня́ться 'to feel shy'	*кого́?* 'before whom?'	*чего́?* 'before what?'	(Gen.)
стыди́ться 'to be ashamed'	*кого́?* 'of whom?'	*чего́?* 'of what?'	(Gen.)
тре́бовать 'to demand'		*чего́?* 'what?'	(Gen.)
увлека́ться 'to take a great interest'	*кем?* 'in whom?'	*чем?* 'in what?'	(Instr.)

уделя́ть внима́ние 'to give attention'	кому́? 'to whom?'	чему́? 'to what?'	(Dat.)
удивля́ться 'to be surprised'	кому́? 'at whom?'	чему́? 'at what?'	(Dat.)
управля́ть 'to manage'	кем? 'whom?'	чем? 'what?'	(Instr.)
хвали́ться 'to boast'	кем? 'of whom?'	чем? 'of what?'	(Instr.)
хоте́ть 'to want'		чего́? 'what?'	(Gen.)
явля́ться 'to be'	кем? 'whom?'	чем? 'what?'	(Instr.)

(For examples, see tables on the use of the cases.)

Table 39

Verbs requiring the Prepositions на, в
(denoting relations other than those of space)

Verb plus the preposition **на** followed by the accusative:

1. влия́ть *на кого? на что?* 'to influence *whom? what?'*
повлия́ть (perfective) *на кого? на что?* 'to influence *whom? what?'*
ока́зывать влия́ние *на кого? на что?* 'to exert influence *on whom? on what?'*

    на това́рища 'a friend', *на аудито́рию* 'an audience', *на здоро́вье* '(one's) health', *на настрое́ние* '(one's) mood'

2. возлага́ть отве́тственность *на кого?* 'to hold responsible *whom?'*
возложи́ть (perfective) отве́тственность *на кого?* 'to hold responsible *whom?'*

    на руководи́теля 'the leader'

3. возлага́ть наде́жды *на кого? на что?* 'to place hopes *in whom? in what?'*
возложи́ть (perfective) наде́жды *на кого? на что?* 'to place hopes *in whom? in what?'*

    на молодёжь 'in the youth', *на пое́здку* 'in a journey'

4. ворча́ть *на кого? на что?* 'to grumble *at whom? at what?'*
поворча́ть (perfective) *на кого? на что?* 'to grumble *at whom? at what?'*

    на дете́й 'at children'

5. смотре́ть *на кого? на что?* 'to look *at whom? at what?'*
посмотре́ть *на кого? на что?* 'to look *at whom? at what?'*

    Ма́льчик умоля́юще посмотре́л на *мать*. 'The boy looked entreatingly at his mother.'

6. жа́ловаться *на кого́? на что?* 'to complain *of whom? of what?*'
   пожа́ловаться (perfective) *на кого́? на что?* 'to complain *of whom? of what?*'

   на челове́ка 'of a person', *на боль* 'of a pain', *на непра́вильные де́йствия* 'of wrong actions'

7. клевета́ть *на кого́?* 'to slander *whom? what?*'
   (but: оклевета́ть (perfective) 'to slander' *кого́?* used without the preposition *на*)
   наклевета́ть (perfective) *на кого́?* 'to slander *whom?*'

8. крича́ть *на кого́?* 'to shout *at whom?*'
   накрича́ть (perfective) *на кого́?* 'to shout *at whom?*'

   Нельзя́ *крича́ть на дете́й.* 'One must not shout at children.'

9. наде́яться *на кого́? на что?* 'to rely *on whom? on what?*', 'to hope *for what?*'
   понаде́яться (perfective) *на кого́? на что?* 'to rely *on whom? on what?*', 'to hope *for what?*'

   на това́рища '(to rely) on a friend', *на по́мощь* 'on help', *на успе́х* '(to hope) for success', *на улучше́ние* 'for an improvement'

10. обраща́ть внима́ние *на кого́? на что?* 'to pay attention *to whom? to what?*'
    обрати́ть (perfective) внима́ние *на кого́? на что?* 'to pay attention *to whom? to what?*'

    на карти́ну 'to a picture,' *на поведе́ние кого́-нибудь* 'to somebody's behaviour'

11. опира́ться *на кого́? на что?* 'to rely *on whom? on what?*'
    опере́ться (perfective) *на кого́? на что?* 'to rely *on whom? on what?*'

    на ма́ссы 'on the masses', *на фа́кты* 'on the facts'

12. покуша́ться *на кого́? на что?* 'to make an attempt *on whom? on what?*'
    соверши́ть (perfective) покуше́ние *на кого́? на что?* 'to make an attempt *on whom? on what?*'

    на челове́ка 'on a person', *на жизнь* 'on (one's) life'

13. полага́ться *на кого́? на что?* 'to rely *on whom? on what?*'
    положи́ться (perfective) *на кого́? на что?* 'to rely *on whom? on what?*'

    на това́рища 'on a friend', *на пого́ду* 'on the weather'

14. посягáть *на что?* 'to encroach *on what?*' посягнýть (perfective) *на что?* 'to encroach *on what?*' — *на правá* 'on (one's) rights', *на чужóе имýщество* 'on other people's property'

15. походи́ть *на когó? на что?* 'to resemble *whom? what?*' — *на отцá* '(one's) father', *на сестрý* '(one's) sister'

быть похóжим *на когó? на что?* 'to look like *whom? what?*' — Это ни на что *не похóже.* 'This is like nothing on earth.'

16. производи́ть впечатлéние *на когó?* 'to make an impression *on whom?*' произвести́ (perfective) впечатлéние *на когó?* 'to make an impression *on whom?*' — *на слýшателей* 'on the listeners', *на зри́телей* 'on the spectators', *на аудитóрию* 'on the audience'

17. решáться *на что?* 'to make up one's mind *as to what?*' реши́ться (perfective) *на что?* 'to make up one's mind *as to what?*' — *на разговóр* 'as to having a conversation', *на поéздку* 'as to making a trip'

18. рассчи́тывать *на когó? на что?* 'to count *on whom? on what?*' — *на поддéржку* 'on (one's) support', *на свобóдное врéмя* 'on (one's) free time'

Note the following: — When used in the above sense, the verb *рассчи́тывать* 'to count' has no perfective aspect. The verb *рассчитáть* is a perfective verb, but its meaning is 'to calculate' and it is used without the preposition *на:* Я плóхо *рассчитáл своё врéмя* 'I calculated my time badly.'

---

19. соглашáться *на что?* 'to agree *to what?*' согласи́ться (perfective) *на что?* 'to agree *to what?*' (but: соглашáться, согласи́ться *с кем? с чем?* 'to agree *with whom? with what?*') — *на рабóту* 'to work', *на определённые услóвия* 'to definite conditions'

20. серди́ться *на когó? на что?* 'to be angry *with whom? with what?*' — *на брáта* 'with (one's) brother', *на товáрища* 'with (one's) friend'

171

Verb plus the preposition *на* followed by the prepositional:

1. игрáть *на чём?* 'to play *what?*'	*на скрúпке* 'the violin', *на роя́ле* 'the piano' (but: *игрáть в кýклы* 'to play dolls', *игрáть в шáхматы* 'to play chess', *игрáть в футбóл* 'to play football')
2. настáивать *на чём?* 'to insist *on what?*' настоя́ть (perfective) *на чём?* 'to insist *on what?*'	*на решéнии* 'on a decision', *на вы́езде* 'on leaving', *настáивать на своём* 'to try to have it one's own way', *настоя́ть на своём* 'to have it one's own way'
3. оснóвываться *на чём?* 'to be based *on what?*'	*на провéренных дáнных* 'on verified data', *на фáктах* 'on facts'

Verb plus the preposition *в* followed by the accusative:

1. вéрить *в когó? во что?* 'to believe *in whom? in what?*' повéрить (perfective) *в когó? во что?* 'to believe *in whom? in what?*'	*в негó* 'in him', *в неё* 'in her', *в побéду* 'in victory', *в бýдущее* 'in the future', *в свои́ си́лы* 'in one's strength'	**Note.** — When used in the sense of 'to trust' this verb is followed by the dative without any preposition: *вéрить комý?* 'to trust whom?' (*товáрищу* 'one's friend', *врачý* 'the doctor', etc.); but note the use of the preposition *в* followed by the prepositional in *Я увéрен в нём* 'I am sure of him', *в нáшей побéде* 'of our victory'.
2. игрáть *во что?* 'to play *what?*'	*в шáхматы* 'chess', *в мяч* 'a ball', *в футбóл* 'football'	

172

3. обраща́ться *во что?* 'to turn into *what?*', 'to become *what?*' обрати́ться (perfective) *во что?* 'to turn into *what?*', 'to become *what?*'	Он весь *обрати́л-ся в слух.* 'He became all ears.' . . . . Облачко *обрати́-лось в бе́лую ту́чу.* (П.) 'The little cloud had turned into a big white cloud.'	*обрати́ться в бе́гство* 'to take to one's heels'
4. превраща́ться *в кого? во что?* 'to turn *into whom? into what?*' преврати́ться (perfective) *в кого? во что?* 'to turn *into whom? into what?*', 'to become *whom? what?*'	Эта ма́ленькая де-реву́шка ско́ро *пре-врати́тся в большо́й посёлок.* 'This small hamlet will soon turn into a large settle-ment.'	

Verb plus the preposition *в* followed by the prepositional:

1. нужда́ться *в ком? в чём?* 'to be in need *of whom? of what?*'	*в рабо́тниках* 'of workers', *в по́мощи* 'of help', *в поддёрж-ке* 'of support', *в ухо́-де* 'of care', *в са́мом необходи́мом* 'of bare necessities'	
2. обма́нываться *в ком? в чём?* 'to be disappointed *in whom? in what?*' обману́ться (perfective) *в ком? в чём?* 'to be disappointed *in whom? in what?*'	*в челове́ке* 'in a person', *в свои́х на-де́ждах* 'in one's expectations'	

3. одержа́ть (perfective) побе́ду *в чём?* 'to gain a victory *in what?*'	*в борьбе́* 'in a fight', *в спо́ре* 'in an argument', *в соревнова́нии* 'in a competition'	But: *одержа́ть побе́ду над кем? над чем?* 'to gain a victory over whom? over what?'
4. отдава́ть (себе́) отчёт *в чём?* 'to realize *what?*'	*в свои́х посту́пках* 'what one is doing', *в свои́х слова́х* 'what one is saying'	
5. отчи́тываться *в чём?* 'to give an account *of what?*' отчита́ться (perfective) *в чём?* 'to give an account *of what?*'	*в свое́й рабо́те* 'of one's work', *в расхо́дах* 'of the money one has spent', *в выполне́нии пла́на* 'of the fulfilment of a plan'	
6. признава́ться *в чём?* 'to make a declaration *of what?*', 'to admit *what?*' призна́ться (perfective) *в чём?* 'to make a declaration *of what?*' 'to admit *what?*'	*в любви́* 'of love', *в свои́х оши́бках* '(to admit) one's mistakes'	
7. разочаро́вываться *в ком? в чём?* 'to be disappointed *in whom? in what?*' разочарова́ться (perfective) *в ком? в чём?* 'to be disappointed *in whom? in what?*'	*в челове́ке* 'in a person', *в рабо́те* 'in (one's) work', *в наде́ждах* 'in (one's) hopes', *в жи́зни* 'in life', *в дру́ге* 'in a friend'	But: *очаро́вываться кем? чем?* 'to be charmed with whom? with what?' очарова́ться (perfective) *кем? чем?* 'to be charmed with whom? with what?'
8. сознава́ться *в чём?* 'to confess *what?*' созна́ться (perfective) *в чём?* 'to confess *what?*'	*в свое́й вине́* 'one's guilt'	

9. соревнова́ться в чём? 'to compete in what?'	в рабо́те 'in work', в игре́ 'in a game', в бе́ге 'in racing', в прыжка́х 'in jumping'	
10. сомнева́ться в чём? 'to doubt what?'	в зна́ниях '(one's) knowledge', в спосо́бностях '(one's) abilities', в че́стности челове́ка 'a person's honesty'	
11. упрека́ть в чём? 'to reproach *with* what?' упрекну́ть (perfective) в чём? 'to reproach *with* what?'	в бесхозя́йственности 'with bad management', в отста́лости 'with backwardness', в жа́дности 'with being stingy'	
12. убежда́ться в чём? 'to be convinced *of* what?', 'to make sure *of* what?' убеди́ться (perfective) в чём? 'to be convinced *of* what?', 'to make sure *of* what?'	в необходи́мости 'of the necessity', в неизбе́жности 'of the incvitability', в правоте́ де́ла 'of the rightness of one's cause'	
13. уча́ствовать в чём? 'to participate *in* what?' (принима́ть уча́стие, приня́ть уча́стие в чём? 'to take part *in* what?')	в вы́борах 'in elections', в голосова́нии 'in the voting', в рабо́те 'in the work'	Idiomatic expression: принима́ть уча́стие (в ком?) means 'to befriend (whom?)', 'to take an interest (in whom?)'

III. THE ADJECTIVE

GENERAL REMARKS

1. The functions of an adjective in the sentence may be *attributive* or *predicative*. When used attributively an adjective agrees with the noun it qualifies in gender, number and case (Я взял в библиотéке *интерéсную кнúгу.* 'I borrowed an interesting book from the library.'). An exception to this rule is the adjective preceded by a numeral (*два* 'two', *три* 'three' or *четы́ре* 'four') and followed by a noun, e.g., *два крáсных карандашá* 'two red pencils' (see Table 43). When used predicatively an adjective agrees with its noun in gender and number (*Кнúга óчень интерéсна.* 'The book is very interesting.' *Доклáд интерéсен.* 'The report is interesting.').

2. Russian adjectives are divided into *qualitative* (e.g., *крáсный* 'red', *большóй* 'large', *красúвый* 'beautiful') and *relative* adjectives (e.g., *деревя́нный* 'wooden', *желéзный* 'iron', *отцóвский* 'father's', *сéстрин* 'sister's', *у́тренний* 'morning', *апрéльский* 'April').

3. Russian qualitative adjectives may be *long* in form (*красú-вый* мáльчик 'handsome boy', *красúвая* дéвочка 'beautiful girl', *красúвое* дитя́ 'handsome child') or *short* (мáльчик *красúв* 'the boy is handsome', дéвочка *красúва* 'the girl is beautiful', дитя́ *красúво* 'the child is handsome').

4. Long-form adjectives are generally attributive (Налéво чернé-ло *глубóкое ущéлье.* 'On the left a deep gorge showed black.'), but they may also be used predicatively (Сегóдня день *я́сный, тúхий.* 'Today the day is clear, quiet.'). Short-form adjectives can only be used predicatively (Как *вóздух чист!* Как *я́сен небосклóн!* (Бар.) 'How pure is the air! How clear is the sky!').

5. As a rule, an attributive adjective precedes the noun it qualifies (*Прекрáсное апрéльское сóлнце* сúльно грéло. 'The splendid April sun was very warm.'), whereas a predicative adjective follows its noun (*Шоссé бы́ло сýхо.* 'The main road was dry.').

If an adjective occupies any other position in the sentence, it always bears logical stress and is given emphatic intonation: Зимá, *злáя, тёмная, длúнная,* былá ещё так недáвно, веснá пришлá вдруг. (Ч.) 'Not so long ago it had been winter, severe, dark and long; spring had arrived all at once.' This exceptional word-order is most frequently observed in poetry: *Эльбру́с, огро́мный, величáвый, белéл на нéбе голубóм.* (П.) 'Elbrus, enormous and majestic, showed white against the azure sky.'

6. In Modern Russian only those short-form adjectives are declined which end in *-ов, -ин* and express possession (*отцóв* 'the father's', *бáбушкин* 'the grandmother's', *Вáнин* 'Vanya's'); they have certain peculiar forms different from those of long-form adjectives (see Table 46). Case-forms of the short-form qualitative adjective occur in Modern Russian in a few isolated instances (see Table 45).

7. Long-form adjectives may be substantivized, i.e., used as nouns: *Больнóй* пошёл к дóктору. 'The sick man went to a doctor.' (cf.: *больнóй ребёнок* 'a sick child').

A number of adjectives have become completely substantivized: *рабóчий* 'worker', *портнóй* 'tailor', *столóвая* 'dining-room', etc.; these words do not change according to gender, but are declined as adjectives.

Table 40

Gender Endings of Adjectives

Singular		
Masculine	Feminine	Neuter
-ый, -ий, -ой	*-ая, -яя*	*-ое, -ее*
крáсный (платóк) 'red (kerchief)'	крáсная (блýзка) 'red (blouse)'	крáсное (плáтье) 'red (frock)'
послéдний (урóк) 'last (lesson)'	послéдняя (минута) 'last (minute)'	послéднее (усúлие) 'last (effort)'
хорóший (план) 'good (plan)'	хорóшая (земля́) 'good (land)'	хорóшее (решéние) 'good (decision)'
рýсский (язы́к) 'Russian (language)'	рýсская (кни́га) 'Russian (book)'	рýсское (слóво) 'Russian (word)'
большóй (стол) 'large (table)'	большáя (кóмната) 'large (room)'	большóе (окнó) 'large (window)'

Plural (for all genders)

-ые, -ие

крáсные (платки́) 'red (kerchiefs)', крáсные (блýзки) 'red (blouses)', крáсные (плáтья) 'red (frocks)'
послéдние (урóки) 'last (lessons)', послéдние (минýты) 'last (minutes)', послéдние (усилия) 'last (efforts)'
больши́е (столы́) 'large (tables)', больши́е (кóмнаты) 'large (rooms)', больши́е (óкна) 'large (windows)'

Note. — Adjectives whose stem ends in a hard consonant take the endings *-ый, -ой, -ая, -ое, -ые;* those whose stem ends in a soft consonant take *-ий, -яя, -ее, -ие.*

The ending *-ой* of masculine adjectives is invariably stressed: *молодо́й* 'young', *боево́й* 'fighting', *выходно́й* 'free', *большо́й* 'large'.

Note on Spelling. — In masculine adjectives the ending is spelt *-ий* after *г, к, х (убо́гий* 'miserable', *глубо́кий* 'deep', *ти́хий* 'quiet') and after sibilants *(хоро́ший* 'good', *похо́жий* 'resembling'); in neuter adjectives the ending after *ш, ж* is spelt *-ое* when stressed *(большо́е* 'large', *чужо́е* 'strange') and *-ее* when unstressed *(хоро́шее* 'good', *све́жее* 'fresh').

Singular		
-ий	*-ья*	*-ье*
медве́жий (у́гол) 'god-forsaken (hole)'	медве́жья (ла́па) 'bear's (paw)'	медве́жье (у́хо) 'bear's (ear)'
во́лчий (аппети́т) 'wolfish (appetite)'	во́лчья (я́ма) 'wolf (hole)'	во́лчье (се́рдце) 'wolf's (heart)'

Plural (for all genders)
-ьи
медве́жьи (углы́, берло́ги, у́ши) 'god-forsaken (holes)', 'bear's (dens, ears)'; во́лчьи (зу́бы, ла́пы, у́ши) 'wolves' (teeth, paws, ears)'

Note. — A number of relative adjectives, mainly those derived from nouns denoting persons or animals *(каза́чий* 'Cossack's', *поме́щичий* 'landlord's', *во́лчий* 'wolf's', *медве́жий* 'bear's', *ли́сий* 'fox's', *собо́лий* 'sable's', etc.), have the ending *-ий, -ья, -ье* in the singular and *-ьи* in the plural.

DECLENSION OF ADJECTIVES

Table 41

	Masculine and Neuter	Endings	Feminine	Endings
Singular				
Adjectives whose Stem ends in a Hard Consonant				
Nom.	кра́сный (плато́к) 'red (kerchief)'	*-ый*	кра́сная (блу́зка) 'red blouse'	*-ая*
	кра́сное (пла́тье) 'red (frock)'	*-ое*		
	интере́сный (докла́дчик)* 'interesting (speaker)'			
Gen.	кра́сного (платка́, пла́тья)	*-ого*	кра́сной (блу́зки)	*-ой*
Dat.	кра́сному (платку́, пла́тью)	*-ому*	кра́сной (блу́зке)	*-ой*

* See Note (1), p. 180

Acc.	красный (платок)	as Nom.	красную (блузку)	-ую
	красное (платье)			
	интересного (докладчика)	as Gen.		
Instr.	красным (платком, платьем)	-ым	красной (блузкой)	-ой (-ою)
Prep.	(о) красном (платке, платье)	-ом	(о) красной (блузке)	-ой

Adjectives whose Stem ends in a Soft Consonant

Nom.	последний (день) 'last (day)'	-ий	последняя (лекция) 'last (lecture)'	-яя
	последнее (собрание) 'last (meeting)'	-ее		
	последний (докладчик) 'last (speaker)'			
Gen.	последнего (дня, собрания)	-его	последней (лекции)	-ей
Dat.	последнему (дню, собранию)	-ему	последней (лекции)	-ей
Acc.	последний (день), последнее (собрание)	as Nom.	последнюю (лекцию)	-юю
	последнего (докладчика)	as Gen.		
Instr.	последним (днём, собранием)	-им	последней (лекцией)	-ей (-ею)
Prep.	(о) последнем (дне, собрании)	-ем	(о) последней (лекции)	-ей

Plural (for all genders)

Nom.	красные (доски) 'red (boards)'	последние (дни) 'last (days)'	-ые, -ие
Gen.	красных (досок)	последних (дней)	-ых, -их
Dat.	красным (доскам)	последним (дням)	-ым, -им
Acc.	красные (доски)	последние (дни)	as Nom.
	внимательных (учениц) 'attentive (pupils)'	последних (докладчиков, докладчиц)	as Gen.
Instr.	красными (досками)	последними (днями)	-ыми, -ими
Prep.	(о) красных (досках)	(о) последних (днях)	-ых, -их

Table 42

Declension of Adjectives of the *во́лчий, ли́сий* Type

| | Singular | | | |
	Masculine and Neuter	Endings	Feminine	Endings
Nom.	во́лчий во́лчье 'wolf's' ли́сий ли́сье 'fox's'		во́лчья ли́сья	
Gen.	во́лчьего ли́сьего	*-его*	во́лчьей ли́сьей	*-ей*
Dat.	во́лчьему ли́сьему	*-ему*	во́лчьей ли́сьей	*-ей*
Acc.	во́лчий ли́сий во́лчье ли́сье	as Nom.	во́лчью ли́сью	*-ю*
	во́лчьего ли́сьего	as Gen.		
Instr.	во́лчьим ли́сьим	*-им*	во́лчьей ли́сьей	*-ей* (*-ею*)
Prep.	(о) во́лчьем (о) ли́сьем	*-ем*	(о) во́лчьей (о) ли́сьей	*-ей*

	Plural (for all genders)		
Nom.	во́лчьи	ли́сьи	
Gen.	во́лчьих	ли́сьих	*-их*
Dat.	во́лчьим	ли́сьим	*-им*
Acc.		as Nom. or Gen.	
Instr.	во́лчьими	ли́сьими	*-ими*
Prep.	(о) во́лчьих	(о) ли́сьих	*-их*

Note. — 1. Adjectives which qualify nouns denoting animate beings are declined in the same manner as adjectives which qualify nouns denoting inanimate objects, except for the accusative, which is identical with the genitive when referring to animate beings.

2. Adjectives whose stem ends in a hard consonant take in the oblique cases the endings *-ого, -ому, -ым, -ом; -ой, -ую; -ых, -ым, -ыми*. Adjectives whose stem ends in a soft consonant take in the oblique cases the endings *-его, -ему, -им, -ем; -ей, -юю; -их, -им, -ими*.

3. Adjectives of the *во́лчий, во́лчья, во́лчье* 'wolf's'; *ли́сий, ли́сья, ли́сье* 'fox's' type invariably take the soft mark *ь* before the endings (*во́лчьего, во́лчьему*, etc.), except in the nominative singular of the masculine gender (*во́лчий*). The accusative singular of the feminine gender has the final *-ью* (*во́лчью*). (The *-я, -ей, -ю* at the end of the corresponding case-forms of the above adjectives are sounded [йа], [йэй], [йу], the sound [й] belonging to the stem of the adjective.)

4. After the sibilants *ж, ч, ш, щ* the adjective ending takes *о* when it is stressed (*большо́й* 'large', *чужо́й* 'another's', *большо́го, чужо́го, большо́му, чужо́му*, etc.) and *е* when unstressed (*хоро́шего*, gen. of *хоро́ший* 'good', *хоро́шему; похо́жего*, gen. of *похо́жий* 'resembling', *похо́жему*, etc.), except for the nominative, where it takes *и* (*хоро́ший*).

5. In the ending of the genitive of the masculine and neuter genders the letter *г (-ого, -его)* is pronounced [в].

6. The instrumental singular of the feminine gender generally ends in *-ой, -ей;* however, alongside this form an obsolescent form ending in *-ою, -ею* is occasionaly used, e.g., *кра́сною*, instr. of *кра́сная* 'red'; *си́нею*, instr. of *си́няя* 'blue'; *во́лчьею*, instr. of *во́лчья* 'wolf's'.

Table 43

Agreement of an Adjective with its Noun
I.

	Singular		Plural
	Masculine and Neuter	Feminine	
Nom.	*Холóдный вéтер.* 'A cold wind.' *Нúзкое тёмное нéбо.* 'A low dark sky.'	*Грýстная óсень.* 'A sad autumn.'	*Пáсмурные печáльные дни.* 'Gloomy cloudy days.'
Gen.	На полńх идёт рабóта *с рáннего утрá до пóзднего вéчера.* 'Work goes on in the fields from early in the morning till late in the evening.'	*Пóсле дождлúвой погóды* наступúли ńсные дни. 'Fine days followed the spell of rainy weather.'	Лéтом бы́ло мнóго *жáрких дней.* 'There were many hot days in the summer.'
Dat.	Все рáдуются *тёплому осéннему сóлнцу.* 'Everybody rejoices in the warm autumn sun.'	Машúны éдут *по рóвной дорóге.* 'The cars are running along a smooth road.'	Урожáй *благодарń чáстым тёплым дождńм* хорóший. 'Thanks to the frequent warm rains the harvest is good.'
Acc.	Бригáды соревнýются *за отлúчное кáчество* рабóты. 'The brigades compete for excellent quality in work.'	*Через широ́кую рекý* постро́или но́вый мост. 'A new bridge was built across the wide river.'	*На колхóзные полń* вы́шли трáкторы. 'Tractors went to work in the collective-farm fields.'
Instr.	Веснá. Яркое сóлнце. Мы отдыхáем *под тенúстым дéревом.* 'It is spring. The sun is shining bright. We are resting under a shady tree.'	*Пéред берёзовой рóщей* расстилáется ширóкий луг с цветáми. 'In front of the birch grove, there is a large meadow sprinkled with flowers.'	Молодёжь возвращáется с рабóты *с весёлыми пéснями.* 'The young people are coming back from work singing gay songs.'
Prep.	*На зелёном лугý* расцвелú цветы́. 'Flowers had blossomed in a green meadow.'	Кáпли дождń блестńт *на свéжей зéлени.* 'Raindrops glisten on fresh verdure.'	*На колхóзных полńх* зрéет пшенúца. 'The wheat is ripening in the collective-farm fields.'

II.

А. Как *лес хорош поздней осенью*... Ветра нет, и нет ни солнца, ни света, ни тени, ни движения, ни шума; *в мягком воздухе* разлит *осенний запах, подобный* запаху вина; *тонкий туман* стоит вдали *над жёлтыми полями*. Сквозь *обнажённые бурые сучья* деревьев мирно белеет *неподвижное небо;* кой-где на липах висят *последние золотые листья*. *Сырая земля* упруга под ногами; *высокие сухие былинки* не шевелятся; *длинные нити* блестят *на побледневшей траве*... (Т.) 'How pleasant is the forest in late autumn... There is no wind, and neither sun, light, shade, movement, or noise; the soft air is filled with an autumnal fragrance like the aroma of wine; a thin mist is spread in the distance over the yellow fields. Through the bare brown branches of the trees the still sky shows peacefully white; here and there the last golden leaves still cling to the limes. The wet ground is soft underfoot; the tall grass is motionless; long threads glisten on the faded grass...'

Б. *В скромных путешествиях* меня не соблазняют *головокружительные рекорды*. Забыв о цели похода, часами готов я любоваться внезапно *раскрывшейся* перед глазами *прекрасной панорамой*. Подолгу засиживаюсь в лесу. С чувством восторга любуюсь *спокойным течением лесной рыбной речки*, полётом *диких птиц*. Я слушаю пение птиц и радуюсь встречам с *людьми*, поэтически *чувствующими* природу. В *отдалённых* и *глухих окраинах* нашей страны, куда завлекала меня *охотничья, скитальческая страсть*, находил я *таких близких* моему сердцу *людей*. Я встречал их на островах *ледяной Арктики* и на берегах *южного синего моря*. Всегда волновали и радовали меня эти встречи. *В охотничьих скитаниях, в далёких* и *радостных путешествиях* обретал я себе *новых* и *верных друзей*, связь с которыми никогда не обрывалась. (С.-М.)

'During my modest trips I am not tempted by breath-taking records. Forgetting about the purpose of the trip, I am ready to admire for hours a beautiful panorama, which suddenly opens up in front of me. I may stay in a forest for a long time. Delighted, I admire the quiet flowing of a forest river teeming with fish, or the flight of wild birds.

'I listen to the singing of birds, and am glad when I meet people who have a poetical feeling of nature. In the remote out-of-the-way corners of our country, where my sportsman's passion for roving has taken me to, I came across such people, so dear to my heart. I met them on the islands of the frozen Arctic, and on the shore of the blue southern sea. In my sportsman's wanderings, in those long and happy journeys I would find new and faithful friends the ties with whom were never broken off.'

Note. — 1. An adjective used attributively always agrees with the noun it qualifies in gender, number and case. In the plural, an adjective ending does not change for gender. Long-form participles, some pronouns and ordinal numerals agree in the same way with the noun they qualify.

2. An adjective may not agree in number with its noun in the following phrases: the numeral *два* 'two', *три* 'three' or *четыре* 'four' plus adjective plus noun, e. g., *два красных* (plural) *карандаша* (singular) 'two red pencils', *три молодых* (plural) *дерева* (singular) 'three young trees', *четыре маленьких* (plural) *мальчика* (singular) 'four small boys'.

SHORT FORM QUALITATIVE ADJECTIVES

Table 44

Long-form Adjectives		Short-form Adjectives	
Singular	Plural (for all genders)	Singular	Plural (for all genders)
Masculine		Masculine	
ста́рый 'old'		стар	*no endings*
споко́йный 'quiet'		споко́ен	
плохо́й 'bad'		плох	
коро́ткий 'short'		коро́ток	
могу́чий 'mighty'		могу́ч	
Feminine		Feminine	
ста́рая	ста́рые	стара́	ста́ры (стары́) -ы
споко́йная	споко́йные	споко́йна	споко́йны
плоха́я	плохи́е	плоха́ -а	пло́хи -и
коро́ткая	коро́ткие	коротка́	ко́ротки (коротки́)
могу́чая	могу́чие	могу́ча	могу́чи
Neuter		Neuter	
ста́рое		ста́ро (старо́) -о	
споко́йное		споко́йно	
плохо́е		пло́хо	
коро́ткое		ко́ротко	
могу́чее		могу́че -е	

Note. — 1. Qualitative adjectives have both the long and short forms (*ста́рый*, *стар* 'old'). Relative adjectives have only the long form (*деревя́нный* 'wooden', *во́лчий* 'wolf's').

2. Only those short-form adjectives are commonly used which are formed from adjectives whose stem ends in a hard consonant or a sibilant (*широ́к* 'wide', *могу́ч* 'mighty', *хоро́ш* 'good'); short-form adjectives formed from adjectives whose stem ends in a soft consonant are very rarely used (*синь, си́ня, си́не, си́ни* 'blue').

3. In the stem of a masculine short-form adjective there may occasionally appear an unstable *-о* or *-е: больно́й — бо́лен* 'sick', *споко́йный — споко́ен* 'quiet', *интере́сный — интере́сен* 'interesting', *коро́ткий — ко́роток* 'short'.

Table 45

Uses of Short-Form Qualitative Adjectives

1. In modern literary Russian the short form adjective is used only predicatively.

The link-verb in the compound predicate (*был, бу́дет, будь, был бы*) is used in the past and future tenses, in the imperative and in the conditional-subjunctive mood; in the present tenses the link-verb (*есть*) is omitted.

Докла́д *интере́сен* 'the report is interesting', докла́д *был интере́сен* 'the report was interesting', докла́д *бу́дет интере́сен* 'the report will be interesting', докла́д *был бы интере́сен* 'the report would be (would have been) interesting'.

. . . .

Весна́, весна́! Как во́здух *чист!* Как *я́сен* небоскло́н! (Бар.) 'Spring! Spring! How pure is the air! How clear is the sky!'

Хоро́ш ле́тние тума́нные дни. (Т.) 'Good are the hazy summer days.'

Уж и впрямь была́ цари́ца:
Высока́, стройна́, бела́,
И умо́м, и всем взяла́:
Но зато́ *горда́, ломли́ва,*
Своенра́вна и ревни́ва. (П.)

'She was a real queen:
Tall, slender, with white skin,
She was also clever, and had many good qualities,
But, on the other hand, she was proud, liked to pose,
Was wilful and jealous'.

...Оно́

Со́ку спе́лого *полно́,*
Так *свежо́* и так *души́сто,*
Так *румя́но, золоти́сто,*
Бу́дто мёдом налило́сь! (П.)

'(The apple) is full of ripe juice,
So fresh and fragrant,
So rosy, so golden,
As if it were filled with honey!'

Note. — The short-form adjectives *согласен* 'agreeable', *рад* 'glad', *должен* 'obliged' have no long form counterparts (with the same meaning).

The usual forms of polite address are: *будь добр, будь добра, будьте добры* 'would you be so kind as': *Будьте добры,* передайте товарищу книгу. 'Would you be so kind as to give this book to my friend?' *будь любезен, будь любезна, будьте любезны* 'will you please': *Будьте так любезны,* позвоните мне по телефону. 'Will you please ring me up?'

2. In modern colloquial Russian the short-form adjective is never used attributively; however, this use (considered archaic) occurs in folk songs, epics, in poetry and also in certain set expressions (some of the latter are used in the spoken language).

красно солнышко 'beautiful sun' — красну солнышку

красна девица 'bonnie lass' — красну девицу

удал добр молодец 'good brave fellow' — удалу добру молодцу

. . . .

Птичка в дальние страны,*
В тёплый край, *за сине море*
Улетает до весны. (П.)
'The little bird flies away to distant
                                        lands,
To a warm country, beyond the dark-
                                        blue sea,
Till spring comes back.'

У ворот стоят у тесовых
Красны девушки да молодушки. (Л.)
'At the rough-hewn gates
Stand bonnie lasses and young wives.'

Не встречает его *молода жена,*
Не накрыт дубовый стол белой ска-
                                        тертью. (Л.)
'The young wife does not meet him,
The oak table is not covered with a
                                        white cloth.'

* As a rule, the stress in the plural falls on *a (страны)* but in poetry *страны* is occasionally encountered.

185

Госуда́рь ты мой, *кра́сно со́лнышко*,
Иль убе́й меня́, и́ли вы́слушай. (Л.)
'My Sovereign, my beautiful sun,
Either kill me or listen to me.'

Я скажу́ вам, бра́тцы любе́зные,
Что *лиха́ беда́* со мно́ю приключи́лася.

(Л.)

'I'll tell you, my dear brethren,
That a sad misfortune has happened to
me.'

Idiomatic expressions: *по бе́лу све́ту*
'into the wide world', *от ма́ла до вели́ка*
'great and small', *на бо́су но́гу* 'on one's
bare feet'.

Table 46

Declension of Adjectives ending in *-ин, -ов* and denoting Possession

	Singular		
	Masculine	Neuter	Feminine
Nom.	Ма́шин (брат, каранда́ш) 'Masha's (brother, pencil)'	Ма́шино (письмо́) 'Masha's (letter)'	Ма́шина (сестра́) 'Masha's (sister)'
Gen.	Ма́шина (бра́та) ог: Ма́шиного (бра́та)	Ма́шина (письма́)	Ма́шиной (сестры́)
Dat.	Ма́шину (бра́ту) ог: Ма́шиному (бра́ту)	Ма́шину (письму́) ог: Ма́шиному (письму́)	Ма́шиной (сестре́)
Acc.	Ма́шина (бра́та) Ма́шин (каранда́ш)	Ма́шино (письмо́)	Ма́шину (сестру́)
Instr.	Ма́шиным (бра́том)	Ма́шиным (письмо́м)	Ма́шиной (сестро́й)
Prep.	(о) Ма́шином (бра́те)	(о) Ма́шином (письме́)	(о) Ма́шиной (сестре́)

Plural

Nom.	Ма́шины (бра́тья, пи́сьма, кни́ги)
Gen.	Ма́шиных (бра́тьев, пи́сем, книг)
Dat.	Ма́шиным (бра́тьям, пи́сьмам, кни́гам)
Acc.	Ма́шиных (бра́тьев)
	Ма́шины (пи́сьма, кни́ги)
Instr.	Ма́шиными (бра́тьями, пи́сьмами, кни́гами)
Prep.	(о) Ма́шиных (бра́тьях, пи́сьмах, кни́гах)

Note. — 1. In modern colloquial Russian the only short form adjectives declined are those which end in the suffixes *-ин* (*дя́дин* 'uncle's', *Ма́шин* 'Masha's'), *-ов* (*отцо́в* 'father's') and denote possession. The most common of these adjectives are formed from proper names: *Ма́ша* 'Masha' — *Ма́шин* 'Masha's', *Ва́ня* 'Vanya' — *Ва́нин* 'Vanya's', *Са́ша* 'Sasha' — *Са́шин* 'Sasha's', etc.

2. These adjectives are declined partly as adjectives and partly as nouns (viz., as surnames ending in *-ов, -ин*).

3. They take noun endings: (1) in the nominative, genitive and dative singular of the masculine and neuter genders (*Ма́шин брат* 'Masha's brother', *Ма́шино письмо́* 'Masha's letter', *Ма́шина бра́та, Ма́шину бра́ту; отцо́в брат* 'father's brother', *отцо́во письмо́* 'father's letter', *отцо́ва бра́та, отцо́ву бра́ту*); (2) in the nominative and accusative singular of the feminine gender (*Ма́шина сестра́* 'Masha's sister' — *Ма́шину сестру́, отцо́ва сестра́* 'father's sister' — *отцо́ву сестру́*); (3) in the nominative and accusative (similar to the nominative) plural of all genders (*Ма́шины пи́сьма* 'Masha's letters', *отцо́вы кни́ги* 'father's books').

In the rest of the cases these adjectives take adjective endings (Мы говори́ли о *Ма́шином бра́те*, о *Ма́шиной сестре́*. 'We were speaking about Masha's brother, about Masha's sister.').

FORMATION AND USES OF THE COMPARATIVE AND SUPERLATIVE DEGREES

Only qualitative adjectives can be used in the comparative and the superlative degrees.

The comparative and the superlative degrees of qualitative are formed from the stem of the positive degree.

The comparative form is not declined, while the superlative form is declined in the same way as the long-form adjective.

THE COMPARATIVE DEGREE

1. Formation of the Comparative Degree. — The comparative degree generally takes the suffix *-ee* (*ста́рый* 'old' — *старе́е* 'older'); in cases where alternation of consonants occurs in the adjective stem (*сухо́й* 'dry' — *су́ше* 'drier', *дорого́й* 'dear' — *доро́же* 'dearer'), it takes the suffix *-e*. Note the formation of the comparative degree with the suffix *-ше* (*тóнкий* 'thin' — *тóньше* 'thinner') (the suffix *-к-* is dropped).

The comparative degree of a number of adjectives is not formed by means of the suffix *-ее* or *-е* but by the addition of the word *бóлее* 'more' or *мéнее* 'less' (*бóлее гóрький* 'more bitter', *мéнее гóрький* 'less bitter'). This way of forming the comparative degree may be used for qualitative adjectives in general.

2. Use of the Comparative Degree. — Comparatives formed by inflexion, e.g., *сильнéе* 'stronger', *вы́ше* 'higher', do not change according to gender, number or case and are used either predicatively (*э́тот дом красúвее* 'this house is more beautiful', *э́та кóмната бóльше* 'this room is larger') or attributively (*Он получúл кóмнату бóльше моéй.* 'He got a larger room than mine.'). In such cases the comparative degree always follows the word it qualifies.

3. The Case following the Comparative Degree. — The comparative degree may be used either with the conjunction *чем* or without it. When a comparative degree is used without the conjunction *чем,* the noun with which the other is compared takes the genitive: *Москвá бóльше Ленингрáда.* 'Moscow is larger than Leningrad'. But: *Москвá бóльше, чем Ленингрáд.*

If the comparison is expressed by an adjective with the word *бóлее* 'more' or *мéнее* 'less', the conjunction *чем* is obligatory: *Это бóлее красúвый дом, чем тот.* 'This is a more beautiful house than that.'

THE SUPERLATIVE DEGREE

1. Formation of the Superlative Degree. — The superlative degree is formed:

(a) by means of the suffix *-айш-* following sibilants (*высочáйший* 'highest'), or *-ейш-* following other sounds.

Note. — A number of adjectives cannot form their superlative degree by means of the above suffixes.

(b) by adding to the adjective the prefix *наи-* (*наилýчший* 'best', *наихýдший* 'worst').

Note. — A number of adjectives cannot form their superlative degree by adding the above prefix.

(c) by placing before the adjective the pronoun *сáмый* 'most', the adjective being in the positive or the superlative degree (*сáмый красúвый* 'most beautiful', *сáмый лýчший* 'very best').

2. Use of the Superlative Degree. —
(a) The most usual superlative form is that of the *сáмый красúвый* 'most beautiful', *сáмый лýчший* 'very best' type. On this pattern the superlative degree of any adjective can be formed.

(b) Only few adjectives form their superlative degree by means of the suffixes *-ейш-, -айш-* (*важне́йший вопро́с* на́шей совре́менности 'the most important question of our times', *старе́йший член о́бщества* 'the oldest member of a society', *широча́йшие наро́дные ма́ссы* 'the broadest popular masses').

(c) The superlative degree with the prefix *наи-* is not very common in modern colloquial Russian. This form is used when the speaker wants to express the utmost degree of a quality (*наилу́чший* 'very best', *наикраси́вейший* 'most beautiful').

(d) In Modern Russian the adjectives *лу́чший* 'best', *ху́дший* 'worst' and *ни́зший* 'lowest' can be used in the sense of both the comparative and the superlative degree, cf.: *Ивано́в — лу́чший учени́к в кла́ссе.* 'Ivanov is the top pupil in his form.' (the superlative degree) and *Они́ живу́т в лу́чших усло́виях, чем ра́ньше.* 'They live under better conditions than before.' (the comparative degree). In Old Russian the adjectives with the suffixes *-ейш, -айш-, -ш-* were used in the sense of both the superlative and the comparative degree.

Note. — 1. In certain instances, the superlative degree loses the meaning of comparison, e.g., *дальне́йшая рабо́та* 'further work', *в ближа́йшем вре́мени* 'in the immediate future'.

2. The use of a particular superlative form is determined by the sense: compare the use of the two superlative forms of the adjective *высо́кий: высоча́йшее де́рево* 'a very tall tree,' but: *вы́сшая сте́пень* 'the highest degree'.

Positive		Comparative		
Long-form Adjectives	Short-form Adjectives		Suf-fixes	Remarks
краси́вый 'beautiful'	краси́в	краси́вее 'more beautiful'		*-ee* in words where no alternation of consonants occurs
кра́сный 'red'	кра́сен	красне́е 'redder'		
до́брый 'kind'	добр	добре́е 'kinder'	*-ee*	
тени́стый 'shady'	тени́ст	тени́стее 'shadier'		
ста́рый 'old'	стар	старе́е 'older'		
высо́кий 'high'	высо́к	вы́ше 'higher'		*с—ш*	(the suffix *-ок* is dropped)
ни́зкий 'low'	ни́зок	ни́же 'lower'		*з—ж*	*-e* in words where alternation of consonants occurs (the suffix *-e* is always unstressed)
у́зкий 'narrow'	у́зок	у́же 'narrower'			
ти́хий 'quiet'	тих	ти́ше 'quieter'		*х—ш*	
сухо́й 'dry'	сух	су́ше 'drier'			
кре́пкий 'strong'	кре́пок	кре́пче 'stronger'	*-e*	*к—ч*	
гро́мкий 'loud'	гро́мок	гро́мче 'louder'			
дорого́й 'dear'	до́рог	доро́же 'dearer'		*г—ж*	
круто́й 'steep'	крут	кру́че 'steeper'		*т—ч*	
молодо́й 'young'	мо́лод	моло́же 'younger'		*д—ж*	
густо́й 'thick'	густ	гу́ще 'thicker'		*ст—щ*	

Table 47

of Comparison

	Superlative		
	Suffixes	Prefix	
красивейший 'most beauti-ful'			самый краси́вый 'most beau-tiful'
			самый кра́сный 'reddest'
добрейший 'kindest'			самый до́брый 'kindest'
			самый тени́стый 'shadiest'
старейший 'oldest' (член о́бщест-ва 'member of a society')			самый ста́рый 'oldest'
высоча́йший 'highest' вы́сший (сове́т) 'supreme (council)' ни́зший 'lowest'	*-ейш- -айш- -ш-*	наивы́сший 'highest'	самый высо́кий 'highest'
			самый ни́зкий 'lowest' самый у́зкий 'narrowest'
			самый ти́хий 'quietest'
			самый сухо́й 'driest' самый кре́пкий 'strongest'
крепча́йший 'strongest'			самый гро́мкий 'loudest'
			самый дорого́й 'dearest'
			самый круто́й 'steepest'
			самый молодо́й 'youngest'
густе́йший 'thickest'			самый густо́й 'thickest'

Positive		Comparative		
Long-form Adjectives	Short-form Adjectives		Suffixes	Remarks
простóй 'simple'	прост	прóще 'simpler'		(for alternation of consonants, see Table 8)
тóлстый 'thick'	толст	тóлще 'thicker'		
хорóший 'good'	хорóш	лýчше 'better'		Special cases of formation.
плохóй 'bad'	плох	хýже 'worse'	-e	
большóй 'large'		бóльше 'larger'		
велúкий 'great'	велúк			
мáленький 'little' мáлый 'little'	мал	мéньше 'less'		

		Superlative	
	Suffixes	Prefix	
простéйший 'simplest'			сáмый простóй 'simplest'
			сáмый тóлстый 'thickest'
лýчший 'best'	*-ейш-*	наилýчший 'very best'	сáмый хорóший 'best'
хýдший 'worst'	*-айш-*	наихýдший 'worst'	сáмый лýчший 'best'
	-ш-		сáмый плохóй 'worst'
			сáмый большóй 'largest'
величáйший 'greatest' (учёный 'scientist', гéний 'genius')			
			сáмый мáленький 'smallest'

IV. THE PRONOUN

GENERAL REMARKS

1. Some Russian pronouns change according to gender, while others remain unchanged.

2. The following pronouns do not change according to gender: the personal pronouns of the 1st and 2nd person (*я* 'I', *ты* 'you'), the reflexive pronoun *себя* 'oneself', the interrogative pronouns *кто* 'who', *что* 'what', and also pronouns compounded with *кто*, *что* (*кто-то* 'somebody', *что-то* 'something', *кто-нибудь* 'somebody', *что-нибудь* 'something', *некто* 'somebody', *нечто* 'something', etc.).

3. According to the gender of the noun which the personal pronoun *я* 'I' or *ты* 'you' replaces, the words depending on this personal pronoun (adjectives, participles, pronouns, numerals, past tense verbs) take the form of either the masculine or the feminine gender: *я сказал* 'I said', *я сказала* 'I said'; *со мной первым* 'first with me', *со мной первой* 'first with me'; *мы обратились к тебе самому* 'we appealed to you yourself', *мы обратились к тебе самой* 'we appealed to you yourself'.

4. All words in the sentence which depend on the pronoun *кто* 'who' or on pronouns compounded with *кто* take the form of the masculine gender: *Кто приехал?* 'Who came?' *Кто-то пришёл.* 'Somebody has come.' (even when the person in question is a woman).

All words in the sentence which depend on the pronoun *что* 'what' or on pronouns compounded with *что* take the form of the neuter gender: *Что-то виднелось вдали.* 'Something was visible in the distance.' *Что двигалось по дороге?* 'What was moving along the road?'

5. Pronouns changing according to gender may be used in the sentence either attributively or predicatively (in the same manner as adjectives).

PRONOUNS: DECLENSION AND USES

Table 48

The Personal Pronouns

	1st Person	2nd Person	3rd Person		
			Masculine	Neuter	Feminine
Nom.	я 'I'	ты 'you'	он 'he'	оно́ 'it'	она́ 'she'
Gen.	меня́	тебя́	его́	его́ (у него́)	её
Dat.	мне	тебе́	ему́ (к нему́)	ему́ (к нему́)	ей (к ней)
Acc.	меня́	тебя́	его́ (на него́)	его́ (на него́)	её (на неё)
Instr.	мной	тобо́й	им (с ним)	им (с ним)	ей, е́ю (с ней, с не́ю)
Prep.	(обо) мне	(о) тебе́	(о) нём	(о) нём	(о) ней

Plural

	1st Person	2nd Person	3rd Person
Nom.	мы 'we'	вы 'you'	они́ 'they'
Gen.	нас	вас	их (у них)
Dat.	нам	вам	им (к ним)
Acc.	нас	вас	их (на них)
Instr.	на́ми	ва́ми	и́ми (с ни́ми)
Prep.	(о) нас	(о) вас	(о) них

Note. — 1. The oblique forms of the personal pronouns *он* 'he', *она́* 'she', *оно́* 'it', *они́* 'they' take *н-* at the beginning when preceded by a preposition (e.g., Я пошёл *к нему́*. 'I went to see him.' Я наде́юсь *на него́*. 'I rely on him.'), while the possessive pronouns *его́* 'his', *её* 'her(s)', *их* 'their(s)' do not.

2. The personal pronoun of the second person plural *вы* 'you' is also used as a form of polite address for one person.

Table 49

Use of the Reflexive Pronoun *себя́*

Когда́ я верну́лся домо́й, я нашёл *у себя́* на столе́ запи́ску. 'When I returned home, I found a note on my desk.' Я купи́л *себе́* кни́гу. 'I bought myself a book.' Захвати́ *с собо́й* докуме́нты. 'Take the documents with you.'	In all the cases the pronoun *себя́* always refers to the agent of the clause in which it stands.

7*

Он недоволен *собóй*. 'He is displeased with himself.'

Мы взя́ли *с собóй* в доро́гу всё необходи́мое. 'We took with us everything we needed on the way.'

Мы купи́ли *себé* не́сколько книг и журна́лов. 'We bought ourselves some books and magazines.'

Они́ рассказа́ли *о себé* мно́го интере́сного. 'They told a lot of interesting things about themselves.'

Note. — In the oblique cases the reflexive pronoun *себя́* 'myself', 'yourself', 'himself', 'herself', 'itself', 'ourselves', 'yourselves', 'themselves' is declined as the pronoun *ты*, i.e., *себя́*, *себе́*, etc. (*себя́* has no nominative).

Table 50

The Possessive Pronouns

	Singular				Plural
	Masculine and Neuter	Feminine	Masculine and Neuter	Feminine	(for all genders)
Nom.	мой моё 'my, mine'	моя́	наш на́ше 'our(s)'	на́ша	мой на́ши
Gen.	моего́	мое́й	на́шего	на́шей	мои́х на́ших
Dat.	моему́	мое́й	на́шему	на́шей	мои́м на́шим
Acc.	as Nom. or Gen.| моё	мою́	as Nom. or Gen.|на́ше	на́шу	as Nom. or Gen.
Instr.	мои́м	мое́й	на́шим	на́шей	мои́ми на́шими
Prep.	(о) моём	(о) мое́й	(о) на́шем	(о) на́шей	(о) мои́х (о) на́ших

Note. — 1. The pronoun *твой* 'thy', 'thine', 'your(s)' and *свой* 'one' s own' are declined in the same way as *мой* 'my (mine)'.
2. The pronoun *ваш* 'your(s)' is declined in the same way as *наш* 'our(s)'.

196

Table 51

Uses of the Pronoun *свой*

Я кончáю *свою* рабóту. 'I am finishing my work.' *Ты* кончáешь *свою* рабóту. 'You are finishing your work.' *Он* кончáет *свою* рабóту. 'He is finishing his work.' *Онá* кончáет *свою* рабóту. 'She is finishing her work.' *Мы* кончáем *свою* рабóту. 'We are finishing our work.' *Вы* кончáете *свою* рабóту. 'You are finishing your work.' *Они́* кончáют *свою* рабóту. 'They are finishing their work.'

The pronoun *свой* indicates the possession of an object by the agent and is used in this sense only in the oblique cases. Note the difference between the following sentences: Поручи́ емý послáть телегрáмму *своемý брáту*. 'Ask him to send a wire to his brother' and Поручи́ емý послáть телегрáмму *твоемý брáту*. 'Ask him to send a wire to your brother.'

When used in the nominative, the pronoun *свой* has a different meaning: Это *свой* человéк. 'He is a friend.'

Table 52

The Pronouns *егó, её, их* used as Possessive Pronouns

Я знáю *егó брáта, егó брáтьев, её брáта, её брáтьев, их брáта, их брáтьев.* 'I know his brother, his brothers, her brother, her brothers, their brother, their brothers.'

Я пошёл к *егó брáту, к егó брáтьям, к её брáту, к её брáтьям, к их брáту, к их брáтьям.* 'I went to his brother, his brothers, her brother, her brothers, their brother, their brothers.'

Я встрéтился *с егó брáтом, с егó брáтьями, с её брáтом, с её брáтьями, с их брáтом, с их брáтьями.* 'I met his brother, his brothers, her brother, her brothers, their brother, their brothers.'

Я говори́л *о егó брáте, о егó брáтьях, о её брáте, о её брáтьях, об их брáте, об их брáтьях.* 'I spoke about his brother, his brothers, her brother, her brothers, their brother, their brothers.'

The possessive pronouns *егó, её, их* do not change according to case and number and they never take an *н-* at the beginning when preceded by a preposition: Я был у *егó брáта.* 'I was at his brother's.' The personal pronoun always takes an *н-* in this case: Я был у негó. 'I was at his place.'

Table 53

The Interrogative and Negative Pronouns

	Interrogative Pronouns что, кто		Negative Pronouns with and without a Preposition			
Nom.	кто 'who'	что 'what'	никто́ 'nobody'		ничто́ 'nothing'	
Gen.	кого́	чего́	никого́	ни у кого́	ничего́	ни для чего́
Dat.	кому́	чему́	никому́	ни к кому́	ничему́	ни к чему́
Acc.	кого́	что	никого́	ни за кого́	ничто́	ни за что
Instr.	кем	чем	нике́м	ни с кем	ниче́м	ни с чем
Prep.	(о) ком	(о) чём		ни о ком		ни о чём

Note. — 1. The negative pronouns *никто́* 'nobody', *ничто́* 'nothing' are declined as *кто* 'who', *что* 'what'.

2. If a negative pronoun or the pronoun *кое-кто́* 'somebody' or *кое-что́* 'something' is used with a preposition, the component parts of the compounds are separated and the preposition placed between them: *ни к кому́* 'not to anybody', *кóе к кому́* 'to somebody' (Я *ни с кем* не говори́л. 'I did not speak to anybody.' Я *ни у кого́* нé был. 'I did not visit anybody.').

Table 54

Uses of Indefinite Pronouns with Particles

Я ви́дел това́рища: он стоя́л и *с ке́м-то* разгова́ривал. 'I saw my friend: he was standing, speaking to somebody.'

По э́тому де́лу поговори́ *с ке́м-нибудь*. 'Speak to somebody about that business.'

Он *что́-то* сказа́л мне, но я забы́л что. 'He told me something, but I forgot what it was.'

Скажи́ мне *что́-нибудь*. 'Tell me something.'

В э́той ко́мнате *кто́-то* кури́л. 'Somebody has been smoking in this room.'

Скажи́, чтоб *кто́-нибудь* пришёл. 'Tell somebody to come here.'

Там *кто́-то* пришёл. 'Somebody has come there.'

When the speaker means a certain definite person (or thing) unknown to himself he uses a pronoun compounded with the particle *-то* (*кто́-то* 'somebody', *что́-то* 'something'). When the speaker means any unspecified person (or thing) the pronoun is compounded with the particle *-нибудь* or *-либо* (*кто́-нибудь* 'somebody', *что́-нибудь* 'something'; *кто́-либо* 'somebody', *что́-либо* 'something').

Дéти спóрят *о чём-то*. 'The children are arguing about something.'

Ктó-нибудь звонил мне? 'Did anybody ring me up?'

Тебé *ктó-то* звонил. 'Somebody rang you up.'

Note. — Indefinite pronouns formed by compounding the particles *-то, -либо, -нибýдь, кóе-* with *кто* 'who', *что* 'what' (*ктó-то* 'somebody', *ктó-нибудь* 'somebody', *ктó-либо* 'somebody', *кое-ктó* 'somebody', *чтó-то* 'something', *чтó-либо* 'something', *чтó-нибудь* 'something', *кое-чтó* 'something') are declined as *кто, что.*

Table 55

The Demonstrative Pronouns *тот, этот, то, это, та, эта, те, эти*

	Singular				Plural (for all genders)	
	Masculine and Neuter		Feminine			
Nom.	тот то 'that'	этот это 'this'	та	эта	те	эти
Gen.	того	этого	той	этой	тех	этих
Dat.	тому	этому	той	этой	тем	этим
Acc.	as Nom. or Gen. | то	as Nom. or Gen. | это	ту	эту	as Nom. or Gen.	
Instr.	тем	этим	той	этой	теми	этими
Prep.	(о) том	(об) этом	(о) той	(об) этой	(о) тех	(об) этих

The Pronouns *сам* and *самый*

The pronoun *сам* 'myself', 'yourself', 'himself', 'itself', *самá* 'myself', 'yourself', 'herself', 'itself', *самó* 'itself', *сáми* 'ourselves', 'yourselves', 'themselves' follow the declension of the pronouns *этот* 'this', *эта* 'this', *это* 'this', *эти* 'these', but they are stressed on the ending.

The forms and meanings of the pronouns *сам, самá, самó, сáми* should not be confused with those of the pronouns *сáмый, сáмая, сáмое, сáмые* 'very'. The latter pronouns cannot be used independently; they are used only with adjectives to form their superlative degree (*сáмый большóй, сáмая большáя* 'the very largest', etc.) or as part of pronouns (*тот же сáмый, та же сáмая, то же сáмое* 'the very same one', *те же сáмые* 'the very same ones').

Table 56

		Singular		Plural
		Masculine *сам*	Feminine *сама*	*сами*
Nom.		*Он* пришёл *сам.* 'He came himself.'	*Она* пришла *сама.* 'She came herself.'	*Они* пришли *сами.* 'They came themselves.'
Gen.	Ещё нет	*его самого.* 'He himself has not come yet.' *самого преподавателя.* 'The teacher himself has not come yet.'	*её самой.* 'She herself has not come yet.' *самой преподавательницы.* 'The teacher herself has not come yet.'	*их самих.* 'They themselves have not come yet.' *самих преподавателей.* 'The teachers themselves have not come yet.'
Dat.	Я передал письмо	*ему самому.* 'I gave the letter to him personally.' *самому преподавателю.* 'I gave the letter to the teacher himself.'	*ей самой.* 'I gave the letter to her personally.' *самой преподавательнице.* 'I gave the letter to the teacher herself.'	*им самим.* 'I gave the letter to them personally.' *самим преподавателям.* 'I gave the letter to the teachers themselves.'
Acc.	Я видел	*его самого.* 'I saw him personally.' *самого преподавателя.* 'I saw the teacher himself.'	*её самоё (её саму).* 'I saw her personally.' *самоё (саму) преподавательницу.* 'I saw the teacher herself.'	*их самих.* 'I saw them personally.' *самих преподавателей.* 'I saw the teachers themselves.'

200

		Singular		Plural
		Masculine *сам*	*Feminine* *самá*	*сáми*
Instr.	Я говорил	*с ним самим.* 'I spoke to him personally.' *с самим преподавателем.* 'I spoke to the teacher himself.'	*с ней самóй.* 'I spoke to her personally.' *с самóй преподавательницей.* 'I spoke to the teacher herself.'	*с ними самими.* 'I spoke to them personally.' *с самими преподавателями.* 'I spoke to the teachers themselves.'
Prep.	Мы говорили	*о нём самóм.* 'We spoke about him personally.' *о самóм преподавателе.* 'We spoke about the teacher himself.'	*о ней самóй.* 'We spoke about her personally.' *о самóй преподавательнице.* 'We spoke about the teacher herself.'	*о них самих.* 'We spoke about them personally.' *о самих преподавателях.* 'We spoke about the teachers themselves.'

		сáмый, сáмое (Masculine and Neuter)	*сáмая* (Feminine)	*сáмые* (Plural)
Nom.	Это	*сáмый лучший ученик.* 'He is the very best pupil.' *сáмое интересное задáние.* 'This is the most interesting assignment.'	*сáмая лучшая ученица.* 'She is the very best pupil.'	*сáмые лучшие ученики.* 'They are the very best pupils.' *сáмые интересные задáния.* 'These are the most interesting assignments.'
Gen.	Сегóдня нет	*сáмого лучшего ученика.* 'Today the very best pupil is not here.'	*сáмой лучшей ученицы.* 'Today the very best pupil is not here.'	*сáмых лучших ученикóв.* 'Today the very best pupils are not here.'

201

		самый, самое (Masculine and Neuter)	самая (Feminine)	самые (Plural)
Dat.	Мы дали премию	самому лучшему ученику. 'We gave a prize to the very best pupil.'	самой лучшей ученице. 'We gave a prize to the very best pupil.'	самым лучшим ученикам. 'We gave prizes to the very best pupils.'
Acc.	Мы премировали	самого лучшего ученика. 'We awarded a prize to the very best pupil.'	самую лучшую ученицу. 'We awarded a prize to the very best pupil.'	самых лучших учеников. 'We awarded prizes to the very best pupils.'
	Я получил	самое интересное задание. 'I got the most interesting assignment.'		самые интересные задания. 'I got the most interesting assignments.'
Instr.	Мы беседовали	с самым лучшим учеником. 'We talked to the very best pupil.'	с самой лучшей ученицей. 'We talked to the very best pupil.'	с самыми лучшими учениками. 'We talked to the very best pupils.'
Prep.	Мы говорили	о самом лучшем ученике. 'We spoke about the very best pupil.'	о самой лучшей ученице. 'We spoke about the very best pupil.'	о самых лучших учениках. 'We spoke about the very best pupils.'

Note. — 1. The pronouns самый, самая, самое, самые 'very' are declined as adjectives.

2. In all the cases the forms of the pronouns сам 'myself', 'yourself', 'himself', 'itself', сама 'myself', 'yourself', 'herself', 'itself', само 'itself', сами 'ourselves', 'yourselves', 'themselves' are stressed differently from those of the pronouns самый, самая, самое, самые and in some cases they have different endings.

3. In the declension of the pronouns тот же самый, та же самая 'that very same', etc. the words тот, та, то 'that' are declined in the same way as the pronouns этот, эта, это 'this' and the word самый 'very' in the same way as an adjective: тому же самому, той же самой, etc.

Table 57

The Pronouns *весь, вся, всё, все*

	Singular		Plural (for all genders)
	Masculine and Neuter	Feminine	
Nom.	весь всё 'all'	вся	все
Gen.	всего́	всей	всех
Dat.	всему́	всей	всем
Acc.	as Nom. or Gen.	всю	as Nom. or Gen.
Instr.	всем	всей(-éю)	всéми
Prep.	(о) всём	(о) всей	(о) всех

Table 58

Pronouns declined as Adjectives

(1) *Какóй* 'what', *котóрый* 'which' and all the pronouns formed from them by means of particles or the negative particle (*какóй-то* 'some', *какóй-нибудь* 'some', *никакóй* 'no', 'none').

Ни к какóму реше́нию он ещё не пришёл. 'He has not come to any decision yet.'	In the declension of the negative pronouns, the negative particle is separated from the pronoun and the preposition is placed between the two component parts of the compound.

(2) The pronouns *чей, чья, чьё, чьи* 'whose'; *ничéй, ничья́, ничьё, ничьи́* 'nobody's' are declined as adjectives of the *вóлчий, вóлчья, вóлчье, вóлчьи* 'wolf's' 'wolves' type.

	Singular		Plural (for all genders)
	Masculine and Neuter	Feminine	
Nom.	чей чьё 'whose'	чья	чьи
Gen.	чьего́	чьей	чьих
Dat.	чьему́	чьей	чьим
Acc.	as Nom. or Gen.	чью	as Nom. or Gen.
Instr.	чьим	чьей(-éю)	чьи́ми
Prep.	(о) чьём	(о) чьей	(о) чьих

V. THE NUMERAL

GENERAL REMARKS

1. In Russian there are *cardinal* numerals (*один* 'one', *два* 'two', *три* 'three', *пятнáдцать* 'fifteen', etc.), *ordinal* numerals (*пéрвый* 'first', *второй* 'second', etc.) and *collective* numerals (*двóе* 'two', *трóе* 'three', *чéтверо* 'four', etc.).

2. Collective numerals are used as follows:

(a) With masculine and neuter nouns denoting persons: *трóе студéнтов* 'three students', *пятеро рабóчих* 'five workers', *двóе детéй* 'two children', *сéмеро мáльчиков* 'seven boys', etc. (but one cannot say, for example, *двóе волкóв* 'two wolves'). However, collective numerals occasionally occur in fiction with nouns denoting the young offspring of animals, e.g., *Волчáта, все трóе*, крéпко спáли. (Ч.) 'The wolf-cubs—all three of them—were fast asleep.'

Collective numerals denoting persons can be used in the sentence independently, i.e., without any noun: *Трóе стоя́ли* на углу́. 'Three people were standing at the corner' (or: *Трóе стоя́ло* на углу́). Я ви́дел *двои́х*, потóм ещё *трои́х*. 'I saw two, then three more.' Нас бы́ло *двóе* — брат и я. (П.) 'There were two of us — my brother and myself.' *Все чéтверо* выхóдят вмéсте. (П.) 'All four of them come out together.' *Сéмеро* одногó не ждут. (Proverb) Cf.: 'For one that is missing there's no spoiling a wedding.'

(b) With nouns used only in the plural: *трóе нóжниц* 'three pairs of scissors', *двóе сýток* 'two days', *чéтверо часóв* 'four watches', *двóе брюк* 'two pairs of trousers', etc.

3. Russian numerals are declined.

Cardinal numerals have certain peculiarities in their declension which are characteristic only of the numerals as a part of speech.

Ordinal numerals are declined as adjectives (in both singular and plural):

4. Russian numerals agree with the noun they refer to in all the cases, except for the nominative and the accusative (identical with the nominative): Он поéхал на экскýрсию *с двумя́ товáрищами*. 'He went on an excursion with two of his friends.' Он рассказáл мне *о трёх свои́х товáрищах*. 'He told me about three of his friends.' A noun following a numeral (from *два* 'two' on) in the nominative case, takes the genitive: *два товáрища* 'two friends', *пять товáрищей* 'five friends' (see Table 25).

5. Cardinal numerals do not change according to number or gender, with the exception of *оди́н* 'one' (masc.), *одна́* 'one' (fem.), *одно́* 'one' (neuter), *два* 'two', *о́ба* 'both' (masc. and neuter), *две* 'two', *о́бе* 'both' (fem.) (*два ма́льчика* 'two boys', *два окна́* 'two windows', *две де́вочки* 'two girls'), *полтора́* 'one and a half' (masc. and neuter), *полторы́* 'one and a half' (fem.) (*полтора́ стака́на* 'one and a half glasses', *полторы́ ча́шки* 'one and a half cups').

6. The following numerals may be used in the plural: *ты́сяча* 'a thousand' — *ты́сячи* 'thousands', *миллио́н* 'a million' — *миллио́ны* 'millions', *миллиа́рд* 'a milliard' — *миллиа́рды* 'milliards'. These numerals are declined as nouns.

Cardinal and Collective Numerals

Table 59

Cardinal		Collective
оди́н (masc.), одна́ (fem.), одно́ (neut.) 'one'	сто 'one hundred'	дво́е 'two'
два (masc. and neut.), две (fem.) 'two'	сто оди́н (одна́, одно́) 'one hundred and one'	о́ба ⎫ о́бе ⎬ 'both'
три 'three'	сто два (две) 'one hundred and two', etc.	тро́е 'three'
четы́ре 'four'	две́сти 'two hundred'	че́тверо 'four'
пять 'five'	три́ста 'three hundred'	пя́теро 'five'
шесть 'six'	четы́реста 'four hundred'	ше́стеро 'six'
семь 'seven'	пятьсо́т 'five hundred'	се́меро 'seven'
во́семь 'eight'	шестьсо́т 'six hundred'	
де́вять 'nine'	семьсо́т 'seven hundred'	
де́сять 'ten'	восемьсо́т 'eight hundred'	
оди́ннадцать 'eleven'	девятьсо́т 'nine hundred'	
двена́дцать 'twelve'	ты́сяча 'one thousand'	
трина́дцать 'thirteen'	ты́сяча оди́н (одна́, одно́) 'one thousand and one'	
четы́рнадцать 'fourteen'	ты́сяча два (две) 'one thousand and two', etc.	
пятна́дцать 'fifteen'	две ты́сячи 'two thousand'	
шестна́дцать 'sixteen'	три ты́сячи 'three thousand'	
семна́дцать 'seventeen'	четы́ре ты́сячи 'four thousand'	
восемна́дцать 'eighteen'	пять ты́сяч 'five thousand'	
девятна́дцать 'nineteen'	шесть ты́сяч 'six thousand', etc.	
два́дцать 'twenty'	два́дцать одна́ ты́сяча 'twenty-one thousand'	
два́дцать оди́н 'twenty-one'	два́дцать две ты́сячи 'twenty-two thousand', etc.	
два́дцать два 'twenty-two', etc.		
три́дцать 'thirty'		
со́рок 'forty'		
пятьдеся́т 'fifty'		
шестьдеся́т 'sixty'		
се́мьдесят 'seventy'		
во́семьдесят 'eighty'		
девяно́сто 'ninety'		

Note. — 1. From some cardinal numerals corresponding feminine nouns can be formed: *единица* 'one', *двойка* 'two', *тройка* 'three', *четвёрка* 'four', *пятёрка* 'five', *шестёрка* 'six', *семёрка* 'seven', *восьмёрка* 'eight', *девятка* 'nine', *десятка* (fem.) and *десяток* (masc.) 'ten', *сотня* (fem.) 'a hundred'. These words may take the plural form and are declined as nouns.

2. The words *тысяча* (fem.) 'a thousand'., *миллион* (masc.) 'a million', *миллиард* (masc.) 'a milliard' are declined as nouns with the same endings. *Тысяча, миллион* or *миллиард* do not agree with the nouns they refer to; a noun following *тысяча, миллион* or *миллиард* generally takes the genitive: Нам привезли *тысячу* книг. 'They brought a thousand books for us.' Расстояние измеряется *тысячами* километров. 'The distance is thousands of miles.'

NUMERALS: DECLENSION AND USES

Table 60

The Numerals *один, одна, одно*

	Singular		Plural (for all genders)
	Masculine and Neuter	Feminine	
Nom.	один одно 'one'	одна	одни 'only'
Gen.	одного	одной	одних
Dat.	одному	одной	одним
Acc.	as Nom. or Gen. | одно	одну	as Nom. or Gen.
Instr.	одним	одной (-ою)	одними
Prep.	(об) одном	(об) одной	(об) одних

Note. — 1. The numeral *один* is used in the plural (одни, одних, одним, etc.) in the following instances:

(a) in the sense of *только* 'only'; На собрании были *одни женщины*. 'Only women attended the meeting';

(b) in a sense close to that of the word *некоторые* 'some': Я взял сначала *одни книги*, потом другие. 'At first I took some books, then I took others';

(c) with a noun used only in the plural: Я купил *одни часы* и *одни ножницы*. 'I bought one watch and one pair of scissors'.

2. *Один* is used in a sense close to that of the word *некоторый* 'certain': Есть у меня *один знакомый*, который очень хорошо играет в шахматы. 'I have a certain acquaintance who plays chess very well.'

The Numerals *два* (masc. and neuter), *две* (fem.) *три, четыре* (for all genders)

Nom.	два две 'two'	три 'three'	четыре 'four'
Gen.	двух	трёх	четырёх
Dat.	двум	трём	четырём
Acc.		as Nom. or Gen.	
Instr.	двумя	тремя	четырьмя
Prep.	(о) двух	(о) трёх	(о) четырёх

Note. — The numerals *два* 'two' (masc. and neut.: *два стола* 'two tables', *два окна* 'two windows') and *две* 'two' (fem.: *две лампы* 'two lamps') take different endings according to gender only in the nominative and the accusative (similar to the nominative).

Collective Numerals

Nom.	óба 'both'	óбе	двóе 'two'	трóе 'three'	чéтверо 'four'
Gen.	обóих	обéих	двоúх	троúх	четверы́х
Dat.	обóим	обéим	двоúм	троúм	четверы́м
Acc.			as Nom. or Gen.		
Instr.	обóими	обéими	двоúми	троúми	четверы́ми
Prep.	(об) обóих	(об) обéих	(о) двоúх	(о) троúх	(о) четверы́х

Note. — 1. The numerals *óба* 'both', *двóе* 'two', *трóе* 'three' follow the same pattern of declension.
2. The numerals *пя́теро* 'five', *шéстеро* 'six', *сéмеро* 'seven' follow the declension pattern of the numeral *чéтверо* 'four'.
3. For the use of collective numerals, see p. 204.

The Numerals *сóрок, сто, полтора́, полторы́*

			Masculine and Neuter	Feminine
Nom.	сóрок 'forty'	сто 'one hundred'	полтора́ 'one and a half'	полторы́
Gen.	сорока́	ста	полу́тора	
Dat.	сорока́	ста	полу́тора	
Acc.	сóрок	сто	as Nom.	
Instr.	сорока́	ста	полу́тора	
Prep.	(о) сорока́	(о) ста	(о) полу́тора	

Note. — The numerals *сто* 'one hundred', *сóрок* 'forty' take identical endings in the genitive, dative, instrumental and prepositional: Я поéхал на экску́рсию *со ста рубля́ми*. 'I went on an excursion with one hundred roubles.' На́ша дере́вня *в сорока́ киломéтрах* от гóрода. 'Our village is forty kilometres from the town.'
2. *Девянóсто* 'ninety' follows the declension pattern of *сто* 'one hundred'.

The Numerals *пять, пятьдеся́т, пятьсóт*

Nom.	пять 'five'	пятьдеся́т 'fifty'	пятьсóт 'five hundred'
Gen.	пятú	пятúдесяти	пятисóт
Dat.	пятú	пятúдесяти	пятистáм
Acc.	пять	пятьдеся́т	пятьсóт
Instr.	пятью́	пятью́десятью	пятьюстáми
Prep.	(о) пятú	(о) пятúдесяти	(о) пятистáх

Note:

1. All the numerals from *пять* 'five' to *двáдцать* 'twenty' and the numeral *трúдцать* 'thirty' follow the declension pattern of *пять*. They all follow the declension of feminine nouns ending in a soft consonant (e.g., *плóщадь* 'square').

2. *Шестьдеся́т* 'sixty' and *се́мьдесят* 'seventy' follow the declension pattern of *пятьдеся́т* 'fifty'. Both parts of these numerals are declined, each following the declension pattern of nouns.

3. *Шестьсóт* 'six hundred', *семьсóт* 'seven hundred', *восемьсóт* 'eight hundred', *девятьсóт* 'nine hundred' follow the declension pattern of *пятьсóт* 'five hundred'. Both parts of which these numerals consist are declined.

The Numerals *двéсти, трúста, четы́реста*

Nom.	двéсти 'two hundred'	трúста 'three hundred'	четы́реста 'four hundred'
Gen.	двухсóт	трёхсóт	четырёхсóт
Dat.	двумстáм	трёмстáм	четырёмстáм
Acc.	двéсти	трúста	четы́реста
Instr.	двумястáми	тремястáми	четырьмястáми
Prep.	(о) двухстáх	(о) трёхстáх	(о) четырёхстáх

Note. — The parts of compound numerals are declined separately, e.g., 942—*девятьсóт сóрок два* 'nine hundred and forty-two', *у девятисóт сорокá двух*, *к девятистáм сорокá двум*, etc.

Table 61

Cardinal Numerals used with Nouns and Adjectives

I. When the numeral is in the nominative or the accusative (similar to the nominative):

(1) following the numeral *одúн, однá* or *однó* 'one' or a compound numeral whose last part is *одúн, однá* or *однó*, both the noun and the adjective take the nominative or the accusative singular (as the numeral):

Комúссия провéрила *двáдцать одúн договóр*. 'The commission checked twenty-one contracts.'

На заводе *двáдцать однá молодёжная бригáда*. 'There are twenty-one youth brigades at the plant.'

Я получúл за год *трúдцать однó письмó*. 'I received thirty-one letters in a year.'

208

(2) following the numeral *два*, *две* 'two', *три* 'three', *четыре* 'four' or a compound numeral whose last part is *два*, *две*, *три* or *четыре*, the numeral *оба*, *обе* 'both' or *полтора́*, *полторы́* 'one and a half', the noun takes the genitive singular:

If the adjective refers to a masculine or neuter noun it generally takes the genitive plural:

If the adjective refers to a feminine noun it generally takes the nominative plural:

Да́йте, пожа́луйста *два каранда́ша, три тетра́ди.* 'Please give two pencils, three exercise-books.'

Да́йте, пожа́луйста, *два си́них карандаша́ и три о́бщих тетра́ди.* 'Please give two blue pencils and three thick exercise-books.'

Я возьму́ *оба а́тласа.* 'I'll take both the atlases.'

Я возьму́ *оба географи́ческих а́тласа.* 'I'll take both the geographical atlases.'

Полтора́ после́дних ме́сяца он хорошо́ рабо́тал. 'For the last one and a half months he's been working well.'

Постро́ено *четыре но́вых больши́х до́ма.* 'Four large new houses have been built.'

Сего́дня в газе́те *два ва́жных изве́стия.* 'Today there are two important items in the newspaper.'

Учени́к реши́л *две тру́дные зада́чи.* 'The pupil solved two difficult problems.'

Для заня́тий нам предоста́вили *четыре све́тлые аудито́рии.* 'Four light rooms were placed at our disposal for our studies.'

Две больши́е стра́ны заключи́ли догово́р о дру́жбе. 'Two large countries concluded a treaty of friendship.'

(3) following numerals other than those mentioned in (1) and (2), both the noun and the adjective take the genitive plural:

Постро́ено *семь больши́х зда́ний.* 'Seven large buildings have been built.'

Прие́хало *три́дцать шесть но́вых делега́тов.* 'Thirty-six new delegates have arrived.'

II. When the numeral is in any case other than the nominative or the accusative (similar to the nominative) it always agrees with the noun it refers to in number and case: Пре́мия бу́дет дана́ *трём лу́чшим* ученика́м. 'The prize will be awarded to the three best pupils.' Я встре́тился *с двумя́ ста́рыми това́рищами.* 'I met two old friends.'

Note. — 1. Following the fractional numerals *полови́на* 'a half', *треть* 'one third', *че́тверть* 'a quarter' and after *ты́сяча* 'one thousand', *миллио́н* 'one million', *миллиа́рд* 'one milliard', the noun invariably takes the genitive: К нам привезли́ *ты́сячу книг.* 'They have brought us a thousand books.' Я прочита́л *полови́ну кни́ги.* 'I read half the book.' На постро́йку истра́тили *о́коло четырёх миллио́нов рубле́й.* 'Over four million roubles was spent on the construction.'

2. Substantivized adjectives (*рабо́чий* 'worker', *портно́й* 'tailor', *столо́вая* dining-room', *мастерска́я* 'workshop', *насеко́мое* 'insect', *живо́тное* 'animal') following the numerals *два* 'two', *три* 'three', *четы́ре* 'four', etc. take the genitive plural: *два рабо́чих (дво́е рабо́чих)* 'two workers', *две столо́вых* 'two dining-rooms', *две мастерски́х* 'two workshops', but one can also say: *две столо́вые, две мастерски́е.*

Table 62

Ordinal Numerals

пе́рвый 'first'	шестидеся́тый 'sixtieth'
второ́й 'second'	семидеся́тый 'seventieth'
тре́тий 'third'	восьмидеся́тый 'eightieth'
четвёртый 'fourth'	девяно́стый 'ninetieth'
пя́тый 'fifth'	со́тый 'the hundredth'
шесто́й 'sixth'	сто пе́рвый 'one hundred and first'
седьмо́й 'seventh'	сто второ́й 'one hundred and second', etc.
восьмо́й 'eighth'	
девя́тый 'ninth'	сто девяно́сто девя́тый 'one hundred and ninety-ninth'
деся́тый 'tenth'	
оди́ннадцатый 'eleventh'	двухсо́тый 'two-hundredth'
двена́дцатый 'twelfth'	две́сти пе́рвый 'two hundred and first'
трина́дцатый 'thirteenth'	
четы́рнадцатый 'fourteenth'	две́сти второ́й 'two hundred and second', etc.
пятна́дцатый 'fifteenth'	
шестна́дцатый 'sixteenth'	две́сти девяно́сто девя́тый 'two hundred and ninety-ninth'
семна́дцатый 'seventeenth'	
восемна́дцатый 'eighteenth'	трёхсотый 'three-hundredth'
девятна́дцатый 'nineteenth'	три́ста пе́рвый 'three hundred and first'
двадца́тый 'twentieth'	
два́дцать пе́рвый 'twenty-first'	три́ста второ́й 'three hundred and second', etc.
два́дцать второ́й 'twenty-second', etc.	
	четырёхсо́тый 'four-hundredth'
тридца́тый 'thirtieth'	четы́реста пе́рвый 'four hundred and first'
три́дцать пе́рвый 'thirty-first', etc.	
	четы́реста второ́й 'four hundred and second', etc.
сороково́й 'fortieth'	
пятидеся́тый 'fiftieth'	

тысячный 'the thousandth', тысяча пе́рвый 'one thousand and first', etc., ты́сяча девятьсо́т девяно́сто девя́тый 'one thousand nine hundred and ninety-ninth', двухты́сячный 'two-thousandth', две ты́сячи пе́рвый 'two thousand and first', etc., две ты́сячи девятьсо́т девяно́сто девя́тый 'two thousand nine hundred and ninety-ninth', трёхты́сячный 'three-thousandth', три ты́сячи пе́рвый 'three thousand and first', etc., миллио́нный 'the millionth'.

Note. — 1. Ordinal numerals are formed from the stem of the genitive of the corresponding cardinal numerals, i.e., they are obtained by dropping the case-ending of the genitive (-*a* or -*u*), and adding, instead, the adjective ending: *пят*||*ый*, -*ая*, -*ое*, -*ые* 'fifth', *девяно́ст*||*ый*, -*ая*, -*ое*, -*ые* 'ninetieth'. The numerals *пе́рв*||*ый*, -*ая*, -*ое*, -*ые* 'first', *втор*||*о́й*, -*а́я*, -*о́е*, -*ы́е* 'second', *тре́т*||*ий*, -*ья*, -*ье*, -*ьи* 'third', *четвёрт*||*ый*, -*ая*, -*ое*, -*ые* 'fourth', *седьм*||*о́й*, -*а́я*, -*о́е*, -*ы́е* 'seventh', *сороков*||*о́й*, -*а́я*, -*о́е*, -*ы́е* 'fortieth' are formed in a special manner.

2. From the words *ты́сяча* 'one thousand', *миллио́н* 'one million', *миллиа́рд* 'one milliard' the ordinal numerals are formed by means of the suffix -*н*-: *ты́-сячный* 'the thousandth', *миллио́нный* 'the millionth', *миллиа́рдный* 'the mil-liardth'.

Uses of Ordinal Numerals

1. Ordinal numerals change in the same way as adjectives.

2. In declining a compound ordinal numeral whose component parts are not spelt as one word, only the last part is changed as in: *в ты́сяча девятьсо́т пя́том году́* 'in the year nineteen hundred and five'.

3. Ordinal numerals are used:

(a) to denote the denominator of a fraction: одна́ *пя́тая* 'one-fifth', две *пя́тых* 'two-fifths', пять *восьмы́х* 'five-eighths'.

(b) to denote time:
че́тверть *пе́рвого* 'a quarter past twelve'⎱ the ordinal numeral takes the
10 мину́т *пя́того* 'ten minutes past four' ⎰ genitive of the masculine gender

(c) to denote dates: *Седьмо́го ию́ля* я уе́ду. 'I leave on the seventh of July.' *Пе́рвого сентября́* начина́ются заня́тия. 'The lessons begin on the first of September' (both the noun and the numeral stand in the genitive).

Note that in Russian the year is denoted by an ordinal numeral: *в 1938 году́* = *в ты́сяча девятьсо́т три́дцать восьмо́м году́* 'in (the year) nineteen hundred and thirty-eight'

VI. THE VERB

GENERAL REMARKS

1. In Russian there are *transitive* verbs, which require an object in the accusative without a preposition (*читáть кнúгу* 'to read a book', *организовáть кружóк* 'to form a society', *объяснúть слóво* 'to explain a word') and *intransitive* verbs (*стоя́ть* 'to stand', *бéгать* 'to run', *встречáться* 'to meet').

2. There are a number of verbs ending in *-ся* (*умывáться* 'to wash', *трудúться* 'to work', *находúться* 'to be', *борóться* 'to fight', *смеркáться* 'to get dark', etc.). All these verbs are intransitive. Some verbs ending in *-ся* have a reflexive meaning (*умывáться* 'to wash oneself', *одевáться* 'to dress oneself') (see Table 104).

3. Russian verbs have the *infinitive*, and the *indicative*, the *imperative* and the *conditional-subjunctive moods;* the indicative mood has three tenses, with one form for the present, one for the past and two for the future; some verbs taking the simple future form (*прочитáю* 'I shall read to the end') and others, the compound future form (*бýду читáть* 'I shall read'). In the present and future tenses, Russian verbs change for person and for number. In the past tense, Russian verbs have no special personal forms but they change for number and, in the singular, also for gender (*он читáл* 'he read', *онá читáла* 'she read', *дитя́ читáло* 'the child read'). The plural form in the past does not change for gender (*онú читáли* 'they read').

The Russian verb has also special forms, namely, the *participle* and the *verbal adverb* (see Tables 114-122).

4. In Russian there are impersonal verbs which change neither for person (in the present and the future) nor for gender or number (in the past). These verbs are used without any subject (see Table 105).

5. The main peculiarity of the Russian verb is that it has *aspects.* There are two aspects: the *imperfective aspect* (*читáть* 'to read', *писáть* 'to write', *стрóить* 'to build', *изучáть* 'to learn', *выполня́ть* 'to fulfil', *идтú* 'to go') and the *perfective aspect* (*прочитáть* 'to read (to the end)', *написáть* 'to write (to the end)', *пострóить* 'to build (completely)', *изучúть* 'to study (thoroughly)', *вы́полнить* 'to fulfil (completely)', *пойтú* 'to go').

Perfective verbs* denote complete actions, i.e., actions which were completed, brought to an end in the past or will be completed in the future.

In the past:

Я прочита́л кни́гу means 'I read the whole book'; *я написа́л письмо́* means 'I wrote the letter to the end (I finished writing it)'; *я изучи́л ру́сский язы́к* means 'I learned Russian (I got a thorough knowledge of it)'; *мы спе́ли пе́сню* means 'we sang the song (from beginning to end)', while the sentences *я чита́л кни́гу* 'I read a book', *я писа́л письмо́* 'I wrote a letter', *я изуча́л ру́сский язы́к* 'I studied the Russian language', *мы пе́ли пе́сню* 'we sang the song' merely state the fact that the actions expressed in them occurred, but do not specify whether they were completed or not. *Чита́л* 'I read', *писа́л* 'I wrote', *изуча́л* 'I studied', *пе́ли* 'we sang' are verbs of the imperfective aspect.

In the future tense:

Я прочита́ю кни́гу means 'I shall read the whole book (from beginning to end)', *я напишу́ письмо́* means 'I shall write the whole letter (I shall finish writing it)', etc., while the sentences *я бу́ду чита́ть кни́гу* 'I shall read a book', *я бу́ду писа́ть письмо́* 'I shall write a letter', etc. merely state the fact that the actions they express will occur in the future, but do not specify whether they willl be completed or not; it is, therefore, quite possible that the book will not be read to the end, the letter will remain unfinished, etc.

Some verbs of the perfective aspect convey not only the idea that the action is completed, brought to an end, but also that the action is only performed once (on a single occasion) or is completed "at one go", thus, *он толкну́л стул* means 'he pushed the chair (once)', *он махну́л руко́й* means 'he waved his hand (once)', while the verbs in the sentences *он толка́л стул* 'he pushed the chair', *он маха́л руко́й* 'he waved his hand' convey continuity or repetition of the action. *Толка́л* 'he pushed', *маха́л* 'he waved' are verbs of the imperfective aspect.

Imperfective verbs* denote only an action or a state without any reference to its completion.

Besides, some imperfective verbs convey the idea that the action took place more than once, having thus an iterative meaning, e.g., *ха́живал* 'used to go'. Iterative verbs are rarely used in either colloquial speech or the literary language.

Many imperfective verbs are primary verbs, while many perfective verbs are derivative. There are few primary perfective verbs; some. are monosyllabic (*дать* 'to give', *лечь* 'to lie down', *сесть* 'to sit down', *стать* 'to become', *деть* 'to put') and some have the

---

* We use this term instead of "verbs of the perfective aspect". Likewise, for brevity's sake, verbs of the imperfective aspect will be referred to as "imperfective verbs".

suffix *-и-:* *кóнчить* 'to finish', *решúть* 'to solve', *брóсить* 'to throw', etc.

Perfective verbs are formed from the corresponding imperfective ones by affixing prefixes or by substituting one suffix for another (*писáть* 'to write — *написáть* 'to write (from beginning to end)', *толкáть* 'to push' — *толкнýть* 'to push (once)'); imperfective verbs are formed from the corresponding perfective ones by affixing suffixes to the stem or by substituting one suffix for another (*овладéть* 'to master (thoroughly)' — *овладевáть* 'to master', *изучúть* 'to learn (thoroughly)' — *изучáть* 'to study').

Besides, when a verb is changed from one aspect to the other there may be alternation of root vowels (*перестрóить* 'to rebuild [to finish rebuilding]' — *перестрáивать* 'to rebuild', *опоздáть* 'to be late [on one occasion]' — *опáздывать* 'to be late [more than once]') or consonants (*отвéтить* 'to reply [once]' — *отвечáть* 'to reply [more than once]' as well as shifting of the stress (*разрéзать* 'to cut [once]' — *разрезáть* 'to cut [more than once]').

Each of the verbs — the primary one and its derivative — is independent and has all the verb forms, i.e., the infinitive, the forms of the moods, the tense forms, etc.

Imperfective verbs have three tenses (*читáю* 'I read', *читáл* 'I read', *бýду читáть* 'I shall read'), while perfective ones have only two, namely, the past and the future (*прочитáл* 'I read [to the end]', *прочитáю* 'I shall read [to the end]'); they have no present tense.

In Russian there are two forms of the future tense: the compound and the simple.

Imperfective verbs have the compound future, formed by means of the future form of the auxiliary verb and the infinitive of the principal verb: *я бýду читáть* 'I shall read', *я бýду изучáть* 'I shall study'.

Perfective verbs have the simple future: *я прочитáю* 'I shall read (to the end)', *я изучý* 'I shall study (thoroughly)'. The endings in the simple future are similar to those in the present tense of imperfective verbs.

The sentences *мы бýдем стрóить дом* 'we shall build a house', *мы бýдем изучáть рýсский язы́к* 'we shall study the Russian language' imply that the actions expressed by the verbs will be performed but they do not specify whether these actions will be completed or not, while the sentences *мы пострóим дом* 'we shall build a house', *мы изýчим рýсский язы́к* 'we shall learn the Russian language' state that the actions expressed by the verbs will be carried on till their completion, i.e., that the building of the house will be completed and that the learners of the language will get a thorough knowledge of it.

The different formation of tense forms resulting from the two different aspects of Russian verbs leads to a number of typical mistakes often made by foreigners; namely, using the present tense instead of the future, the future instead of the present, and also to an incorrect formation of the future tense from perfective verbs (instead of the correct future tense *я скажу́* 'I shall say', *я пойду́* 'I shall go', *я возьму́* 'I shall take', *я начну́* 'I shall begin', etc. foreigners often say incorrectly *я бу́ду сказа́ть*, *я бу́ду пойти́*, *я бу́ду взять*, *я бу́ду нача́ть*, etc.).

Note. — For some peculiarities in the use of verbs of different aspects in the infinitive, the past and the future tense, the imperative and the conditional-subjunctive mood, see Tables 96-98.

ASPECTS OF THE VERB

Table 63

FORMATION OF PERFECTIVE VERBS BY MEANS OF PREFIXES

A. Prefixes may add to the verb a meaning of completion, without altering its principal lexical meaning.

Imperfective Aspect	Perfective Aspect	Pre-fixes	Remarks
стро́ить 'to build' Рабо́чие стро́или дом. 'The workers were building a house.'	*постро́ить* Рабо́чие постро́или дом. 'The workers had built a house.'	*по-*	*Стро́или дом* — the verb merely indicates. the fact that the action took place. *Постро́или дом* means 'the building of the house was started and finished'.
чита́ть 'to read' Я чита́л кни́гу. 'I was reading a book.'	*прочита́ть* Я прочита́л кни́гу. 'I read the book.'	*про-*	*Чита́л кни́гу* — the verb merely indicates the fact that the action took place. *Прочита́л кни́гу* means 'read the whole book (to the end)'.

215

Imperfective Aspect	Perfective Aspect	Pre-fixes	Remarks
писа́ть 'to write' Това́рищ *писа́л письмо́.* 'My friend was writing a let-ter.'	*написа́ть* Това́рищ *написа́л письмо́.* 'My friend wrote a letter (to the end).'	*на-*	*Писа́л письмо́* does not specify whether the letter was finished or not. *Написа́л письмо́* means 'the let-ter was written from beginning to end'.
де́лать 'to do' Учени́к *де́лал уро́ки.* 'The pupil was doing his les-sons.'	*сде́лать* Учени́к *сде́-лал уро́ки.* 'The pupil did his lessons.'	*с-*	*Де́лал уро́ки* — the verb merely states that the action took place without any reference to its being completed or not. *Сде́лал уро́ки* means 'began and finished the lessons'.
петь 'to sing' Мы *пе́ли песню.* 'We were singing a song.'	*спеть* Мы *спе́ли песню.* 'We sang a song.'		*Спе́ли песню* means 'sang the song (to the end)'.
гло́хнуть 'to go deaf' Стари́к *на́-чал гло́хнуть.* 'The old man began to go deaf.'	*огло́хнуть* Стари́к *ог-ло́х.* 'The old man went quite deaf.'	*о-*	*Стари́к огло́х* means 'went deaf', 'lost his hearing completely'.
сле́пнуть 'to go blind' Он *сле́пнет.* 'He goes blind.'	*осле́пнуть* Больно́й *осле́п.* 'The patient went quite blind'.		*Больно́й осле́п* means 'went blind', 'lost his sight completely'.

Imperfective Aspect	Perfective Aspect	Pre-fixes	Remarks
делúть 'to divide'	*разделúть*	**раз-**	
Онú *делúли дьíню* на рáвные чáсти. 'They divided the melon into equal parts.'	Онú *разделúли дьíню* на рáвные чáсти. 'They had divided the melon into equal parts.'		*Делúли дьíню* — the verb does not specify whether the action was completed or not. *Разделúли дьíню* — the process of dividing was finished.
будúть 'to wake up'	*разбудúть*		
Я дóлго *будúл товáрища.* 'I tried for a long time to wake my friend up.'	Наконéц я *разбудúл егó.* 'At last I succeeded in waking him up.'		*Будúл* — the verb does not specify whether the action was completed or not. *Разбудúл* means 'woke (the friend) up'.

Note. — Imperfective verbs denoting a gradual change of state (mainly a change of colour) generally form their perfective aspect, denoting completion of the change, by means of the prefix *по-: желтéть — пожелтéть* 'to turn yellow' (Сентя́брь. Уж *пожелтéли лúстья.* 'It is September. The leaves have already turned yellow.'); *чернéть — почернéть* 'to turn black' (Идёт дождь. *Почернéли дорóги.* 'It is raining. The roads have become black.'); *седéть — поседéть* 'to turn grey' (Её *вóлосы поседéли.* 'Her hair turned grey.'); *краснéть — покраснéть* 'to become red, 'to blush' (Ученúк *покраснéл* от волнéния. 'The pupil blushed from nervousness.'), etc.

B. Besides adding to the lexical meaning of the verb the notion of completion, some prefixes may add various shades of meaning in relation to time.

1. The prefix **по-** attached to some verbs adds a meaning of limitation in time:

Imperfective Aspect	Perfective Aspect	Pre-fixes	Remarks
читáть 'to read'	*почитáть*	**по-**	*Почитáл* means 'read for a while (and then stopped reading)'.

Imperfective Aspect	Perfective Aspect	Prefixes	Remarks
рабо́тать 'to work'	*порабо́тать*		*Порабо́тал* means 'worked for a while (and then stopped working)'.
гуля́ть 'to go for walks'	*погуля́ть*		*Погуля́л* means 'walked for a while'.
	Вчера́ я *порабо́тал, почита́л,* пото́м *погуля́л.* 'Yesterday I worked and read for a while and then went for a walk.'		

2. The prefixes **за-, по-** add to some verbs the notion of the beginning of action or state (an inchoative meaning):

Imperfective Aspect	Perfective Aspect	Prefixes	Remarks
петь 'to sing' Мы *пе́ли* пе́сню. 'We were singing a song.'	*запе́ть* Все сра́зу *запе́ли* пе́сню. 'They all began singing the song at once.'	**за-**	*запе́ли* 'began to sing'
шуме́ть 'to rustle' Лес *шуме́л.* 'The wood rustled.'	*зашуме́ть* Лес вдруг *зашуме́л.* 'The wood began to rustle all of a sudden.'		*зашуме́л* 'began to rustle'
говори́ть 'to speak' Он *говори́л* до́лго. 'He spoke for a long time.'	*заговори́ть* Он неожи́данно *заговори́л.* 'He suddenly began to speak.'		*заговори́л* 'began speaking'
пла́кать 'to cry' Ребёнок *пла́кал.* 'The child was crying.'	*запла́кать* Ребёнок *запла́кал.* 'The child began to cry.'		*запла́кал* 'started crying'

Imperfective Aspect	Perfective Aspect	Prefixes	Remarks
ходи́ть 'to pace' Мой оте́ц *ходи́л* по ко́мнате. 'My father was pacing the room.'	*заходи́ть* Мой оте́ц в волне́нии *заходи́л* по ко́мнате. 'My father began pacing the room in excitement.'		*заходи́л* 'began pacing (the room)'
лете́ть 'to fly' Самолёт *лете́л.* 'The plane was flying.'	*полете́ть* Самолёт *полете́л.* 'The plane flew off.'	*по-*	*Полете́л* shows the commencement of the action: '(took off and) started flying'.

Орля́та *засвиста́ли* и *запища́ли* ещё жа́лобнее. Тогда́ орёл вдруг сам гро́мко *закрича́л,* распра́вил кры́лья и тяжело́ *полете́л* к мо́рю. (Л. Т.) 'The eaglets began piping and cheeping still more piteously. Then the eagle itself gave a sudden scream, spread out its wings and flew heavily towards the sea.'

> Лес *зазвене́л, застона́л, затреща́л,*
> За́яц *послу́шал* и вон *побежа́л.* (Некр.)
> 'The forest began ringing, moaning, crackling,
> The hare listened for a while and then ran away.'

...И по реке́, стыдли́во сине́вшей из-под реде́ющего тума́на, *полили́сь* сперва́ а́лые, пото́м кра́сные, золоты́е пото́ки молодо́го, горя́чего све́та... Всё *зашевели́лось,* просну́лось, *запе́ло, зашуме́ло, заговори́ло.* Всю́ду лучи́стыми алма́зами *зарде́лись* кру́пные ка́пли росы́. (Т.) '...And down along the river, which shamefully showed blue in the thinning mist, streams of young, hot light began pouring, first scarlet, then red and golden... Everything began moving, awoke from slumber, began singing, making noise, talking. Large dewdrops shone everywhere like sparkling diamonds.'

Note. — 1. The prefix *за-* with an inchoative meaning is generally affixed to verbs denoting sounds (Ребёнок *запла́кал.* 'The child began crying.'), motion (Его́ рука́ *задрожа́ла.* 'His hand began to shake.') or luminous effects (Мо́лния *засверка́ла* над ле́сом. 'Lightning flashed (began to flash) over the wood.'). In a number of verbs the prefix *за-* has only the meaning of the beginning of action (Ребёнок *закрича́л.* 'The child began crying.'), in other verbs it shows that the action, once started, continues (Он *заговори́л* взволно́ванно и горячо́. 'He began (and continued) speaking excitedly and with warmth.').

2. (a) When affixed to verbs of "definite" motion the prefix *по-* adds the meaning of the beginning of action. (Де́ти *побежа́ли* к реке́. 'The children started running to the river.' Самолёт *полете́л* в Ленингра́д. 'The plane flew to Leningrad.')

(b) When affixed to verbs of "indefinite" motion the prefix *по-* adds the notion of limitation in time (Де́ти во вре́мя переры́ва *побе́гали* по́ двору. 'During the interval the children ran about in the yard.' Самолёт *полетáл* над гóродом и скрылся. 'The plane flew over the town for a while and then disappeared.').

(For verbs of "indefinite" and "definite" motion, see Table 73.)

3. There are many verbs which cannot express inchoative meaning by the perfective aspect. In such cases this meaning is conveyed by the verbs *начáть*, *стать* 'to begin', 'to start': e.g., Я *нáчал занимáться* рýсским языкóм. 'I began to study the Russian language.' Я *нáчал читáть* рýсскую литератýру. 'I began to read Russian literature.' Ребёнок *стал развивáться*. 'The child began to develop.'

C. Besides the idea of completion, prefixes may add to the verb various shades of meaning pertaining to space, etc.:

Imperfective Aspect	Perfective Aspect	Prefixes
идти́ 'to go'	*войти́* 'to come in', 'to enter' Учи́тель *вошёл* в класс. 'The teacher came into the classroom.'	*в- (во-)*
	вы́йти 'to go out' Учи́тель *вы́шел* из клáсса. 'The teacher went out of the classroom.'	*вы-*
	уйти́ 'to go away', 'to leave' Брáта нет дóма; он *ушёл*. 'The brother is not at home; he has left.'	*у-*
	дойти́ 'to come to', 'to reach' Я *дошёл* до шкóлы за 10 минýт. 'I reached the school in ten minutes.'	*до-*
	отойти́ 'to step aside' Учени́к *отошёл* от доски́. 'The pupil stepped aside from the blackboard.'	*от-(ото-)*
	сойти́ 'to step down', 'to go down', 'to alight' Доклáдчик *сошёл* с трибýны. 'The speaker stepped down from the rostrum.'	*с- (со-)*
	прийти́ 'to come' Ко мне *пришёл* товáрищ. 'A friend came to see me.'	*при-*
	зайти́ 'to call on' Он *зашёл* за мной. 'He called for me.'	*за-*
	перейти́ 'to cross' Мы *перешли́* рéчку вброд. 'We forded the river.'	*пере-*
писáть 'to write'	*списáть* 'to copy' Учени́к хорошó *списáл* текст. 'The pupil copied the text well.'	*с-*
	дописáть 'to finish writing' Он *дописáл* письмó. 'He finished his letter.'	*до-*

Imperfective Aspect	Perfective Aspect	Prefixes
	вы́писать 'to write out', 'to copy out'	*вы-*
	Студе́нт *вы́писал* цита́ты из статьи́. 'The student wrote out quotations from the article.'	
	вписа́ть 'to write in', 'to insert'	*в-*
	Я *вписа́л* не́сколько пропу́щенных слов. 'I inserted a few missing words.'	
	переписа́ть 'to copy'	*пере-*
	Я *переписа́л* рабо́ту. 'I copied the work.'	
	приписа́ть 'to add'	*при-*
	Оте́ц *приписа́л* не́сколько слов к письму́. 'The father added a few words to the letter.'	
	записа́ть 'to write down', 'to take down'	*за-*
	Я хорошо́ *записа́л* ле́кцию. 'I wrote down the lecture well.'	
	исписа́ть 'to cover with writing'	*из-(ис-)*
	Мой сын *исписа́л* весь лист бума́ги. 'My son covered the whole sheet of paper with writing.'	
	подписа́ть 'to sign'	*под-*
	Учи́тель *подписа́л* рабо́ты ученико́в. 'The teacher signed the pupils' papers.'	
	надписа́ть 'to dedicate (a book)'	*над-*
	Мой друг подари́л мне кни́гу и *надписа́л* её. 'My friend gave me a book and wrote a dedication on it.'	
	прописа́ть 'to prescribe'	*про-*
	До́ктор *прописа́л* лека́рство от ка́шля. 'The doctor prescribed a cough medicine.'	
	описа́ть 'to describe'	*о-*
	Поэ́т *описа́л* приро́ду своего́ кра́я. 'The poet described his native countryside.'	
	расписа́ть 'to paint'	*раз-(рас-)*

Note. — 1. Verbs formed by affixing prefixes to imperfective verbs are usually of the perfective aspect.

2. The prefixes *в-, вы-, от-, до-, из-, у-, с-, за-, под-, над-, о-, пере-, при-, раз-,* etc. when affixed to verbs add various meanings to them, thus forming new words (in dictionaries such verbs preceded by prefixes are given as new words).

3. One and the same prefix affixed to different verbs may add to the verbs different meanings, e.g., *перебежа́ть у́лицу (че́рез у́лицу)* 'to run across the street'; *перечита́ть письмо́* 'to re-read a letter' (i.e., to read it once more); *перестро́ить дом* 'to rebuild a house' (i.e., to change its architecture, to dismantle some parts of it and then build them differently); *перестара́лся* 'he overdid it'; *переломá́л игру́шки* 'he broke the toys' (i.e., broke all of the toys); *переночева́л в лесу́* 'he spent the night in the forest' (i.e., spent the whole night in the forest).

4. Some of the above prefixes add to verbs not a notion pertaining to space but one of completed action: *вы́лечить больно́го* 'to cure a patient completely', *вы́учить стихи́* 'to learn verses by heart'

FORMATION OF VERBS IMPERFECTIVE AND PERFECTIVE ASPECTS BY MEANS OF SUFFIXES

Table 64

Verbs with the Suffixes -ива-, -ыва-

Imperfective Aspect	Perfective Aspect	Imperfective Aspect	Suffixes
стро́ить 'to build'	*достро́ить* 'to complete building' Вчера́ рабо́чие *достро́или* дом. 'Yesterday the workers finished building the house.'	*достра́ивать* Вчера́ рабо́чие ещё *достра́ивали* дом. 'Yesterday the workers were still finishing building the house.'	*-ива-*
	перестро́ить 'to rebuild' Этот дом *перестро́или*. 'This house was rebuilt.'	*перестра́ивать* Этот дом *перестра́ивали* три ра́за. 'This house was rebuilt three times.'	
	надстро́ить 'to build additional storeys' В Москве́ *надстро́или* мно́гие дома́. 'They built additional storeys to many houses in Moscow.'	*надстра́ивать* В Москве́ ле́том *надстра́ивали* не́которые дома́. 'In summer they built additional storeys to some houses in Moscow.'	
писа́ть 'to write'	*переписа́ть* 'to copy' Я *переписа́л* рабо́ту. 'I copied the work.'	*перепи́сывать* Я не́сколько раз *перепи́сывал* рабо́ту. 'I copied the work several times.'	*-ыва-*

Imperfective Aspect	Perfective Aspect	Imperfective Aspect	Suffixes
	дописа́ть 'to finish writing' Я *дописа́л* письмо́ и вложи́л его́ в конве́рт. 'I finished writing the letter and put it in an envelope.'	*допи́сывать* Я *допи́сывал* письмо́, когда́ он вошёл в ко́мнату. 'I was finishing the letter when he entered the room.'	*-ыва-*
	вы́писать 'to copy out' Я *вы́писал* из те́кста мно́го но́вых слов. 'I copied out many new words from the text.'	*выпи́сывать* Я чита́л и *выпи́сывал* незнако́мые слова́. 'I was reading, copying out the new words.'	
	подписа́ть 'to sign' Он *подписа́л* все бума́ги. 'He signed all the papers.'	*подпи́сывать* Он всегда́ *подпи́сывал* все бума́ги. 'He always signed all the papers.'	
чита́ть 'to read'	*дочита́ть* 'to finish reading' Я как раз *дочита́л* газе́ту, когда́ он вошёл. 'I had just finished reading the newspaper when he came in.'	*дочи́тывать* Я *дочи́тывал* газе́ту, когда́ он вошёл. 'I was finishing reading the newspaper when he came in.'	
	перечита́ть 'to re-read' Я вчера́ *перечита́л* э́тот расска́з. 'I re-read this story yesterday.'	*перечи́тывать* Я ча́сто *перечи́ты-вал* э́тот расска́з. 'I often re-read this story.'	

Note. — 1. Perfective verbs formed by affixing prefixes imparting to them a new lexical meaning can once again be turned into imperfective ones by means of the suffixes *-ива-, -ыва-*. However, if the prefix imparts to the verb only the idea of completion or of beginning of action and does not essentially alter its meaning, the verb cannot be turned into an imperfective one. There are a few exceptions to this rule, for example, *чита́ть* 'to read' — *прочита́ть* 'to read to the end' — *прочи́тывать* 'to read to the end (a number of times)' and *гово-ри́ть* 'to talk' — *заговори́ть* 'to begin talking' — *заговаривать* 'to begin talking (several times)'.

2. Verbs with the suffixes *-ива-, -ыва-* are always imperfective; perfective verbs with two prefixes plus the suffix *-ива-* or *-ыва-* (*повытáлкивать* 'to push out all or many severally') are used very rarely.

3. The suffixes *-ива-, -ыва-* also occur in verbs without prefixes: *лáвливать* 'to catch (on and off)' (Мы *лáвливали* и ершéй. (Кр.) 'We used to catch even ruff'), *хáживать* 'to walk (on and off)'. Such verbs express actions repeated in the past (cf. 'used to...'). Most of them are archaic, but they are encountered in 19th century literary works.

Я *вúдывал* частéнько, что ры́льце у тебя́ в пуху́... (Кр.)
'I often saw down on your snout...'

. . . . Та́ня да́ле;
Стару́шка ей: А вот ками́н;
Здесь ба́рин *сúживал* оди́н,
Здесь с ним *обéдывал* зимо́ю
Поко́йный Лéнский, наш сосéд... (П.)

. . . . 'Tanya went on;
The old woman said, "There is the fireplace;
The master used to sit there alone,
The late Lensky, our neighbour,
Used to come to us to dinner in winter..."'

Table 65

Verbs with the Suffix *-ну-*

Imperfective Aspect	Perfective Aspect	Suffix	Remarks
исчезáть 'to disappear (gradually)' Со́лнце постепéнно *исчезáло.* 'The sun was slowly disappearing.'	*исчéзнуть* 'to disappear (completely)' Наконéц оно́ совсéм *исчéзло.* 'Finally it disappeared completely.'	*-ну-*	*Со́лнце исчезáло* means that the setting sun was still visible. *Со́лнце исчéзло* ·means that the sun was no longer visible.
достигáть 'to reach' Мы ужé *достигáли* вершúны горы́, когда́ пошёл дождь. 'We were already arriving at the top of the mountain when it began raining.'	*достúгнуть* 'to reach' Мы ужé *достúгли* вершúны горы́, когда́ пошёл дождь. 'We had already reached the top of the mountain when it began raining.' Нау́ка *достúгла* огро́мных успéхов. 'Science has achieved great successes.'		*Мы ужé достигáли вершúны* means that we had not yet reached the top of the mountain. *Доcтúгли вершúны* means that we had reached the top of the mountain. *Нау́ка достúгла успéхов* — the successes are already have been achieved.

Imperfective Aspect	Perfective Aspect	Suffix	Remarks
мелькáть 'to gleam'	мелькнýть 'to gleam (once and then go out)'	-ну-	
Вдалú мелькáли огонькú. 'Lights were gleaming in the distance.'	Вдалú мелькнýл огонёк. 'A light gleamed for a moment in the distance (and then went out).'		*Мелькáли огонькú*—repeated, recurrent action. *Мелькнýл огонёк* — a light showed only once and then went out.
толкáть 'to push'	толкнýть 'to push (once)'		
Мáльчик толкáл телéжку. 'The boy was pushing the cart.'	Мáльчик толкнýл телéжку. 'The boy gave the cart a push.'		*Толкáл телéжку* — the action was repeated. *Толкнýл телéжку* — gave the cart a push.
махáть 'to wave'	махнýть 'to wave (once)'		
Он махáл рукóй на прощáнье. 'He was waving his hand in parting.'	Он махнýл рукóй. 'He waved his hand (once).'		*Махáл рукóй* means 'waved his hand several times.' *Махнýл рукóй*—'waved his hand only `once'.
кричáть 'to cry'	крúкнуть 'to cry (once)'		
Ребёнок кричáл не переставáя. 'The child was crying incessantly.'	Ребёнок крúкнул и замóлк. 'The child gave a cry and was silent.'		*Кричáл* — the action is not limited in time. *Крúкнул* denotes an action which took place only once.

Note. — 1. Most verbs, whether prefixed or unprefixed, with the suffix **-ну-** are perfective.

2. Perfective verbs with the suffix **-ну-**: (a) denote completion of action, attainment of a result (*достúгнуть* 'to reach', *исчéзнуть* 'to disappear'); (b) convey the idea that the action was performed only once, on a single occasion, that it was of a momentary character (*толкнýть* 'to push', *махнýть* 'to wave', *крúкнуть* 'to cry').

3. Some unprefixed verbs with the suffix **-ну-** are imperfective, e.g., *вя́нуть* 'to fade', *вя́знуть* 'to stick', *сóхнуть* 'to dry', *мóкнуть* 'to become wet', *гúбнуть* 'to perish', *крéпнуть* 'to become stronger', *мёрзнуть* 'to freeze', *зя́бнуть* 'to suffer from the cold', *глóхнуть* 'to go deaf'. Most of these verbs express gradual intensification of a state. Their perfective counterparts are formed by means of the prefixes *вы-, за-, о-, у-: завя́нуть* 'to fade (completely)', *увя́нуть* 'to fade (completely)', *увя́знуть* 'to stick', *вы́сохнуть* 'to dry (completely)', *вы́мокнуть* 'to get wet through', *погúбнуть* 'to perish', *окрéпнуть* 'to become stronger', *замёрзнуть* 'to freeze', *оглóхнуть* 'to go deaf'. These verbs,

in their turn, have imperfective counterparts: *увядáть* 'to fade', *увязáть* 'to stick', *засыхáть* 'to dry', *вымокáть* 'to become wet', *погибáть* 'to perish', *замерзáть* 'to freeze'.

4. The suffix *-ну-* of imperfective verbs is never stressed, the only exception being the verb *тянýть* 'to pull'.

Table 66

Verbs with the Suffix -ва-

Perfective Aspect	Imperfective Aspect	Suffix
дать 'to give' Он *дал* мне книгу. 'He lent me a book.'	*давáть* Он *давáл* мне книги. 'He always lent me books.'	-ва-
создáть 'to create', 'to build' Мы *сóздали* тяжёлую промышленность. 'We have built our heavy industry.'	*создавáть* Мы *создавáли* тяжёлую промышленность в течéние ряда лет. 'We were building our heavy industry for a number of years.'	
осознáть 'to realize' Он *осознáл* свои ошибки. 'He realized his mistakes.'	*осознавáть* Он дóлго не *осознавáл* своих ошибок. 'He did not realize his mistakes for a long time.'	
признáть 'to admit' Он *признáл* свою винý. 'He admitted his guilt.'	*признавáть* Он сначáла не *признавáл* своéй винь. 'At first he would not admit his guilt.'	
встать 'to get up' Мáльчик *встал* рáно ýтром. 'The boy got up early in the morning.'	*вставáть* Я всегдá *вставáл* рáно ýтром. 'I always got up early in the morning.'	
застáть 'to find' Вчерá он не *застáл* никогó дóма. 'Yesterday he did not find anybody in.'	*заставáть* Я обычно *заставáл* всех дóма. 'I usually found everybody in.'	
преодолéть 'to overcome' Мы *преодолéли* все препятствия. 'We have overcome all the obstacles.'	*преодолевáть* Мы с трудóм *преодолевáли* препятствия. 'We overcame the obstacles with difficulty.'	
добиться 'to achieve' Мы *добились* успéхов. 'We achieved success.'	*добивáться* Мы упóрно *добивáлись* успéхов. 'We were persistently trying to achieve success.'	-ва-

Perfective Aspect	Imperfective Aspect	Suffix
забы́ть 'to forget' Я *забы́л* сего́дня взять слова́рь. 'Today I forgot to take a dictionary with me.'	*забыва́ть* Я всегда́ *забыва́л* взять слова́рь. 'I always forgot to take a dictionary with me.'	
откры́ть 'to open' Магази́н *откры́ли* в 8 часо́в. 'The shop opened at 8 o'clock.'	*открыва́ть* Магази́н всегда́ *открыва́ли* во́время. 'The shop always used to open on time.'	
покры́ть 'to cover', 'to spread (over)' Утром густо́й тума́н *покры́л* поля́. 'In the morning a thick mist spread over the fields.'	*покрыва́ть* По утра́м густо́й тума́н *покрыва́л* поля́. 'In the mornings a thick mist would spread over the fields.'	
зали́ть 'to flood' Вода́ *залила́* луга́. 'The water flooded the meadows.'	*залива́ть* Вода́ всегда́ *залива́ла* луга́. 'The water always used to flood the meadows.'	

Note. — 1. Imperfective verbs with the suffix *-ва-* (*дава́ть* 'to give', *забыва́ть* 'to forget') are formed from the stem (or root) of their perfective counterparts (*дать* 'to give', *забы́ть* 'to forget', etc.). The suffix *-ва-* always follows a vowel.

2. Verbs with the suffix *-ва-* generally remain imperfective even if prefixes are affixed, e.g., *передава́ть* 'to pass', *продава́ть* 'to sell', *отдава́ть* 'to return', *выдава́ть* 'to deliver', etc.

Bear in mind that (a) the verbs *быть* 'to be' and *быва́ть* 'to be' are both imperfective, while *побы́ть* 'to stay' and *побыва́ть* 'to stay' are both perfective: Я хочу́ *побыва́ть* в дере́вне. 'I want to stay in the country.' Я хочу́ *побы́ть* в дере́вне с ме́сяц. 'I want to stay in the country for about a month.'; (b) if the prefix *по-* imparting the notion of completion is affixed to a prefixed verb with the suffix *-ва-,* the verb turns into a perfective one (В аудито́рии *пооткрыва́ли* все о́кна. 'They opened all the windows in the classroom.'); however, such verbs with two prefixes are not very common in the literary language.

3. To this group belong all the verbs whose roots are *-да-, -зна-, -ста-* (*признать—признава́ть* 'to admit', *отда́ть—отдава́ть* 'to return', *приста́ть—приставать* 'to stick').

The peculiarity of the conjugation of these verbs is that in the present tense they have no suffix *-ва-,* (*отдаёшь* 'you return', *пристаёшь* 'you stick', *встаёшь* 'you get up', etc.).

4. Verbs formed by affixing prefixes to monosyllabic verbs form their imperfective aspect by means of the suffix *-ва-,* e.g.:

> *крыть—покры́ть—покрыва́ть* 'to cover'
> *лить—зали́ть—залива́ть* 'to pour'
> *греть—нагре́ть—нагрева́ть* 'to warm'

8*

Table 67

Verbs with the Suffixes -*и*-, -*a*-

Perfective Aspect	Suffix	Imperfective Aspect	Suffix
изучи́ть 'to study' Мы уже́ *изучи́ли* дре́внюю исто́рию. 'We have already studied ancient history.'	-*и*-	*изуча́ть* Мы *изуча́ли* дре́внюю исто́рию в пя́том кла́ссе. 'We studied ancient history in the fifth form.'	-*a*- (-*я*-)
получи́ть 'to get', 'to receive' Сего́дня я *получи́л* письмо́. 'Today I received a letter.'		*получа́ть* Ле́том я ча́сто *получа́л* пи́сьма. 'In summer I often used to receive letters.'	
реши́ть 'to settle' Наконе́ц они́ *реши́ли* э́тот вопро́с. 'They finally settled that question.'		*реша́ть* Они́ до́лго *реша́ли* э́тот вопро́с. 'They tried for a long time to settle that question.'	
ко́нчить 'to finish' Сего́дня они́ *ко́нчили* рабо́ту в 7 часо́в. 'Today they finished work at 7 o'clock.'		*конча́ть* Они́ обы́чно *конча́ли* рабо́ту в 6 часо́в. 'They usually finished work at 6 o'clock.'	
вы́полнить 'to fulfil' Мы *вы́полнили* план. 'We have fulfilled the plan.'		*выполня́ть* Мы *выполня́ли* план ка́ждый год. 'We used to fulfil the plan every year.'	
прове́рить 'to correct' Учи́тельница *прове́рила* тетра́ди ученико́в. 'The teacher had corrected the pupils' note-books.'		*проверя́ть* Учи́тельница *проверя́ла* тетра́ди ученико́в ка́ждый день. 'The teacher corrected the pupils' note-books every day.'	

Note. — 1. When a pair of verbs have the same principal meaning, the verb with the suffix -*и*- is perfective and the verb with the suffix -*a*- imperfective. To determine aspect of a given verb, one must find out if there exists the other verb of the pair.

Bear in mind that the verb *купи́ть* 'to buy' is perfective, whereas *покупа́ть* 'to buy' is imperfective (in this case the imperfective verb is formed by means of both a suffix and a prefix).

Он купил книги (the verb conveys the idea of completion of the action) 'He bought the books.' *Я его видел в магазине, где он покупал книги* (the verb conveys no idea of completion; he may not have bought the books after all) 'I saw him in a shop; he was buying books there.'

2. Some verbs of this group may have alternating consonants in the stem:

> ответить 'to answer' — отвечать
> защитить 'to defend' — защищать
> проводить 'to see off' — провожать
> победить 'to defeat' — побеждать
> простить 'to forgive' — прощать
> обновить 'to renovate' — обновлять
> укрепить 'to strengthen' — укреплять
> пустить 'to let' — пускать

3. Some perfective verbs differ from their imperfective counterparts not only in that they have different suffixes, but also in that they are stressed on different syllables; thus, verbs ending in *-ить* are stressed on the root, while verbs ending in *-ать* are stressed on the suffix:

> кончить 'to finish' — кончать
> бросить 'to throw' — бросать
> ответить 'to answer' — отвечать

4. Prefixes affixed to unprefixed imperfective verbs of this group do not generally turn them into perfectives: *пускать* 'to let' — *выпускать* 'to let out', *отпускать* 'to let go', *запускать* 'to throw', *допускать* 'to admit'; *решать* 'to settle' — *разрешать* 'to allow', *предрешать* 'to predetermine' (but: *бросать* 'to throw' (imperfective) — *набросать* (perfective) везде бумажек 'to throw scraps of paper all around', *разбросать* (perfective) игрушки 'to scatter toys', *забросать* (perfective) докладчика вопросами 'to shower the speaker with questions'.

In the above examples, the prefixes *на-, раз-, за-* attached to the verb *бросать* 'to throw' impart to it the notion of completion.

Table 68

Verbs with Changes occurring in the Root and the Stem

Imperfective Aspect	Perfective Aspect
избирать, выбирать 'to elect'	*избрать, выбрать*
Собрание *выбирало* президиум 10 минут. 'The meeting was ten minutes electing its presidium.'	Собрание *выбрало* в президиум трёх человек. 'The meeting elected three people to the presidium.'
призывать 'to call'	*призвать*
Учитель *призывал* учеников к порядку. 'The teacher was calling the pupils to order.'	Учитель *призвал* учеников к порядку. 'The teacher called the pupils to order.'
засыпать 'to fall asleep'	*заснуть*
Ребёнок обычно плохо *засыпал*. 'Usually the child did not fall asleep easily.'	Вчера он *заснул* быстро. 'Yesterday he fell asleep quickly.'

Imperfective Aspect	Perfective Aspect
поднима́ть 'to raise'	*подня́ть*
Спортсме́н легко́ *поднима́л* 180 кг. 'The sportsman easily lifted 180 kg.'	Ма́льчик *по́днял* тяжёлый чемода́н. 'The boy lifted the heavy suit-case.'
понима́ть 'to understand'	*поня́ть*
Снача́ла я не понима́ла ле́кций на ру́сском языке́, тепе́рь понима́ю. 'At first I did not understand lectures in Russian, now I do.'	Сего́дня он всё *по́нял*. 'Today he understood everything.'
начина́ть 'to begin	*нача́ть*
Мы всегда́ *начина́ем* рабо́ту в 9 часо́в. 'We always begin work at 9 o'clock.'	Вчера́ мы *на́чали* рабо́ту в 8 часо́в. 'Yesterday we began work at 8 o'clock.'
помога́ть 'to help'	*помо́чь*
Он всегда́ *помога́л* мне. 'He always helped me.'	Он *помо́г* мне сего́дня зако́нчить рабо́ту. 'He helped me to finish the work today.'
предостерега́ть 'to warn'	*предостере́чь*
Я его́ не раз *предостерега́л* от опа́сности. 'I warned him more than once against the danger.'	Я его́ *предостерёг* от опа́сности. 'I warned him against the danger.
увлека́ть 'to carry away'	*увле́чь*
Он всегда́ *увлека́л* слу́шателей свое́й ре́чью. 'He always captivated his listeners by his speeches.'	Докла́д всех *увлёк*. 'Everyone was carried away by the report.'
приобрета́ть 'to buy'	*приобрести́*
Он всегда́ *приобрета́л* ре́дкие кни́ги. 'He was always buying rare books.'	Сего́дня он *приобрёл* ре́дкую кни́гу. 'He has bought a rare book today.'
пропада́ть 'to be absent'	*пропа́сть*
Он *пропада́л* не́сколько дней. 'He was absent for several days.'	Он *пропа́л* бе́з вести. 'He was missing.'

Imperfective Aspect	Perfective Aspect
спаса́ть 'to save' Он не раз *спаса́л* утопа́ющих. 'He saved drowning people more than once.'	*спасти́* Он *спас* утопа́ющего. 'He saved the drowning man.'
ложи́ться 'to lie down' Ле́том я *ложи́лся* спать в 10 часо́в. 'In summer I used to go to bed at 10 o'clock.'	*лечь* Вчера́ я *лёг* спать в 12 часо́в. 'Yesterday I went to bed at 12 o'clock.'
сади́ться 'to sit down', 'to set' Со́лнце ме́дленно *сади́лось*. 'The sun was setting slowly.'	*сесть* Со́лнце *се́ло*. 'The sun had set.'
станови́ться 'to become' Он постепе́нно *станови́лся* бо́лее споко́йным ребёнком. 'He gradually became a quieter child.'	*стать* Он *стал* споко́йным ма́льчиком. 'He had become a quiet boy.'

Table 69

Summary Table of Alternation of Root Vowels in Different Aspects of the Verb

Alternating Vowels	Perfective Aspect	Imperfective Aspect	Remarks
o—a	опозда́ть 'to be late' вскочи́ть 'to jump', 'to jump up' вздро́гнуть 'to start' осмотре́ть 'to examine'	опа́здывать вска́кивать вздра́гивать осма́тривать	The imperfective aspect has the suffixes *-ыва-, -ива-;* the root vowel is stressed.
o—a	изложи́ть 'to set forth' предложи́ть 'to offer' приложи́ть 'to append'	излага́ть предлага́ть прилага́ть	Roots: *-лож- — -лаг-*

Alternating Vowels	Perfective Aspect	Imperfective Aspect	Remarks
	косну́ться 'to touch'	каса́ться	Roots: *-кос- — -кас-*
	прикосну́ться 'to touch'	прикаса́ться	
е—и	собра́ть 'to gather' — соберу́ 'I shall gather'	собира́ть	Roots: *-бр- — -бер- — -бир-*
	вы́брать 'to choose' — вы́беру 'I shall choose'	выбира́ть	
	разобра́ть 'to disassemble' — разберу́ 'I shall disassemble'	разбира́ть	
	удра́ть 'to take to one's heels' — удеру́ 'I shall take to my heels'	удира́ть	*-др- — -дер- — -дир-*
	расстели́ть 'to spread out' — разостла́ть	расстила́ть	Roots: *-стел- — -стил- — -стл-*
	постели́ть 'to spread' — постла́ть	постила́ть	
	стере́ть 'to wipe off' — сотру́ 'I shall wipe off'	стира́ть	Roots: *-тер- — -тр- — -тир-*
	умере́ть 'to die' — умру́ 'I shall die'	умира́ть	*-мер- — -мр- — -мир-*
	запере́ть 'to lock' — запру́ 'I shall lock'	запира́ть	*-пер- — -пр- — -пир-*

232

Alternating Vowels	Perfective Aspect	Imperfective Aspect	Remarks
	заже́чь 'to light'— зажгу́ 'I shall light' — зажёг 'I lighted'	зажига́ть	Roots: *-жег- — -жг- — -жиг-*
	подже́чь 'to set fire (to)' — подожгу́ 'I shall set fire (to)'	поджига́ть	
о — ы	вздохну́ть 'to heave a sigh'	вздыха́ть	Roots: *-дох- — -дых-*
я — им	поня́ть 'to under-stand'	понима́ть	*-ня- — -ним-*
а — ин	нача́ть 'to begin'	начина́ть	*-ча- — -чин-*

Note. — 1. In some cases alternation of vowels occurs only in spelling: the unstressed *о—а, е—и* sound identical.

2. A perfective verb with the root *-лож-* has not necessarily an imperfective counterpart with the root *-лаг-*; in some cases a perfective verb with the root *-лож-* has an imperfective counterpart with the root *-клад-*, e.g., *доло-жи́ть* о рабо́те 'to report about the work done' — *докла́дывать* о рабо́те; *отло-жи́ть* собра́ние 'to put off a meeting' — *откла́дывать* собра́ние.

3. There are instances when in certain meanings perfective verbs with the root *-лож-* have imperfective counterparts with the root *-клад-* and in other meanings, with the root *-лаг-*, e.g., *сложи́ть* ве́щи 'to pack the things' — *скла́-дывать* ве́щи; *сложи́ть* пе́сню 'to make up a song' — *слага́ть* пе́сню; *приложи́ть* лёд к голове́ 'to apply ice to one's head' — *прикла́дывать* лёд к голове́; *прило-жи́ть* докуме́нты 'to enclose documents' — *прилага́ть* докуме́нты; *обложи́ть* больно́го гре́лками 'to put hot water bottles all round the sick man' — *обкла́-дывать* больно́го гре́лками; *обложи́ть* населе́ние нало́гами 'to tax the population' — *облага́ть* населе́ние нало́гами.

Table 70

Formation of Different Aspects by Shifting the Stress

Imperfective Aspect	Perfective Aspect
разреза́ть 'to cut up' Мать *разреза́ла* торт на куски́. 'The mother was cutting the cake into slices.'	*разре́зать* Мать разре́зала торт и дала́ кусо́к ребёнку. 'The mother cut the cake and gave a slice to her child.'
среза́ть 'to cut' Она́ ка́ждое у́тро *среза́ла* цветы́ и ста́вила их в ва́зу. 'Every morning she used to cut some flowers and put them in a vase.'	*сре́зать* Она́ сре́зала цвето́к и подари́-ла его́ мне. 'She cut off a flower and gave it to me.'

233

засыпа́ть 'to cover', 'to bury' Снег всё бо́льше и бо́льше *за-сыпа́л* доро́гу. 'The snow kept on burying the road.'	*засы́пать* Снег совсе́м *засы́пал* доро́гу. 'The snow had completely buried the road.'
посыпа́ть 'to sprinkle' Ну́жно ка́ждый день *посыпа́ть* доро́жки .песко́м. 'The paths should be sprinkled with sand every day.'	*посы́пать* В не́сколько мину́т садо́вник *посы́пал* все доро́жки песко́м. 'In a few minutes the gardener sprinkled all the paths with sand.'

Note. — 1. The aspect of some verbs is changed by shifting the stress.

2. In the infinitive and the forms derived from it such verbs differ only in the place of stress: imperfectives: *посыпа́ть* 'to sprinkle'—*посыпа́л* (I, he) sprinkled' — *посыпа́вший* '(who) was sprinkling'; perfectives: *посы́пать* 'to sprinkle'—*посы́пал* '(I, he) sprinkled' — *посы́павший* '(who) (had) sprinkled' — *посы́панный* 'sprinkled'— *посы́пан* 'sprinkled'— *посы́пав* 'having sprinkled'; imperfectives: *раз-реза́ть* 'to cut' — *разреза́л* '(I, he) cut' — *разреза́вший* '(who) was cutting'; perfectives: *разре́зать* 'to cut' — *разре́зал* '(I, he) cut' — *разре́завший* '(who) had cut' — *разре́занный* 'cut' — *разре́зан* 'cut' — *разре́зав* 'having cut'.

In the present, the simple future and the forms derived from the present or future tense stem, these verbs, besides being stressed differently, have different stems: *посыпа́ю* 'I sprinkle' — *посыпа́й* 'sprinkle', *посыпа́ющий* 'sprinkling', *по-сыпа́емый* 'being sprinkled', *посыпа́я* 'sprinkling' but *посы́плю* 'I shall sprinkle'— *посы́пь* 'sprinkle'; *разреза́ю* 'I cut'— *разреза́й* 'cut', *разреза́ющий* 'cutting', *раз-реза́емый* 'being cut', *разреза́я* 'cutting' but *разре́жу* 'I shall cut'— *разре́жь* 'cut'.

Note that in some cases shifting of the stress results not only in a change of aspect but also in a change of meaning: *сбега́ть* (imperfective) 'to run down': Ма́льчик *сбега́л* с ле́стницы и упа́л. 'The boy fell as he ran downstairs'; *сбе́-гать* (perfective) 'to run to some place and back': Ма́льчик *сбе́гал* в магази́н и купи́л хле́ба. 'The boy ran to the shop and bought some bread.' (For details, see Table 73, dealing with verbs of motion.)

Table 71

Expressing Different Aspects by Different Words

Imperfective Aspect	Perfective Aspect
говори́ть 'to speak' Он *говори́л* два часа́. 'He spoke for two hours.'	*сказа́ть* Он *сказа́л* мне всё, что хо-те́л. 'He told me all he wanted to.'
брать 'to borrow' Я всегда́ *брал* кни́ги в э́той библиоте́ке. 'I always borrowed books from this library.'	*взять* Сего́дня я *взял* сочине́ния Пу́шкина. 'Today I borrowed Pushkin's works.'
класть 'to put' Часть зарпла́ты я бу́ду еже-ме́сячно *класть* в сберка́ссу. 'Every month I'll put part of my salary in the savings-bank.'	*положи́ть* За́втра я *положу́* в сберка́ссу часть зарпла́ты. 'Tomorrow I'll put part of my salary in the savings-bank.'

Table 72

Verbs Having No Imperfective or Perfective Counterpart

I. Most common imperfective verbs having no perfective counterparts of the same meaning:

зави́сеть 'to depend'
зна́чить 'to mean'
недоумева́ть 'to be puzzled'
нужда́ться 'to need'
облада́ть 'to possess'
ожида́ть 'to expect'
отрица́ть 'to deny'
отсу́тствовать 'to be absent'
повествова́ть 'to narrate'
полага́ть 'to suppose'
предви́деть 'to foresee'
предчу́вствовать 'to have a presentiment'
преоблада́ть 'to prevail'
пресле́довать 'to persecute'
приве́тствовать 'to greet'
принадлежа́ть 'to belong'
прису́тствовать 'to be present'
содержа́ть 'to contain'
(Кни́га *содержит* 5 глав. 'The book contains five chapters.')

содержа́ться 'to be contained',
 'to have'
(В кни́ге *содержится* 5 глав.
'The book has five chapters.')
сожале́ть 'to be sorry'
состоя́ть, состоя́ть в..., состоя́ть из... 'to be (a member) of..., to belong to..., to consist of...'
(Он *состои́т* чле́ном э́той организа́ции. 'He is a member of this organization.' Он *состои́т* в э́той организа́ции. 'He belongs to this organization.' Организа́ция *состои́т* из 40 чле́нов. 'The organization consists of 40 members.')
соотве́тствовать 'to correspond'
сто́ить 'to be worth'
угнета́ть 'to oppress'
управля́ть 'to govern'
утвержда́ть 'to state'
уча́ствовать 'to participate'

Note. — 1. The verb *утвержда́ть*, with the meaning 'to confirm' (*утвержда́ть в до́лжности*, *утверди́ть в до́лжности*), 'to confirm one's appointment' has a perfective counterpart (*утверди́ть*); it has no such counterpart with the meaning 'to assert' (Я э́то категори́чески *утвержда́ю*. 'I state that categorically.').

2. The verb *полага́ть* has no perfective counterpart with the meaning 'to think', 'to suppose' (Я *полага́ю*, что... 'I think that...'); but its derivatives *предполага́ть* and *предположи́ть* are imperfective and perfective respectively.

3. The verb *уча́ствовать* 'to participate' has no perfective counterpart, but the expression *принима́ть уча́стие* 'to take part', which is imperfective, has a perfective counterpart: *приня́ть уча́стие*.

II. Most common perfective verbs having no imperfective counterparts of the same meaning:

гря́нуть 'to break out'	ри́нуться 'to rush'
заблуди́ться 'to lose one's way'	состоя́ться 'to take place'
опо́мниться 'to come to one's senses'	(совеща́ние *состоя́лось* 'the conference took place')
отпря́нуть 'to start back'	стать 'to begin'
очути́ться 'to find oneself'	хлы́нуть 'to gush out'

Note. — The verb *заблужда́ться* 'to be mistaken', 'to err' cannot be regarded as the imperfective counterpart of the verb *заблуди́ться* 'to lose one's way': these two verbs have different lexical meanings: Мы *заблуди́лись* в лесу́. 'We lost our way in the wood.' Вы *заблужда́етесь*. 'You are mistaken.'

III. Most common verbs having one form for both the imperfective and the perfective aspect:

атакова́ть 'to attack'	обеща́ть 'to promise'
веле́ть 'to order'	образова́ть 'to form'
жени́ть(ся) 'to marry'	организова́ть 'to organize'
испо́льзовать 'to use'	сочета́ть 'to combine'
иссле́довать 'to investigate'	телеграфи́ровать 'to telegraph'
ликвиди́ровать 'to liquidate'	

Note. — 1. These verbs may be perfective or imperfective according to the context, e.g.:

Он всегда́ выполня́ет всё, что *обеща́ет* (imperfective). 'He always does what he promises.'

Сего́дня он *обеща́л* (perfective) прийти́ ро́вно в 8 часо́в и пришёл во́время. 'Today he promised to come at 8 o'clock and he came on time.'

За́втра мы *организу́ем* (future tense of the perfective aspect) лы́жные соревнова́ния. 'Tomorrow we shall organize a skiing competition.'

Ка́ждый год мы *организу́ем* (present tense of the imperfective aspect) лы́жные соревнова́ния. 'Every year we organize skiing competitions.'

2. Most verbs with the same form for both the imperfective and the perfective aspects have the suffix *-ова-* or *-ирова-*: *образова́ть* 'to form', *организова́ть* 'to organize', *телеграфи́ровать* 'to telegraph', *национализи́ровать* 'to nationalize', etc.

3. In Modern Russian, the imperfective aspect can be formed from some of the above verbs by means of the suffix *-ыва-* (*организо́вывать* 'to organize', *образо́вывать* 'to form').

To emphasize their perfective meaning, some verbs are used with prefixes: *сорганизова́ть* 'to organize', *пообеща́ть* 'to promise', *пожени́ть* 'to marry', *пожени́ться* 'to get married'.

4. The verb *телеграфи́ровать* means 'to send a wire'; in colloquial speech, the expressions дава́ть телегра́мму, дать телегра́мму are generally used, especially in the perfective meaning: Вчера́ я *дал телегра́мму*. 'I sent a wire yesterday ' За́втра я *дам телегра́мму*. 'I'll send a wire tomorrow.'

VERBS OF MOTION WITH DIFFERENT STEMS

Table 73

Imperfective Aspect	Perfective Aspect
носи́ть 'to carry', выноси́ть 'to carry out', относи́ть 'to carry (to some place)', приноси́ть 'to bring', переноси́ть 'to transfer', etc. *нести́* 'to carry'	вы́нести 'to carry out', отнести́ 'to carry (to some place)', принести́ 'to bring', перенести́ 'to transfer', etc.
води́ть 'to lead', доводи́ть 'to take (to some place)', отводи́ть 'to take away', приводи́ть 'to bring', переводи́ть 'to lead across', etc. *вести́* 'to lead'	вы́вести 'to lead out', довести́ 'to take (to some place)', отвести́ 'to take away', привести́ 'to bring', перевести́ 'to lead across', etc.
вози́ть 'to carry (from one place to another) in a vehicle', довози́ть 'to carry (up to some place)', вывози́ть 'to carry out', ввози́ть 'to carry in', привози́ть 'to bring', перевози́ть 'to carry across', etc. *везти́* 'to carry'	вы́везти 'to carry out', ввезти́ 'to carry in', привезти́ 'to bring', перевезти́ 'to carry across', etc.
ходи́ть 'to go', 'to walk', уходи́ть 'to go away', приходи́ть 'to come', выходи́ть 'to go out', переходи́ть 'to go across', etc. *идти́* 'to go', 'to walk'	вы́йти 'to go out', уйти́ 'to go away', прийти́ 'to come', перейти́ 'to go across', etc.
лета́ть 'to fly', вылета́ть 'to fly out', прилета́ть 'to come flying', улета́ть 'to fly away', etc. *лете́ть* 'to fly'	вы́лететь 'to fly out', прилете́ть 'to come flying', улете́ть 'to fly away', etc.
бе́гать 'to run', убега́ть 'to run away', прибега́ть 'to come running', выбега́ть 'to run out', etc.	

Imperfective Aspect	Perfective Aspect
бежа́ть 'to run'	вы́бежать 'to run out', убе-жа́ть 'to run away', прибежа́ть 'to come running', etc.
по́лзать 'to crawl', выполза́ть 'to crawl out', приполза́ть 'to come crawling', уполза́ть 'to crawl away', etc.	
ползти́ 'to crawl'	вы́ползти 'to crawl out', при-ползти́ 'to come crawling', уполз-ти́ 'to crawl away', etc.
е́здить 'to go', 'to drive', въез-жа́ть 'to drive in', выезжа́ть 'to drive out', уезжа́ть 'to drive away', приезжа́ть 'to come driv-ing', переезжа́ть 'to drive across' (see Note 7)	
е́хать 'to drive'	въе́хать 'to drive in', вы́ехать 'to drive out', уе́хать 'to drive away', прие́хать 'to come driving', перее́хать 'to drive across', etc.

Note. — 1. The verbs *носи́ть* 'to carry', *води́ть* 'to lead', *вози́ть* 'to carry', *ходи́ть* 'to go', 'to walk', *лета́ть* 'to fly', *бе́гать* 'to run', *по́лзать* 'to crawl', etc. and the verbs *нести́* 'to carry', *вести́* 'to lead', *везти́* 'to carry', *идти́* 'to go', 'to walk', *лете́ть* 'to fly', *бежа́ть* 'to run', *ползти́* 'to crawl' are imper-fective. The difference between them is as follows.

(1) The verbs *носи́ть* 'to carry (from one place to another)', *ходи́ть* 'to go', 'to walk', *води́ть* 'to lead', etc. denote movement which takes place habitually:

Почтальо́н *но́сит* по́чту.	The postman brings the post.
Пти́цы *лета́ют*.	Birds fly.
Зме́и *по́лзают*.	Snakes crawl.

or a motion which is repeated at different times and in different directions:

Учи́тель ча́сто *во́дит* нас на экску́р-сии.	The teacher often takes us on excursions.
Челове́к *хо́дит* по ко́мнате.	The man paces the room.
Де́ти *бе́гают* во дворе́.	The children run about in the courtyard.

These verbs are generally called verbs of "indefinite" motion.

(2) The verbs *нести́* 'to carry', *вести́* 'to lead', *везти́* 'to carry (in a vehicle)', *идти́* 'to go', 'to walk', etc. denote a movement performed on a single occasion and in a definite direction:

Смотри́, почтальо́н *несёт* по́чту.	Look, the postman is bringing the post.
Сего́дня я *иду́* в теа́тр.	Today I am going to the theatre.
Самолёт *лети́т* на по́люс.	The plane is flying to the Pole.
Сюда́ *бежи́т* ма́льчик.	A boy is running here.

These verbs are generally called verbs of "definite" motion.

2. When verbs of the first type — *носи́ть, води́ть, вози́ть, ходи́ть,* etc. — have prefixes affixed, they remain imperfective if the prefix adds a meaning of relation in space: *выходи́ть из ко́мнаты* 'to go out of the room', *входи́ть в ко́мнату* 'to go into the room', *уходи́ть из до́му* 'to leave the house', *переходи́ть у́лицу* 'to cross the street', etc.

3. If the prefixes affixed to these verbs indicate relation in time (beginning or continuity of action), i.e., if they show that the action began, continued for some time and then ceased, these verbs become perfective, e.g., (a) Он в волне́нии *заходи́л (забе́гал)* по ко́мнате. 'In his excitement he began pacing (running up and down) the room.' In this example *заходи́л, забе́гал* are perfective verbs; but they are imperfective in the sentence Он ко мне ча́сто *заходи́л (забега́л)* ле́том. 'He often called on me (dropped in) in summer.' Note that the perfective verb is stressed on the root *(забе́гал)*, while in the imperfective verb the stress falls on the suffix *(забега́л)*; (b) Я *походи́л* по ко́мнате и присе́л. 'I paced the room for a while and then sat down.' Он *полета́л* над го́родом и опусти́лся. 'He flew over the city for a while and then landed.' (*походи́л, полета́л* are perfective verbs).

4. If the prefixes affixed to imperfective verbs indicate completion of action, these verbs become perfective: in *сходи́ть куда́-нибудь и верну́ться* 'to go somewhere and return' the verb *сходи́ть* is perfective, while in *сходи́ть отку́да-нибудь* (с горы́, с ле́стницы) 'to go down (a hill, stairs)' the verb *сходи́ть* is imperfective; in *исходи́л* всё по́ле '(he) walked all over the field', *избе́гал* весь сад '(he) ran all over the garden' the verbs are perfective since they denote actions extending to a whole surface and carried to completion; the stress in the verb *избе́гал* is on the root.

Note that in the verb *избе́гал* the stress falls on the suffix *-а-* and that the meaning of the word is different: *он избега́л люде́й* means 'he tried to avoid people'.

5. If verbs are used in a figurative sense, a perfective verb with a meaning of completion of action is formed by means of a prefix: *выходить больно́го* 'to nurse the patient back to health', *заноси́ть пла́тье* or *износи́ть пла́тье* 'to wear clothes till they are threadbare', etc.

6. The verbs of the second type — *нести́, вести́, везти́, идти́,* etc. — always become perfective when a prefix is attached to them. When the prefix *вы-* is affixed to these verbs it is always stressed: *вы́нести* 'to carry out', *вы́вести* 'to lead out', *вы́бежать* 'to run out', etc.

7. The verb *е́здить* 'to go', 'to travel' (imperfective) exists, but prefixes are affixed to the verb *езжа́ть* which is rarely used now without prefixes: *приезжа́ть* 'to come', 'to arrive', *выезжа́ть* 'to go out', 'to leave', etc.

Note that prefixed verbs of "indefinite" motion in the past may imply movement proceeding in the direction of some place or object and away from it:

Ко мне *приходи́л* кто́-нибудь? — Has anyone been to see me?

Да, к тебе *приходи́л* това́рищ. — Yes, there was your friend (he came and went away).

Он *входи́л* в ко́мнату? — Did he enter the room?

Да, он *входи́л* в ко́мнату и оста́вил запи́ску. — Yes, he did, and he left a note for you (he entered the room and then left it).

Prefixed verbs of "definite" motion indicate motion effected in one direction and completed:

К тебе́ *пришёл* това́рищ. — A friend has come to see you (he is here).

В ко́мнату кто́-то *вошёл.* — Somebody entered the room (and is still there).

Table 74

Comparative Table of Verbs of the Imperfective and Perfective Aspects

Infinitive	Imperfective Aspect		Perfective Aspect	
	строить 'to build'	изучать 'to study'	построить 'to build (from beginning to end)'	изучить 'to study (thoroughly)'
Indicative Mood — Present Tense	я строю ты строишь он, она, оно строит мы строим вы строите они строят	изучаю изучаешь изучает изучаем изучаете изучают	No present tense form	
Indicative Mood — Past Tense	я, ты, он строил я, ты, она строила оно строило мы вы они } строили	изучал изучала изучало изучали	построил построила построило построили	изучил изучила изучило изучили

Infinitive	Imperfective Aspect		Perfective Aspect	
	строить	*изучать*	*построить*	*изучить*
Future Tense / Compound	я буду строить ты будешь строить он, она, оно будет строить мы будем строить вы будете строить они будут строить	буду изучать будешь изучать будет изучать будем изучать будете изучать будут изучать	**Simple** я построю ты построишь он, она, оно построит мы построим вы построите они построят	изучу изучишь изучит изучим изучите изучат
Conditional-Subjunctive Mood	Я, ты, он строил бы Я, ты, она строила бы оно строило бы мы, вы, они строили бы	изучал бы изучала бы изучало бы изучали бы	построил бы построила бы построило бы построили бы	изучил бы изучила бы изучило бы изучили бы
Imperative Mood	строй стройте	изучай изучайте	построй постройте	изучи изучите

241

Table 75

Conjugation of the Verb *быть* 'to be'

Present Tense	Past Tense	Future Tense
See Note	я, ты, он был я, ты, она́ была́ оно́ бы́ло мы вы } бы́ли они́	я бу́ду ты бу́дешь он, она́, оно́ бу́дет мы бу́дем вы бу́дете они́ бу́дут
Conditional-Sub-junctive Mood	был бы, была́ бы, бы́ло бы, бы́ли бы	
Imperative Mood	будь, бу́дьте	

Note. — The verb *быть* 'to be' is generally not used in the present tense, except in certain cases in the third person singular (*есть* 'is') and plural (*суть* 'are').

Table 76

Uses of the Present Tense of the Verb *быть (есть, суть)*

1. In Modern Russian *есть* 'is' — the third person singular, present tense, of the verb *быть* 'to be' — is used:

(a) In scientific definitions as the link-verb of a compound predicate:

Пряма́я ли́ния *есть* кратча́йшее расстоя́ние ме́жду двумя́ то́чками. 'A straight line is the shortest distance between two points.'

In other cases the link-verb *есть* is generally omitted:

Я студе́нт университе́та. 'I am a student of the University.'

Мой брат — до́ктор. 'My brother is a doctor.'

(b) To state the existence of somebody or something (in this instance *есть* is used for both singular and plural):

У меня́ *есть* бра́тья и сёстры. 'I have brothers and sisters.'

Сего́дня у меня́ *есть* вре́мя пойти́ в теа́тр. 'Today I have enough time to go to the theatre.'

However, if the thing existing with a person or object is some feature or interior or exterior quality, emotional state or disease, the verb *есть* is always omitted:

У мое́й сестры́ све́тлые во́лосы. 'My sister has fair hair'

У моего́ бра́та о́чень хоро́ший хара́ктер. 'My brother is very good-natured.'

У певи́цы хоро́ший го́лос. 'The singer has a good voice.'

У дру́га го́ре: у́мер оте́ц. 'My friend is in grief: his father has died.'

Он не придёт на заня́тия: у него́ грипп. 'He will not attend the classes: he has the 'flu.'

2. The form *суть* 'are' for the third person plural occurs very rarely and mostly in the classics:

Сий столь оклеве́танные смотри́тели вообще́ *суть* лю́ди ми́рные, от приро́ды услу́жливые, скло́нные к общежи́тию. (П.) 'These much slandered station-masters are generally peaceful people, by nature obliging, inclined to be sociable.'

In Modern Russian *суть* is used very rarely, chiefly in scientific definitions.

THE INFINITIVE

Table 77

-ть	*-ти*	*-чь*
изуча́ть 'to study'	нести́ 'to carry'	бере́чь 'to take care of'
рабо́тать 'to work'	идти́ 'to go', 'to walk'	стере́чь 'to guard'
говори́ть 'to speak'	расти́ 'to grow'	вовле́чь 'to draw (in to)'
стро́ить 'to build'	спасти́ 'to save'	толо́чь 'to pound'
смотре́ть 'to look'	вести́ 'to lead'	лечь 'to lie down'
ви́деть 'to see'	везти́ 'to carry (in a vehicle)'	мочь 'can', 'to be able'
тяну́ть 'to pull'	найти́ 'to find'	печь 'to bake'
поги́бнуть 'to perish'	пойти́ 'to go', 'to walk'	
сесть 'to sit down'		
влезть 'to climb'		
-ть	*-ти*	*-чь*
after vowels, sometimes after the consonants *с, з*.	after consonants and *й*.	after vowels.
Position of stress varies.	Stress falls on the last syllable.	Stress falls on the last syllable.

Note. — 1. -*ть* is mainly found following a vowel, but it may also occur after the consonants *с, з* (*сесть* 'to sit down', *счесть* 'to consider', *влезть* 'to climb', etc.), -*ти* occurs after consonants and *й,* and -*чь* after vowels.

2. If the verb ends in -*ти* or -*чь* the stress invariably falls on the last syllable. Exceptions are perfective verbs with the stressed prefix *вы-*: *вы́нести* 'to carry out', *вы́везти* 'to carry out (in a vehicle)', *вы́печь* 'to bake'.

3. The stem of the infinitive is used to form: the past tense (*чита́л* 'read', *взял* 'took'), past participles active (*чита́вший* 'reading', *взя́вший* 'who took'), past participles passive (*прочи́танный* 'read', *взя́тый* 'taken'), and perfective verbal adverbs (*прочита́в* 'having read', *взяв* 'having taken').

Table 78

Uses of the Infinitive

The infinitive is used:

I. (a) with verbs expressing the beginning, continuity or end of an action:

Я *начинаю изучать* русский язык. 'I begin to study the Russian language.'
Он *стал писать*. 'He began to write.'
Я *продолжаю работать*. 'I go on working.'
Сестра *кончила читать*. 'The sister had finished reading.'
Девочка *перестала заниматься*. 'The girl stopped going to school.'

(b) with verbs expressing possibility or impossibility, ability or inability to perform an action:

Я *могу (не могу)* правильно *произносить* русские слова. 'I can (cannot) pronounce Russian words correctly.'
Я *умею (не умею) рисовать*. 'I can (cannot) draw.'
Я *хочу работать*. 'I want to work.'

(c) with numerous verbs expressing the attitude of the subject towards the action denoted by the infinitive:

Я *люблю читать.* 'I like to read.'
Я *стремлюсь учиться*. 'I strive to learn.'
Я *мечтаю поехать* на море. 'I dream of going to the seaside.'
Я *намереваюсь заниматься* спортом. 'I am going to take up sport.'
Я *предполагаю выехать* завтра. 'I plan to leave tomorrow.'
Он *решил отказаться* от поездки. 'He decided to give up his trip.'
Я *стесняюсь говорить*. 'I feel shy to speak.'
Я *стараюсь быть* сдержанным. 'I am trying to restrain myself.'
Я *отказываюсь понимать* вас. 'I refuse to understand you.'
Я *боюсь простудиться*. 'I am afraid of catching cold.'

(But one cannot say: *интере-
су́юсь рабо́тать, увлека́юсь чи-
та́ть.*)

II. With verbs expressing persuasion, request, prohibition, etc.
to perform an action:

Прошу́ вас *сесть*. 'I ask you
to sit down.'

Разреша́ю вам *кури́ть*. 'I allow
you to smoke.'

Прика́зываю вам *собра́ться*. 'I
order that you should gather.'

Запреща́ю им *уходи́ть*. 'I for-
bid them to leave.'

Я *угова́риваю* их *оста́ться*.
'I am trying to persuade them to
stay.'

Я *заставля́ю* их *слу́шать*. 'I
make them listen.'

Я *убежда́ю* их *не волнова́ть-
ся*. 'I am trying to persuade them
not to be nervous.'

Я *предлага́ю* ей *уе́хать*. 'I sug-
gest that she should leave.'

Сове́тую вам *занима́ться* спо́р-
том. 'I advise you to take up sport.'

Я *помога́ю* им *рабо́тать*. 'I
help them to work.'

Я *учу́* его́ *чита́ть*. 'I teach
him to read.'

III. With verbs of motion to
express purpose:

Я *иду́ занима́ться*. 'I am going
to my lessons.'

Я *пое́хал отдыха́ть*. 'I went
on a holiday.'

Я *побежа́л купа́ться*. 'I ran to
have a bathe.'

IV. With the adjectives:
до́лжен 'must'
обя́зан '(am, is) obliged', 'have
(has)'
вы́нужден '(am, is) forced', 'have
(has)'
гото́в '(am, is) ready'

наме́рен 'intend'

рад '(am, is) glad'

Я *до́лжен идти́*. 'I must go.'

Я *обя́зан сказа́ть*. 'I have to
say.'

Он *вы́нужден лечь* в посте́ль.
'He has to go to bed.'

Я *гото́в защища́ть* свою́ то́чку
зре́ния. 'I am ready to defend
my point of view.'

Я *наме́рен уе́хать*. 'I intend
to leave.'

Я *рад ви́деть* вас. 'I am glad
to see you.'

V. With the words:
на́до 'must'

ну́жно 'must'

необходи́мо 'necessary', 'must'

мо́жно 'may'
(*невозмо́жно* 'must not')
нельзя́ 'must not'

VI. With the dative case to express inevitability or impossibility:

VII. With:
(a) adverbs formed from qualitative adjectives and ending in -*о* (*тру́дно* 'it is difficult', *ве́село* 'it is gay', *хорошо́* 'it is good', etc.)

(b) negative adverbs and pronouns in some of the oblique cases:

Вам *на́до учи́ться*. 'You must study.'

Нам *ну́жно пойти́* в библиоте́ку. 'We must go to the library.'

Им *необходи́мо занима́ться* спо́ртом. 'They must take up sport.'

Ей *мо́жно занима́ться* спо́ртом. 'She may go in for sport.'

Вам *нельзя́ опа́здывать*. 'You must not be late.'

Набежа́ли ту́чи: *быть дождю́!* 'The sky has become overcast: it will raining!'

Не́бо я́сно: *не быть дождю́!* 'The sky is clear: it won't rain!'

Быть грозе́ вели́кой! 'There will· be a great storm!'

Не быть войне́! 'There shall be no war!'

Тру́дно бежа́ть в го́ру, *легко́ бежа́ть* с горы́. 'It is difficult to run uphill, it is easy to run downhill.'

Ве́село рабо́тать в коллекти́ве. 'It is fun to work in a collective.'

Гру́стно расстава́ться с дру́гом. 'One is sorry to part with his friend.'

Мне *не́куда идти́*. 'I have nowhere to go.'

Мне *не́откуда ждать* пи́сем. 'There is nowhere for me to expect letters from.'

Мне *не́кому э́то сказа́ть*. 'I've nobody to tell that.'

Ей *не́ с кем поговори́ть*. 'She has nobody to speak to.'

Ему́ *не́ о ком вспо́мнить*. 'He has no one to remember.'

Note. — The infinitive may also follow numerous nouns having the same lexical meaning as the verbs listed in I (b), I (c) and II: *возмо́жность (невозмо́жность) рабо́тать* 'a possibility (an impossibility) of working', *уме́ние (неуме́ние) рисова́ть* 'an ability (an inability) to draw', *жела́ние, стремле́ние учи́ться* 'a wish, an aspiration, a desire to learn', *мечта́ пое́хать* 'a dream of going', *наме́рение занима́ться* спо́ртом 'intention to take up sport', *разреше́ние вы́ехать* 'permission to leave', *боя́знь простуди́ться* 'the fear of catching cold', *про́сьба сесть* 'a request to take a seat', *разреше́ние кури́ть* 'permission to smoke', *прика́з собра́ться* 'an order to assemble,' *запреще́ние уходи́ть* 'prohibition to leave', *предложе́ние уе́хать* 'a suggestion to leave', *сове́т занима́ться* спо́ртом 'advice to take up sport.'

(For the use of the imperfective and perfective infinitives, see following tables.)

Table 79

Use of the Imperfective Infinitive

The verbs given below may be followed only by an imperfective infinitive:

нача́ть, начина́ть 'to begin'	Вчера́ мы *на́чали занима́ться* в 8 часо́в утра́. 'Yesterday our classes began at 8 o'clock in the morning.'
	Обы́чно мы *начина́ем занима́ться* в 9 часо́в утра́. 'Our classes usually begin at 9 o'clock in the morning.'
стать 'to begin'	Мы *ста́ли занима́ться* физкульту́рой. 'We began doing P.T. exercises.'
ко́нчить, конча́ть 'to finish'	Вчера́ мы *ко́нчили занима́ться* в 6 часо́в ве́чера. 'Yesterday our classes were over at 6 o'clock in the evening.'
	Обы́чно мы *конча́ем занима́ться* в 5 часо́в ве́чера. 'Our classes are usually over at 5 o'clock in the evening.'
прекрати́ть, прекраща́ть 'to cease', 'to stop'	*Прекрати́те разгова́ривать!* 'Stop talking!'
переста́ть, перестава́ть 'to stop'	Больно́й *переста́л стона́ть.* 'The patient stopped groaning.'
продолжа́ть 'to continue'	Мы *продолжа́ли* оживлённо *разгова́ривать* и на у́лице. 'We continued our animated conversation even in the street.'
привы́кнуть, привыка́ть 'to get used'	Я *привы́к встава́ть* ле́том в 6 часо́в утра́. 'I am used to get-

247

ting up at 6 o'clock in the morning in summer.'

Я постепе́нно *привыка́л встава́ть* ра́но у́тром. 'I gradually got used to getting up early in the morning.'

отвы́кнуть, отвыка́ть 'to grow out (fall out) of the habit of'

Я *отвы́к встава́ть* ра́но. 'I've lost the habit of getting up early.'

Я постепе́нно *отвыка́л встава́ть* ра́но. 'I gradually lost the habit of getting up early.'

полюби́ть 'to grow fond of'

Я *полюби́л гуля́ть* вечера́ми вдоль реки́. 'I grew fond of walking along the river bank in the evening.'

разлюби́ть 'to cease to like'

Я *разлюби́л чита́ть* стихи́. 'I ceased to like reading poetry.'

научи́ться 'to learn'

Сестра́ с де́тства *научи́лась бе́гать* на конька́х и лы́жах. 'My sister learnt to skate and ski when a child.'

разучи́ться 'to forget (how to do)'

Я *разучи́лся говори́ть* по-неме́цки. 'I have forgotten how to speak German.'

Я постепе́нно *разучи́лся говори́ть* по-неме́цки. 'I gradually forgot how to speak German.'

надое́сть, надоеда́ть 'to be tiring', 'to be boring'

К концу́ ле́та нам *надое́ло отдыха́ть.* 'Towards the end of the summer we got tired of resting.'

Обы́чно к концу́ ле́та нам *надоеда́ло отдыха́ть.* 'We usually got tired of resting towards the end of summer.'

уста́ть, устава́ть 'to get tired'

Больно́й *уста́л сиде́ть.* 'The patient got tired of sitting up.'

Больно́й обы́чно о́чень ско́ро *устава́л сиде́ть.* 'Usually the patient very soon got tired of sitting up.'

избега́ть 'to avoid'

Я *избега́ю встреча́ться* с ним. 'I avoid meeting him.'

Note. — 1. The verbs *продолжáть* 'to continue' and *избегáть* 'to avoid' are followed by an infinitive only when they are in the imperfective aspect. When in the perfective aspect, they can be followed only by a verbal noun, e.g., Мы *продóлжили обсуждéние* вопрóса. 'We continued discussing the problem.' Я *избежáл встрéчи* с ним. 'I avoided meeting him.'

A verbal noun may also follow an imperfective verb: Мы *продолжáли обсуждéние* вопрóса. 'We continued discussing the question.' Я *избегáл встрéчи* с ним. 'I avoided meeting him.'

2. The perfective verbs *полюбúть* 'to grow fond (of),' *разлюбúть* 'to cease to like', and *научúться* 'to learn', *разучúться* 'to forget (how to do)' are followed by an imperfective infinitive (Я *полюбúл говорúть* с ним. 'I grew fond of speaking to him.' Я *разлюбúл читáть* стихú. 'I ceased to like reading poetry.' etc.), but the corresponding imperfective verbs may be followed by either an imperfective or perfective infinitive (я *любúл говорúть* с ним 'I liked to talk with him', я *любúл поговорúть* с ним 'I liked to have a chat with him'; я *любúл читáть* стихú 'I liked to read poetry', я *любúл почитáть* стихú 'I liked to read some poetry').

Table 80

Use of Only the Imperfective Aspect in the Compound Predicate after Words denoting Inexpediency

не нáдо (не нýжно) 'one should not', 'one must not'	*Не нáдо* так грóмко *говорúть*: ты мне мешáешь. 'You must not speak so loud: you are disturbing me.'
не слéдует 'one should not'	*Не слéдует задéрживать* кнúгу: онá всем нужнá. 'You should not keep the book too long: everybody wants it.'
не стóит '(it is) not worth'	*Не стóит смотрéть* этот фильм: он неинтерéсный. 'This film is not worth seeing: it's not interesting.'
достáточно '(it is) enough'	*Достáточно говорúть* на эту тéму: всё ясно. 'Enough speaking on this subject: everything is clear.'
нé к чему *нéзачем* *нé за что* *нéчего* } in the sense of *не нáдо*	*Нé к чему* с ним *спóрить*. 'It's no use arguing with him.'
	Нéзачем тебé *уезжáть*. 'You should not leave.'
	Нé за что меня *благодарúть*. 'There's nothing to thank me for.'
	Нéчего меня *уговáривать*: я не пойдý в кинó. 'It's no use trying to persuade me: I won't go to the cinema.'

| *вре́дно* '(it is) harmful' | Тебе́ *вре́дно кури́ть*. 'Smoking is bad for you.' |
| *бесполе́зно* '(it is) useless' | *Бесполе́зно учи́ть* его́ пе́нию: у него́ о́чень плохо́й слух. 'It is useless to teach him singing: he has a very bad ear for music.' |

Note. — 1. Since interrogative sentences of the type *Не на́до ли нам навести́ть больно́го?* 'Shouldn't we visit the sick man? *Не сле́дует ли посла́ть поздравле́ние?* 'Shouldn't a message of congratulation be sent?' convey persuasion or a desire to perform an action, the perfective infinitive is used, just as in sentences of the type: *Нам на́до навести́ть больно́го.* 'We must visit the sick man.' *Сле́дует посла́ть поздравле́ние.* 'A message of congratulation must be sent.'
2. Since interrogative sentences of the type *Заче́м его́ ждать? Сам придёт.* 'Why should you (we) wait for him? He'll come by himself.' *Заче́м ему́ обо всём расска́зывать?* Он о́чень расстро́ится. 'Why should you (we) tell him about everything? He'll get upset,' convey the idea of inexpediency (*не на́до ждать* 'you (we) should not wait', *не на́до расска́зывать* 'you (we) should not tell') the imperfective infinitive is used.

Table 81

Use of the Imperfective or Perfective Infinitive in Sentences expressing Prohibition or Impossibility to Perform an Action

I. Meaning of the word *нельзя́* according to the Aspect of the Infinitive:

Нельзя́ + an imperfective infinitive (*нельзя́* has the meaning of 'it is prohibited', 'one must not', 'one should not'):	*Нельзя́* + a perfective infinitive (*нельзя́* has the meaning of 'it is impossible', 'one cannot'):
Нельзя́ переходи́ть у́лицу во вре́мя движе́ния маши́н. 'One must not cross the street when there is traffic.'	У́лицу по́сле дождя́ *нельзя́ бы́ло перейти́:* посреди́ была́ огро́мная лу́жа. 'It was impossible to cross the street after the rain: there was a huge puddle in the middle of the roadway.'
В ко́мнату *нельзя́ входи́ть* в пальто́. 'It is not allowed to (one must not) enter the room in one's overcoat.'	В ко́мнату *нельзя́ войти́:* дверь заперта́. 'You cannot enter the room: the door is locked.'
Нельзя́ дотра́гиваться до электри́ческих проводо́в. 'You must not touch electric wires.'	До утюга́ *нельзя́ дотро́нуть-ся:* тако́й он горя́чий. 'It is impossible to touch the iron: it is so hot.'

II. Prohibition of an Action:	Impossibility of an Action:
Туда́ *не подходи́ть!* Опа́сно! 'You must not go near there! It is dangerous!' *Не брать* ничего́ со стола́! 'Nothing must be taken from the table!' *Не сади́ться* в э́том ряду́! 'You must not sit in this row!'	Туда́ *не подойти́,* там мно́го наро́ду. 'You cannot go near there as there are too many people!' *Не взять* мне сего́дня биле́та: опозда́л. 'I shan't manage to get a ticket today: I am late.' *Не сесть* в э́том ряду́: все места́ за́няты. 'I shan't be able to take a seat in this row: all the seats have been taken'.

Table 82

Use of the Imperfective or Perfective Infinitive after Verbs denoting Persuasion or Intention to Perform an Action

1. Comparative Table on the Use of Imperfective and Perfective Infinitives (preceded by the negative *не* or not):

Infinitive Not Preceded by the Negative	Infinitive Preceded by the Negative
Мать *проси́ла вы́звать* до́ктора. 'The mother asked for a doctor to be called.' Врач *посове́товал* больно́му *приня́ть* снотво́рное. 'The doctor advised the patient to take a sleeping drug.' Он *уговори́л* меня́ *оста́ться.* 'He persuaded me to stay.' Ма́тери *разреши́ли провести́* э́ту ночь о́коло больно́го. 'The mother was allowed to stay at the patient's bedside that night.' Дире́ктор шко́лы *распоряди́л-ся измени́ть* расписа́ние заня-	Мать *проси́ла не вызыва́ть* до́ктора. 'The mother asked that the doctor should not be called.' Врач *посове́товал* больно́му *не принима́ть* снотво́рного. 'The doctor advised the patient not to take the sleeping drug.' Он *уговори́л* меня́ *не оста-ва́ться.* 'He persuaded me not to stay.' Санита́рке *разреши́ли не про-води́ть* э́ту ночь (э́той но́чи) о́коло больно́го. 'The hospital nurse was allowed to stay away from the patient's bedside that night.' Дире́ктор шко́лы *распоряди́л-ся не изменя́ть* расписа́ние за-

251

Infinitive Not Preceded by the Negative	Infinitive Preceded by the Negative
тий. 'The director of the school ordered the time-table to be changed.'	нятий. 'The director of the school ordered the time-table not to be changed.'
Я *просил* его *познакомить* меня с этим человеком. 'I asked him to introduce me to that man.'	Я *просил* его *не знакомить* меня с этим человеком. 'I asked him not to introduce me to that man.'
Товарищ *убедил* меня *купить* телевизор. 'My friend persuaded me to buy a T.V. set.'	Товарищ *убедил* меня *не покупать* телевизора. 'My friend persuaded me not to buy a T.V. set.'
Я *обещал вернуться* сегодня домой до пяти часов вечера. 'I promised to be back home before 5 o'clock in the evening.'	Я *обещал не возвращаться* сегодня домой до пяти часов вечера. 'I promised not to be back home before 5 o'clock in the evening.'
Я *даю* тебе *слово написать* ему о нашей встрече. 'I give you my word that I'll write to him about our meeting.'	Я *даю* тебе *слово не писать* ему о нашей встрече. 'I give you my word that I won't write to him about our meeting.'
Мы *условились встретиться* завтра. 'We agreed to meet tomorrow.'	Мы *условились не встречаться* завтра. 'We agreed not to meet tomorrow.'
Мы *решили уехать* после экзаменов домой. 'We decided to go home after the examinations.'	Мы *решили не уезжать* после экзаменов домой. 'We decided not to go home after the examinations.'
Я *хотел бы провести* лето на берегу моря. 'I should like to spend the summer at the seaside.'	Я *хотел бы не проводить* лета на берегу моря, а провести его в горах. 'I should like to spend the summer not at the seaside, but in the mountains.'
Преподаватель *намерен увеличить* количество занятий в неделю. 'The teacher intends to increase the number of lessons a week.'	Преподаватель *намерен не увеличивать* количества занятий в неделю. 'The teacher does not intend to increase the number of lessons a week.'
Отец *дал* мне твёрдое *обещание взять* меня на охоту. 'My father promised me quite definitely to take me to a hunting party.'	Отец *дал* матери твёрдое *обещание не брать* меня на охоту. 'My father promised my mother quite definitely not to take me to the hunting party.'

Note. — 1. If an infinitive used with verbs expressing persuasion to perform an action (*просить* 'to ask' — *попросить, советовать* 'to advise' — *посоветовать, разрешать* 'to allow' — *разрешить*, etc.) or with verbs expressing intention to perform an action (*решать* 'to decide' — *решить, обещать* 'to promise', *хотеть* 'to want' — *захотеть*, etc.) is not preceded by the negative particle, it may be either in the perfective or the imperfective aspect, according to the general meaning of the statement, e.g., Я обещал всегда *возвращаться* (imperfective) домой к пяти часам (recurrent action) 'I promised always to be back home by five o'clock', but: Я обещал *вернуться* (perfective) домой к пяти часам (action performed on a single occasion) 'I promised to be back home by five o'clock.'

Матери разрешили *проводить* (imperfective) ночи около больного (the statement implies that the mother was allowed to stay at the patient's bedside all the time, i.e., without limitation of time) 'The mother was allowed to stay at the patient's bedside at night'; but: Матери разрешили *провести* (perfective) около больного две ночи, несколько ночей (in this statement a definite time limit is implied) 'The mother was allowed to stay at the patient's bedside two nights, several nights.'

2. If an infinitive referring to the above verbs (*просить* 'to ask', *советовать* 'to advise', *решить* 'to decide', *обещать* 'to promise', etc.) is preceded by the negative particle *не,* it is generally imperfective. (For examples, see the above table.)

One cannot say Мать *просила не вызвать* доктора or Товарищ *убедил* меня *не купить* телевизор, but must say instead: Мать *просила не вызывать* доктора. 'The mother asked that the doctor should not be called.' Товарищ *убедил* меня *не покупать* телевизор. 'My friend persuaded me not to buy a T.V. set.' (For some uses of the perfective infinitive preceded by the negative particle and a verb, see the following table.)

II. Meaning of Sentences depending on the Aspect of the Infinitive preceded by the Negative Particle:

Persuasion not to perform an action:		Persuasion not to perform an action plus warning against involuntarily performing the action:	
Imperfective		Perfective	
Прошу тебя 'I ask you' *Советую* тебе 'I advise you' *Приказываю* тебе 'I order you' *Предлагаю* тебе 'I suggest that you' *Требую* от тебя 'I insist that you'	*не говорить* никому о болезни нашего друга. 'not to tell anybody about our friend's illness.' *не говорить* никому о болезни нашего друга. 'should not tell anybody about our friend's illness.'	*Прошу* вас 'I ask you' *Советую* вам 'I advise you'	(как-нибудь случайно) *не проговориться, не сказать* о болезни нашего друга. 'not to say anything (by accident) about our friend's illness to anyone.' (See Note 1)

253

A desire or determination not to perform an action:	A desire not to perform an action plus apprehension that the undesired action may take place:

Стара́юсь 'I try'
Пыта́юсь 'I try'
Обеща́ю 'I promise'
Обязу́юсь 'I pledge'
Кляну́сь 'I swear'
} *не де́лать* оши́бок. 'not to make any mistakes.'

Стара́юсь 'I try'
Пыта́юсь 'I try'
} (ка́к-нибудь случа́йно) *не сде́лать* оши́бок, 'not to make any mistakes by accident.'

(see Note 2)

Note. — 1. The meaning of warning is not generally expressed by an infinitive with a verb denoting an explicit order (*прика́зывать* 'to order', *тре́бовать* 'to demand').

2. Apprehension that an undesired action may take place is not generally expressed by an infinitive with a verb denoting a firm promise (*обязу́юсь* 'I pledge', *кляну́сь* 'I swear', *даю́ че́стное сло́во* 'I give my word of honour').

THE PRESENT TENSE

Table 83

Verbs of the First Conjugation			Verbs of the Second Conjugation		
		Endings			Endings
идти́ 'to go'	*рабо́тать* 'to work'		*стуча́ть* 'to knock'	*стро́ить* 'to build'	
я иду́	рабо́таю	*-у, -ю*	стучу́	стро́ю	*-у, -ю*
ты идёшь	рабо́таешь	*-ёшь, -ешь*	стучи́шь	стро́ишь	*-ишь*
он она́ } идёт оно́	рабо́тает	*-ёт, -ет*	стучи́т	стро́ит	*-ит*
мы идём	рабо́таем	*-ём, -ем*	стучи́м	стро́им	*-им*
вы идёте	рабо́таете	*-ёте, -ете*	стучи́те	стро́ите	*-ите*
они́ иду́т	рабо́тают	*-ут, -ют*	стуча́т	стро́ят	*-ат, -ят*

Note. — 1. The present tense has a stem of its own which is not formed regularly from other verb stems; therefore, to make verbal forms correctly, one must know not only the stem of the infinitive but also the stem of the present tense. Verbs having identical infinitive stems may have different present tense stems (*писа́ть* 'to write' — *пишу́* 'I write', *чита́ть* 'to read' — *чита́ю* 'I read'; *лить* 'to pour' — *лью* 'I pour'; *гнить* 'to rot' — *гнию́* 'I rot' (see Tables 106-107). The first and the second person singular of the present tense may have different stems, the third person singular and all the persons plural being formed from the stem of the second person singular (*люблю́* 'I love', *лю́бишь* 'you love' — *лю́бит* 'he loves', etc.).

According to the peculiarities of these two stems, all Russian verbs may be classed into several groups (see Tables 106-107).

2. From the stem of the present tense are formed: the imperative mood (*изу-чáй* 'study'), the present participles active and passive (*изучáющий* 'studying', *изучáемый* 'studied') and the imperfective verbal adverb (*изучáя* 'studying'). Exception: the verbal adverb of the verbs with the suffix *-ва-* after the roots *да-, зна-, ста-* is formed from the stem of the infinitive (see Table 121).

3. According to their personal endings verbs are classed into two groups: (1) verbs of the first conjugation, with the personal endings *-у (-ю), -ешь, -ет; -ем, -ете, -ут (-ют)* (or *-ёшь, -ёт; -ём, -ёте,* when the endings are stressed) and (2) verbs of the second conjugation, with the personal endings *-у (-ю), -ишь, -ит; -им, -ите, -ат (-ят)*.

Some forms of the verbs *хотéть* 'to want', *бежáть* 'to run', *чтить* 'to honour' conform to the first conjugation and others to the second conjugation.

хотéть		бежáть		чтить	
я хочý ты хóчешь он онá } хóчет онó	мы хотúм вы хотúте онú хотя́т	я бегý ты бежúшь он онá } бежúт онó	мы бежúм вы бежúте онú бегýт	я чту ты чтишь он онá } чтит онó	мы чтим вы чтúте онú чтут

Table 84

Verbs with Unstressed Endings

If the stress does not fall on the personal endings, the conjugation (first or second) to which a verb belongs may be determined from the infinitive:

Verbs of the First Conjugation	Verbs of the Second Conjugation
1. One verb with the infinitive ending in *-ить:* *брить* 'to shave' (*брéешь, брéют*).	1. All verbs with the infinitive ending in *-ить* (with the single exception of *брить* 'to shave'): *стрóить* 'to build' (*стрóю, стрóишь, стрóят*) *ходúть* 'to walk' (*хожý, хóдишь, хóдят*) *белúть* 'to whitewash' (*белю́, бé-лишь, бéлят*)
2. All verbs with the infinitive ending in *-еть:* *краснéть* 'to redden' (*краснéю, краснéешь, краснéют*) *белéть* 'to turn white' (*белéю, белéешь, белéют*) (with the exception of seven verbs).	2. Seven verbs with the infinitive ending in *-еть:* *смотрéть* 'to look' (*смотрю́, смóтришь, смóтрят*) *вúдеть* 'to see' (*вúжу, вúдишь, вúдят*)

Verbs of the First Conjugation	Verbs of the Second Conjugation
	ненави́деть 'to hate' (*ненави́жу, ненави́дишь, ненави́дят*)
	терпе́ть 'to endure' (*терплю́, те́рпишь, те́рпят*)
	оби́деть 'to offend' (*оби́жу, оби́дишь, оби́дят*)
	верте́ть 'to turn round' (*верчу́, ве́ртишь, ве́ртят*)
	зави́сеть 'to depend' (*зави́шу, зави́сишь, зави́сят*)
	as well as their derivatives formed by means of prefixes: *посмотре́ть* 'to have a look', *уви́деть* 'to see', *вы́терпеть* 'to endure', etc.
3. All verbs with the infinitive ending in *-ать:*	3. Four verbs with the infinitive ending in *-ать:*
отвеча́ть 'to answer' (*отвеча́ю, отвеча́ешь, отвеча́ют*)	*дыша́ть* 'to breathe' (*дышу́, ды́шишь, ды́шат*)
лома́ть 'to break' (*лома́ю, лома́ешь, лома́ют*)	*слы́шать* 'to hear' (*слы́шу, слы́шишь, слы́шат*)
(with the exception of four verbs).	*держа́ть* 'to hold' (*держу́, де́ржишь, де́ржат*)
	гнать 'to drive' (*гоню́, го́нишь, го́нят*)
	as well as their derivatives formed by means of prefixes: *поды-ша́ть* 'to breathe', *услы́шать* 'to hear', *вы́держать* 'to endure', *согна́ть* 'to drive off'.

All other verbs belong to the first conjugation.

Note. — Perfective verbs with the prefix *вы-* are invariably stressed on the prefix; verbs with the stressed prefix *вы-*(*вы́беру* 'to choose' — *вы́берешь, вы́берут*) belong to the same conjugation as corresponding verbs without the prefix (*беру́* 'I take' — *берёшь, берёт*).

Table 85

Uses of the Present Tense

1. To express an action taking place at the moment of speaking:	Куда́ вы *идёте?* 'Where are you going?' Иду́ домо́й. 'I am going home.' Что вы *де́лаете?* 'What are you doing?' Пишу́ письмо́. 'I am writing a letter.'
2. To express a habitual or recurrent action:	Каки́е ле́кции вы *посеща́ете?* 'What lectures do you attend?' Я *посеща́ю* ле́кции профе́ссора N. 'I attend Professor N.'s lectures.' Уже́ год я *занима́юсь* ру́сским языко́м. 'I have been studying Russian for a year already.' Что вы *де́лаете* в свобо́дные дни? 'What do you do on your days off?' *Хожу́* в теа́тр, *посеща́ю* музе́и, вы́ставки. 'I go to the theatre, visit museums, exhibitions.'
3. To express an action: (a) permanently characterizing its agent:	Пти́цы *лета́ют.* 'Birds fly.' Зме́и *по́лзают.* 'Snakes crawl.' Зо́лото *не ржа́веет.* 'Gold does not rust.'
(b) which indicates an ability (inability) or capacity (incapacity) of a person or thing:	Он хорошо́ *говори́т* по-ру́сски. 'He speaks Russian well.' Ма́льчик вырази́тельно *чита́ет* стихи́. 'The boy recites poetry with expression.' Я *не ката́юсь* на конька́х. 'I don't skate.'

Table 86

Use of the Present Tense to Express a Past or Future Action

1. The present tense is used with a past meaning to lend vividness to the narration:	Вчера́ я *был* у това́рища. *Сиди́м* мы, *разгова́риваем,* вдруг *слы́шим:* кто́-то *сту́чится...* 'Yesterday I was at my friend's. We sat talking, suddenly we heard someone knocking...'

. . . .

Пе́рвый день я *провёл* о́чень ску́чно; на друго́й день у́тром *въезжа́ет* во двор пово́зка... А! Макси́м Макси́мыч!... Мы *встре́тились* как ста́рые прия́тели. (Л.) 'The first day I spent there was very dull; next morning a carriage drove into the yard... Ah! It was Maxim Maximych!.. We greeted each other like old pals.'

Сего́дня я *встал* по́здно: *прихожу́* к коло́дцу — никого́ уже́ нет. (Л.) 'I got up late today: I came to the well — there was already nobody there.'

Приходи́л он к нам ча́сто. *Сиди́т, быва́ло, и расска́зывает*... 'He used to come to see us often. He would sit and tell us...'

. . . .

...*Быва́ло*, он меня́ *не замеча́ет*, а я *стою́* у две́ри и *ду́маю*:
Бе́дный, бе́дный стари́к! Нас мно́го, мы *игра́ем*, нам ве́село, а он — оди́н-одинёшенек... (Л. Т.) '...He would fail to notice me, and I would stand at the door and think:
"Poor, poor old man! There are so many of us, and we play and feel gay and happy, and he — he is all alone..."'

За́втра *лети́м* в Ленингра́д. 'We fly to Leningrad tomorrow.'

Сего́дня ве́чером *иду́* в теа́тр. 'Tonight I am going to the theatre.'

. . . .

Я *реши́ла* бесповоро́тно. Жре́бий бро́шен, я *поступа́ю* на сце́ну. За́втра меня́ уже́ не бу́дет здесь. Я *ухожу́* от отца́, *покида́ю* всё, *начина́ю* но́вую жизнь... Я *уезжа́ю*, как и вы, в Москву́... (Ч.) 'I decided irrevocably. The die is cast, I go on the stage. Tomorrow I will have left here. I leave my father, abandon all and everything and begin a new life... I leave for Moscow, as you do...'

To express a recurrent action which took place a long time ago (in this case the present tense is combined with the word *быва́ло* 'used to', 'would'):

2. The present tense is used with a future meaning when it denotes an action (mainly expressed by a verb of motion) firmly decided upon:

THE PAST TENSE

Infinitive: *изучáть, изучúть* 'to study', *стрóить, построúть* 'to build'

Imperfective Aspect		Perfective Aspect		
я, ты, он изучáл	стрóил	изучúл	построúл	*-л*
я, ты, онá изучáла	стрóила	изучúла	построúла	*-л-а*
онó изучáло	стрóило	изучúло	построúло	*-л-о*
мы вы они изучáли	стрóили	изучúли	построúли	*-л-и*

Note. — 1. The past tense is formed from the stem of the infinitive by adding the suffix *-л* (*рабóтать* 'to work' — *рабóтал, мыть* 'to wash' — *мыл*).
2. Verbs in the past tense change according to number: *я рабóтал* 'I worked', *мы рабóтали* 'we worked' and, in the singular, according to gender: *он рабóтал* 'he worked', *онá рабóтала* 'she worked', *онó рабóтало* 'it worked', but not according to person.

Table 88

Some Peculiarities in the Formation of the Past Tense

1. Verbs ending in *-сти* (*-зти*)	2. Verbs ending in *-чь*	3. Verbs ending in *-нуть*
Infinitive		
нестú 'to carry' везтú 'to carry (in a vehicle)' грестú 'to row' вестú 'to lead' плестú 'to weave'	мочь 'to be able', 'can' печь 'to bake' стерéчь 'to guard'	погúбнуть 'to perish' исчéзнуть 'to disappear' ослéпнуть 'to go blind'
Past Tense		
я, ты, он нёс, вёз, грёб, вёл, плёл	мог, пёк, стерёг	погúб, исчéз, ослéп
я, ты, онá неслá, везлá, греблá, велá, плелá	моглá, пеклá, стереглá	погúбла, исчéзла, ослéпла
онó неслó, везлó, греблó, велó, плелó	моглó, пеклó, стереглó	погúбло, исчéзло, ослéпло
мы, вы, они неслú везлú, греблú, велú, плелú	моглú, пеклú, стереглú	погúбли, исчéзли, ослéпли

Note. — 1. Verbs ending in *-сти* in the infinitive and having no *д, т* at the end of the present tense stem (*нести* 'to carry' — *несу́*, *везти́* 'to carry (in a vehicle)' — *везу́*) do not take the past tense suffix *-л* in the masculine singular, but end in the stem consonant. For example: *нести́ — несу́ — нёс; везти́ — везу́ — вёз*.

However, if verbs ending in *-сти* in the infinitive have *д* or *т* at the end of the present tense stem, the suffix *-л* of the past tense immediately follows the stem vowel. For example: *вести́* 'to lead' — *веду́ — вёл; плести́* 'to weave' — *плету́ — плёл*.

2. Verbs ending in *-чь* in the infinitive (*бере́чь* 'to take care', *печь* 'to bake') have the past tense stem ending in *г, к (берёг, пёк)* and do not take the suffix *-л* in the masculine.

3. A number of verbs with the suffix *-ну-* drop this suffix in the past (*погибнуть* 'to perish' — *погиб; исчезнуть* 'to disappear' — *исчез*). *-ну-* is dropped in the past tense mainly in verbs which, when unprefixed, are imperfective: *сохнуть* 'to dry' — *сох*, *мёрзнуть* 'to freeze' — *мёрз*, *крепнуть* 'to get stronger' — *креп*.

The suffix *-л* does not occur in the masculine if the stem ends in a consonant.

4. *-л* does not occur in the past tense in the masculine gender of verbs having *-ере-* in the infinitive (*умере́ть* 'to die' — *у́мер*, *запере́ть* 'to lock' — *за́пер*, *тере́ть* 'to rub' — *тёр*).

Table 89

Comparative Table on the Uses of the Past Tense of Imperfective and Perfective Verbs

Imperfective Aspect	Perfective Aspect
I. Used to express an action which lasted a certain time or recurred in the past:	**I.** Used to express a completed action or an action which occurred on a single occasion:
В э́том году́ я мно́го *чита́л, писа́л* диссерта́цию. 'This year I have been reading a lot and have been writing my thesis.'	В э́том году́ я *прочита́л* мно́го книг, *написа́л* диссерта́цию. 'This year I read many books and wrote my thesis.'
Я обы́чно *встава́л* в 7 часо́в, *умыва́лся, одева́лся, за́втракал* и *шёл* на ле́кцию. 'I usually got up at 7 o'clock, washed, dressed, had my breakfast and went to attend a lecture.'	Сего́дня я *встал* в 7 часо́в, *умы́лся, оде́лся, поза́втракал* и *пошёл* на ле́кцию. 'Today I got up at 7 o'clock, washed, dressed, had my breakfast and went to attend the lecture.'
Шуме́ли дере́вья, *лил* дождь, река́ *волнова́лась*. 'The trees were rustling, the rain was pouring, the river was agitated.'	*Зашуме́ли* дере́вья, *поли́л* дождь, река́ *заволнова́лась*. 'The trees began to rustle, it started raining, the river got agitated.'
II. Used to denote an action which occurred in the past and is wholly unconnected with the present:	**II.** Used to denote an action completed in the past but associated by its result with the present (perfective meaning):

Imperfective Aspect	Perfective Aspect
К вам кто́-то *приходи́л* (means that the person who called on you is not here now). Я *брал* э́ту кни́гу у това́рища (means that I have already given the book back to my friend). Я *открыва́л* окно́ (means that the window was opened but is now closed).	К вам кто́-то *пришёл* (means that someone has come to see you and is now at your place). Я *взял* э́ту кни́гу у това́рища (means that I have borrowed the book from my friend and I still have it). Я *откры́л* окно́ (means I opened the window and it is still open).

Note. — The past tense of perfective verbs used in a perfective meaning often occurs, alongside verbs in the present tense, in descriptions of the present: Осень. Лес опусте́л. Ве́тер кача́ет верху́шки дере́вьев. Ли́стья пожелте́ли и па́дают. 'It is autumn. The wood is deserted. The wind is shaking the crowns of the trees. The leaves have turned yellow and are falling.'

Table 90

Use of the Past Tense with the Words *быва́ло* and *бы́ло*

1. The past tense of imperfective verbs is used with the word *быва́ло* to express an action which recurred a long time ago: 2. The past tense of imperfective and perfective verbs is used with the word *бы́ло* to express actions which were intended but were not performed or actions whose performance was interrupted:	Он, *быва́ло*, *приходи́л* к нам по вечера́м, *сади́лся* в саду́ и *расска́зывал* нам что́-нибудь интере́сное из свое́й жи́зни. 'He used to come to see us in the evening, he would sit in the garden and tell us something interesting from his life.' Я *хоте́л было* сказа́ть ему́ де́рзость, но сдержа́лся. 'I wanted to say something rude to him but checked myself.' Я *собира́лся было* пое́хать э́тим ле́том на́ море, но обстоя́тельства помеша́ли. 'I intended to go to the seaside this summer, but circumstances did not allow me to.' Мы *пошли́ было* в кино́, но нас задержа́ли. 'We wanted to go to the cinema, but were detained.'

Note. — The infinitive used with a past tense form plus the word *бы́ло* is usually a perfective one (хоте́л было *сказа́ть* 'I (he) wanted to say', собира́лся было *пое́хать* 'I (he) intended to go').

Table 91

Use of the Past Tense with Future Meaning

In colloquial Russian, the past tense of perfective verbs (usually verbs of motion) is occasionally used with a future meaning to make the statement more categoric:	Я *пошёл*, вернусь скоро. 'I am going, I'll be back soon.' Ну, я *поехал* на вокзал за билетами, а ты приедешь к отходу поезда. 'Well, I am off to the station to get tickets, and you'll come before the train leaves.' Если нам не помогут, мы *пропали.* 'If they don't help us we are done for.'

THE FUTURE TENSE

Table 92

Compound Future			Simple Future	
я буду читать			прочитаю	
ты будешь читать			прочитаешь	
он, она, оно будет читать			прочитает	
мы будем читать			прочитаем	
вы будете читать			прочитаете	
они будут читать			прочитают	
я буду	изучать	выполнять	изучу	выполню
ты будешь	изучать	выполнять	изучишь	выполнишь
он она } будет оно	изучать	выполнять	изучит	выполнит
мы будем	изучать	выполнять	изучим	выполним
вы будете	изучать	выполнять	изучите	выполните
они будут	изучать	выполнять	изучат	выполнят

Note. — 1. Only imperfective verbs have the compound future.

2. The compound future is formed by means of the future tense of the auxiliary verb (*буду, будешь*, etc.) plus the infinitive of the verb to be conjugated.

Note. — 1. Only perfective verbs have the simple future.

2. The personal endings of the simple future are identical with those of the present tense of imperfective verbs.

Table 93

Meaning of the Simple and the Compound Future

1. The compound future expresses an action which will occur in the future but it does not specify whether that action will be completed: я *бу́ду чита́ть* кни́гу 'I shall read the book' я *бу́ду изуча́ть* язы́к 'I shall study the language' я *бу́ду писа́ть* письмо́ 'I shall write a letter'	1. The simple future shows either that the action will be completed in the future: я *прочита́ю* кни́гу 'I shall read the book (from beginning to end)' я *изучу́* язы́к 'I shall learn the language (thoroughly)' я *напишу́* письмо́ 'I shall write a letter (from beginning to end)' or that it will begin: я *запою́* 'I shall begin singing' я *закричу́* 'I shall begin shouting'
2. The compound future is never used to mean any other tense.	2. For the uses of the simple future, see the following table.

Table 94

Uses of the Simple Future

I. To denote the possibility or impossibility of an action.

1. To express the possibility of an action, the ability to perform an action:	То́лько он *отве́тит* на э́тот вопро́с. 'Only he can answer this question.' Он на все ру́ки ма́стер: и электри́чество *проведёт*, и часы́ *почи́нит*, и ме́бель *смастери́т*. 'He is a Jack-of-all-trades: he can wire up electricity, mend a watch or a clock, make furniture.'
2. To express the impossibility of an action, the inability to perform an action (in this sense the simple future is widely used	*Не пойму́* ника́к, что ты говори́шь. 'I just can't understand what you are saying.' Ищу́ каранда́ш, ника́к *не найду́*. 'I am looking for the pencil, I just can't find it.'

263

in generalized personal sentences*):	Ему́ *не угоди́шь.* 'There is no pleasing him.' Про́шлого *не вернёшь.* 'The past cannot be revived.' Слеза́ми го́рю *не помо́жешь.* 'Tears are no help in sorrow.' Без труда́ *не вы́нешь* и ры́бку из пруда́. (Proverb) Cf. 'No pains, no gains.' . . . . — Нам придётся здесь ночева́ть, — сказа́л он с доса́дою, — в таку́ю мете́ль че́рез го́ры *не перее́дешь.* (Л.) ' "We'll have to stay here overnight," he said, much annoyed. "You can't cross the mountains in such a snow-storm." '

II. In the meaning of the present or past tense.

1. To denote momentaneous recurrent actions occurring against the background of another action:	
(a) the future used with present meaning:	Бу́ря мгло́ю не́бо кро́ет, Ви́хри сне́жные крутя́, То, как зверь, она́ *заво́ет,* То *запла́чет,* как дитя́. (П.) 'The storm spreads a haze all over the sky, Driving the blizzards, Now it howls like a beast, Now it whimpers like a child.'

---

* Generalized personal sentences are sentences in which the verb is in the second person singular (less frequently in another personal form), present or future tense, but applies to any person, singular or plural: *Лю́бишь ката́ться — люби́ и са́ночки вози́ть.* Cf. 'After the feast comes the reckoning.' *Что име́ем, не храни́м, потеря́вши — пла́чем.* Cf. 'We never know the value of water until the well is dry.'

(b) the future used with past meaning:

Ночь была́ ти́хая, сла́вная, са́мая удо́бная для езды́. Ве́тер то *прошелести́т* в куста́х, *закача́ет* ве́тки, то совсе́м *замрёт*. (Т.) 'The night was still and pleasant, very good for travelling. The wind would now rustle in the bushes, swaying the branches, now die down altogether.'

2. To denote momentaneous actions which take place regularly (or took place regularly in the past):

(a) the future used with present meaning:

Свой обы́чный день провожу́ таки́м о́бразом: встаю́ в 8 часо́в, бы́стро *оде́нусь*, *поза́втракаю* и е́ду на заня́тия. Занима́юсь до обе́да, пото́м обе́даю, *отдохну́* и иду́ в библиоте́ку. 'I spend my working day in this way: I get up at 8 o'clock, dress quickly, have my breakfast and go to my classes. I study till lunch time, then I have lunch, rest a while and go to the library.'

(b) the future used with past meaning:

Бы́ло у него́ [Бе́ликова] стра́нное обыкнове́ние — ходи́ть по на́шим кварти́рам. *Придёт* к учи́телю, *ся́дет* и молчи́т; *посиди́т* эдак мо́лча час-друго́й и *уйдёт*. (Ч.) 'He had a queer habit of coming to see us at home. He would come to a teacher's house, sit down and remain silent; and having sat thus silently for an hour or even longer he would go away.'

(The present tense *молчи́т* is also used in the sense of the past.)

(c) to denote actions which recurred a long time ago, the simple future is often used with *быва́ло* 'used to', 'would':

...И так жа́лко ста́нет, что, *быва́ло*, *подойдёшь* к нему́, *возьмёшь* за́ руки и *ска́жешь*: «Lieber Карл Ива́нович!» Он люби́л, когда́ я ему́ говори́л так: всегда́ прила́скает, и ви́дно, что растро́ган. (Л. Т.) 'And I would feel so sorry for him that I would come up to him, take his hands in mine and say: "Lieber Karl Ivanovich!" He liked it when I said that to him: he would always caress me, it was obvious he was moved.'

3. Used with the negative particle *не* in expressing absence of action in the present or the past: (a) the future used with present meaning:	Со́лнце стои́т неподви́жно над головой и жжёт траву́. Ни де́рево, ни вода́ *не шелохну́тся*, над дере́вней и по́лем лежи́т невозмути́мая тишина́. (Гонч.) 'The sun hung immovable overhead and scorched the grass. Neither a tree, nor the water stirred; an unruffled silence reigned over the village and the field.'
(b) the future used with past meaning:	Всё бы́ло ти́хо, волна́ *не поды'мется*, листо́к *не шелохнётся*. (Акс.) 'All was quiet: neither a wave would rise, nor a leaf would stir.'
4. To denote a swift and unexpected action (in combination with the particle *как*): the future used with past meaning:	Иду́ я вчера́ по у́лице, и вдруг кто́-то *как схва́тит* меня́ за́ руку. 'I was going along a street yesterday and suddenly somebody grasped my hand.' (The present tense form *иду́* is also used here in the sense of the past.) · · · · · · · · · · Гера́сим гляде́л, гляде́л, да *как засмеётся* вдруг. (Т.) 'Gerasim kept looking and suddenly burst out laughing.'

Table 95

Use of Imperfective and Perfective Verbs in a Context

Imperfective Aspect	Perfective Aspect
(a) 1. Гроза́ *надвига́лась*. Впереди́ огро́мная лило́вая ту́ча ме́дленно *поднима́лась* из-за ле́су; надо мно́ю и мне навстре́чу *несли́сь* дли́нные се́рые	(b) 1. Си́льный ве́тер внеза́пно *загуде́л* в вышине́, дере́вья *забушева́ли*, кру́пные ка́пли дождя́ ре́зко *застуча́ли*, *зашлёпали* по ли́стьям. (Т.) 'A strong wind

облака́; раки́ты трево́жно *шеве-ли́лись* и *лепета́ли*. (Т.)

'A storm was coming.

A huge violet rain-cloud was slowly rising ahead of me from behind the forest; long grey clouds were racing overhead in the direction opposite to the one I was going in; the brooms were swaying and ˄prattling in alarm.'

2. *Был* ве́чер. Не́бо *ме́ркло.* Во́ды *струи́лись* ти́хо. Жук *жужжа́л.* (П.) 'It was evening. The sky was growing dark. The waters were streaming silently. A beetle was buzzing.'

3. Между́ колёсами теле́г,
Полузаве́шанных ковра́ми,
Гори́т ого́нь; семья́ круго́м
Гото́вит у́жин; в чи́стом
по́ле
Пасу́тся ко́ни; за шатро́м
Ручно́й медве́дь *лежи́т* на
во́ле. (П.)
'Between the wheels of the
waggons,
Half-hung with rugs,
A fire is seen burning; the family
gathered round it
Are cooking their supper; the
horses are grazing
In the open field; behind the
tent
A tamed bear is lying, un-
chained and unleashed.'

4. *Приводи́ли* обыкнове́нно новичка́ к две́ри э́той ко́мнаты, неча́янно *вта́лкивали* его́ к медве́дю, две́ри *запира́лись,* и не-сча́стную же́ртву *оставля́ли* на-

suddenly began to howl in the sky, the trees began to sway violently, and large raindrops began to patter and splash on the leaves.'

5. Всё *зашевели́лось, просну́-лось, запе́ло, зашуме́ло, загово-ри́ло.* (Т.) 'Everything began to move, arose from slumber, began singing, making noise, chattering.'

6. Роня́ет лес багря́ный свой
убо́р,
Сребри́т моро́з увя́нувшее
по́ле,
Прогля́нет день как бу́дто
понево́ле,
И *скро́ется* за край окру́ж-
ных гор. (П.)
'The woods were shedding their
scarlet attire,
The frost had covered the faded
field with silver,
Daylight would appear, as if
unwillingly,
And would vanish beyond the
edge of the surrounding mountains.'

7. Дефо́рж *вы́нул* из карма́на ма́ленький пистоле́т, *вложи́л* его́ в у́хо голо́дному зве́рю и *вы́-стрелил.* Всё *сбежа́лось,* две́ри *отвори́лись* — Кири́ла Петро́вич *вошёл,* изумлённый развя́зкою свое́й шу́тки. (П.) 'Deforge took a small pistol out of his pocket, put it to the hungry beast's ear and fired. The bear fell. Everybody came running, the door was opened — Cyril Petrovich stepped in, flabbergasted at such an outcome of his joke.'

едине́ с косма́тым пусты́нником. (П.) 'They used to take a new guest to the door of that room and would push him in, as if by accident, to meet the bear; the door was then locked and the unlucky victim had to face the shaggy hermit.'

но всё *погля́дывал* на восто́к.
Ло́шади *бежа́ли* дру́жно. Ве́тер между те́м час о́т часу *станови́лся* сильне́е.
'but he kept looking at the east on and off.
The horses ran at full speed. Meanwhile the wind was growing stronger every minute.'

кото́рая тяжело́ *подыма́лась*, *росла́* и постепе́нно *облега́ла* не́бо.
'which was rising slowly, growing, and was gradually spreading all over the sky.'

8. Ямщи́к *поскака́л*;
'The coachman set the horses at a gallop'

Облако *обрати́лось* в бе́лую ту́чу,
'The cloud turned into a white snow-cloud'

Пошёл ме́лкий снег — и вдруг *повали́л* хло́пьями. Ве́тер *завы́л*, *сде́лалась* мете́ль. В одно́ мгнове́нье тёмное не́бо *смеша́лось* с сне́жным мо́рем. Всё *исче́зло*. «Ну, ба́рин, — *закрича́л* ямщи́к, — беда́: бура́н!»
Я *вы́глянул* из киби́тки:
'Fine snowflakes began to fall — and all of a sudden it began snowing hard. The wind started howling, and a snow-storm broke out. In a moment the dark sky had merged with this sea of snow. One could see nothing

around him. "Well, Your Honour," the coachman shouted, "we've come to grief: it's a blizzard." I looked out of my hooded sleigh:

всё *бы́ло* мрак и вихрь. Ве́тер *выл* с тако́й свире́пой вырази́тельностью, что *каза́лся* одушевлённым; снег *засыпа́л* меня́ и Саве́льича; ло́шади *шли* ша́гом 'all around was darkness and whirling snow. The wind was moaning with such a vicious expression that it seemed to come from a living being; the snow was burying Savelyich and myself; the horses went at a walk,

и ско́ро *ста́ли*. (П.) and presently they stopped altogether.'

Note. — Imperfective and perfective verbs are used to express consecutiveness and simultaneousness of actions:

(1) To express absolute simultaneousness, verbs of only one aspect — imperfective or perfective (generally verbs denoting the beginning of an action) — are used (for the former, see examples 1 (a), 2, 3; for the latter, see example 5).

(2) To express partial simultaneousness (when one action seems to take place against the background of another), only verbs of different aspects are used (see examples 1 (a, b), 6 and in example 8: Ве́тер между тём *станови́лся* сильне́е. Облако *обрати́лось* в бе́лую ту́чу...).

(3) To express consecutiveness of actions, (a) either only perfective verbs are used denoting consecutive completed actions (see example 7) or only imperfective ones denoting actions repeated in a certain order (see example 4); or (b) verbs of different aspects are used (see example 8: Облако *обрати́лось* в бе́лую ту́чу, кото́рая тяжело́ *подыма́лась*, *росла́* и постепе́нно *облега́ла* не́бо...).

Table 96

The Conditional-Subjunctive Mood

Imperfective Aspect			Perfective Aspect	
я, ты, он	стро́ил бы	изуча́л бы	постро́ил бы	изучи́л бы
я, ты, она́	стро́ила бы	изуча́ла бы	постро́ила бы	изучи́ла бы
оно́	стро́ило бы	изуча́ло бы	постро́ило бы	изучи́ло бы
мы вы они́	стро́или бы	изуча́ли бы	постро́или бы	изучи́ли бы

Note. — To form the conditional-subjunctive mood, the form of the past tense is used with the particle *бы*.

Table 97

Uses of the Conditional-Subjunctive Mood

1. (a) To denote an action which may take place under certain circumstances: (b) To denote a desired or planned action:	Если бы у меня было время, я *пошёл бы* сегодня в театр. 'If I had time, I should go to the theatre today.' Сегодня я занят, но завтра я с удовольствием *пошёл бы* в театр. 'Today I am busy, but tomorrow I should be very glad to go to the theatre.'
2. To express a wish, a request or a mild order:	Скорей *бы пришло* лето! 'I wish summer would come sooner!' *Пошёл бы* ты гулять! 'Why don't you go for a walk!' *Почитал бы* книгу! 'Why don't you read a book!'

Note – 1. The particle *бы* is not attached to the verb: it may take different positions in the sentence: Я с удовольствием *пошёл бы* в театр or Я *бы* с удовольствием *пошёл* в театр. 'I should be very glad to go to the theatre.'

In a complex sentence with the verb in the conditional-subjunctive mood the particle *бы* is used both in the principal and the subordinate clauses: Если *бы* у меня *было время*, я *пошёл бы* в театр. 'If I had (had) time, I should (have) go (gone) to the theatre.'

2. In impersonal sentences, an infinitive or a predicative adverb can be used with the particle *бы* in the sense of the conditional-subjunctive mood to express a desired or planned action:

Поехать бы летом на море! 'Oh, to go to the seaside in summer!'

Хорошо бы поехать летом на море! 'It would be grand to go to the seaside in summer!'

Table 98

Use of Imperfective and Perfective Verbs preceded by the Negative Particle *не* in the Conditional-Subjunctive Mood

Imperfective Aspect	Perfective Aspect
Expressing a desire not to perform an action or a wish that it should not be performed:	Expressing apprehension that an undesirable action may take place:
Не выходил бы ты сегодня на улицу: очень холодно. 'I wish you would not go out today: it is very cold.'	*Не вышел бы* больной слишком рано. 'I fear the patient may go out too early.'

Не бéгал бы ты так бы́стро: упадёшь. 'I wish you wouldn't run so fast: you may fall.'

Не éхать бы никудá! 'I wish I didn't have to go anywhere!'

Никогдá бы не ви́деть и не слы́шать э́того! 'I wish I hadn't had to see and hear all that!'

Не убежáл бы он кудá-нибудь. (*Как бы он не убежáл* кудá-нибудь.) 'Provided he does not run away somewhere.'

Не проéхать бы остано́вку. (*Как бы не проéхать* остано́вку.) 'If only I don't miss my stop.'

Не проспáть бы. (*Как бы не проспáть.*) 'If only I don't oversleep.'

Не урони́ть бы вáзу. (*Как бы не урони́ть* вáзу.) 'If only I don't drop the vase.'

Не забы́ть бы его́ телефóна. (*Как бы не забы́ть* его́ телефóна.) 'If only I don't forget his telephone number.'

Note. — 1. In expressing a wish that an action should not be performed, imperfective verbs are generally used in the conditional-subjunctive mood: *Не éхал бы* ты оди́н! *Не éхать бы* тебé одному́! 'You shouldn't go alone!'

2. In expressing apprehension that an undesirable action may take place, only perfective verbs are used in the conditional-subjunctive mood: *Не проéхал бы* ты остано́вку! *Не проéхать бы* тебé остано́вку! 'I am afraid you may miss your stop!'

3. Apprehension that an undesirable action may take place is often rendered by *как бы не* with a perfective verb: *Как бы* ты *не проéхал* остано́вку. *Как бы* тебé *не проéхать* остано́вку. 'Take care you don't miss your stop.'

Table 99

The Imperative Mood

Singular					
иди́	'go'	рабóтай	'work'	встань	'stand up'
изучи́	'learn'	изучáй	'learn'	пригото́вь	'prepare'
говори́	'speak up'	организу́й	'organize'	брось	'give up'
исчéзни	'disappear'	выполня́й	'carry out'	режь	'cut'

Note. — The imperative mood is formed from the present tense stem for imperfective verbs (*идти́* 'to go' — *идёшь* — *иди́*; *рабóтать* 'to work' — *рабóтаешь* — *рабóтай*; *рéзать* 'to cut' — *рéжешь* — *режь*) and from the future tense stem for perfective verbs (*изучи́ть* 'to learn' — *изучишь* — *изучи́*; *брóсить* 'to throw' — *брóсишь* — *брось*; *пригото́вить* 'to prepare' — *пригото́вишь* — *пригото́вь*, etc.)

The ending **-и** occurs:	**-й** at the end of the stem occurs:	A soft consonant or sibilant occurs at the end of the stem (in spelling the softness in the final stem consonant or sibilant is rendered by a **ь**):
1. In verbs which, in the first person singular, present or future tense, have a consonant before the personal endings, and which are stressed on those endings: иду́ — иди́ изучу́ — изучи́ говорю́ — говори́ If the stressed prefix **вы-** is attached to these verbs (*вы́йду* 'I shall go out', *вы́учу* 'I shall learn', *вы́скажу* 'I shall speak up', etc.) the ending is still **-и** (*вы́йди, вы́учи, вы́скажи*). 2. In verbs whose first person singular, present or simple future tense, has an **н** (before the ending) preceded by another consonant: дости́гну — дости́гни исче́зну — исче́зни све́ргну — све́ргни	1. In verbs whose first person singular, present or future tense, ends in **-ю** preceded by a vowel: рабо́таю — рабо́тай изуча́ю — изуча́й организу́ю—организу́й выполня́ю —выполня́й броса́ю — броса́й 2. In monosyllabic verbs with **и** in the stem of the infinitive (*пить* 'to drink', *лить* 'to pour', *шить* 'to sew', *бить* 'to beat'): пью — пей лью — лей шью — шей бью — бей This rule holds good when a prefix is attached to the verbs (*вы́пей, вы́лей*).	In verbs whose first person singular, present or future tense, has a consonant preceding an unstressed personal ending: вста́ну — встань ре́жу — режь бро́шу — брось пригото́влю-пригото́вь ся́ду — сядь
Plural		
иди́те изучи́те говори́те исче́зните	рабо́тайте изуча́йте организу́йте выполня́йте	вста́ньте пригото́вьте бро́сьте ре́жьте

Note. — The plural of the imperative mood is formed from the singular by adding the ending *-те*: *идú* — *идúте* 'go', *изучáй* — *изучáйте* 'learn', *встань* — *встáньте* 'stand up', etc.

Table 100

Aspect of the Imperative with and without *не*

The Imperative without *не*	The Imperative with *не*
Пожáлуйста, *открóй* сейчáс окнó. 'Please open the window now.'	Пожáлуйста, *не открывáй* сейчáс окнá. 'Please don't open the window now.'
Подойдú ко мне. 'Come over to me.'	*Не подходú* ко мне. 'Don't come over to me.'
Положúте кнúги на стол. 'Put the books on the table.	*Не кладúте* кнúги на стол. 'Don't put the books on the table.
Дай товáрищу карандáш. 'Give a pencil to your friend.'	*Не давáй* товáрищу карандáш, пусть он пúшет ручкой. 'Don't give a pencil to your friend, let him write with a pen.'
Возьмú тетрáдь домóй. 'Take the exercise-book home.'	*Не берú* тетрáдь: я дóлжен её провéрить. 'Don't take the exercise-book, I must correct it.'
Пожáлуйста, *отнесú* сегóдня кнúги в библиотéку. 'Please take the books to the library today.'	Сегóдня *не относú* кнúги в библиотéку. 'Don't return the books to the library today.'
Относú кнúги всегдá в срок. 'Always return books in time.'	

Note. — 1. If a verb in the imperative is not preceded by the negative particle *не*, it may be either of the perfective or of the imperfective aspect according to the meaning of the whole sentence, e.g.: Пожáлуйста, *возьмú* кнúги и *отнесú* их в библиотéку. 'Please take the books and return them to the library.' *Берú* кнúги всегдá в этой библиотéке. 'Always borrow books from this library.' Всегдá *относú* кнúги в срок. 'Always return books in time.'

2. If a verb in the imperative is preceded by *не*, it is generally of the imperfective aspect even though it may express an action performed on a single occasion and of very short duration: *Не берú* сейчáс эту кнúгу, я дам тебé её потóм. 'Don't take that book now, I'll let you have it afterwards.' For some uses of perfective verbs following the negative particle *не* in the imperative, see the following table.

Table 101

Aspects of the Negative Imperative

Imperfective Aspect	Perfective Aspect
Persuasion or request not to perform an action:	Warning against an undesirable action with apprehension that it may occur:
Пожа́луйста, *не хло́пай* две́рью! 'Please don't bang the door!'	*Не хло́пни* случа́йно две́рью. 'Don't bang the door by chance.'
Не бери́ мою тетра́дь. 'Don't take my exercise-book.'	*Не возьми́* случа́йно мою тетра́дь. 'Don't take my exercise-book by mistake.'
Не говори́ никому́ о том, что я тебе́ рассказа́л. 'Don't tell anyone what I've told you.'	*Не скажи́* случа́йно кому́-нибудь о том, что я тебе́ рассказа́л. 'Mind you don't tell anyone what I've told you.'
Не уходи́, прошу́ тебя́. 'Don't go, I ask you.'	*Смотри́ не уйди́*, не запере́в две́ри. 'See that you don't leave without locking the door.'
Смотри́ не па́дай, будь осторо́жен! 'See that you don't fall, be careful!'	*Смотри́ не упади́*, здесь о́чень ско́льзко. 'See you don't fall, it's very slippery here.'
Смотри́ не забыва́й нас! 'See you don't forget us!'	*Смотри́ не забу́дь* но́мер моего́ телефо́на. 'See you don't forget my telephone number.'

Note. — If the particle *смотри́* 'take care' is used to warn against an undesirable action, the verb in the imperative may be either perfective or imperfective: *Смотри́ не упади́*, здесь о́чень ско́льзко. 'See you don't fall, it's very slippery here.' *Смотри́ не па́дай*, будь осторо́жен. 'See you don't fall, be careful.'

Table 102

Aspect of the Infinitive with or without *не* used in the Sense of the Imperative

Order, command or demand to do something	Order, command or demand not to do something
Подойти́ ко мне! 'Come over to me!'	*Не подходи́ть* ко мне! 'Don't come over to me!'
Встать! 'Stand up!'	*Не встава́ть!* 'Don't stand up!'

.*Взять* всё необходи́мое в доро́гу! 'Take all the things you may need on your journey!'

Сиде́ть ти́хо! 'Sit quiet!'

Не брать в доро́гу ничего́ ли́шнего! 'Don't take anything which is not necessary on your journey!'

Не шуме́ть! 'Don't make a noise!'

Note. — An order to do something can be expressed not only by a perfective infinitive but also by an imperfective one, e.g.: *Молча́ть!* 'Silence!' *Сиде́ть* ти́хо! 'Sit quiet!' *Лежа́ть!* 'Lie!' An order not to do something is expressed only by imperfective verbs.

VERBS ENDING IN -*СЯ*

Table 103

		Imperfective Aspect				Perfective Aspect
	Infinitive	*занима́ться* 'to study'		*учи́ться* 'to study'		*доби́ться* 'to succeed'
Indicative Mood	Present Tense	я занима́юсь	-*ю-сь*	учу́сь	-*у-сь*	No present tense
		ты занима́ешься	-*ешь-ся*	у́чишься	-*ишь-ся*	
		он, она́, оно́ занима́ется	-*ет-ся*	у́чится	-*ит-ся*	
		мы занима́емся	-*ем-ся*	у́чимся	-*им-ся*	
		вы занима́етесь	-*ете-сь*	у́читесь	-*ите-сь*	
		они́ занима́ются	-*ют-ся*	у́чатся	-*ат-ся*	
	Past Tense	я, ты, он занима́лся		учи́лся		доби́лся
		я, ты, она́ занима́лась		учи́лась		доби́лась
		оно́ занима́лось		учи́лось		доби́лось
		мы вы они́ } занима́лись		учи́лись		доби́лись

275

	Infinitive	Imperfective Aspect		Perfective Aspect
		занима́ться 'to study'	*учи́ться* 'to study'	*доби́ться* 'to succeed'

Indicative Mood / Future Tense

	занима́ться	*учи́ться*	*доби́ться*	
я бу́ду		бу́ду	добью́сь	*-ю-сь*
ты бу́дешь		бу́дешь	добьёшься	*-ёшь-ся*
он, она́, оно́ бу́дет		бу́дет	добьётся	*-ёт-ся*
мы бу́дем		бу́дем	добьёмся	*-ём-ся*
вы бу́дете		бу́дете	добьётесь	*-ёте-сь*
они́ бу́дут		бу́дут	добью́тся	*-ют-ся*

Conditional-Subjunctive Mood

я, ты, он занима́лся бы	учи́лся бы	доби́лся бы
я, ты, она́ занима́лась бы	учи́лась бы	доби́лась бы
оно́ занима́лось бы	учи́лось бы	доби́лось бы
мы, вы, они́ занима́лись бы	учи́лись бы	доби́лись бы

Imperative Mood

занима́йся	учи́сь	добе́йся
занима́йтесь	учи́тесь	добе́йтесь

Note. — 1. Verbs ending in *-ся* build their forms just as verbs without *-ся*. *-ся* is added after the verb endings.

2. *-ся* is pronounced and written after consonants (*занима́ешься, учи́лся*), while *-сь* is pronounced and written after vowels (*занима́юсь, занима́лась*, etc.).

Table 104

Meaning and Use of Verbs ending in -ся

Group 1	*-ся* has the meaning of *себя́* 'oneself': the action of the verb is directed towards its agent:	одева́ться 'to dress (oneself)' умыва́ться 'to wash (oneself)' причёсываться 'to comb (oneself)'

276

Group 2	Verbs ending in **-ся** denote a reciprocal action of two or more agents:	боро́ться 'to fight' встре́титься 'to meet' совеща́ться 'to confer' ссо́риться 'to quarrel'	Друзья́ *встре́тились* на вокза́ле. 'The friends met at the railway station.'
Group 3	**-ся** is used to obtain passive forms of transitive verbs:	стро́иться 'to be built' управля́ться 'to be governed' охраня́ться 'to be guarded' обсужда́ться 'to be discussed'	Прое́кт но́вого зда́ния *обсужда́ется* молоды́ми архите́кторами. 'The plan of the new building is being discussed by young architects.' (the active construction is: Молоды́е архите́кторы *обсужда́ют* прое́кт но́вого зда́ния. 'Young architects are discussing the plan of the new building.')
Group 4	The addition of the particle **-ся** may form an entirely new verb with a new meaning:	доби́ть 'to finish off' — доби́ться 'to achieve' находи́ть 'to find' — находи́ться 'to be found'	Охо́тники *доби́ли* во́лка. 'The hunters finished off the wolf.' Мы *доби́лись* успе́хов. 'We achieved success.' В э́той ме́стности всегда́ *нахо́дят* мно́го зо́лота. 'They always find a lot of gold in this locality.' В э́той ме́стности *нахо́дится* зо́лото. 'There is gold in this locality.'

Group 5	The verb is not used without *-ся:*	боя́ться 'to be afraid' труди́ться 'to work' распоряжа́ться 'to order'	Мы *не бои́мся* тру́дностей. 'We are not afraid of hardships.'
		наде́яться 'to hope' горди́ться 'to be proud' наслажда́ться 'to enjoy' смея́ться 'to laugh' улыба́ться 'to smile' случи́ться 'to happen' очути́ться 'to find oneself'	Мы *наде́емся* на успе́х. 'We hope for success.' Мы *наслажда́емся* жи́знью. 'We enjoy life.'
Group 6	*-ся* occurs in impersonal verbs: (a) which can be used without *-ся* as personal verbs: (b) which cannot be used without *-ся:*	(a) хо́чется 'to want' ду́мается 'to think' (b) ка́жется 'to seem' нездоро́вится 'to feel unwell' смерка́ется 'to get dark'	Мне *хо́чется* рабо́тать. 'I want to work.' Зимо́й *смерка́ется* ра́но. 'In winter it gets dark early.'

Note. — 1. *-ся* is the old short form of the accusative of the reflexive pronoun *себя.* In the course of time *-ся* merged with the verb into one word, retaining a reflexive meaning only in some verbs (see verbs of Group 1).

2. Verbs with *-ся* are intransitive.

3. Passive forms can be obtained only from transitive verbs.

4. A Russian passive construction can be formed not only by adding the particle *-ся* to transitive verbs (Прое́кт *обсужда́ется, обсужда́лся, бу́дет обсужда́ться* архите́кторами. 'The plan is, was, will be discussed by the architects.') but also by means of the passive participle (Прое́кт *обсуждён, был обсуждён, бу́дет обсуждён* архите́кторами. 'The plan is, was, will be discussed by the architects.')

Passive forms with the particle *-ся* are mainly formed from imperfective verbs (*обсужда́ться* 'to be discussed', *стро́иться* 'to be built'), whereas passive participles are formed mainly from perfective verbs (*постро́ен* 'was built', *прочи́тан* 'was read', *взят* 'was taken'), e.g.: Мост *постро́ен.* 'The bridge has been built.' Кни́га *прочи́тана.* 'The book has been read.'

Table 105

Impersonal Verbs

Impersonal verbs are used in all tenses only in the third person singular, and in the past tense only in the neuter gender.

Present Tense		Past Tense	Future Tense	
смеркáется 'it gets dark'		смеркá- лось	смеркáть- ся	These impersonal verbs denote phenomena (generally natural) which occur without the interference of any person or object.
светáет 'it gets light'		светáло	светáть	
вечерéет 'the day draws to a close'		вечерéло	будет вечерéть	
сквозúт 'there is a draught'		сквозúло	сквозúть	
морóзит 'it freezes'		морóзило	морóзить	
пáрит 'it is sultry'		пáрило	пáрить	
With the dative case:				
мне 'I' тебé 'you' емý 'he' ей 'she'	нездо- рóвится 'feel(s) un- well',	нездорó- вилось	нездорó- виться хотéться дýматься	These impersonal verbs denote a state or a mood of a person; they are usually used with the dative case, but some verbs require the accusative.
нам 'we' вам 'you'	хóчется 'want(s)',	хотéлось	будет	
товáрищу 'the comrade'	дýмается 'think(s)',	дýмалось		
товáрищам 'the comrades', etc.	не спúтся 'cannot sleep'	не спа- лóсь	не бýдет спáться	
With the accusative case:				
меня 'I' тебя 'you' егó 'he' её 'she' нас 'we'	тошнúт 'feel(s) sick',	тошнúло	тошнúть	
вас 'you' их 'they'	мутúт 'feel(s)sick',	мутúло	мутúть	
товáрища 'the comrade'	лихорá- дит 'am, is, are in a fever',	лихорá- дило	будет лихорá- дить	
товáрищей 'the comrades', etc.	знобúт 'am, is, are feverish'	знобúло	знобúть	

MAIN TYPES OF VERBS

(Productive and Non-Productive)

Productive types of verbs are those which can serve as living patterns in the modern language. Since all newly-formed verbs are conjugated according to one of the productive types, the number of verbs belonging to these types is constantly growing. Non-productive types of verbs were inherited from older periods and they no longer serve as living patterns. Each non-productive type of verbs includes a definite number of verbs formed in the language a long time ago (the number of verbs in some types is quite considerable). There are productive and non-productive types of verbs in both the first and second conjugations.

Table 106

Productive Types of Verbs

Types	Infinitive	Present (or Simple Future) Tense	Remarks
		First Conjugation	
1.	*-а-ть* *(-я-ть)* читáть 'to read' изучáть 'to study' рабóтать 'to work' являть 'to be' влиять 'to influence' знать 'to know'	First person singular *-а-ю (-я-ю)*. Second person singular *-а-ешь (-я-ешь)*. читáю — читáешь изучáю — изучáешь рабóтаю — рабóтаешь являю — являешь влияю — влияешь знáю — знáешь	As a rule, *-а-* is a suffix, but in some instances it belongs to the verb root (*знá-ть* 'to know')
2.	*-е-ть* белéть 'to whiten' краснéть 'to redden' богатéть 'to become rich' зреть 'to ripen' спеть 'to ripen'	First person singular *-е-ю*. Second person singular *-е-ешь*. белéю — белéешь краснéю — краснéешь богатéю — богатéешь зрéю — зрéешь спéю — спéешь	As a rule, *-е-* is a suffix, but in some instances it belongs to the verb root (*зре-ть* 'to ripen').

First Conjugation

3.	-*ов-а-ть* -*ев-а-ть*	First person singular -*у-ю* (-*ю-ю*). Second person singular -*у-ешь* (-*ю--ешь*), . -*у-ёшь* (-*ю-ёшь*).	-*ов-а-* occurs after hard consonants, -*ев-а-* after soft consonants and sibilants. In some instances -*ов-*, -*ев-* in the infinitive and -*у-* in the present tense are suffixes (*рисовать* 'to draw' — *рисую*), in others they belong to the verb root (*ковать* 'to forge' — *кую*, *жевать* 'to chew' — *жую*).
	рисова́ть 'to draw' существова́ть 'to exist' организова́ть 'to organize' кова́ть 'to forge' горева́ть 'to grieve' ночева́ть 'to spend the night' жева́ть 'to chew' плева́ть 'to spit'	рису́ю — рису́ешь существу́ю — суще- ству́ешь организу́ю — орга- низу́ешь кую́ — куёшь горю́ю — горю́ешь ночу́ю — ночу́ешь жую́ — жуёшь плюю́ — плюёшь	
4.	-*ну-ть*	First person singular -*н-у*. Second person singular -*н-ешь* (-*н-ёшь*).	
	толкну́ть 'to push' махну́ть 'to wave' дви́нуть 'to move'	толкну́ — толкнёшь махну́ — махнёшь дви́ну — дви́нешь	

Second Conjugation

5.	-*и-ть*	First person singular -*у* (-*ю*). Second person singular -*ишь*.	The ending of the present (simple future) tense is added to the verb root. At the end of the stem of the present tense there is a soft consonant or a sibilant. If the root in the infinitive ends in *т, д, с, з* or a bilabial consonant,
	мочи́ть 'to wet' кружи́ть 'to turn' реши́ть 'to decide' пои́ть 'to water' вари́ть 'to boil'	мочу́ — мо́чишь кружу́ — кру́жишь решу́ — реши́шь пою́ — пои́шь варю́ — ва́ришь	

молить 'to entreat'	молю — мо́лишь	an alternation of conso-
уронить 'to drop'	уроню́ — уро́нишь	nants takes place, a dif-
молоти́ть 'to thresh'	молочу́ — моло́тишь	ferent sound (or combi-
укроти́ть 'to tame'	укрощу́ — укроти́шь	nation of sounds) occur-
грусти́ть 'to be sad'	грущу́ — грусти́шь	ring in the stem of the
ходи́ть 'to walk'	хожу́ — хо́дишь	first person singular,
проси́ть 'to ask'	прошу́ — про́сишь	present (simple future)
грози́ть 'to threat- en'	грожу́ — грози́шь	tense. The alternations of
топи́ть 'to heat'	топлю́ — то́пишь	consonants are as fol- lows:
люби́ть 'to love'	люблю́ — лю́бишь	*т — ч (т — щ), ст —*
лови́ть 'to catch'	ловлю́ — ло́вишь	*щ, д — ж, с — ш, з —*
графи́ть 'to rule'	графлю́ — графи́шь	*ж, п — пл, б — бл,*
корми́ть 'to feed'	кормлю́ — ко́рмишь	*в — вл, ф — фл, м — мл.*

Table 107

Non-Productive Types of Verbs

Types	Infinitive	Present (or Simple Future) Tense	Remarks
		First Conjugation	
1.	*-а-ть*	First person singu- lar *-у (-ю).* Second person sin- gular *-ешь.*	There is no *a* in the stem of the present tense. In the infinitive a hard consonant occurs before *-а-ть;* the stem of the present tense ends in a sibilant or a soft conso- nant.
	пла́кать 'to cry'	пла́чу — пла́чешь	There is alternation of
	паха́ть 'to plough'	пашу́ — па́шешь	consonants (the final con-
	иска́ть 'to seek'	ищу́ — и́щешь	sonants of the roots of
	пря́тать 'to hide'	пря́чу — пря́чешь	the infinitive and of the
	глода́ть 'to gnaw'	гложу́ — гло́жешь	present tense alternate).
	писа́ть 'to write'	пишу́ — пи́шешь	The alternation follows
	ре́зать ·to cut'	ре́жу — ре́жешь	the normal pattern: *к — ч,*
	сы́пать 'to pour'	сы́плю — сы́плешь	*х — ш, ск — щ, т — ч,*
	колеба́ть 'to shake'	колеблю́ — колеб- лешь	*д — ж, с — ш, з — ж, п — пл, б — бл, в — вл,*
	дрема́ть 'to doze'	дремлю́ — дре́млешь	*м — мл,. л — л* (soft).
	стлать 'to spread'	стелю́ — сте́лешь	An unstable vowel may occur; it does not occur in the infinitive (*стла́ть* 'to spread' — *стелю́*).

2.	**-я-ть** (following the root vowel)	First person singular **-ю** Second person singular **-ешь** (**-ёшь**) } following the root vowel.	**я** = [йа], of which [й] is the final consonant of the root, whereas [a] is the suffix of the infinitive and does not occur in the stem of the present tense.
	ла́ять 'to bark' та́ять 'to thaw' ве́ять 'to blow' смея́ться 'to laugh'	ла́ю — ла́ешь та́ю — та́ешь ве́ю — ве́ешь смею́сь — смеёшься	
3.	**-а-ть**	First person singular **-у**. Second person singular **-ёшь**.	There is no *a* in the stem of the present tense. There is a hard consonant in the stem of the infinitive and of the first person singular (*ждать* — *жду*). An unstable *e* or *o* may occur in the root (no unstable vowel occurs in the infinitive). In the present tense back-palatal consonants at the end of the stem alternate with sibilants (the only exception is the verb *ткать* 'to weave', in which *к* does not alternate with *ч*).
	брать 'to take' звать 'to call' ждать 'to wait' лгать 'to tell lies' ткать 'to weave'	беру́ — берёшь зову́ — зовёшь жду — ждёшь лгу — лжёшь тку — ткёшь	
4.	**-ть** (following the *о* of the root)	First person singular **-ю(-сь)**. Second person singular **-ешь(-ся)**.	**-оло-, -оро-** occur in the root of the infinitive; the stem of the present tense ends in a soft consonant (the second *o* is dropped). The alternation *o — e* may occur: (*молоть* 'to grind' — *мелю́*).
	коло́ть 'to chop' поло́ть 'to weed' моло́ть 'to grind' боро́ться 'to fight'	колю́ — ко́лешь полю́ — по́лешь мелю́ — ме́лешь борю́сь — бо́решься	
5.	**-ть** (following the *e* of the root)	First person singular **-у**. Second person singular **-ёшь**.	The root of the infinitive contains the combination **-ере-**; the stem of the present tense in the first person singular ends

	тере́ть 'to grate' умере́ть 'to die'	тру — трёшь умру́ — умрёшь	in a hard consonant (in the present tense only one *e* remains). There is an unstable *e* (it does not occur in the stem of the present tense).
6.	*-а-ть* *-я-ть* жать 'to reap' нача́ть 'to begin' мять 'to crumple' жать 'to press' взять 'to take' поня́ть 'to understand'	First person singular *-н-у (-м-у)*. Second person singular *-н-ёшь (-м-ёшь)*. жну — жнёшь начну́ — начнёшь мну — мнёшь жму — жмёшь возьму́ — возьмёшь пойму́ — поймёшь	*a* in the infinitive belongs to the root; *м*, *н* in the stem of the present (simple future) tense belong to the root. The verb *поня́ть* 'to understand' has in the root of the infinitive an *н*, which does not occur in the simple future tense.
7.	*-ть* (following the root vowel) стать 'to become' оде́ть 'to dress'	First person singular *-н-у*. Second person singular *-н-ешь*. ста́ну — ста́нешь оде́ну — оде́нешь	There is an *н* at the end of the stem of the future tense (of perfective verbs); *н* does not occur in the stem of the infinitive.
8.	*-и-ть* *-у-ть* гнить 'to rot' дуть 'to blow'	First person singular *-ю*. Second person singular *-ешь (-ёшь)*. гнию́ — гниёшь ду́ю — ду́ешь	*и, у* in the stems of the infinitive and of the present tense belong to the root.
9.	*-и-ть* *(-ы-ть)* *-е-ть* пить 'to drink' бить 'to beat'	First person singular *-ю (-ью)*. Second person singular *-ешь (-ёшь, -ьёшь)*. пью — пьёшь бью — бьёшь	The vowels *и, ы, е* in the stem of the infinitive belong to the root. There are different vowels in the stem of the present tense and in the stem of the infinitive

	мыть 'to wash' брить 'to shave' петь 'to sing'	мо́ю — мо́ешь бре́ю — бре́ешь пою́ — поёшь	(alternation of vowels); in some verbs the vowel may be dropped. The stem of the present tense ends in *й* (in spelling, the ending of the first person singular is *-ю* after a vowel and *-ью* after a consonant).
10.	*-ва-ть* (following the *а* of the root) дава́ть 'to give' встава́ть 'to stand up' сознава́ть 'to realize'	First person singular *-ю*. Second person singular *-ёшь*. } following a vowel. даю́ — даёшь встаю́ — встаёшь сознаю́ — сознаёшь	*-ва-* does not occur in the stem of the present tense, which ends in *й:* [дай-у́] (in spelling — *даю*).
11.	*-и-ть* *(-ы-ть)* жить 'to live' плыть 'to swim' слыть 'to have a reputation (for)'	First person singular *-у*. Second person singular *-ёшь*. } following *в*. живу́ — живёшь плыву́ — плывёшь слыву́ — слывёшь	*и(ы)* belongs to the root; the stem of the present tense ends in *в* following the root vowel *и(ы)*.
12.	*-сти (-сть)* *-зти (-зть)* нести́ 'to carry' вести́ 'to lead' плести́ 'to plait' грести́ 'to row' везти́ 'to carry'	First person singular *-у*. Second person singular *-ешь* *(-ёшь)*. } following the root consonant. несу́ — несёшь веду́ — ведёшь плету́ — плетёшь гребу́ — гребёшь везу́ — везёшь	The ending of the infinitive is *-сти (-зти)* with the stress on *и*. The stem of the first person singular in the present tense ends in a hard consonant.

	прясть 'to spin' лезть 'to get (into)'	пряду́ — прядёшь ле́зу — ле́зешь	
13.	**-чь** печь 'to bake' бере́чь 'to take care' стере́чь 'to guard' мочь 'to be able', 'can' жечь 'to burn'	First person singular **-у.** Second person singular **-ешь (-ёшь).** пеку́ — печёшь берегу́ — бережёшь стерегу́ — стережёшь могу́ — мо́жешь жгу — жжёшь	A back-palatal consonant (*к* or *г*) occurs in the stem of the present tense before the ending of the first person singular; in the present tense back-palatal consonants alternate with sibilants *(к — ч, г — ж).* An unstable vowel may occur (*жечь* 'to burn' — *жгу*).

Second Conjugation

14.	**-е-ть** горе́ть 'to burn' веле́ть 'to order' сиде́ть 'to sit' ви́деть 'to see' висе́ть 'to hang' скрипе́ть 'to creak' терпе́ть 'to endure'	First person singular **-у (-ю).** Second person singular **-ишь.** горю́ — гори́шь велю́ — вели́шь сижу́ — сиди́шь ви́жу — ви́дишь вишу́ — виси́шь скриплю́ — скри- пи́шь терплю́ — те́рпишь	The stem of the first person singular in the present tense ends in a soft consonant or a sibilant. If the stem of the infinitive ends in a dental or bilabial consonant, alternation of consonants occurs in the stem of the present tense: a sibilant in the first person singular — a dental consonant in all the other forms, a combination of a bilabial consonant with a soft *л* in the first person singular — a bilabial consonant in all the other forms.
15.	**-ать (-ять) (-ся)** спать 'to sleep' гнать 'to drive' крича́ть 'to cry' молча́ть 'to be silent'	First person singular **-у (-ю) (-сь).** Second person singular **-ишь (-ся).** сплю — спишь гоню́ — го́нишь кричу́ — кричи́шь молчу́ — молчи́шь	*a* does not occur in the stem of the present tense. **-ать** in the infinitive is preceded by a hard consonant, a sibilant or *й* (*боя́ться* [байа́цца] 'to be afraid'). There is a soft consonant, a sibilant or *й* at the end of the stem of the present tense.

стуча́ть 'to knock' бо́яться 'to be afraid'	стучу́ — стучи́шь бою́сь — бои́шься	An unstable vowel may occur in the conjugation (*гна́ть* 'to drive' — *гоню́*). Alternation of consonants (*п — пл, н —* soft *н*) may occur.

Note. — Productive type 4, with the infinitive ending in *-ну-ть* and the present (simple future) tense ending in *-н-у, -н-ешь, -н-ёшь,* should not be confused with the non-productive type which has a similar infinitive and present (simple future) tense (for which reason it is not given separately in the foregoing tables) but a different form for the past tense. The stem of the past tense of the productive type verbs ending in *-ну-ть* coincides with the stem of the infinitive (infinitive: *толк-ну́-ть* 'to push', *дви-ну-ть* 'to move'; past tense: *толк-ну́-л, дви-ну-л*), whereas that of the non-productive verbs has no suffix *-ну-* (infinitive: *мёрз-ну-ть* 'to freeze', *сóх-ну-ть* 'to dry'; past tense: *мёрз, сох*).

Table 108

Verbs which do not Conform to Any Type

Infinitive	Present (Simple Future) Tense	Remarks
бежа́ть 'to run'	бегу́ — бежи́шь	The third person plural is *бегу́т*, whereas verbs ending in the second person singular in *-ишь* generally take *-ат*.
быть 'to be'	бу́ду — бу́дешь	*Бу́ду, бу́дешь* are the forms of the future tense; the present tense is formed from a different root, and the third person singular (*есть* 'is') and the third person plural (*суть* 'are') are the only forms used (though very rarely) in Modern Russian.
дать 'to give' есть 'to eat'	дам — дашь ем — ешь	The ending of the first person singular of these two verbs is different from those of all other verbs.
éхать 'to go'	éду — éдешь	

идти́ 'to walk'	иду́ — идёшь	The stem of the infinitive ends in *д*. The past tense is formed irregularly (from a different root): *шёл*.
расшиби́ть 'to hurt'	расшибу́ — расшибёшь	A hard consonant occurs before the ending in the first person singular. The only verbs conjugated according to this type are prefixed verbs formed from the root *-шиб-* (they are all perfective verbs).
реве́ть 'to roar'	реву́ — ревёшь	A hard consonant occurs before the ending of the first person singular; there is no *е* at the end of the stem of the present tense.
надое́сть 'to bore'	надое́м — надое́шь	Historically, this verb was formed from the verb *есть* 'to eat': *ем — ешь* (see above), by means of a prefix; the modern meanings of the two verbs, however, are altogether different.
созда́ть 'to create'	созда́м — созда́шь	This verb has the same forms as the verb *дать* 'to give': *дам — дашь*.
чтить 'to revere'	чту — чтишь	This verb differs from all the other verbs of the second conjugation in that the stem of the first person singular ends in a hard consonant.
хоте́ть 'to want'	хочу́ — хо́чешь	In the present tense plural this verb follows the second conjugation (*хоти́м, хоти́те, хотя́т*).

MAIN TYPES OF STRESS IN VERBS

1. The stress is fixed, i.e., it falls either on the same syllable (counting from the beginning of the word) in the infinitive and in all persons of the present (simple future) tense: *читáть* 'to read' — *читáю* — *читáешь*, etc., or on the last syllable in the infinitive and in all persons (except the second person plural) of the present (simple future) tense: *прожúть* 'to live' — *проживý*, *проживёшь*... *проживёте* (second person plural).

2. The stress falls on the last syllable in the infinitive and in the first person singular, present tense, but is shifted one syllable nearer the beginning of the word in all the other persons: *носúть* 'to carry' — *ношý* — *нóсишь*, etc.

3. In a few cases the stress falls on the last syllable in the infinitive, in the first person singular and in all persons plural, present tense, but is shifted one syllable nearer the beginning of the word in the second and third persons singular: *хотéть* 'to want' — *хочý* — *хóчешь* — *хóчет* — *хотúм* — *хотúте* — *хотя́т*.

4. In many verbs ending in **-овáть, -евáть** the stress falls on the last syllable in the infinitive, and on the penultimate syllable in all persons in the present (simple future) tense: *рисовáть* 'to draw' — *рисýю* — *рисýешь*; *горевáть* 'to grieve' — *горю́ю* — *горю́ешь*.

Note: — When in the following Tables the stress is shown as falling on the last syllable in the forms of the present (simple future) tense, this applies to all persons, except the second person plural, where the stress falls on the penultimate syllable.

MAIN TYPES OF STRESS-SHIFT IN VERBAL FORMS*

Productive Types   *Table 109*

Types	Infinitive	First Person Singular of the Present (Simple Future) Tense		Second Person Singular of the Present (Simple Future) Tense		Remarks
		The stress falls on the penultimate syllable	The stress falls on the last syllable	The stress falls on the penultimate syllable	The stress falls on the last syllable	
1.	читáть 'to read'	читáю		читá-ешь		Fixed Stress
2.	белéть 'to whiten'	белéю		белé-ешь		Fixed Stress

* Here we follow the order of the main types of verbs (see Tables 106-107).

3.	ковáть 'to forge'		ку́ю		куёшь	The stress in the infinitive falls on the last syllable, in some verbs it also falls on the last syllable in the present tense; other verbs are stressed on the penultimate syllable in all the persons.
	жевáть 'to chew'		жую́		жуёшь	
	рисовáть 'to draw'	рису́ю		рису́ешь		
	горевáть 'to grieve'	горю́ю		горю́ешь		
4.	толкну́ть 'to push'		толкну́		толк-нёшь	Almost all the verbs have fixed stress. Perfective verbs (without prefixes) are generally stressed on the last syllable (except *двúнуть* 'to move'); imperfective verbs are stressed on the penultimate syllable. The stress is shifted only in four verbs (*тяну́ть* 'to pull', *взгляну́ть* 'to look', *обману́ть* 'to deceive', *помяну́ть* 'to pray [for]'); it falls on the last syllable in the infinitive and in the first person singular, present (simple future) tense, and on the penultimate syllable in all the other persons of the present (simple future) tense.
	двúнуть 'to move'	двúну		двú-нешь		
	со́хнуть 'to dry'	со́хну		со́х-нешь		
	тяну́ть 'to pull'		тяну́	тя́нешь		
5.	реши́ть 'to decide'		решу́		реши́шь	A number of verbs have fixed stress on the ending. In a number of verbs the stress is shifted, falling on the last syllable in the infinitive and in the first person singular, and on the penultimate syllable in all the other persons in the present tense.
	гости́ть 'to stay'		гощу́		гос-ти́шь	
	графи́ть 'to rule'		графлю́		гра-фи́шь	
	вари́ть 'to boil'		варю́	ва́ришь		
	урони́ть 'to drop'		уроню́	уро́-нишь		
	молоти́ть 'to thresh'		молочу́	моло́-тишь		

	First Person Singular of the Present (Simple Future) Tense		Second Person Singular of the Present (Simple Future) Tense	
топи́ть 'to light'		топлю́	то́пишь	
люби́ть 'to love'		люблю́	лю́бишь	

Table 110

Non-Productive Types

Types	Infinitive	First Person Singular of the Present (Simple Future) Tense		Second Person Singular of the Present (Simple Future) Tense		Remarks
		The stress falls on the penultimate syllable	The stress falls on the last syllable	The stress falls on the penultimate syllable	The stress falls on the last syllable	
1.	иска́ть 'to seek' писа́ть 'to write' колеба́ть 'to shake'	коле́б-лю	ищу́ пишу́	и́щешь пи́шешь коле́б-лешь		In verbs stressed in the infinitive on the last syllable the stress is shifted, generally falling on the last syllable in the first person singular, present tense, and on the penultimate syllable in all the other persons. In two verbs (*колеба́ть* 'to shake', *колыха́ть* 'to rock') the stress falls on the penultimate syllable in all the persons.
2.	ла́ять 'to bark'	ла́ю		ла́ешь		Fixed stress
3.	брать 'to take'		беру́		берёшь	Fixed stress
4.	коло́ть 'to chop'		колю́	ко́лешь		Stress shifts
5.	умере́ть 'to die'		умру́		умрёшь	Fixed stress

6.	нача́ть 'to begin'		начну́		нач- нёшь	Fixed stress
7.	оде́ть 'to dress'	оде́ну		оде́- нешь		Fixed stress
8.	гни́ть 'to rot'		гнию́		гниёшь	Fixed stress
	дуть 'to blow'	ду́ю		ду́ешь		
9.	мыть 'to wash'	мо́ю		мо́ешь		Fixed stress
	петь 'to sing'		пою́		поёшь	
10.	дава́ть 'to give'		даю́		даёшь	Fixed stress
11.	жить 'to live'		живу́		живёшь	Fixed stress
12.	нести́ 'to carry'		несу́		несёшь	Fixed stress. If the infinitive ends in -*сти* (-*зти*) the stress in the present tense falls on the last syllable; if the infinitive ends in -*сть* (-*зть*) the stress in the present tense falls on the last syllable in some verbs, and on the penultimate syllable in others.
	прясть 'to spin'		пряду́		пря- дёшь	
	лезть 'to get'	ле́зу		ле́зешь		
13.	печь 'to bake'		пеку́		печёшь	The stress is mostly fixed: it falls on the last syllable in the present tense; but in the verb *мочь* 'to be able', 'can' the stress is shifted.
	бере́чь 'to take care (of)'		берегу́		бере- жёшь	
	мочь 'to be able', 'can'		могу́	мо́- жешь		

14.	горе́ть 'to burn' ви́деть 'to see терпе́ть 'to endure'	ви́жу	горю́ терплю́	гори́шь ви́дишь тёр- пишь		The stress is fixed in most cases, but is shifted in the verbs *терпе́ть* 'to endure', *верте́ть* 'to turn'.
15.	крича́ть 'to shout' гнать 'to drive'		кричу́ гоню́	го́нишь	кри- чи́шь	The stress is fixed in most cases, falling on the last syllable; but in the verb *гнать* 'to drive' the stress is shifted.

Table 111

LIST OF THE MOST IMPORTANT VERBS
OF NON-PRODUCTIVE TYPES

Most of the verbs listed are unprefixed. Verbs with a prefix are given only if they are not used otherwise. The figure following a verb indicates the type it belongs to according to Table 107; the word "isolated" after some verbs means that these verbs are isolated cases not belonging to any type (see Table 108).

бежа́ть 'to run' — isolated
бере́чь 'to take care (of)' — 13
бить 'to beat' — 9
бле́ять 'to bleat' — 2
бормота́ть 'to mutter' — 1
боро́ться 'to fight' — 4
боя́ться 'to be afraid' — 15
брать 'to take' — 3
брести́ 'to stroll' — 12
брить 'to shave' — 9
быть 'to be' — isolated

везти́ 'to carry' — 12
веле́ть 'to order' — 14
верте́ть 'to turn' — 14
вести́ 'to lead' — 12
ви́деть 'to see' — 14
визжа́ть 'to yelp' — 15
висе́ть 'to hang' — 14
вить 'to weave' — 9
влечь 'to attract' — 13

воло́чь 'to drag' — 13
врать 'to lie' — 3
встава́ть 'to stand up' — 10
выть 'to howl' — 9
вы́честь 'to deduct' — 12
вяза́ть 'to knit' — 1

глода́ть 'to gnaw' — 1
гнать 'to drive' — 15
гнить 'to rot' — 8
горе́ть 'to burn' — 14
грести́ 'to row' — 12
грохота́ть 'to peal' — 1
грызть 'to nibble' — 12

дава́ть 'to give' — 10
дать 'to give' — isolated
деть 'to put' — 7
драть 'to tear' — 3
дрема́ть 'to doze' — 1
дрожа́ть 'to tremble' — 15

293

дуть 'to blow' — 8
дыша́ть 'to breathe' — 15

есть 'to eat' — isolated
е́хать 'to go', 'to travel' — isolated
жать 'to press' (жму) — 6
жать 'to reap' (жну) — 6
ждать 'to wait' — 3
жечь 'to burn' — 13
жить 'to live' — 11
жужжа́ть 'to buzz' — 15

зави́сеть 'to depend' — 14
запря́чь 'to harness' — 13
застря́ть 'to stick' — 7
звать 'to call' — 3
звуча́ть 'to sound' — 15

идти́ 'to go', 'to walk' — isolated

класть 'to put' — 12
кля́сть 'to curse' (кляну́) — 12
коло́ть 'to chop' — 4
красть 'to steal' — 12
крича́ть 'to shout' — 15
кры́ть 'to cover' — 9

лгать 'to tell lies' — 3
лежа́ть 'to lie' — 15
лезть 'to get (into)' — 12
лепета́ть 'to prattle' — 1
лете́ть 'to fly' — 14
лечь 'to lie down' (ля́гу) — 13
лиза́ть 'to lick' — 1
лить 'to pour' (лью) — 9

ма́зать 'to soil' — 1
маха́ть 'to wave' — 1
мести́ 'to sweep' — 12
моло́ть 'to grind' — 4
молча́ть 'to be silent' — 15
мочь 'to be able', 'can' — 13
мыть 'to wash' — 9
мыча́ть 'to low' — 15

надое́сть 'to bore' — isolated
ненави́деть 'to hate' — 14
нести́ 'to carry' — 12

ныть 'to whimper' (но́ю) — 9

оби́деть 'to offend' — 14
обня́ть 'to embrace' (обниму́) — 6
обрести́ 'to find' (обрету́) — 12
обу́ть 'to put on somebody's shoes for him' — 8
обяза́ть 'to oblige' — 1
ора́ть 'to yell' — 3
отре́чься 'to renounce' — 13

пасти́ 'to graze' — 12
пасть 'to fall' — 12
паха́ть 'to plough' — 1
петь 'to sing' — 9
печь 'to bake' — 13
писа́ть 'to write' — 1
пить 'to drink' — 9
пища́ть 'to squeak' — 15
пла́кать 'to cry' — 1
плеска́ть 'to splash' — 1
плести́ 'to weave' — 12
плыть 'to swim' — 11
пляса́ть 'to dance' — 1
ползти́ 'to crawl' — 12
поло́ть 'to weed' — 4
поро́ть 'to flog' — 4
пренебре́чь 'to ignore' — 13
прясть 'to spin' — 12

разу́ть 'to take off somebody's shoes for him' — 8
расти́ 'to grow' (расту́) — 12
рвать 'to tear' — 3
реве́ть 'to roar' — isolated
ржать 'to neigh' — 3
рыть 'to dig' (ро́ю) — 9
рыча́ть 'to growl' — 15
свиста́ть 'to whistle' — 1
свисте́ть 'to whistle' — 14
сесть 'to sit down' (ся́ду) — 12
сиде́ть 'to sit' — 14
скака́ть 'to gallop' — 1
скрести́ 'to scratch' (скребу́) — 12
скрипе́ть 'to creak' — 14
слать 'to send' (шлю) — 1

слыть 'to have a reputation (for)' — 11
смея́ться 'to laugh' — 2
смотре́ть 'to look' — 14
создава́ть 'to create' — 10
созда́ть 'to create' — isolated
соса́ть 'to suck' — 3
спать 'to sleep' — 15
стать 'to become' — 7
стере́чь 'to guard' — 13
стлать 'to spread' — 1
стона́ть 'to groan' — 1
стоя́ть 'to stand' — 15
стри́чь 'to cut' (стригу́) — 13
стуча́ть 'to knock' — 15
сы́пать 'to pour' — 1

тере́ть 'to grate' — 5
терпе́ть 'to endure' — 14
теса́ть 'to hew' — 1
ткать 'to weave' — 3
толо́чь 'to pound' (толку́) — 13
топта́ть 'to trample down' — 1
торча́ть 'to jut out' — 15
трепета́ть 'to flicker' (трепещу́) — 1

треща́ть 'to crackle' — 15
трясти́ 'to shake' (трясу́) — 12

узнава́ть 'to recognize' — 10
умере́ть 'to die' — 5
ушиби́ть 'to hurt' — isolated

хлеста́ть 'to lash' — 1
хлопота́ть 'to bustle about' — 1
хны́кать 'to whimper', 'to snivel' — 1
хоте́ть 'to want' — isolated
хохота́ть 'to roar with laughter' — 1

цвести́ 'to bloom' (цвету́) — 12

чеса́ть 'to scratch' — 1
чтить 'to revere' — isolated

шепта́ть 'to whisper' — 1
шить 'to sew' (шью) — 9
шуме́ть 'to make a noise' — 14

щебета́ть 'to twitter' — 1
щекота́ть 'to tickle' — 1
щипа́ть 'to pinch' — 1

Table 112

LIST OF MOST FREQUENTLY USED VERBS WITH THE SUFFIX -НУ- FORMING THEIR PAST TENSE WITHOUT THIS SUFFIX

(Forms without prefixes are mostly given)

воздви́гнуть (воздви́г) 'to errect'
вя́знуть (вяз) 'to stick'
вя́нуть (вял) 'to fade'
га́снуть (гас) 'to die out'
ги́бнуть (гиб) 'to perish'
гло́хнуть (глох) 'to go deaf'
зя́бнуть (зяб) 'to freeze'
исся́кнуть (исся́к) 'to run short'
исче́знуть (исче́з) 'to disappear'
ки́снуть (кис) 'to run sour'
кре́пнуть (креп) 'to become strong'

мёрзнуть (мёрз) 'to freeze'
ме́ркнуть (мерк) 'to grow dark'
па́хнуть (пах) 'to smell'
продро́гнуть (продро́г) 'to be chilled'
све́ргнуть (сверг) 'to overthrow'
сле́пнуть (слеп) 'to go blind'
со́хнуть (сох) 'to dry'
сты́нуть (стыл) 'to grow cold'
ту́хнуть (тух) 'to go bad'
ча́хнуть (чах) 'to wither'

Table 113

Isolated Verbs having Certain Peculiarities in Conjugation

Infinitive	Present Tense	Past Tense	Future Tense	Remarks
идти́ 'to go', 'to walk' (imperfective)	я иду́ ты идёшь, etc.	я, ты, он шёл я, ты, она́ шла оно́ шло мы, вы, они́ шли	Formed regularly бу́ду идти́	The compound future is бу́ду идти́ (used very rarely).
пойти́ 'to go', 'to walk' (perfective)	No present tense	я пошёл, etc.	я пойду́ ты пойдёшь, etc.	
éхать 'to go', 'to travel'	я éду ты éдешь он, она́, оно́ éдет мы éдем вы éдете они́ éдут	Formed regularly éхал	Formed regularly бу́ду éхать	Бу́ду éхать is used very rarely.
есть 'to eat'	я ем ты ешь он, она́, оно́ ест мы еди́м вы еди́те они́ едя́т	я, ты, он ел я, ты, она́ éла оно́ éло мы, вы, они́ éли	Formed regularly бу́ду есть	
дать 'to give' (perfective)	No present tense	Formed regularly дал	я дам мы дади́м ты дашь вы дади́те он, оно́ даст они́ даду́т	

Infinitive	Present Tense	Past Tense	Future Tense	Remarks
давáть 'to give' (imperfective)	я даю́ мы даём ты даёшь вы даёте он, она́ они́ даю́т онó даёт	Formed regularly давáл	Formed regularly бýду давáть	
взять 'to take'	No present tense	Formed regularly взял	я возьмý ты возьмёшь, etc.	
понять 'to understand'	No present tense	Formed regularly пóнял	я поймý ты поймёшь, etc.	
спать 'to sleep'	я сплю ты спишь, etc.	Formed regularly спал	Formed regularly бýду спать	
гнать 'to drive'	я гоню́ ты гóнишь, etc.	Formed regularly гнал	Formed regularly бýду гнать	
брить 'to shave'	я брéю, ты брéешь, etc.	Formed regularly брил	Formed regularly бýду брить	

For peculiarities in the conjugation of other verbs, such as the frequently used *жить* 'to live' — *живý*, *мочь* 'to be able', 'can' — *могý* and of verbs ending in *-сти (-зти)*: *нести* 'to carry', *везти* 'to carry (in a vehicle)', etc., see Table 107. For the verb *хотéть* 'to want' — *хочý*, see Table 108.

VII. THE PARTICIPLE AND THE VERBAL ADVERB

Two special forms are derived from the Russian verb: (1) *the participle* (*выполня́ющий* 'fulfilling', *выполня́вший* '(that) fulfilled', *выполня́емый* 'being fulfilled' — from the imperfective verb *выполня́ть* 'to fulfil ', and *вы́полнивший* '(that) fulfilled', *вы́полненный* 'having been fulfilled' — from the perfective verb *вы́полнить* 'to fulfil') and (2) *the verbal adverb* (*выполня́я* 'fulfilling' — from the imperfective verb *выполня́ть*, and *вы́полнив* 'having fulfilled' — from the perfective verb *вы́полнить*).

THE PARTICIPLE

I. The participle is a verbal form which has both verbal and adjectival characteristics.

A. VERBAL CHARACTERISTICS OF THE PARTICIPLE

1. Like verbs, participles may be transitive or intransitive: the participles *выполня́ющий* 'fulfilling', *чита́ющий* 'reading', *лю́бящий* 'loving', derived from the transitive verbs *выполня́ть* 'to fulfil', *чита́ть* 'to read', *люби́ть* 'to love', retain the transitive meaning: *выполня́ть план* 'to fulfil a plan' (*что* выполня́ть? план 'to fulfil what? a plan') — *заво́д, выполня́ющий план* 'the mill fulfilling its plan' (выполня́ющий *что?* план 'fulfilling what? its plan'); *чита́ть кни́гу* 'to read a book' (*что* чита́ть? кни́гу 'to read what? a book') — *ма́льчик, чита́ющий кни́гу* 'the boy reading a book' (чита́ющий *что?* кни́гу 'reading what? a book'); *люби́ть отца́* 'to love one's father' (*кого́* люби́ть? отца́ 'to love whom? one's father') — *ма́льчик, лю́бящий отца́* 'the boy loving his father' (лю́бящий *кого́?* отца́ 'loving whom? his father'). Thus, it is obvious that the verbs *выполня́ть, чита́ть, люби́ть* and the participles *выполня́ющий, чита́ющий, лю́бящий* express actions which pass over to their object, which, therefore, takes the accusative without any preposition (questions: *кого́?* 'whom?', *что?* 'what?')

The verbs *идти́* 'to go', 'to walk', *сиде́ть* 'to sit', *отдохну́ть* 'to have a rest' are intransitive and so are the participles *иду́щий, сидя́щий, отдохну́вший*.

2. The participle governs the same case as the verb from which it is formed; thus, the Russian verb *занима́ться* 'to study' requires the instrumental (*Я занима́юсь ру́сским языко́м.* 'I study the Russian language.') and the participles *занима́ющийся, занима́вшийся* also require the same case (*занима́ющийся ру́сским языко́м, занима́вшийся ру́сским языко́м*; other examples: *Я увлека́юсь исто́рией* 'I take a great interest in history' — *увлека́ющийся исто́рией; Я руковожу́ кружко́м* 'I direct a study-group' — *руководя́щий кружко́м; Я тре́бую выполне́ния* 'I demand the fulfilment' — *тре́бующий выполне́ния, тре́бовавший выполне́ния; достиг результа́та* '(I, he) achieved the result' — *дости́гший результа́та*, etc.).

The participle requires the same preposition as the verb from which it is formed: *надею́сь на успе́х* 'I hope for success' — *наде́ющийся на успе́х; убеди́лся в пра́вильности реше́ния э́того вопро́са* '(I, he) made sure of the correctness of the solution of this question' — *убеди́вшийся в пра́вильности реше́ния э́того вопро́са.*

3. The participle retains the aspect of the verb it is derived from: thus, the verbs *чита́ть* 'to read', *люби́ть* 'to love' are imperfective and so are the participles *чита́ющий, любя́щий;* the verbs *прочита́ть* 'to read', *полюби́ть* 'to love', *дости́гнуть* 'to achieve' are perfective and so are the participles *прочита́вший, полюби́вший, дости́гший.*

4. There are present and past participles; cf. *чита́ющий* — a present participle (*ма́льчик, чита́ющий кни́гу* means 'the boy who is reading a book') and *чита́вший* — a past participle (*ма́льчик, чита́вший кни́гу* means 'the boy who was reading a book'); *любя́щий* — a present participle (*ма́льчик, любя́щий отца́* means 'the boy who loves his father') and *люби́вший* — a past participle (*ма́льчик, люби́вший отца́* means 'the boy who loved his father'). Unlike the verb, the participle has no future tense.

B. ADJECTIVAL CHARACTERISTICS OF THE PARTICIPLE

Like the adjective, the participle changes according to gender, number and case and agrees with the singular noun it qualifies in gender, number and case, and with the plural noun in number and case. Thus, in the sentence *Я получи́л письмо́ от това́рища, живу́щего в Москве́* 'I received a letter from a friend living in Moscow' the participle *живу́щего* is masculine just as the noun *това́рища* which it qualifies, and it takes the genitive singular just as the noun does.

Active and Passive Participles

II. There are active and passive participles in Russian.

The active participle is used to qualify a noun denoting the performer of the action expressed by the participle, e.g., *Профе́ссор, прочита́вший ле́кцию, прие́хал из друго́го го́рода.* 'The professor who delivered the lecture came from another town.' (in this example *профéссор* 'the professor' is the performer of the action expressed by the participle *прочитáвший* 'who delivered'.)

The passive participle is used to qualify a noun denoting the object upon which the action expressed by the participle is performed, e.g., *Лéкция, прочúтанная профéссором*, заинтересовáла всех слýшателей. 'The lecture delivered by the professor aroused the interest of all the listeners.' Here *лéкция* stands for the object acted upon.

Active participles can be formed from both transitive and intransitive verbs, whereas passive participles can be formed only from transitive verbs, i.e., from verbs whose action passes over to their object.

Active participles have only long forms, whereas passive participles have both long and short forms.

Long-form passive participles: *вы́полненный план* 'a plan which had been fulfilled', *организóванное хозя́йство* 'an economy which had been organized'.

Short-form passive participles: *план вы́полнен* 'the plan has been fulfilled', *хозя́йство организóвано* 'the economy has been organized'.

Like the short-form adjective the short-form participle fulfils the function of predicate in the sentence and agrees with the noun it qualifies only in gender and number: *письмó напúсано* 'the letter is written', *доклáд напúсан* 'the report is written', *статья́ напúсана* 'the article is written'; *пúсьма, доклáды, статьú напúсаны* 'the letters, reports, articles are written'.

Table 114

The Active Participle

| | Singular | | Plural | Suffixes |
Masculine	Feminine	Neuter		
		Present Tense		
пúшущий 'writing'	пúшущая	пúшущее	пúшущие	*-ущ-*
читáющий 'reading'	читáющая	читáющее	читáющие	*-ющ-*
кричáщий 'shouting'	кричáщая	кричáщее	кричáщие	*-ащ-*
говоря́щий 'speaking'	говоря́щая	говоря́щее	говоря́щие	*-ящ-*

Singular			Plural	Suffixes
Masculine	Feminine	Neuter		
Past Tense				
писа́вший 'who wrote'	писа́вшая	писа́вшее	писа́вшие	-вш-
чита́вший 'who read'	чита́вшая	чита́вшее	чита́вшие	
крича́вший 'who shouted'	крича́вшая	крича́вшее	крича́вшие	
говори́вший 'who spoke'	говори́вшая	говори́вшее	говори́вшие	
нёсший 'who carried'	нёсшая	нёсшее	нёсшие	-ш-
засо́хший 'which dried'	засо́хшая	засо́хшее	засо́хшие	

Table 115

Formation of Active Participles

The present participle is formed from the stem of the present tense by means of the suffixes *-ущ-*, *-ющ-* for verbs of the first conjugation:

пи́шут—пи́шущий
чита́ют—чита́ющий

and of the suffixes *-ащ-*, *-ящ-* for verbs of the second conjugation:

стуча́т—стуча́щий
говоря́т—говоря́щий

Note.—The present participle can easily be obtained in the following manner: drop the final *-т* of the verb in the third person plural, present tense (пи́шу-т), and add *-щий* (for the masculine gender), *-щая* (for the feminine), *-щее* (for the neuter).

The past participle is formed from the stem of the past tense by means of the suffixes *-вш-* for verbs whose stem ends in a vowel:

чита́л—чита́вший
говори́л—говори́вший

and *-ш-* for verbs whose stem ends in a consonant:

нёс—нёсший
вёз—вёзший
засо́х—засо́хший
лёг—лёгший

Note. — The past participle can easily be obtained in the following manner: drop the suffix *-л* of the verb in the past tense (чита́-л) and add *-вший* (for the masculine gender), *-вшая* (for the feminine gender) and *-вшее* (for the neuter gender).

If the past tense has no suffix *-л* (the stem ending in a consonant), the suffix *-ший* is added for the masculine gender (нёсший), *-шая* for the feminine (нёсшая) and *-шее* for the neuter (несшее).

If the stem in the past tense ends in a vowel (*вёл* 'I (he) led', *расцвёл* 'I (he) bloomed)' and the present tense in *-д, -т* (*веду́, расцвету́*) the suffix *-ший* of the past participle is added to the stem of the present tense (*ве́дший, расцве́тший*, etc.).

Note. — Participles formed from verbs ending in *-ся* (*занима́ющийся, занима́вшийся*) take the particle *-ся* at the end.

Table 116

The Long-Form Passive Participle

Singular			Plural	Suffixes
Masculine	Feminine	Neuter		
Present Tense				
чита́емый 'read'	чита́емая	чита́емое	чита́емые	*-ем-*
изуча́емый 'studied'	изуча́емая	изуча́емое	изуча́емые	*-ем-*
люби́мый 'loved'	люби́мая	люби́мое	люби́мые	*-им-*
Past Tense				
чи́танный 'read'	чи́танная	чи́танное	чи́танные	*-нн-*
изу́ченный 'studied'	изу́ченная	изу́ченное	изу́ченные	*-енн-*
взя́тый 'taken'	взя́тая	взя́тое	взя́тые	*-т-*

Table 117

Formation of Passive Participles

The present participle is formed from the stem of the present tense by means of the suffix *-ем-* for verbs of the first conjugation:
чита́ем 'we read' — чита́емый 'read'
изуча́ем 'we study' — изуча́емый 'studied'

The past participle is formed from the stem of the past tense:
by means of the suffix *-нн-* or *-т-* if the stem ends in a vowel:
прочита́л 'I (he) read' —прочи́танный 'read'

by means of the suffix *-енн-* if the stem ends in a consonant or in *и* (not belonging to the root):
изучи́л 'I (he)

and the suffix **-им-** for verbs of the second conjugation: любим 'we love' — любимый 'loved' руководим 'we direct'—руководимый 'directed'	видел 'I (he) saw'— виденный 'seen' взял 'I (he) took'— взятый 'taken' бил 'I (he) beat'— битый 'beaten' мыл 'I (he) washed' —мытый 'washed' дул 'I (he) blew'— дутый 'inflated'	studied' — изученный 'studied' принёс 'I (he) brought'—принесённый 'brought' возвратил 'I (he) returned' — возвращённый 're-turned' (alternation: *т-щ*).

Note. — 1. Only transitive verbs have passive participles.

2. Verbs with the suffix *-ва-* (following the roots *да-*, *зна-*) form their present participles from the stem of the infinitive: *передавать* 'to pass'—*передаваемый*, *признавать* 'to recognize'—*признаваемый*.

3. The present passive participles of many verbs are not used, e.g., of the verbs *брать* 'to take', *шить* 'to sew', *мыть* 'to wash', *пить* 'to drink', *лить* 'to pour', *бить* 'to beat', *портить* 'to spoil', etc.

4. Past passive participles are mainly formed from perfective verbs. Only a few imperfective verbs have passive past participles: *читать* 'to read'—*читанный*, *видеть* 'to see'—*виденный*, etc.

Table 118

The Short-Form Passive Participle

	Long Form	Short Form	Long Form	Short Form
	Present Tense		Past Tense	
Masculine	угнетаемый 'oppressed'	угнетаем	прочитанный 'read' взятый 'taken'	прочитан взят
Feminine	угнетаемая	угнетаема	прочитанная взятая	прочитана взята
Neuter	угнетаемое	угнетаемо	прочитанное взятое	прочитано взято
Plural	угнетаемые	угнетаемы	прочитанные взятые	прочитаны взяты

Note. — 1. Short-form participles are not declined. Like short-form adjectives they are used in compound predicates: *Книга взята.* 'The book is taken.' *Книга была прочитана* в два дня. 'The book was read in two days.' *Книга будет напечатана.* 'The book will be printed.' Short-form participles agree with the subject in gender and number.

2. In Modern Russian short-form present passive participles are formed only from some verbs, e.g., Этот писатель всеми *любим*, *уважаем*. 'This writer is liked and respected by all.'

Table 119

Summary Table of Formation of Participles

		Active		Passive		Remarks
		Present Tense	Past Tense	Present Tense	Past Tense	
Transitive	**Imperfective** читáть 'to read' вѝдеть 'to see' слýшать 'to listen'	читáющий вѝдящий слýшающий	читáвший вѝдевший слýшавший	читáемый вѝдимый слýшаемый	чѝтанный вѝденный —	The past passive participles of many transitive verbs of the imperfective aspect are not used.
	Perfective прочитáть увѝдеть прослýшать	— — —	прочитáвший увѝдевший прослýшав- ший	— — —	прочѝтанный увѝденный прослýшан- ный	Perfective verbs have no present participles.
Intransitive	**Imperfective** éхать 'to go'	éдущий	éхавший	—	—	Passive participles are not formed from intransitive verbs.
	Perfective приéхать 'to come'	—	приéхавший	—	—	

As is seen from the above table, some verbs have all four forms of participles, others, three forms, still others, two forms, whereas a number of verbs have only one form of participle.

Note. — The verb слышáть 'to hear' has a past participle (слышанный), whereas the verb слýшать 'to listen' has none.

Table 120

Declension of Participles

Masculine and Neuter Gender	Endings	Feminine Gender	Endings	Plural	Endings
Nom. читающий 'reading', читавший читавшее, читавшее занимающийся 'studying', занимавшийся, занимающееся, занимавшееся	*-ий(ся)* *-ее(ся)*	читающая, читавшая занимающаяся, нимавшаяся	*-ая(ся)*	читающие, читавшие занимающиеся, нимавшиеся	*-ие(ся)*
Gen. читающего, читавшего занимающегося, занимавшегося	*-его(ся)*	читающей, читавшей занимающейся нимавшейся	*-ей(ся)*	читающих, читавших занимающихся нимавшихся	*-их(ся)*
Dat. читающему, читавшему занимающемуся, занимавшемуся	*-ему(ся)*	читающей, читавшей занимающейся нимавшейся	*-ей(ся)*	читающим, читавшим занимающимся нимавшимся	*-им(ся)*
Acc. as Nom. or Gen. (masc.) as Nom. (neuter)		читающую, читавшую занимающуюся, занимавшуюся	*-ую(ся)*	as Nom. or Gen.	

Masculine and Neuter Gender	Endings	Feminine Gender	Endings	Plural	Endings
Instr. читающим, читавшим занимающимся, занимавшимся	-им(ся)	читающей, читавшей занимающейся, занимавшейся	-ей(-ею)(ся)	читающими, читавшими занимающимися, занимавшимися	-ими(ся)
Prep. (о) читающем, читавшем (о) занимающемся, занимавшемся	-ем(ся)	(о) читающей, читавшей (о) занимающейся, занимавшейся	-ей(ся)	(о) читающих, читавших (о) занимающихся, занимавшихся	-их(ся)
Nom. прочитанный 'read', прочитанное	-ый -ое	прочитанная	-ая	прочитанные	-ые
Gen. прочитанного	-ого	прочитанной	-ой	прочитанных	-ых
Dat. прочитанному	-ому	прочитанной	-ой	прочитанным	-ым
Acc. { as Nom. or Gen. (masc.) as Nom. (neuter)		прочитанную	-ую	as Nom. or Gen.	
Instr. прочитанным	-ым	прочитанной (-ою)	-ой(-ою)	прочитанными	-ыми
Prep. (о) прочитанном	-ом	(о) прочитанной	-ой	(о) прочитанных	-ых

Note. — 1. Participles are declined as adjectives.

2. Active participles, both present and past, take case-endings identical with those of adjectives whose stem ends in a sibilant followed by an unstressed ending (хороший 'good', хорошего, etc.; хорошая, хорошей, хорошую, etc.).

3. Passive participles, both present and past, take case-endings identical with those of adjectives whose stem ends in a hard consonant (красный 'red', красного, etc.).

4. Participles formed from verbs ending in -ся always take the particle -ся at the end (занимающийся 'studying', занимающегося, etc.).

POSITION OF THE PARTICIPLE IN THE SENTENCE

The participle does not necessarily precede the noun it qualifies (Я навестил *приехавшего* из деревни *товарища.* 'I visited a friend who had come from· the country.'), it may follow it (Я навестил *товарища, приехавшего* из деревни).

THE VERBAL ADVERB

GENERAL REMARKS

The verbal adverb is a verbal form which has both verbal and adverbial characteristics.

A. Verbal Characteristics of the Verbal Adverb

1. Like verbs, verbal adverbs may be transitive or intransitive; thus, the verbal adverbs *читая* 'reading', *любя* 'loving', formed from the transitive verbs *читать* 'to read', *любить* "to love', retain their transitive meaning (*Читать книгу.* 'To read a book.'· Он сидел в саду, *читая книгу.* 'He sat in the garden, reading a book'. Любить отца. 'To love one's father.' *Любя отца.* 'Loving one's father.'), i.e., like the verbs *читать, любить* the verbal adverbs *читая, любя* govern the accusative case without any preposition (question: *что?* 'what?' *кого?* 'whom?'): читать *что?* — книгу, читая *что?* — книгу; любить *кого?* — отца, любя *кого?* — отца.

The verbs *отдыхать* 'to have a rest', *сидеть* 'to sit' are intransitive·and so are the verbal adverbs *отдыхая, сидя.*

2. Verbal adverbs govern the same cases as the verbs from which they are formed: thus, the Russian *интересоваться* 'to be interested' requires the instrumental (*интересоваться археологией* 'to be interested in archaeology') and so does the verbal adverb (*интересуясь археологией* 'being interested in archaeology'); the same is true of the verbs *командовать* 'to command', *управлять* 'to direct' and the verbal adverbs *командуя, управляя* (*командовать отрядом* 'to command a detachment' — *командуя отрядом* 'commanding a detachment'; *управлять хозяйством* 'to direct an economy' — *управляя хозяйством* 'directing an economy').

The verbal adverb requires the same preposition as the verb from which it is formed: *нуждаться в помощи* 'to be in need of help', *нуждаясь в помощи* 'being in need of help.'

3. The verbal adverb has the same aspect as the verb from which it is formed: thus, the verbs *читать* 'to read', *любить* 'to love' are imperfective and so are the verbal adverbs *читая, любя;* the verbs *овладеть* 'to master', *превратиться* 'to turn (into)' are perfective and so are the verbal adverbs *овладев, превратившись.*

B. Adverbial Characteristics of the Verbal Adverb

Like the adverb, the verbal adverb does not change in the sentence and it indicates various circumstances (*как?* 'how?', *когда?* 'when?', *почему?* 'why?', *при каких условиях?* 'in what circumstances?') attending an action.

1. Он говорил *волнуясь и спеша*. 'He spoke excitedly and hurriedly.' (*как* говорил? *волнуясь и спеша*).

2. *Окончив* занятия, мы уедем на практику. 'On finishing our classes we shall have practice.' (*когда* мы уедем на практику? *окончив занятия*).

3. *Желая* скорее уехать, он торопится закончить работу. 'Wishing to leave as soon as possible, he is in a hurry to finish his work.' (*почему* он торопится закончить работу? *желая скорее уехать*).

4. *Занимаясь* систематически гимнастикой, можно укрепить здоровье. 'Doing P. T. exercises regularly, you can strengthen your health.' (*при каких условиях* можно укрепить здоровье? *занимаясь систематически гимнастикой*).

In a sentence, the verbal adverb modifies the verb and denotes some additional action.

Table 121

Formation of Verbal Adverbs

Imperfective Aspect		Perfective Aspect	
живя 'living' читая 'reading' кончая 'finishing' сидя 'sitting' стуча 'knocking' занимаясь 'studying'	*-а, -я*	прочитав 'having read' закончив 'having finished' посидев 'having sat' постучав 'having knocked' запершись 'having locked oneself up' позанимавшись 'having studied'	*-в, -ши, -вши*
Verbal adverbs of the imperfective aspect are formed from the stem of the present tense.		Verbal adverbs of the perfective aspect are formed from the stem of the past tense.	

Imperfective Aspect	Perfective Aspect

To obtain an imperfective verbal adverb, the ending of the verb in the present tense is dropped and the suffix *-a* or *-я* is added (the suffix *-a* is used only after the sibilants):

жив-у́т 'they live' — жив-я́
чита́-ют 'they read' — чита́-я
тре́бу-ют 'they demand'—тре́бу-я
занима́-ют-ся 'they study' — —занима́-я-сь
сид-я́т 'they sit'—си́д-я
стуч-а́т 'they knock' — стуч-а́

(Exception: verbal adverbs of verbs with the suffix *-ва-* following the roots *-да-, -зна-, -ста-* are formed from the stem of the infinitive: дава́ть 'to give'—дава́я, сознава́ть 'to realize' — сознава́я, встава́ть 'to stand up' — встава́я.

Note. — 1. Verbal adverbs are not formed from imperfective verbs with the suffix *-ну-* (*тяну́ть* 'to pull', *завя́знуть* 'to stick', *со́хнуть* 'to dry', *мо́кнуть* 'to become wet').

2. Verbal adverbs of some verbs are not used, e.g., of the verbs *ждать* 'to wait', *петь* 'to sing', *бежа́ть* 'to run', *писа́ть* 'to write', *пить* 'to drink', *бить* 'to beat', *жать* 'to press', *мять* 'to crumple', *тере́ть* 'to grate', *печь* 'to bake', *стере́чь* 'to guard', *паха́ть* 'to plough', *ре́зать* 'to cut'.

3. In the popular language the forms of the verbal adverb ending in *-учи, -ючи* have been preserved (*и́дучи* 'going', *гля́дючи* 'looking').

In the modern literary language such forms occur very rarely, with the exception of *бу́дучи* (verbal adverb of the verb *быть* 'to be').

To obtain a perfective verbal adverb, the suffix *-л* of the verb in the past tense is dropped and *-в* or *-вши* is added to the stem vowel:

прочита́-л 'I (he) read'—прочита́-в
взя́-л-ся 'I (he) undertook'—взя́-в- ши-сь
or *-ши* to the final consonant of the stem:
за́перся 'I (he) locked myself (himself)'—запер-ши́-сь
(but: за́пер 'I (he) locked'—запе-ре́в)
вы́сох 'it dried'—вы́сох-ши

Note. — 1. Verbal adverbs of perfective verbs with the suffix *-ну-* may in some cases be formed both from the stem of the infinitive and from the stem of the past tense:
  окре́пнуть 'to become strong' — окре́пнув, окре́пши
  вы́сохнуть 'to dry up' — вы́сохнув, вы́сохши.

2. Verbal adverbs of a few verbs can be formed from the stem of the simple future:
уви́д-ят 'they will see'—уви́д-я (уви́дев is more frequently used)
пройд-у́т 'they will pass'—пройд-я́.

Table 122

Uses of Verbal Adverbs

Imperfective Aspect	Perfective Aspect
Ученик отвечает урок, *стоя* у доски. 'The pupil recites his lesson, standing at the blackboard.' *Возвращаясь* из театра, мы встретили товарища. 'Returning from the theatre, we met a friend.' Завтра, *возвращаясь* с прогулки, я зайду к товарищу. 'When I come back from my walk tomorrow I shall call on a friend.' *Желая* скорее уехать, он торопится кончить работу. 'Wishing to leave as soon as possible, he is in a hurry to finish his work.'	*Вернувшись* из театра, я нашёл на столе письмо. 'On coming back from the theatre I found a letter on the table.' *Закончив* работу, он уедет. 'On finishing his work he will leave.' *Закончив* работу, он будет отдыхать. 'On finishing his work he will have a rest.'
Note. — Verbal adverbs of imperfective verbs are used to denote an action which is simultaneous with that of the predicate.	**Note.** — Verbal adverbs of perfective verbs are used to denote an action which precedes that of the predicate.

The verbal adverb can be used only if the action it denotes is performed by the same agent as the action of the verb of the clause in which it stands.

VIII. THE ADVERB

FORMATION OF ADVERBS

Table 123

PRINCIPAL WAYS OF FORMING ADVERBS

Part of speech from which adverbs are formed	Meaning	Examples
I. From adjectives: (a) from qualitative adjectives adverbs ending in *-o, -e* are formed. (Their form is identical with that of the short form adjectives ending in *-o, -e*): хоро́ший 'good' — хорошо́ 'well', могу́чий 'powerful' — могу́че 'powerfully':	Denoting manner (question *как?* 'how?'): хорошо́ 'well' пло́хо 'badly' я́сно 'clearly' краси́во 'beautifully' могу́че 'powerfully' и́скренне 'frankly'	Он *хорошо́* написа́л сочине́ние. 'He wrote his composition well.' Ла́сточки лета́ли *высоко́*. 'Swallows were flying high.' Он говори́т *и́скренне*.' He speaks frankly.'
(b) from relative adjectives and from some qualitative ones by means of the prefix *no-* and the ending of the dative singular of the masculine gender:	по-весе́ннему 'as in spring' по-зи́мнему 'as in winter' по-доро́жному 'as when travelling' по-вое́нному 'like a military man' по-настоя́щему 'really' по-хоро́шему 'in a friendly way' по-но́вому 'in a new way'	Он был оде́т *по-доро́жному*. 'He had travelling clothes on.' Мы разошли́сь *по-хоро́шему*. 'We parted as friends.'

(c) from relative adjectives ending in **-ский** (*дру́жеский* 'friendly', *ру́сский* 'Russian', etc.) adverbs ending in **-и** are formed by means of the prefix **по-**; from a number of adjectives adverbs are formed without the prefix:	по-челове́чески 'as people do' по-дру́жески 'in a friendly way' по-това́рищески 'in a friendly way' по-прия́тельски 'as an acquaintance would do' по-ру́сски 'in Russian' по-англи́йски 'in English' крити́чески 'critically' полити́чески 'politically' теорети́чески 'theoretically' практи́чески 'practically' тво́рчески 'creatively' геро́ически 'heroically' геро́йски 'heroically'	Он поступи́л *по-това́рищески*. 'He acted as a friend.' Студе́нт хорошо́ говори́т *по-ру́сски*. 'The student speaks Russian well.' Он уме́ет относи́ться *крити́чески* к свои́м посту́пкам. 'He is capable of taking a critical attitude to his actions.' Партиза́ны сража́лись *геро́ически*. 'The guerrillas fought heroically.'
(d) from relative adjectives in **-ий, -ья, -ье** (*медве́жий* 'bear's', *медве́жья, медве́жье*) adverbs ending in **-и**, generally with the prefix **по-**, are formed:	по-медве́жьи 'like a bear' по-во́лчьи 'like a wolf' по-ли́сьи 'like a fox' по-за́ячьи 'like a hare'	Соба́ка завы́ла *по-во́лчьи*. 'The dog howled like a wolf.'
(e) from some qualitative long and short form adjectives adverbs are formed by means of various prefixes:	Denoting place or manner: спра́ва (*где?* 'where?') 'on the right' сле́ва 'on the left'	*Спра́ва* шуме́ла ро́ща, *сле́ва* колыха́лась рожь. 'On the right, a grove was rustling; on the left, rye was swaying.'

	издалека́ (*отку́да?* 'where from?') 'from afar'	
	до́красна́ (*как?* 'how?') 'red-hot' добела́ (*как?* 'how?') 'white-hot'	Желе́зо раскали́-лось *до́красна́*. 'The iron became red-hot.'
	на́бело (*как?* 'how?') 'clean' на́чисто (*как?* 'how?') 'clean' сно́ва (*как?* 'how?') 'again'	Учени́к переписа́л дома́шнюю рабо́ту *на́-бело (на́чисто)*. 'The pupil made a fair copy of his homework.'
	вкра́тце (*как?* 'how?') 'in brief' впусту́ю (*как?* 'how?') 'for nothing'	Он рассказа́л нам *вкра́тце* содержа́ние статьи́. 'He gave us a brief outline of the article.'
	вплотну́ю (*как?* 'how?') 'close'	Он подошёл ко мне *вплотну́ю*. 'He came close up to me.'
(f) from active participles adverbs ending in *-e* are formed:	Denoting manner (question: *как?* 'how?'):	
	торжеству́юще 'triumphantly'	Пе́сня звуча́ла *тор-жеству́юще*. 'The song sounded triumphant.'
	вызыва́юще 'defiantly'	Он вёл себя́ *вызы-ва́юще*. 'He behaved defiantly.'
	умоля́юще 'imploringly'	Ребёнок *умоля́юще* смотре́л на мать. 'The child was looking at his mother imploringly.'

	блестя́ще 'brilliantly'	Он говори́л блестя́ще. 'He spoke brilliantly.'
II. From nouns: (a) by putting them in the instrumental singular without a preposition:	Denoting time (question: когда́? 'when?'): у́тром 'in the morning' днём 'in the daytime' ве́чером 'in the evening' но́чью 'at night'	
	ле́том 'in summer' весно́й 'in spring'	Ле́том мы мно́го купа́лись. 'We bathed a lot in summer'
(the Russian adverbs босико́м 'barefoot', пешко́м 'on foot' also have the form of the instrumental singular, although they have no corresponding nouns):	Denoting manner (question: как? 'how?'): верхо́м 'on horseback' бего́м 'running'	Люблю́ ле́том бе́гать босико́м. 'I like to run about barefoot in summer.' Путеше́ственники всю доро́гу е́хали верхо́м. 'All the way the travellers went on horseback.'
	ша́гом 'at a walk' ры́сью 'at a trot'	Ло́шадь шла ша́гом, пото́м побежа́ла ры́сью. 'The horse went at a walk, then it broke into a trot.'
(b) from other oblique cases with prepositions:	Generally denoting place: вдали́ (где? 'where?') 'in the distance' и́здали (отку́да? 'from where?') 'from a distance'	Вдали́ серебряной бахромо́й сверка́ли го́ры. (Л.) 'In the distance there glittered the silver tringle of the mountains.'

	свéрху (*откýда?* 'from where?') 'from top' наверхý (*гдé?* 'where?') 'above' внизý (*гдé?* 'where?') 'be-low' вниз (*кудá?* 'where to?') 'down' дóма (*гдé?* 'where?') 'at home'	Молодóй зелёный лес покры́л гóры *свéр-ху дóнизу.* 'Young green woods covered the mountains from top to bottom.' *Внизý* журчáли про-вóрные ручьи́. 'Below there murmured swift streams.' Весь день я сидéл *дóма.* 'I stayed at home all day long.'
III. From possessive pro-nouns: from · the dative singular of the masculine gender of possessive pronouns adverbs with the prefix **по-** are formed:	Denoting man-ner (question *как?* 'how?') по-мóему 'as I wish(ed)' по-твóему 'as you would have it' по-свóему 'in one's own way' по-нáшему 'as we wish(ed)'	Он сдéлал всё *по-свóему.* 'He did eve-rything in his own way.'
IV. From numerals: (a) from ordinal numerals adverbs are formed by means of the prefixes *в-, во-*: (b) from cardinal and col-lective numerals:	во-пéрвых 'first-ly' во-вторы́х 'sec-ondly' в-трéтьих 'third-ly', etc. однáжды 'once' двáжды 'twice' трúжды 'three times' вдвоём 'two (to-gether)'	*Однáжды* я возвра-щáлся с охóты... (Т.) 'One day I was return-ing after a shooting expedition...' Этот вопрóс ужé обсуждáлся *двáжды.* 'This question has been debated twice.'

	втроём 'three (together)'	Эта книга стоит *втрое* дороже, чем та. 'This book is three times as dear as that.'
	вчетвером 'four (together)'	
	вдвое 'twice'	
	втрое 'three times'	
V. Adverbs may be formed from other adverbs:		
(a) by means of a prefix:	позавчера 'the day before yesterday'	Куда ни оглянусь, *повсюду* рожь густая. (M.) 'Wherever I look, there's thick rye on all sides.'
	послезавтра 'the day after tomorrow'	
	отсюда 'from here'	
	оттуда 'from there'	
	повсюду 'everywhere'	
(b) by means of the particles *не-, ни-, -то, -либо, -нибудь, кое-:*	никогда 'never'	Я *никогда* не был на Урале. 'I've never been to the Urals.'
	некогда 'long ago'	
	нигде 'nowhere'	
	негде '(there is) no place'	
	никуда 'nowhere'	Я сегодня *никуда* не пойду: мне *некуда* идти. 'I shan't go anywhere today; I've nowhere to go to.'
	некуда 'nowhere'	
	где-то 'somewhere'	
	когда-нибудь 'sometime'	*Когда-нибудь* поеду на Урал. 'Sometime I'll go to the Urals'.
	куда-либо 'somewhere'	
	кое-где 'here and there'	

Besides derivative adverbs, there are simple ones, e.g., *здесь* 'here', *там* 'there', *сюда* 'here', *туда* 'there', *очень* 'very (much)' and others.

IX. THE CONJUNCTION

Table 124

Conjunctions	Examples	Remarks
A. Coordinating Conjunctions (used in a sentence to connect words or clauses):		
Coordinating conjunctions: *и* 'and':	Ра́достно, мо́лодо бы́ло *и* на не́бе, *и* на земле́, *и* в се́рдце челове́ка. (Л. Т.) 'Happy and young felt the heaven, and the earth, and man's heart'. Надо всём стоя́ла тень лёгкой ту́чки, *и* всё жда́ло ти́хого весе́ннего до́ждика. (Л. Т.) 'The shadow of a light cloud overhung everything, and all yearned for a gentle spring shower.'	
да (meaning *и* 'and'):	Со́сны лишь *да* е́ли Верши́нами шуме́ли... (П.) 'Only the crowns of pines and fir-trees were rustling'. По́ле с ро́жью то́чно гори́т огнём, *да* ре́чка блести́т, сверка́ет на со́лнце. (Гонч.) 'The rye-field seems to be ablaze with fire, and the river glistens and sparkles in the sun.'	1. The conjunction *да* meaning *и* 'and' occurs rarely and is mainly used in colloquial speech.
ни... ни 'neither... nor':	Сего́дня я не получи́л *ни* пи́сем, *ни* газе́т. 'Today I have received neither letters nor newspapers.'	2. The conjunction *ни... ни* is used in negative sentences to emphasize the negation.

	Ни я не посла́л бра́ту письма́, *ни* он мне не написа́л. 'Neither I sent a letter to my brother nor he wrote to me.'	
a 'but':	Не геро́и де́лают исто́рию, *a* исто́рия де́лает геро́ев. 'It is not heroes that make history, but history that makes heroes.'	
	. . . . Челове́ку ну́жно не три арши́на земли́, не уса́дьба, *a* весь земно́й шар, вся приро́да. (Ч.) 'Man needs not three arshins* of land, not a farmstead, but the whole of the earth, the whole of nature.'	
но 'but':	Ни́зкое со́лнце не гре́ет, *но* блести́т я́рче ле́тнего. (Т.) 'The low sun is not warm, but it shines brighter than a summer sun does.' Со́лнце зашло́ за го́ры, *но* бы́ло ещё светло́. (Л. Т.) 'The sun had set beyond the mountains, but it was still light.'	
да (meaning *но* 'but'):	Я хоте́л отве́тить тебе́ на письмо́, *да* позабы́л твой а́дрес. 'I wanted to answer your letter, but I've forgotten your address.' Давно́ собира́лся написа́ть тебе́, *да* всё вре́мени не́ было. 'I intended to write to you a long time ago, but I always had no time.'	3. The conjunction *да* (meaning *но* 'but') occurs rarely and is mainly used in colloquial speech.

* arshin, an old Russian measure of length, equal to 28 inches

и́ли 'or', *ли́бо* 'or', *и́ли... и́ли* *(ли́бо... ли́бо)* 'either... or':	Да́йте мне, пожа́луйста, кни́гу *и́ли* журна́л. 'Please give me a book or a magazine.' В воскресе́нье *и́ли* я пойду́ к това́рищу, *и́ли* он придёт ко мне. 'On Sunday, either I'll go to my friend's or he'll come to my place.'	4. The conjunctions *и́ли* and *ли́бо* are synonymous. *Ли́бо* is rarely used.
то... то 'now... now':	Лёгкий ветеро́к *то* просыпа́лся, *то* утиха́л. (Т.) 'A light breeze now rose, now fell.' То хо́лодно, *то* о́чень жа́рко, То со́лнце спря́чется, То све́тит сли́шком я́рко. (Кр.) 'Now it's cold, now it's very hot, Now the sun is hidden, Now it shines too bright.'	5. The conjunction *то... то* is used to indicate sequence of actions.

B. Subordinating Conjunctions (used to connect clauses):

Explanatory conjunctions: *что* 'that'; *что́бы (чтоб)* (usually rendered in English by the infinitive of a verb or by a clause):	Скажи́ ему́, *что* я приду́ за́втра. 'Tell him that I'll come tomorrow.' Скажи́ ему́, *что́бы* он пришёл за́втра. 'Tell him to come tomorrow.' Мы написа́ли бра́ту, *что́бы* он встре́тил нас на вокза́ле. 'We wrote to our brother that he should meet us at the station.'	1. In these instances the conjunction *что́бы* is used to connect two clauses one of which completes and explains the other.

Conjunctions
of purpose:
чтóбы (чтоб)
'in order to':
***для тогó чтó-
бы*** 'in order to',
'in order that':

Я зашёл к товáрищу, *чтóбы* рассказáть ему об экскýрсии. 'I called on my friend to tell him about the excursion.'

Я зашёл к товáрищу, *чтóбы* он рассказáл мне *об* экскýрсии. 'I called on my friend so that he might tell me about the excursion.'

. . . .

Чтóбы сократúть путь, мы пошлú к рéчке напрямúк чéрез Сырые лугá. (Гайдáр) 'To take a short cut, we went to the river straight across Damp Meadows.'

Для тогó чтóбы хорошó изобразúть, худóжник дóлжен прекрáсно вúдеть и дáже предвúдеть. (М.Г.) 'To portray well, the artist must see well, he must even foresee.'

Для тогó чтóбы литератýрное произведéние заслужúло тúтул худóжественного, необходúмо придáть ему совершéнную словéсную фóрму. (М. Г.) 'For a work of literature to deserve the name of a work of art, it must be perfectly worded.'

Conjunctions
of cause:
потомý что
'because'; ***так
как*** 'as', 'since';
úбо 'for'; ***оттогó что*** 'because';
***из-за тогó,
что*** 'because of',
'on account of';

Одéнься теплéе, *потомý что* сегóдня хóлодно. 'Put on your warm clothes because it's cold today.'

Я не пришёл на занятия, *так как* заболéл. 'I didn't come to the classes as I had fallen ill.'

. . . .

2. In these instances the conjunction ***чтóбы*** is used to connect two parts of a sentence, one of which expresses the purpose of the action in the other.

3. In a construction introduced by ***чтóбы***, the only verbal forms that can be used are an infinitive or a past tense.

4. The infinitive is used to express an action the agent of which is the same as that of the action expressed by the principal verb.

5. The past tense is used to express an action the agent of which is different from that of the action expressed by the principal verb.

6. In colloquial speech the conjunctions ***потомý что*** and ***так как*** are most frequently used.

в си́лу того́ что 'owing to', 'because of', 'by virtue of'; ввиду́ того́ что 'in view of the fact that', 'as'; всле́дствие того́ что 'in consequence of':

Спать ему́ не хоте́лось, и́бо на душе́ бы́ло неспоко́йно и тяжело́. (Ч.) 'He was not sleepy, for he felt uneasy and miserable.'

Оттого́ что мы вста́ли о́чень ра́но и пото́м ничего́ не де́лали, э́тот день каза́лся о́чень дли́нным, са́мым дли́нным в мое́й жи́зни. (Ч.) 'We having got up very early and been doing nothing ever since, that day seemed very long, the longest in my life.'

Из-за того́ что я в ука́занный срок не верну́л книг в библиоте́ку, у меня́ бы́ли неприя́тности. 'I had some trouble, because I had failed to return the books to the library in time.'

Ввиду́ того́ что я во вре́мя о́тпуска был бо́лен (всле́дствие того́ что я был бо́лен..., в си́лу того́ что я был бо́лен), прошу́ продли́ть мне о́тпуск на две неде́ли. 'Owing to the fact that I was ill during my holiday, I ask you to extend it for two weeks.'

7. The conjunction *и́бо* is rarely used in colloquial speech; it more often occurs in scientific contexts.

8. The conjunctions *всле́дствие того́ что, ввиду́ того́ что* and *в си́лу того́ что* are mainly used in business and official language.

Conjunctions of condition: *е́сли* 'if'; *е́сли бы* 'if'; *раз* 'once'; *коль ско́ро* 'once', 'as soon as'; *ко́ли* 'if'; *коль* 'if':

Е́сли я получу́ о́тпуск ле́том, я пое́ду в дере́вню. 'If I get a holiday in summer, I'll go to the country.'

Е́сли бы я получи́л о́тпуск ле́том, я пое́хал бы в дере́вню. 'If I (had) got a holiday in summer, I should (have) go (gone) to the country.'

9. The conjunctions *ко́ли (коль)* and *коль ско́ро* are rarely used.

11–118

Conjunctions
of time:
когда́ 'when';
как то́лько 'as
soon as', 'the
moment'; *лишь
то́лько* 'as soon
as'; *в то вре́мя
как* 'while';
едва́ 'hardly';
пока́ 'while';
пока́ не 'till',
'until':

Раз дал сло́во (*е́сли* дал сло́во, *коль ско́ро* дал сло́во, *ко́ли* дал сло́во), до́лжен его́ сдержа́ть. 'Once you pledged your word, you must keep it.'

Когда́ мы тро́нулись в путь, свети́ло я́ркое со́лнце. 'When we set out, the sun was shining bright.'

Лишь то́лько скры́лось со́лнце, ста́ло о́чень хо́лодно. 'The moment the sun disappeared, it became very cold.'

Как то́лько со́лнце скры́лось за горизо́нтом, сра́зу поду́л ре́зкий, холо́дный ве́тер. 'The very moment the sun set beyond the horizon, a sharp, cold wind began blowing.'

В то вре́мя как в по́ле ду́ет ве́тер, в лесу́ ти́хо и тепло́. 'While it is windy in the fields, it is quiet and warm in the wood.'

Едва́ мы добрали́сь до ле́са, как пошёл дождь. 'Hardly had we reached the wood when it began raining.'

Мы стоя́ли под де́ревом, *пока́* шёл дождь. 'We stood under a tree while it was raining.'

Мы стоя́ли под де́ревом, *пока́* дождь *не* переста́л. 'We stood under a tree till the rain stopped.'

10. The conjunction *пока́ не* is used to connect two clauses, the clause containing *пока́ не* expressing a time limit before which the action expressed in the other clause cannot take place.

	Часа́ три мы шли без о́тдыха, *пока́* в стороне́ *не* послы́шался шум воды́. 'We had been walking without a rest for about three hours till we heard the noise of water not far away.'	
	. . . .	
	Мину́т два́дцать я бесце́льно броди́л по одному́ ме́сту, *пока́ не* успоко́ился. (Арс.) 'For about twenty minutes I walked about the same place aimlessly, till I calmed down.'	
Conjunctions of result: *так что* 'so that'; *всле́дствие чего́* 'in consequence of':	Лёд на реке́ места́ми уже́ тро́нулся, *так что* идти́ на лы́жах бы́ло опа́сно. (Павл.) 'The ice on the river had broken in some places, so that it was dangerous to ski.'	11. The conjunction *всле́дствие чего́* is generally used in business and official language.
Conjunctions of comparison: *как* 'as'; *как бу́дто* 'as if', 'as though'; *бу́дто* 'as if', 'as though'; *бу́дто бы* 'as though'; *то́чно, сло́вно* 'as though', 'like', 'as if':	Тёмные верши́ны колыха́лись, *как** гре́бни волн в гро́зную непого́ду. (Кор.) 'The dark summits were swaying like wave-crests in terrible weather.' ...Нева́ мета́лась, *как* больно́й В свое́й посте́ли беспоко́йной. (П.) 'The Neva was tossing about like a sick man In his restless bed.'	12. The most frequently used conjunctions of comparison are *как* and *как бу́дто*.

---

* In this case *как* is synonymous with *то́чно* and *сло́вно*.

Сего́дня я чу́вствую себя́ так, *как бу́дто** гора́ свали́-лась с мои́х плеч. (Гарш.) 'Today I feel as if a heavy load has been taken off my mind.'

Conjunctions of concession: *хотя́* 'though', 'although'; *несмотря́ на то что* 'in spite of', 'despite'; *как ни* 'no matter how', 'however':

Хотя́ мы о́чень торопи́-лись до темноты́ верну́ться домо́й, ночь заста́ла нас в пути́. 'Though we hurried very much in order to get home before dark, night fell as we were still on our way.'

Несмотря́ на то что бы́ло уже́ совсе́м темно́, мы продолжа́ли свой путь. 'In spite of it being quite dark, we continued on our way.'

Как ни тру́ден был путь, мы шли о́чень бы́стро. 'However hard the road was, we went fast.'

---

* In this case *как бу́дто* is synonymous with *бу́дто* and *бу́дто бы*.

X. WORD-BUILDING

GENERAL REMARKS

Various words can be derived from one and the same root by adding different suffixes and prefixes.

уч-и́-ть 'to study' — вы́-учить 'to study thoroughly', на-учи́ть 'to teach', за-учи́ть 'to learn (by heart)', etc.
уч-и́-тель 'teacher', 'schoolmaster'
уч-и́-тель-ниц(а) 'teacher', 'schoolmistress'
уч-е-ни́к 'pupil', 'schoolboy'
уч-е-ни́ц(а) 'pupil', 'schoolgirl'
уч-а́щ-ий-ся 'student'
уч-ён-ый 'scientist'
уч-е́ни(е) 'teaching'

стро́-ить 'to build' — по-стро́ить 'to finish building', пере-стро́ить 'to rebuild', за-стро́ить 'to build up', etc.
стро-и́-тель 'builder'
стро-и́-тель-ств(о) 'building', 'construction'
строй-к(а) 'building' — по-стро́йка 'building', пере-стро́йка 'rebuilding', за-стро́йка 'building'
стро́й-н-ый 'well-proportioned'
стро-е́ни(е) 'building', 'structure'
стро́-ящ-ий-ся 'being built'

Note. — The root of all the words is *-строй-*, but *й* is dropped before *и*. The combination [йэ] is rendered in spelling by the letter *е*.

In forming new words, some sounds in the stem may undergo certain changes:
друг 'friend' — друзья́ 'friends'
дружи́ть 'to be friends'
дру́жба 'friendship'
дру́жный 'friendly'
дру́жеский 'friendly'
дру́жественный 'friendly'

alternation: *г — з; г — ж*

MOST PRODUCTIVE NOUN-FORMING SUFFIXES

Table 125

Suffixes used to Form Nouns denoting the Agent or Performer of an Action

	Suffixes forming Masculine Nouns		Suffixes forming Feminine Nouns	Remarks
-тель	читáтель 'reader' писáтель 'writer' руководúтель 'leader' строúтель 'builder'	**-ниц-а**	читáтельница писáтельница руководúтель- ница	1. Nouns with the suffix **-тель** are chiefly derived from the stem of the infinitive of a verb: *читá-ть* 'to read' — *читá-тель* 'reader' *руководú-ть* 'to lead' — *руководú-тель* 'leader' 2. In words derived from a verb stem ending in **-а,** the stress of the verb is retained: *читáть* 'to read' — *читáтель* 'reader' *писáть* 'to write' — *писáтель* 'writer' In words derived from a verb stem ending in **-и,** the stress invariably falls on **-и:** *руководúть* 'to lead' — *руководúтель* 'leader' *стрóить* 'to build' — *стрóитель* 'builder' 3. In corresponding feminine nouns, the suffix **-тель** is retained and the suffix **-ниц-а** is added. The stress in feminine nouns falls on the same syllable as in the corresponding masculine ones.

Note. — From the stem of the infinitive, nouns can also be formed which do not denote persons (e.g. числи́тель 'numerator', знамена́тель 'denominator', мно́житель 'multiplier', дели́тель 'diviser', дви́гатель 'engine', истреби́тель 'fighter-plane', etc.). Such nouns generally retain the stress of the verb, except for a very few words: чи́слить 'numerate' — числи́тель 'numerator'.

Suffix	Examples	Feminine suffix	Feminine examples
-щик	набо́рщик 'type-setter' конто́рщик 'clerk' нату́рщик 'model' ка́менщик 'stonemason' стеко́льщик 'glazier' бараба́нщик 'drummer' часовщи́к 'watch-maker'	-щиц-а	набо́рщица конто́рщица нату́рщица
-ов-щик -ёв-щик	старьёвщик 'old-clothes man'		
-ль-щик	носи́льщик 'carrier', 'porter'		
-чик (after д, т, з, с, ж)	лётчик 'flyer' пулемётчик 'machine-gunner' разве́дчик 'scout' перево́дчик 'translator'	-чиц-а	лётчица пулемётчица разве́дчица перево́дчица

1. Nouns with the suffixes -щик, -чик, -щиц-а, -чиц-а are derived from noun and verb stems:

барабан 'drum' — бараба́нщик 'drummer'
носи́ть 'to carry' — носи́льщик 'carrier', 'porter'
переписывать 'to copy' — перепи́счик 'copyist'
ответ 'response' — отве́тчик 'respondent'

2. In nouns with the suffix -чик the stress always falls on the penultimate syllable (разве́дчик 'scout', перево́дчик 'translator').

3. In nouns with the suffix -щик the stress may fall on different syllables. In some cases it falls on the same syllable as in the word the noun is derived from, e.g.:

ка́мень 'stone' — ка́менщик 'stonemason'
старьё 'old clothes' — старьёвщик 'old-clothes man'

Suffixes forming Masculine Nouns	Suffixes forming Feminine Nouns		Remarks
перепи́счик 'copyist' во́зчик 'carter' перебе́жчик 'deserter'		перепи́счица	In other cases it falls on the last syllable, (часовщи́к 'watch-maker'). If the noun is not stressed on the last syllable, the stress remains fixed. If the noun is stressed on the last syllable, the stress is shifted in declension according to the type as in Table 24, group C, I (стари́к 'old man', дождь 'rain').
			4. Feminine nouns are stressed on the same syllable as the corresponding masculine nouns.
-ник	-ниц-а		
колхо́зник 'collective farmer'		колхо́зница	1. Nouns with the suffix -ник are derived from adjective or noun stems:
рабо́тник 'worker' отли́чник 'excellent pupil'		рабо́тница отли́чница	отли́чный 'excellent' — отли́чник 'excellent pupil'. мя́со 'meat' — мясни́к 'butcher', 'dealer in meat'
учени́к 'pupil', 'school-boy'		учени́ца	2. Feminine nouns are stressed on the same syllable as the corresponding masculine nouns.
помо́щник 'assistant' сапо́жник 'shoe-maker' мясни́к 'butcher' печни́к 'stovemaker'		помо́щница	Nouns with the suffix -ник denoting a man's trade (сапо́жник 'shoe-maker', мясни́к 'butcher', печни́к 'stovemaker') have no corresponding feminine nouns.
			3. The stress in some nouns falls on the penultimate syllable (дво́рник 'yard-keeper',

пильщик 'sawyer', *помо́щник* 'assistant', *ко́нник* 'cavalryman'); in others, on the last syllable (*лесни́к* 'forester', *печни́к* 'stove-maker'). If the stress falls on the penultimate syllable, it remains fixed in declension; if it falls on the last syllable, it is shifted according to the type as in Table 24, group C, I.

Note. — By means of the suffixes *-ник, -ниц-а* nouns are also formed which denote things (*ча́йник* 'teakettle', 'teapot', *кофе́йник* 'coffee-pot', *са́харница* 'sugar-basin', *пе́пельница* 'ash-tray').

-ик	1. Nouns with the suffix *-ик* are generally formed from nouns. 2. The suffix *-ик* generally denotes speciality (*исто́рик* 'historian', *фи́зик* 'physicist', etc.). 3. Nouns with the suffix *-ик* may also denote things (*грузови́к* 'lorry', *боеви́к* 'thriller', etc.).	математик 'mathematician', историк 'historian' физик 'physicist' химик 'chemist'
-ов-ик (-ев-ик)	4. Nouns with the suffix *-ови́к (-еви́к)* are stressed on the last syllable: *фронтови́к* 'front-line soldier'. In their declension the	фронтовик 'front-line soldier'

Suffixes forming Masculine Nouns	Suffixes forming Feminine Nouns		Remarks
передовúк 'foremost worker'			stress is generally shifted according to the type as in Table 24, group C, I. Note. — The suffix -uk may also occur in nouns derived from adjectives: стáрый 'old' — старúк 'old man'.
-ец			
комсомóлец 'Young Communist Leaguer' борéц 'fighter' боéц 'fighting-man' гребéц 'rower' ленинградец 'native/resident of Leningrad' сарáтовец 'native/resident of Saratov' испáнец 'Spaniard' голлáндец 'Dutchman' красáвец 'very good-looking man' храбрéц 'brave man' гордéц 'proud man' чтец 'elocutionist'	**-к-а** комсомóлка ленинградка **-и-ца**	испáнка голлáндка красáвица	1. Nouns with the suffix -ец are derived from the stems of nouns (бой 'fight' — боéц 'fighting-man'), adjectives (красúвый 'good-looking' — красáвец 'very good-looking man', хрáбрый 'brave' — храбрéц 'brave man') or verbs (борóться 'to fight' — борéц 'fighter', читáть 'to read' — чтец 'elocutionist'); most frequently from the stems of nouns. 2. Masculine nouns denoting persons belonging to some organization (комсомóлец 'Young Communist Leaguer'), nationality (голлáндец 'Dutchman') or place of residence (ленинградец 'native/resident of Leningrad') form their feminine counterparts by means of the suffix -к- (комсомóлка 'Young Communist Leaguer', голлáндка 'Dutch woman', ленинградка 'native/resident of Leningrad') whereas masculine nouns denoting persons by their activities either have
-ан-ец республикáнец 'republican'	**-к-а** республикáнка		

-ен-ец *-ов-ец* *-л-ец*	бе́женец 'refugee' торго́вец 'merchant' владе́лец 'owner'	бе́женка

no feminine counterparts at all (e.g., *бое́ц* 'fighting-man', *боре́ц* 'fighter', *еребе́ц* 'rower', *храбре́ц* 'brave man') or form them by means of the suffixes *-иц-а*, *-их-а* (*краса́вица* 'beauty', *чти́ца* 'elocutionist', *купчи́ха* 'merchant's wife') and not *-к-*.

3. These nouns are generally stressed on the last syllable: *бое́ц* 'fighting-man', *храбре́ц* 'brave man', *удале́ц* 'daring fellow', *молоде́ц* 'fine fellow', but sometimes on the penultimate syllable: *краса́вец* 'very good-looking man', *ленинера́дец* 'native/resident of Leningrad', *разя́нец* 'native/resident of Ryazan'. Nouns denoting a resident of a town or a citizen of a country retain the stress on the same syllable as the nouns they are derived from: *Ленинера́д* 'Leningrad' — *ленинера́дец*, *Севасто́поль* 'Sevastopol' — *севасто́полец*, *Испа́ния* 'Spain' — *испа́нец*. If these nouns are not stressed on the last syllable, the stress remains fixed. If they are stressed on the last syllable, the stress is shifted in declension according to the type as in Table 24, group C, I. Nouns with the suffixes *-ен-ец* are generally stressed on the penultimate syllable: *посе́ленец* 'settler', *пересе́ленец* 'immigrant'. In this case the stress is fixed.

Suffixes forming Masculine Nouns		Suffixes forming Feminine Nouns		Remarks
-ин	болга́рин 'Bulgarian' грузи́н 'Georgian' тата́рин 'Tatar' гражда́нин 'citizen'	**-ка-**	болга́рка грузи́нка тата́рка гражда́нка	1. The suffixes **-ин, -анин (-янин)** are generally used to indicate nationality (*боле́-рин* 'Bulgarian') or place of birth or residence (*волжа́нин* 'native/resident of the Volga region').
-ан-ин (-я-ч-ин)	горожа́нин 'resident of a city or town' волжа́нин 'native/resi-dent of the Volga region' харьковча́нин 'native/resident of Kharkov' крестья́нин 'peasant' киевля́нин 'native/resi-dent of Kiev'	**-к-а**	горожа́нка волжа́нка харьковча́нка крестья́нка киевля́нка	2. These nouns are stressed either on the penultimate syllable (*тата́рин, горожа́нин, крестья́нин*) or on the last syllable (*грузи́н, граждан//н*). The stress is fixed, except in the word *гражда́нин* which, in all the forms of the plural, is stressed on the first syllable: *гра́ждане, гра́ждан, гра́жданам*, etc.
-ич	москви́ч 'Moscovite' костроми́ч 'native/resi-dent of Kostroma' вя́тич 'native/resident of Vyatka'	**-к-а**	москви́чка костроми́чка	1. Nouns with the suffix **-ич, -ак (-як)** or **-як** are derived from noun and adjective stems: (*Москва́* 'Moscow' — *москви́ч, Сиби́рь* 'Siberia' — *сибиря́к, бе́дный* 'poor' — *бед-ня́к*).

-ак (-як)	сибиряк 'native/resident of Siberia'	-к-а	сибирячка
	пермяк 'native/resident of Perm'		пермячка
	земляк 'fellow-townsman'		землячка
-ач	бедняк 'poor man'		беднячка
	батрак 'farm-hand'		батрачка
	скрипач 'violinist'		скрипнячка
	трубач 'trumpet-player'		

2. No special words are formed from the names of some towns to denote their residents or natives: the latter are denoted in a descriptive manner: *житель/уроженец Омска* 'native/resident of Omsk', *житель/уроженец Каширы* 'native/resident of Kashira', etc.

3. Masculine nouns are generally stressed on the last syllable. In their declension the stress is shifted according to the type as in Table 24, group C, I. Feminine nouns are stressed on the same syllable as their masculine counterparts (*москвич* 'Moscovite' — *москвичка*). The stress remains fixed. Nouns with the suffix *-ак (-як)* (*батрак* 'farm-hand', *бедняк* 'poor man') or *-ач* (*избач* 'village librarian') are stressed on the last syllable. In their declension the stress is shifted according to the type as in Table 24, group C, I.

In feminine nouns derived from masculine nouns with the siffixes *-ак*, *-ач* the stress is retained on the same syllable as in the masculine ones (e.g., *рыбак* 'fisherman' — *рыбачка*). The stress is fixed.

Suffixes forming Masculine Nouns	Suffixes forming Feminine Nouns	Remarks
-ун болту́н 'chatterer' шалу́н 'naughty boy' хвасту́н 'braggart' крику́н 'squaller' ворчу́н 'grumbler'	болту́нья шалу́нья хвасту́нья крику́нья ворчу́нья	1. Nouns with the suffix **-ун** are generally derived from verbal stems: *болта́ть* 'to chatter' — *болту́н* 'chatterer'; *шали́ть* 'to be naughty' — *шалу́н* 'naughty boy'; *ворча́ть* 'to grumble' — *ворчу́н* 'grumbler'. 2. The stress is on the last syllable (*шалу́н*); in declension the stress is shifted according to the type as in Table 24, group C, I. In feminine nouns the stress falls on the same syllable as in their masculine counterparts (*шалу́н — шалу́нья*). The stress is fixed.
-арь секрета́рь 'secretary' библиоте́карь 'librarian' пе́карь 'baker' па́харь 'ploughman' то́карь 'turner'		1. The stress generally falls on the last syllable (*врата́рь* 'goal-keeper', *дика́рь* 'savage', *звона́рь* 'bell-ringer', *секрета́рь* 'secretary'), but some words are stressed on the root (*пе́карь* 'baker', *ле́карь* 'doctor', *сле́сарь* 'metal craftsman'). In the declension of these nouns the stress is shifted according to the type as in Table 24, group C, I.

Suffixes of Foreign Origin

Suffix		-к-а	
-ист	марксист 'Marxist', коммунист 'communist', материалист 'materialist', трактористt 'tractor-driver'	-к-а	коммунистка, трактористка
-ионер	революционéр 'revolutionary'		революционéр-ка
-ент	корреспондéнт 'correspondent'		корреспондéнт-ка
-ант	дилетáнт 'amateur', организáтор 'organizer'	-к-а	дилетáнтка
-тор	дирéктор 'director', дóктор 'doctor'		
-атор	новáтор 'innovator'		

Note. — In the declension of nouns with the suffixes -*ар*, -*яр* (*столяр* 'joiner', *маляр* 'house-painter', *гончáр* 'potter') the stress is generally shifted according to the type as in Table 24, group C, I.

2. Feminine nouns of the *секретáрша* 'librarian' type, though frequently used in colloquial speech, do not occur in the literary language; to denote persons of the female sex, masculine nouns are generally used: *секретáрь, библиотé-карь*, etc.

1. The stress invariably falls on the last syllable (*марксист* 'Marxist', *социалист* 'socialist') and remains fixed.

2. Nouns with the suffix -*тор* are stressed on the penultimate syllable (*дóктор* 'doctor', *дирéктор* 'director', *новáтор* 'innovator'). In most words the stress is fixed. The words *дóктор* and *дирéктор* ending in the nominative plural in -*а* (*доктора́, директора́*) are stressed on the ending in all cases in the plural.

3. Nouns with the suffixes -*ист*, -*ент*, -*ант* are invariably stressed on the suffix; nouns with the suffix -*ионер* are stressed on the last syllable (*революционéр* 'revolutionary').

Table 126

Suffixes forming Abstract Nouns

	Suffixes forming Feminine Nouns	Remarks
-ость **(-есть)**	акти́вность 'activity' реши́тельность 'determination' хра́брость 'bravery' го́рдость 'pride' промы́шленность 'industry' организо́ванность 'organization' дисциплини́рованность 'discipline' све́жесть 'freshness' теку́честь 'fluidity'	1. These words are derived from the stems of adjectives (*го́рдый* 'proud' — *го́рдость* 'pride') and passive participles (*организо́ванный* 'organized' — *организо́ванность* 'organization'). 2. The stress never falls on the suffix; as a rule, it falls on the same syllable in the derivative word as it does in the word from which it is derived (*го́рдый* 'proud'—*го́рдость* 'pride', *промы́шленный* 'industrial' — *промы́шленность* 'industry', *ко́лкий* 'biting' — *ко́лкость* 'biting remark'). The word *мо́лодость* 'youth' is, in fact, not an exception from the general rule, since the short-form adjective is *мо́лод* 'young' (long-form adjective *молодо́й*). The stress in these words is fixed.
-от-а **-ет-а**	беднота́ 'the poor' краснота́ 'redness' чернота́ 'blackness' полнота́ 'stoutness' темнота́ 'darkness' высота́ 'height' нищета́ 'poverty'	1. These nouns are generally derived from adjective stems (*бе́дный* 'poor' — *беднота́* 'the poor'). 2. The stress generally falls on the last syllable (*темнота́* 'darkness', *нищета́* 'poverty'); a number of nouns with the suffix *-от-а* are stressed on the penultimate syllable (*зево́та* 'yawning').
-ин-а	ширина́ 'width' глубина́ 'depth' вышина́ 'height'	1. The suffix is added to the root.

		2. The stress invariably falls on the last syllable; in declension it is shifted according to the type as in Table 24, group A, 2 (if the noun has a plural at all).
-изн-а	белизна́ 'whiteness' дешеви́зна 'cheapness' дорогови́зна 'expensiveness'	1. These nouns are derived from adjective stems (*бе́лый* 'white' — *белизна́* 'whiteness'). 2. In some words the stress falls on the last syllable (*белизна́*), in others, on the penultimate syllable (*дешеви́зна* 'cheapness', *укори́зна* 'reproach'). The stress is always fixed.
-к-а	стро́йка 'building' подгото́вка 'preparation' нахо́дка 'find'	1. These nouns are derived from verb stems (*подгото́вить* 'to prepare' — *подгото́вка*). 2. The stress never falls on the last syllable.
-б-а	борьба́ 'fighting' ходьба́ 'walking' молотьба́ 'threshing'	1 These words are derived from verb stems (*ходи́ть* 'to walk' — *ходьба́*). 2. The stress generally falls on the last syllable, and is fixed (but *проси́ть* — *про́сьба*).
Suffix of Foreign Origin		
-ация (-изация)	организа́ция 'organization' коллективиза́ция 'collectivization' квалифика́ция 'qualification' воениза́ция 'militarization' яровиза́ция 'yarovization'	1. The corresponding verbs are *организова́ть* 'to organize', *коллективизи́ровать* 'to collectivize', etc. 2. The suffix is also used to form nouns from Russian stems (*воениза́ция* 'militarization').

Suffixes forming Neuter Nouns		
-а-ни-е	внима́ние 'attention' собра́ние 'meeting', 'gathering' преподава́ние 'teaching' стара́ние 'endeavour'	1. These nouns are derived from the stem of the infinitive (*собра́ть* 'to gather' — *собра́ние*). 2. Nouns with the suffix *-а-ни-е* are stressed on the same syllable as the verbs they are formed from (*внима́ть* 'to listen attentively' — *внима́ние*, *преподава́ть* 'to teach' — *преподава́ние*).
-е-ни-е ***-енье***	чте́ние 'reading' удивле́ние 'surprise' уче́ние ⎫ 'learn-(уче́нье)⎭ ing' сужде́ние 'judgement'	3. Nouns with the suffix *-е-ни-е* are generally stressed on the *е* of the suffix (*ударе́ние* 'stress', *уточне́ние* 'specification', *упуще́ние* 'dereliction', etc., but: *наме́рение* 'intention', *упро́чение* 'consolidation', *обеспе́чение* 'ensuring', *сосредото́чение* 'concentration').
-ти-е	взя́тие 'taking' откры́тие 'opening' поня́тие 'idea'	1. These nouns are generally derived from verbs whose passive participles have the suffix *-т-ый*: (*откры́ть* 'to open' — *откры́тый* 'opened' — *откры́тие* 'opening'). 2. The stress never falls on the suffix. In most instances it falls on the same syllable as in the word from which the noun is derived (on the third syllable from the end of the word): *наи́тие* 'inspiration', *прибы́тие* 'arrival'. Exception: *бытие́* 'being'. The stress is invariably fixed.
-ств-о	произво́дство 'production' строи́тельство 'building', 'construction'	These nouns are derived from various stems: *производи́ть* 'to produce' — *произво́дство*, *строи́тель* 'builder' — *строи́тельство*. In some words the stress falls on the penultimate syllable (*госпо́дство* 'supremacy', *превосхо́дство* 'superiority'); in others on the last syllable (*мастерство́* 'mastery', *кумовство́* 'favouritism', *колдовство́* 'witchcraft'). The stress is invariably fixed.

Suffixes forming Masculine Nouns		
Suffix of Foreign Origin		
-*изм*	коммуни́зм 'communism' материали́зм 'materialism' маркси́зм 'Marxism' ленини́зм 'Leninism'	The stress invariably falls on the last syllable, i.e., on the suffix, and is fixed.

Table 127

Diminutive and Augmentative Noun Suffixes

Diminutive Suffixes

Suffixes	Masculine	Neuter	Feminine	Manner of Formation
-*ик*	стол 'table' — сто́лик дом 'house' — до́мик			Suffixes added to the stem.
		плечо́ 'shoulder' — пле́чико лицо́ 'face' — ли́чико		Alternation *ц — ч.*
-*чик*	шкаф 'cupboard' — шка́фчик па́лец 'finger' — па́льчик			An unstable *e* plus alternation *ц — ч.*
-*ок (-ёк)*	лист 'leaf' — листо́к па́рень 'fellow' — паренёк сук 'bough' — сучо́к стари́к 'old man' — старичо́к			Alternation *к — ч.*

Diminutive Suffixes				
Suffixes	Masculine	Neuter	Feminine	Manner of Formation
-ец	брат 'brother' — брáтец			
-к-а			головá 'head' — голóвка	
			кóмната 'room' — кóмнатка	
			вѝшня 'cherry' — вѝшенка	An unstable *е.*
-иц-а			водá 'water' — водѝца	
			сестрá 'sister' — сестрѝца	
-иц-е		плáтье 'frock' — плáтьице		
-ич-к-а			сестрá 'sister' — сестрѝчка	
			лисá 'fox' — лисѝчка	
-онк-, -ёнк-	мáльчик 'boy' — мальчóнка		сестрá 'sister' — сестрёнка	
			дéвочка 'girl' — девчóнка	An unstable *о.*
-оньк-а			берёза 'birch' — берёзонька	
-еньк-а			рукá 'hand' — рýченька	Alternation *к — ч.*
-ц-е		окнó 'window' — окóнце		An unstable *о.*
-ечк-а			уздá 'bridle' — уздéчка	

340

Diminutive Suffixes

Suffixes	Masculine	Neuter	Feminine	Manner of Formation
-ечк-о -очк-о, -а -ушк-а, -о -юшк-о	дед 'grand-father' — дéдушка хлеб 'bread' — хлéбушко	сéмя 'seed' —сéмечко я́блоко 'apple' — я́блочко гóре 'sorrow' — гóрюшко мóре 'sea' — мóрюшко	рубáшка 'shirt' — рубáшечка кóшка 'cat' — кóшечка тарéлка 'plate' — тарéлочка стару́ха 'old-woman' — стару́шка рекá 'river' — речу́шка избá 'hut' — избу́шка	The suffix -ух- is replaced by the suffix -ушк-. Alternation к—ч.
-ишк-а, -о -ышк-о	мáльчик 'boy' — мальчи́шка плут 'swindler'—плути́шка гóрод 'city'— городи́шко дом 'house'— доми́шко	сóлнце 'sun' —сóлнышко гнездó 'nest' —гнёздышко	земля́ 'land' — земли́шка	Note.—Nouns with the suffixes -ушк-, -ышк-, -ишк- always take the ending -а (голóвушка 'poor dear head', земли́шка 'poor land') if they are feminine or -о if they are neuter (сóлнышко 'dear sun'); if they are masculine and denote animate beings or inanimate things the ending is -а (мальчи́шка 'urchin') or -о (доми́шко 'poor small house') respectively.

Diminutive Suffixes

Suffixes	Masculine	Neuter	Feminine	Manner of Formation
Two or three suffixes: *-уш-ечк-а* *-уш-он-* *-очк-а* *-онк-а* *-иш-ечк-а* *-он-очк-а*	 мальчи́шечка 'laddie'		избу́шечка 'little hut' старушо́ноч-ка 'little old woman' старушо́нка 'small old woman' девчо́ночка 'girlie'	Two or three suffixes.

Augmentative Suffixes

Suffixes	Masculine	Neuter	Feminine	Manner of Formation
-ищ-е, -а	дом 'house'— доми́ще нож 'knife' — ножи́ще	письмо́ 'letter' — письми́ще	кни́га 'book' — кни́жи-ща нога́ 'foot' — ножи́ща рука́ 'hand' — ручи́ща	Alternation *г — ж.* Alternation *к — ч.*
-ин-а	дом 'house' — доми́на		ры́ба 'fish' — ры́бина	**Note.** — Feminine nouns with the suffix *-ищ-* take the ending *-а (ру-чи́ща)*, whereas neuter and masouline nouns take the ending *-е (пись-ми́ще, доми́-ще)*.

-ик   The stress is generally on the penultimate syllable (*дóмик* 'little house', *стóлик* 'little table', *óслик* 'little donkey') and is fixed.

-ок (-ёк)   The stress is on the last syllable (*листóк* 'little leaf', *уголёк* 'small piece of coal'). In declension the stress is shifted according to the type as in Table 24, group C, I.

-к-а   If in the word from which the given word is derived the stress does not fall on the last syllable, it falls on the same syllable in the derivative word, e.g., *кóмната* 'room' — *кóмнатка* 'little room', *монéта* 'coin' — *монéтка* 'little coin'. If in the word from which the given word is derived the stress falls on the last syllable, the derivative word is stressed on the penultimate syllable, e.g., *рукá* 'hand' — *рýчка, ногá* 'foot' — *нóжка, головá* 'head' — *голóвка.*

-иц-а }
-ичк-а }   The stress falls on the penultimate syllable (*водúца* 'water' — *водúчка*) and is fixed.

-онк-а   The stress falls on the penultimate syllable (*девчóнка* 'little girl', *мальчóнка* 'little boy') and is fixed.

-ц-е, -о   The stress generally falls on the penultimate syllable (*окóнце* 'little window', *волокóнце* 'thin fibre'), it may also fall on the third syllable from the end of the word (*плáтьице* 'light frock', *дéревце* 'little tree'); occasionally it falls on the last syllable *(-цо): пальтецó* 'light overcoat', *ружьецó* 'little gun'. In all cases the stress is fixed.

-ечк-а   The stress in words with this suffix follows the same rule as in words with the suffix *-к-а.*

-ушк-а,
-юшк-а   In some words the stress falls on *-у-* (i.e., on the penultimate syllable), in others on the syllable preceding the suffix (i.e., on the third syllable from the end of the word), the different stress resulting in different meanings: if the stress falls on *-у-* the word may acquire a pejorative meaning, while if the stress is on the syllable preceding *-у-* the word has a meaning of endearment (cf. *Катю́шка* (feminine name) — *Кáтюшка*). The stress in both cases is fixed.

-ышк-о   The stress generally falls on the third syllable from the end of the word (*сóлнышко* 'dear sun', *зёрнышко* 'little grain') and is fixed.

-ишк-а,
-о   The stress generally falls on the penultimate syllable (*мальчúшка* 'urchin', *умúшко* 'poor intellect', *домúшко* 'poor small house').

-ищ-е, -а　　　If the word from which the given word is derived is stressed not on the last syllable, the stress in the derived word generally falls on the same syllable (кни́га 'book' — кни́жища). If the word from which the given word is derived is stressed on the last syllable, the stress in the derivative word falls on the penultimate syllable (рука́ 'hand' — ручи́ща, нога́ 'foot' — ножи́ща, стари́к 'old man' — старичи́ще). But: челове́к 'man' — челове́чище.

Note. — 1. All diminutive suffixes may add to the word a meaning of endearment according to the context.
2. Some diminutive suffixes *(-ик, -ушк-, -ышк-, -онк-, -ёнк-)* may add to the word a meaning of endearment or of contempt according to the context, e.g.:

A Diminutive Meaning or a Meaning of Endearment:

Ма́ленькая *речу́шка* протека́ла о́коло дере́вни. 'A small river ran near the village.'

Ма́ленький *доми́шко* стоя́л в зе́лени. 'The little cottage was submerged in verdure.'

. . . .

Кири́ла Петро́вич заезжа́л за́просто в *доми́шко* своего́ ста́рого това́рища... (П.) 'Cyril Petrovich called on his old friend at his little house without ceremony.'

A Meaning of Contempt:

Это не река́, а кака́я-то *речу́шка* (or *речо́нка*). 'This is not a river, but just a stream.'

Како́й же э́то дом? Это *доми́шко*. 'You call that a house? It's just a shack.'

Приходи́л како́й-то *мальчи́шка*. 'A youngster came.'

. . . .

На краю́ доща́нки стои́т... растрёпанный *мужичо́нка* в рва́ном армяке́... (М. Г.) 'On the edge of the flatbottom stands... a dishevelled smallish peasant wearing a tattered cloth coat.'

Заси́м э́тот съёжившийся *старика́шка* проводи́л его́ со двора́. (Г.) 'After that this wizened old man saw him to the gate.'

3. Endearment diminutives of proper names — both masculine and feminine — are formed by means of the same suffixes:
Masculine names: *Ва́ня — Ваню́ша, Ва́нечка, Ваню́шечка*, etc.; *Ви́тя — Витю́шенька*, etc.
Feminine names: *Та́ня — Таню́ша, Таню́шка, Та́нечка*, etc.; *Ни́на — Нину́ся, Нину́сенька*, etc.

COMPOUND NOUNS

I. A number of nouns contain more than one root; they are called compound nouns. Compound nouns are formed by combining two or more words (generally two nouns, or a noun and a pronoun, or a noun and a numeral, etc.) into one.

A compound word may, in turn, become part of a more complex compound, e.g.:

парово́з (пар + вози́ть) 'steam locomotive'
паровозострое́ние (парово́з + строе́ние) 'locomotive-building'

The parts of a compound word are joined by the link vowel *o* or *e*.

Table 128

Manner of Formation		
паровóз 'steam-engine' паровозострое́ние 'lo- comotive-building' земледе́лие 'agricul- ture' птицево́дство 'poul- try-farming' пешехо́д 'pedestrian' самокри́тика 'self- criticism' самоопределе́ние 'self- determination'	пар-о-во́з паровоз-о-строе́ние земл-е-де́лие птиц-е-во́дство пеш-е-хо́д сам-о-кри́тика сам-о-определе́ние	These words are formed by means of the link vowel *o* or *e.* The link vowel *o* is used after a hard con- sonant, and *e* after a soft consonant or af- ter *ц, ж, ш, ч, щ.*
пятиле́тка 'Five-Year Plan' Ленингра́д 'Lenin- grad'	пяти-ле́тка Ленин-гра́д	These words are formed without a link vowel.

II. In Modern Russian there are special compounds which appeared after the Great October Socialist Revolution and are formed by compounding abbreviated words.

According to the manner of abbreviating and compounding, these words can be classified into several groups:

Manner of Formation		
a) профсою́з стенгазе́та	профессиона́льный сою́з 'trade union' стенна́я газе́та 'wall newspaper'	Only the initial word is abbreviated.
b) комсомо́л колхо́з райко́м	коммунисти́ческий сою́з молодёжи 'Young Communist League' коллекти́вное хо- зя́йство 'collective farm' райо́нный комите́т 'district committee'	All the component words are abbreviated.

c) вуз	вы́сшее уче́бное за-веде́ние 'higher educational institution'	The compound consists of the letters indicating the initial sounds of the component words.
ТАСС	Телегра́фное аге́нтство Сове́тского Сою́за 'Telegraph Agency of the Soviet Union'	
d) СССР (pronounced: эс-эс-эс-эр)	Сою́з Сове́тских Социалисти́ческих Респу́блик 'Union of Soviet Socialist Republics'	A number of compounds consist of the initial letters of the component words pronounced as in the alphabet.
e) Днепрогэ́с	Днепро́вская гидро-электри́ческая ста́нция 'The Dnieper Hydroelectric Power Station'	The compound consists of the abbreviated initial word and the initial letters of the following component words.

Table 129

FORMATION OF ADJECTIVES

A. Formation of Adjectives from Nouns, Adverbs, Verbs and Numerals:

Main Suffixes	Adjectives	Manner of Formation
	Formation by means of Suffixes:	
-н-	ле́тний 'summer' зи́мний 'winter' осе́нний 'autumn' весе́нний 'spring' вече́рний 'evening' фабри́чный 'factory'	From noun stems: ле́то 'summer' зима́ 'winter' о́сень 'autumn' весна́ 'spring' ве́чер 'evening' фа́брика 'factory' (alternation к — ч)

Formation by means of Suffixes:

Main Suffixes	Adjectives	Manner of Formation
(-ш-)-н-	желе́зный 'iron' ме́стный 'local'	желе́зо 'iron' ме́сто 'place' *From adverbs:*
	сего́дняшний 'today's' вчера́шний 'yesterday's' за́втрашний 'tomorrow's' вне́шний 'outside' ны́нешний 'present'	сего́дня 'today' вчера́ 'yesterday' за́втра 'tomorrow' вне 'outside' ны́не 'now' *From noun stems:*
-онн-, **-енн-**	революцио́нный 'revolutionary' хозя́йственный 'economic' жи́зненный 'vital'	револю́ция 'revolution' хозя́йство 'economy' жизнь 'life' *From noun stems:*
-ск-	городско́й 'urban', 'city' сове́тский 'Soviet' моско́вский 'Moscow'	го́род 'city' сове́т 'Soviet' Москва́ 'Moscow'
-к-	пролета́рский 'proletarian' маркси́стский 'Marxist' неме́цкий 'German' бедня́цкий 'poor peasant's' кула́цкий 'kulak'	пролета́рий 'proletarian' маркси́ст 'Marxist' не́мец 'German' бедня́к 'poor peasant' кула́к 'kulak' (alternation *к — ц*) *From noun stems:*
-ан-, -ян-	ко́жаный 'leather' сере́бряный 'silver'	ко́жа 'leather' серебро́ 'silver' (alternation hard *p* — soft *p*)
-ин-	платяно́й 'clothes' лебеди́ный 'swan' соколи́ный 'falcon'	пла́тье 'clothes' ле́бедь 'swan' со́кол 'falcon'
-ов-, -ев-	дубо́вый 'oak' сосно́вый 'pine' боево́й 'battle' плечева́я 'humeral' ключева́я 'spring' столо́вый 'table' домо́вый 'house' га́зовый 'gas'	дуб 'oak' сосна́ 'pine' бой 'battle' плечо́ 'shoulder' ключ 'spring' стол 'table' дом 'house' газ 'gas'

Main Suffixes	Formation by means of Suffixes: Adjectives	Manner of Formation
-овит-	родови́тый 'of high birth'	род 'birth'
	ядови́тый 'poisonous'	яд 'poison'
-ов-	отцо́в 'father's'	оте́ц 'father' ⎱ (an unstable
-ов-(-ск-)	отцо́вский 'paternal', 'father's'	оте́ц 'father' ⎰ *e*)
-ин-	ма́терин 'mother's'	мать 'mother'
	се́стрин 'sister's'	сестра́ 'sister'
	ба́бушкин 'grandmother's'	ба́бушка 'grandmother'
-ин-(-ск)	матери́нский 'maternal', 'mother's'	мать 'mother'
	се́стринский 'filial', 'sister's'	сестра́ 'sister'
		Note. — The words *отцо́в* 'father's', *ма́терин* 'mother's', *се́стрин* 'sister's' have almost completely fallen into disuse; but the words *ба́бушкин* 'grandmother's' and *ма́мин* 'mother's' are frequently used.
-ист-	тени́стый 'shady'	тень 'shade'
	гли́нистый 'clayey'	гли́на 'clay'
-ат-	уса́тый 'moustached'	ус 'moustache'
	бborода́тый 'bearded'	борода́ 'beard'
-чат-	ды́мчатый 'smoky'	дым 'smoke'
-аст-	глаза́стый 'sharp-eyed'	глаз 'eye'
	голова́стый 'brainy'	голова́ 'head'
-ив-	лени́вый 'lazy'	лень 'laziness'
-лив-	приве́тливый 'affable'	приве́т 'greeting'
-чив-	обма́нчивый 'deceptive'	обма́н 'deceit'
		From verb stems:
-уч-, -юч-	лету́чий 'flying'	лета́ть 'to fly'
	горю́чий 'combustible'	горе́ть 'to burn'
	колю́чий 'prickly'	коло́ть 'to prick'
-к-	ло́мкий 'breakable', 'fragile'	лома́ть 'to break'
	ко́лкий 'prickly'	коло́ть 'to prickle'

Formation of Adjectives by means of Prefixes and Suffixes

The Prefix *без-*	безру́кий 'armless' безно́гий 'legless' бездо́мный 'homeless' безвре́дный 'harmless'	From noun stems: рука́ 'arm' нога́ 'leg' дом 'home' вред 'harm'
The Suffixes *-н-, -енн-*	безра́достный 'joyless' бесприю́тный 'shelterless' бессмы́сленный 'senseless'	From noun stems: ра́дость 'joy' прию́т 'shelter' смысл 'sense'
The Prefixes *на-, за-, при-* The Suffixes *-н-, -ск-*	насто́льный 'table' засто́льный 'table' нате́льный 'body' приура́льский 'Ural'	From noun stems: стол 'table' те́ло 'body' Ура́л 'the Urals'

Formation of Adjectives without Prefixes or Suffixes:

	From noun stems: (a) mainly denoting animals:
во́лчий 'wolfish' медве́жий 'bear('s)' пти́чий 'bird('s)' за́ячий 'hare('s)' ли́сий 'fox('s)', 'foxy' собо́лий 'sable('s)' о́тчий 'paternal' поме́щичий 'landowner('s)' рыба́чий 'fishing', 'fisherman's'	волк 'wolf' (alternation *к—ч*) медве́дь 'bear' (alternation *д—ж*) пти́ца 'bird' (alternation *ц—ч*) за́яц 'hare' (alternation *ц—ч*) лиса́ 'fox' со́боль 'sable' (b) denoting persons: оте́ц 'father' (alternation *ц—ч*) поме́щик 'landowner' (alternation *к—ч*) рыба́к 'fisherman (alternation *к—ч*)

B. Formation of Adjectives trom Adjectives:

With an augmentative or diminutive meaning or with a meaning of endearment:

Suffixes: diminutive:		From adjective stems:
-оват- **-еват-**	краснова́тый 'reddish' синева́тый 'bluish'	кра́сный 'red' си́ний 'blue'
expressing endear-ment:		
-еньк- **-оньк-**	бе́ленький 'nice and white' ти́хонький 'nice and quiet'	бе́лый 'white' ти́хий 'quiet'
augmenta-tive:		
-ущ- **-ющ-**	большу́щий 'very large' злю́щий 'very wicked'	большо́й 'large' злой 'wicked'
Prefixes: augmen-tative:		
пре-	пребольшо́й 'awfully large' пренепри́ятный 'extremely unpleasant'	большо́й 'large' неприя́тный 'unpleasant'
of foreign origin:		
архи-	архиреакцио́нный 'archre-actionary'	реакцио́нный 'reactionary'
анти-	антирелиги́озный 'antireli-gious' антифаши́стский 'antifas-cist'	религи́озный 'religious' фаши́стский 'fascist'

C. Formation of Compound Adjectives:

сéро-зелёный 'grey-green' тёмно-крáсный 'dark-red' свéтло-голубóй 'light-blue' сúне-жёлтый 'blue-yellow'	The stem of the first adjective, the link vowel and the second adjective (сéр-о-зелёный, сúн-е-жёлтый).

сероглáзый 'grey-eyed' черноволóсый 'black-haired' остроýмный 'witty' паровозострóйтельный 'locomo- tive-building' чугунолитéйный 'cast-iron'	The stem of the adjective, the link vowel, the stem of the noun and the adjective ending (сер-о-глáз-ый, паровоз-о-стройтель-н-ый, чугун-о-литéй-н-ый).

ИЛЬЗА МАКСИМИЛИАНОВНА ПУЛЬКИНА
КРАТКИЙ СПРАВОЧНИК
ПО РУССКОЙ ГРАММАТИКЕ

(для говорящих на английском языке)
Зав. редакцией Н. Спирина
Редакторы *И. Малахова, С. Власова*
Художественный редактор *Б. Казаков*
Технические редакторы *Е. Лобанцова, О. Скребнева*

ИБ № 5318